Southern Literary Studies

The American South

THE
AMERICAN
SOUTH

Portrait
of a Culture

Edited by LOUIS D. RUBIN, JR.

Louisiana State University Press
Baton Rouge and London

Copyright © 1980 by
Louisiana State University Press
All rights reserved
Manufactured in the
United States of America

Designer: Albert Crochet
Typeface: VIP Trump
Typesetter: LSU Press
Printer and Binder: Thomson-Shore, Inc.

The editor gratefully acknowledges permission to reprint C. Hugh Holman's
essay, "The Southern Provincial in Metropolis," originally published in *Windows
on the World: Essays in American Social Fiction* by C. Hugh Holman, © 1979 by
The University of Tennessee Press, Knoxville 37916.

Second Printing

LIBRARY OF CONGRESS CATALOGING IN PUBLICATION DATA

Main entry under title:

The American South.

   (Southern literary studies)
    1. Southern States—Civilization—Addresses, essays,
lectures. 2. American literature—Southern States—
History and criticism—Addresses, essays, lectures.
I. Rubin, Louis Decimus, 1923–   II. Series.
F209.5.A47   975   79–12316 √
ISBN 0–8071–0562–7

Contents

III. LITERARY IMAGES

Preface

Early in 1977, I was invited by the Voice of America Forum Branch of the United States Information Agency to organize and coordinate a series of presentations on the topic of the American South today. The emphasis would be cultural and literary, since it was through the region's literature that the South was best known to overseas audiences. It seemed a good time for such a project; a southerner had just been inaugurated president of the United States, the first to be elected since the 1840s, and the election was being widely viewed as a sign that the long separation of the South, culturally and politically, from the remainder of the American Union had come to an end. Very well. As viewed through its literature and attendant cultural and social reflectors, what *was* the condition of the South today? Was it disappearing? Was it changing? In what ways had its relations with the nation and the world changed? Or not changed?

My part of the project was to enlist the services of a number of persons, most of them writers, who were interested in the South and knew something about it. The Voice of America would interview each of them and broadcast the interview to overseas audiences. Each participant would then write out a more formal presentation of the subject, and these would be collected and published in an overseas edition by the USIA. There would also be an American edition, but not under the auspices of the USIA. As coordinator, I was to make all these arrangements, and also to contribute an opening presentation, a concluding essay, and at least one additional presentation.

The papers that follow are designed for the informed nonspecialist (though obviously the participants have differed in their estimate of just how informed the nonspecialist was to be.) There is no attempt to present a complete, thorough-going analysis of the South today. What we sought to do was to observe the South and its culture from various perspectives and then to take a look at what its literature has been and now is. Admittedly the presentation that follows is idiosyncratic, even eccentric; I went looking for writers who I thought had things to say about the South today, and I fitted the topics to the participants rather than the other way around. I've no doubt that many quantifying scholars in particular will be disappointed, will find these presentations unrepresentative and (to use the customary code word) *impressionistic*. So be it; impressions were what I wanted, by persons whose perceptions I valued.

If there is one theme that emerges from all these papers and the several transcripts of discussions, it seems to be that of endurance. The South has changed and is changing all the time, both for good and for ill; it is also enduring. It may even be enduring because it is changing.

There is no uniformity of viewpoint here. What is common to all these presentations is a fascination with the place; that, and the ability to communicate it. In describing the colony of Virginia for an English audience in 1705, Robert Beverley wrote, in the *The History and Present State of Virginia*, that "if we consider its natural aptitude to be improved, it may with justice be accounted one of the finest countries in the world." Whatever the aptitude, some of the improvements have come very slowly indeed.

Throughout the conception and the execution of this project, I have at all times enjoyed the help and support of Richard J. Gordon, until recently editor of the Forum Branch of the Voice of America. I am grateful to him and to his associates.

I

INTRODUCTION

LOUIS D. RUBIN, JR.

The American South:
The Continuity of
Self-Definition

If one thing seems certain about the region of the United States of America known as the South, it is that there will always be those of its inhabitants who will be arguing about whether it can continue to exist.

From the time that the states of the early American republic began to identify their concerns along geographical lines, there was a self-conscious South. Nowadays, almost two centuries later, there is still. During those years developments have taken place —economic, social, political, military—that have caused persons to predict the imminent end of the South as a recognizable entity. Most recently, the election of a southerner as president of the United States, one who campaigned for that office *as* a southerner and from a southern base of operations, has led many to declare that there is no longer an importantly separate political and cultural unit known as the South. If there were, the argument runs, Jimmy Carter could not and would not have been elected to national office.

Although no one can say for sure whether the argument is valid, the very fact that there was and is so much being made of Jimmy Carter's identity as a southerner would appear to indicate that it is too early yet to dismiss the importance or the sustaining power of the regional identification. That a southerner could be voted into the highest office in the land for the first time since the 1840s[1]

1. Lyndon B. Johnson of Texas was elected vice-president; he was reelected president after succeeding John F. Kennedy. The last southern president who lived in and had his political base of operations in the South was James Knox Polk (1845–1848).

doubtless signifies a change in the relationship of the South to the rest of the country; that it also means the end of the South as a viable social and cultural unit is another assumption entirely, and by no means a logical inference.

In the period before the secession of the southern states and the formation of the Confederate States of America in 1860–1861, the nature and the well-being of the South were associated with chattel slavery. Even though only one of every three white southern families owned slaves, and of these the majority owned only one or two apiece, the Peculiar Institution was held to be the sine qua non for maintaining and enhancing the unique nature of southern life. The region's foremost politicians devoted their legislative talents to protecting slavery and insisting upon its legality even in those western reaches where it could not possibly be made economically feasible. John Caldwell Calhoun's words, "The South —the poor South! God knows what will become of her!" uttered as he saw his hopes for united southern resistance to northern legislative attack failing, are quintessentially the expression of the slaveholding planter leadership. If the right to own black men and women as property were not protected by strict constitutional construction and by legislative and executive authority, then the unique civilization south of the Potomac and Ohio rivers would surely crumble into ruin.

Indeed, the secession of the southern states in 1860 and 1861, following the election of Abraham Lincoln as president, might best be understood not primarily as a nationalistic endeavor, motivated by the urge to set up a separate republic controlled by slaveholding interests, but as an attempt to preserve southern sectional identity in the face of what seemed imminent destruction by governmental fiat. The South would have been quite content to remain in the Union, if one is to judge by what was written and said at the time, provided that its uniqueness—i.e., slavery—could be thoroughly safeguarded.

If southern sectional identity were dependent upon slavery, then the loss of the war and the end of slavery should have destroyed that identity. They did not. Military defeat brought devastation, catastrophe. The cost was huge and hideous and would not be paid off for generations yet unborn. Yet in defeat the South not only retained its sense of identity, but added to it the mythos of a Lost Cause, a sense of ancestral pieties and loyalties bequeathed through suffering, and a unity that comes through common deprivation and shared hatred and adversity. This was not exactly what those who favored secession had in mind, but if their object was to preserve southern identity there can be no doubt that it worked.

Part of the cost of secession was Reconstruction, and military occupation and government imposed from Washington only added to the intensity of the region's sense of uniqueness. They provided a scapegoat: Negro rule. For almost a century afterward, it would only be necessary to invoke the specter of black men voting to spike the guns of any attempt to ameliorate the disadvantaged economic situation of the lower orders of whites through political action. The Reconstruction failed because in order for it to have worked, a majority of white southerners would have had to participate in the externally imposed Reconstruction state governments. This did not take place, for several reasons. From the standpoint of the southern whites, it meant acquiescing in black political equality. From the standpoint of the Radical Republican government in Washington, it meant that if the white South were completely reenfranchised, the southern states would vote Democratic and that would be the end of a national Republican majority. In any event, the southern states eventually got back into the Union on their own terms, while black southerners, though politically free from slavery, now found themselves eligible for such benefits as tenant farming, sharecropping, lynching, peonage, Jim Crow laws, poll taxes, and economic, social, and political discrimination of all sorts.

Much of the continuing trouble was due to the insufficient wealth now available to provide decent living conditions for the less affluent whites, let alone the blacks as well. The capital of the antebellum South had been invested in land and slaves, and derived from an exportable and commercially marketable cash crop, primarily cotton. With emancipation, the land was now greatly reduced in value, since there were no slaves to work it or cash to pay wages to freedmen, while the demand for the several

southern cash crops also receded considerably, principally because
of tariff policies enacted by a Republican Congress free to legis-
late in favor of protecting manufactures, without any effective
southern agricultural opposition. "Ten cent cotton and forty cent
meat," the song went; "How in the hell can a poor man eat?"

It seemed obvious to southerners such as Henry W. Grady of
the Atlanta *Constitution* that the only way the South could re-
trieve its fortunes was to throw off the habits and attitudes of the
defeated past and set out to pursue commerce, industry, and the
almighty dollar with the same avidity and finesse as the victorious North. Grady called for a New South of bustling cities, prosperous manufactures, and diversified, multicrop agriculture. To
Grady, the wish became the deed. "The old South rested everything on slavery and agriculture, unconscious that these could
neither give nor maintain healthy growth," he orated. "The new
South [now] presents a perfect democracy, the oligarchs leading
in the popular movement—a social system compact and closely
knitted, less splendid on the surface, but stronger at the core—a
hundred farms for every plantation, fifty homes for every palace—
and a diversified industry that meets the complex need of this
complex age." That such a South bore almost no resemblance to
actual conditions, that the manufactures were minor and unim-
portant and the farms mortgaged or worked on shares, did not per-
turb Grady. For he was a promoter and an optimist, and to him
actual facts were of modest significance. Yet even in his high-
hearted zeal for a South that could match the Northeast with factory smokestacks and investment capital and the Midwest with
independent farmers, Grady wished, however illogically, to retain
such southern virtues as religious orthodoxy, strict racial subordi-
nation, government by the better sort, and the traditional pieties
in general. The South, in short, was to welcome manufactures
and the spirit of laissez faire capitalism, but still remain socially
and spiritually unchanged.

In the early twentieth century, the factories and the cities at
last began to make their presence felt, and grudgingly but surely
the old southern establishment, with its stratifications, pieties,
closed social ordering, and generally rural ways of doing things, be-

gan to give way to the new dispensation. The South *had* changed
some since 1865: for one thing, the so-called revolt of the red-
necks,[2] the move of the rural whites to political power in virtually
all southern states, had brought forth a considerable democratiza-
tion (for whites only) of the region, the expenditure of considerably more tax revenue (albeit still not very much) for education
and public services, and a notable lowering of the tone of political
discourse as demagogues learned how to combine appeals to class
consciousness with the worst sort of "nigger-baiting" to gain and
hold office. For another, good roads, the advent of the automobile,
mass communications, and the like were ending the old rural isolation and bringing the South somewhat closer to the American
mainstream. Still another change: the old Confederate heritage,
the political and social hegemony of the generation that had fought
the war and for whom, in Walter Hines Page's words, the war had
"stopped the thought of most of them as an earthquake stops a
clock," was largely concluded. The past, and public fealty to it,
still counted for a great deal, but more in the nature of homage
than as model.

Yet much remained, too. The southern community was still a
viable force, nor did the arrival of cities and factories seem to dis-
lodge it. One "belonged" to a place and did not merely reside there.
Although World War I brought change, the southern sense of family roots, the notion of identity coming from where one lived, the
complex social patterns, were not importantly disturbed. And
economically, the financial gains of the war years, while impressive, did not serve to eliminate the poverty that characterized
much of the region and in particular the rural South, for the South
was still the nation's economic stepchild, a colonial tributary to
the Northeast.

2. A red-neck is a southerner of lower middle-class allegiance, and was so entitled because, supposedly, his neck was sunburned from working behind a plow.
Another term for this group—the average rural white southerner—was "the wool-
hat boys." Nowadays, the term *red-neck* has lost its association with farming, but
its class distinction remains. A term sometimes used today for the same group is
good old boy. Your typical red-neck dotes on country and western music, prides
himself on his powerful automobile, is a devotee of stock-car racing, likes plain ol'
home cooking, is Baptist or perhaps Methodist in upbringing, and, until recently,
had no use for blacks. Needless to say, this is a caricature—so are many red-necks.

Because the ways of big business were still largely alien to the southern scene and because buying and selling was still pretty much on a personal basis, there remained a habit of conducting one's affairs that if not the same thing as leisure seemed nevertheless to involve approaching what one did for a living in something like dignity and deliberation, the *otium cum dignitate* motif. (And if one was black and worked six and a half days a week for a very few dollars, what else might be expected?) Describe it as one might wish, in the South one generally took the easy way, and not merely labor but time itself was cheap. (There was a newspaperman I knew in Charleston, South Carolina, who in the year 1915 greatly vexed the promotional boosters of the Chamber of Commerce by submitting, as his entry in a contest to select a slogan for the city, "Please go 'way and let me sleep.")

The life of the region was still tied to church-going, and modernism and the social gospel were not at home in southern theology. There were mighty few atheists in southern towns, and even fewer Republicans, for the Solid South that was the legacy of Reconstruction was still unbroken.

And there were the black folk. They had begun moving north and west, and during the 1930s and thereafter would depart by the hundreds of thousands yearly for the industrial cities and jobs and welfare rolls of the North. But they were part of the South, and in however disadvantaged a relationship, part of the community, and emphatically no impersonal labor force. By the 1900s, they had been sufficiently removed as a political entity and would remain so for fifty years to come; they were kept in their place by the Jim Crow laws, the emblem of the lower-class white man's social superiority and now acquiesced in without much objection from the "better sort" who had at first disdained such tactics. The incidence of lynching, so high in the 1880s and 1890s, declined during the twentieth century, and except for the more foul-mouthed of the Deep South demagogues the politicians tended to talk a little more circumspectly about lynch law as the population became more sophisticated—lynching was now excused rather than advocated. But until well into the years of World War II and afterward, the mass of black people knew abject poverty, hard work,

and social humiliation for their lot. Yet they endured, even flourished; and they gave to southern life a tone, a tempo, that made it
personal, dramatic, a trifle hedonistic. Well might a young patri-
cian like Quentin Compson, in William Faulkner's *The Sound
and the Fury*, riding home from Harvard on the train for Christmas vacation in 1910, spy a black man on a mule somewhere in
Virginia and realize that he was home in the South again, and also
how greatly he had missed the blacks he knew while he had been
away in the North. The South was indeed inconceivable without
black folk, even in those areas where they were relatively few in
number; but only after several generations would whites come to
realize how much more the blacks could contribute to the community if admitted into full membership.

A region that was economically disadvantaged, and deficient in
all the more desirable economic and social indices—per-capita income, agricultural diversity, value added to commodities by man-
ufacture, worth of land, expenditures for schools and colleges, li-
braries, hospitals, and so on, as documented by Howard W. Odum
in his monumental *Southern Regions of the United States* (1936)
—was quite concerned with catching up, and in the 1910s and
1920s as the factories increased and the towns and cities grew, the
rhetoric was principally of progress and prosperity. Things were
already getting better by the early 1910s, and the boom times of
World War I brought folding money, new people, a surge of prosperity that, though it receded, did not go away entirely. The business community greatly favored the money-making New South,
and formed itself into Chambers of Commerce and civic clubs to
celebrate it (W. J. Cash declared himself "perpetually astonished"
at the fact that the Rotary Club had not been invented in the
South.) The liberals at the newspapers and the universities were
quick to single out all instances of educational, cultural, and social progress attendant upon the economic upsurge as proof that
the South was finished with its dark age of reaction, racial injustice, and religious fundamentalism. Episodes such as the Scopes
trial in Dayton, Tennessee, in which a high school science teacher
was convicted of violating a state law by teaching evolution, were
considered temporary embarrassments on the high road to the en-

lightened, progressive ways of modernity. *The Advancing South: Stories of Progress and Reaction* was what Edwin Mims entitled his paean to progress in 1927. "No one can have too high a hope of what may be achieved in the next quarter of a century," he declared. "Freed from the limitations that have so long hampered it, and buoyant with the energy of a new life coursing through its veins, the South will press forward to a new destiny."

It was not so simple as that. The "limitations" had not exactly disappeared. Economically, the South was still dirt poor except in the cities, and most of the economic and commercial accomplishments were being announced with entire disregard for the depressed condition of southern agriculture, which, once the war boom had ended, was back in the toils of debt. Sharecropping continued to be widespread; in much of the rural South tenant farming was a way of life. Nor did the intellectual enlightenment that Mims and others recognized really go very deep. Theologically, not merely the rural southern churches but the fundamentalist congregations in general, in rural areas, mill villages, towns and cities, were hardly attuned to modernism in religion, or to anything approaching the notion that "being saved" might involve concern for the plight of one's fellow man. The rash of antievolution laws voted or proposed during the 1920s showed where many southern protestants stood on intellectual freedom. And as for the rise of a critical spirit, which Mims and all good southern progressives agreed was essential to the development of an advancing South, there was a barrier that effectively negated anything much in the way of whole-souled southern self-scrutiny: the doctrine of white supremacy. There could be no public questioning of the South's racial imperatives, and since advanced thinking upon economic, religious, and political matters tended to accompany enlightened views of race relations, it remained only necessary to denounce anyone proposing examination of long-unexamined shibboleths in the economic and political realm for also and at the same time desiring to undermine the sacred truths of white supremacy—which indeed was probably so—to discredit his or her political credentials. The South of the 1910s and 1920s was a White Man's Country, and anyone who dissented from that premise had no future in politics. And the politics remained Democratic—the Solid South. Nor could the 1928 aberration, in which five southern states deserted the national party to vote for the Republican Herbert Hoover in preference to the anti-Prohibition, Roman Catholic Al Smith of New York City, be considered the harbinger of a two-party system in Dixie, at least as a progressive manifestation of political change. For it was wholly the result of insularity, fundamentalism, suspicion of the metropolis, and of the popish and/or atheistic hordes of the cities, not the sign of any break-up of the Solid South.

So if the South of the predepression years seemed to be moving closer to the national mainstream so far as progressive allegiances and an industrial, commercial economy were involved, any such identification was still very much a chancey business. There was a long way yet to go, and a great many factors that were working, either actively or through inertia, against any such development. Yet insofar as the South that had in effect rejoined the Union with Woodrow Wilson's election in 1912 may be said to have possessed an ideology, and to have displayed a self-consciousness as to where it was headed, it *was* in the direction of the national business-progressive ethos. Few thinking southerners would have voiced such a notion as the novelist-reformer George W. Cable had done as far back as 1881, when he had declared that what was needed was neither an Old South nor a New South, but instead the No-South. Yet a less peculiarly "southern," more generally "American" South was the assumed ideal of the intelligentsia.

As always, however, there continued to be dissenters, and during the middle and late 1920s, as the cities of the region seemed to be moving considerably closer to the American industrial ideal, there began developing a critical opposition to progress that owed little to theological fundamentalism or lingering aristocratic hauteur. This was the movement, or enterprise, known as Agrarianism, which centered on Vanderbilt University in Nashville, Tennessee. The striking difference between Nashville Agrarianism and previous southern critiques of industrial progress and urban sophistication was that the Nashville version was an intellectual endeavor, an imaginative affair of writers. Although its underlying social and philosophical assumptions were rooted in the humane values of the southern community, it was in motivation and spirit part of the widespread intellectual protest against the materialism and rootlessness of postwar twentieth-century life. In impulse it was closely related to T. S. Eliot's theological attack on scientific materialism and logical positivism in England, the polemics of Lewis Mumford and Ralph Borsodi in the United States, even the *Action Français* of Charles Maurras and others in France. In other words, it was a radical, intellectual formulation of a philosophical conservatism.

Yet by virtue of its roots in the southern community, it was unlike any such endeavors in key respects. It was not remotely High Church in its composition, and so had nothing aristocratic or snobbish in its allegiances. Its community assumptions saved it from intellectual hatred. It had no role for antisemitism or any other sort of xenophobia, either in its principles or its dynamics. Unlike the fascistic thinking such as that characterized by the *Action Français*, the viewpoint of the Agrarians involved an abiding belief in individual liberty and respect for law, and the primacy of the individual over the state. At heart it was not even pro- (or anti-) segregation, though the expected fealty was paid to that staple of white southern enterprise, for race relations were tangential to its concern, which was an assertion of the value of the humane community in protest and rebuke to dehumanization and materialistic, acquisitive society. For all its historical assertion, in spirit it was closer to Henry David Thoreau and *Walden* than to John C. Calhoun's *South Carolina Exposition* of 1828. For although it officially proposed Agrarianism as cure for the evils of industrial capitalism, and called for a restoration and reassertion of the South's small-town and rural community integrity, its practical economic application was sketchy and essentially the symbol for an assertion of humanistic values.

The Agrarians deplored the headlong course of the South, as they saw it, to adopt the national materialistic and commercial spirit. They called upon younger southerners to resist the industrial gospel, and they depicted the older southern agricultural community as exemplary of a harmonious, nonexploitative human relationship to nature. Southerners, they declared, must "be persuaded to look very critically at the advantages of becoming a 'new South' which will be only an undistinguished replica of the usual industrial community."

The Agrarian symposium, *I'll Take My Stand: The South and the Agrarian Tradition* (1930), was not taken seriously by very many southerners. The too-specific, too-concrete Agrarian identification, which was really a pastoral metaphor rather than a program for economic action, seemed highly impractical, flying as it did in the face of the industrial age. Had it not been for the economic depression, which arrived after the book was written but before it was published, the symposium's true identity, as humanistic rebuke to industrialization and depersonalization, might have been more generally grasped. But by the time the book appeared, the South and the nation were sliding into the morass of business collapse, so that the assertion of an Agrarian alternative to 1920s industrial society seemed more topical than it should have. Yet the attitudes and values enunciated by the Twelve Southerners who wrote the book were neither impractical nor transient. For in their concern for individual worth and the humane society they reflected the highest ideals and needs of the southern community, however indifferently reflected in actuality, and the success of the region in holding to those concerns and enhancing them amid growth and change would constitute the South's retention of its identity.

The Agrarians were not the only group actively concerned with the South's future. Centered on the University of North Carolina, at Chapel Hill, was a group of academics and others who desired for the South economic and social betterment that would rescue the region from poverty and ignorance. Temperamentally, the Chapel Hill Regionalists were of a different sort from the Agrarians. They dwelt in statistics, indices, programs; they were social scientists, not poets and philosophers, and they looked to social action, education, and governmental action through the New Deal of Franklin D. Roosevelt as cure for what ailed a South still suffering from its ruinous past and now undergoing the miseries of the depression.

Historians have tended to view Howard W. Odum, Rupert Vance, and their North Carolina coworkers as constituting an alternative, and much more practical and realistic, program to Nashville Agrarianism. The fact is that the two groups were not comparable in any meaningful way. The Tennesseans were aesthetic and moral philosophers; the North Carolinians were social planners. So far as the South's material welfare was involved, the Chapel Hill group represented the wave of the future. Most of what they advocated in the way of agricultural diversification, scientific farming, increased public education expenses, more and higher quality industrial development, an end to industrial and agricultural victimization of both white and black labor, racial justice, and a far greater measure of economic and political opportunity for the black man has come to pass. They were activist prophets, and they led the way out of the swamp—with, however, little concern for whether the swamp might have any attractions of its own that an engineering program might ruin.

The Agrarians were prophets, too, but of a very different sort. The Agrarians were not social planners (it was a term of opprobrium for them); what they were worried about was the preservation of the human virtues of the southern community in the face of an impersonal industrial juggernaut. They foresaw what would happen if an exploitative, acquisitive industrialization were allowed to proceed without hindrance, and all too often what they warned about has indeed taken place, so that the current generation of southerners and indeed of Americans in general now finds itself engaged in an increasingly bitter ecological battle against further rape of the land. There is a contemporaneity to these supposedly impractical visionaries of 1930 that is striking to encounter a half century later, as in John Crowe Ransom's assertion in *I'll Take My Stand* that "our vast industrial machine, with its laboratory centers of experimentation, and its far-flung organs of mass production, is like a Prussianized state which is organized strictly for war and can never consent to peace." The Agrarians were prophetic in their warnings about the perils of dehumanization; they saw what the machine would do to the southern community if not kept subordinate to the human life that it was sup-

posedly designed to serve. The warning was appropriate in 1930;
in 1979 it is hardly less so.

For once the worst rigors of the Great Depression of the early
1930s were done, the industrialization of Dixie got into high gear.
The South made a strong recovery, and the advent of World War II
brought great prosperity, for defense industries mushroomed, and
military and naval installations were set up throughout the region to take advantage of the milder climate to train millions of
fighting men outdoors. Towns became cities almost overnight,
towns and cities became crowded almost beyond recognition, and
from the Texas flatlands to the Chesapeake Bay, the former Confederate States of American experienced a boom time as never before.
Profound changes were taking place in southern agriculture: it
was acquiring a new name, agribusiness. It was being mechanized,
the marginal subsistence farm was phased out, rural electrifica-
tion brought lighting for homes and voltage power for equipment
to the remotest countryside, sharecropping and farm tenantry virtually disappeared, and the surplus labor force, in particular blacks,
went to the expanding southern cities and to the industrial me-
tropolises of the North and West to find jobs.

When the war was concluded, the South experienced no reces-
sion to speak of; the region not only did not falter economically,
but continued right on with an industrial expansion and an urban
development that seemed to increase in geometric ratio as the
years swept along. No longer was Dixie the nation's No. 1 Economic Problem, as it had been termed during the 1930s. Instead it
boomed, and slowly but steadily the gap between the southern
states and the rest of the nation in per-capita income, expenditures for education, and other economic and social indices narrowed. By the mid-1970s, although there was still a discrepancy,
the South was prosperous beyond previous imagining. New industry moved steadily in to take advantage of the climate, now
that air conditioning had minimized the summer sun's disadvan-
tages. Real estate promoters and Chambers of Commerce had a
new name for the region. No longer was it Dixie or the Sunny
South; it was the Sun Belt.

And there was another, and even more astonishing, revolution in the South, too. After two centuries and more of slavery, war, and massive segregation, the black southerner was moving into full political, social, and economic participation in the southern community. The big change had been getting under way in the 1930s, though the signs were seldom openly observable. By the 1940s, inroads in the long-established patterns of white supremacy were clearly visible. Then in the 1950s came the public school decisions of the United States Supreme Court, notably *Brown* v. *Board of Education* in 1954, which declared segregation by race unconstitutional, followed by the bus boycotts and sit-ins, led by black southerners and in particular the Reverend Martin Luther King, Jr., that forced an end to discrimination in all forms of public and semipublic accommodations. A Texas-bred president, Lyndon Baines Johnson, placed a Democratic administration in Washington thoroughly behind a sweeping civil rights law that outlawed racial discrimination in all walks of life. Within a few years, black southerners were making their power felt in elections, and the politicians began coming around.

Resistance to all this by whites was at first massive and determined, occasionally even violent, but there was also a strong element in white sentiment that favored compliance with the law and an end to racial injustice. In a surprisingly brief time the law of the land prevailed. After a decade of struggle, the defense of public segregation was all but over, and by the time of the bicentennial years of American independence the South was integrated —politically, economically, legally, and socially—far beyond the wildest dreams of only a few decades earlier. There were black mayors, black legislators, black sheriffs, black civic leaders, elected not by black voters alone but with white support as well. Economic discrimination is by no means ended, and racial inequalities aplenty remain, but the onetime Confederacy now constitutes the most thoroughly integrated section of the nation. And many of those who had fought bitterly to block it now admitted they had been wrong, and that, as Senator John Stennis of Mississippi put it, the coming of legal desegregation had been for the best.

But was it, after all, the *South* any more? Was an American region now more urban than rural, in which blacks not only voted but joined with whites in overwhelming numbers to elect a white southerner president, in which memories of the War Between The States and the pieties of the Lost Cause were of antiquarian interest alone, which was no longer set apart from the rest of the nation by the fact of poverty, in which the two-party system had replaced the old monolithic Democratic loyalties in many states, in which factories and services now provided far greater revenue than farming—was such a place still appropriately described at all as the South, in anything more than a geographical sense? And if it was, would it remain identifiably so for very long?

Once again, therefore, the old dispute: is there a South? Where is it headed? Can it survive? Should it? The same self-conscious regionalism that had carried import since the days of Jefferson, Madison, Jackson, and Calhoun still has meaning enough remaining to it to cause argument and concern. Apparently it still means something significant to say of a human being that he is a southerner.

The question is, what does it mean now? It doesn't mean that one has a specific view of the race question any more. It doesn't mean that one comes from a rural or village environment. It doesn't mean that one is temperamentally out of place in large cities. It doesn't mean that one is likely to be less prosperous than other Americans. It doesn't involve a relative unfamiliarity with and hostility to the economic artifacts and entities of the machine age. It doesn't even mean that one is almost certain to be a communicant of the Democratic party. And it certainly doesn't indicate that one is likely to maintain an energetic and pious concern for Confederate military history.

It doesn't signify any of these things, even though it was out of these things, and the events and institutions responsible for them, that the regional identity was created, shaped, and nurtured. To be a southerner today is still to be heir to a complex set of attitudes and affinities, assumptions and instincts, that are the product of history acting upon geography, even though much of the history is now forgotten and the geography modified. It is still to a notable extent as Quentin Compson, in William Faulkner's *Ab-*

salom, Absalom!, responded to his Canadian roommate at college when asked what it was that made southerners into what they were: "You cant understand it. You would have to be born there." Or else have lived there a long time. And this whether one is black or white, for the same heritage, however markedly and in part even cruelly different in its impact, formed them both.

What it comes down to is the continued existence, despite (or more properly, because of) time and change, of a social and cultural community in which membership offers a form of self-definition. This is to say that, even allowing for the utmost diversity and extremes of individual experience, and encompassing attributes both good and bad, worthy and unworthy, there is a shared identity involved, and whatever the complexity of the ingredients that go to make it up, it works in direct and palpable ways to cause its members to identify their concerns with those of a particular social and cultural allegiance. Nobody has ever, to my knowledge, succeeded in defining precisely what that entity is, or what goes into the mix. Yet it *is*, and insofar as its manifestations can be quantified for measurement, as John Shelton Reed had done in his book *The Enduring South*, not only have these survived in the face of sweeping social and economic change, but in some ways they even appear to have intensified.

It is easily parodied, and has been. It can take on curious and even grotesque shapes in expressing itself. Sometimes its characteristic performances have been unattractive, sometimes downright ugly and evil. It can be, and has been, sentimentalized, and also exorcized as if it were the foul fiend incarnate. Yet it has outlasted all such abuses and misuses, and seems to move triumphantly onward in historical time, oblivious to all the developments that supposedly were to bring about its demise.

Its chroniclers, the novelists and poets of the South, have made it known throughout the world. The French call it *sudisme*, and French scholars in particular have labored to define it, without notably more success than Americans both northern and southern—for all such success must be partial, since what is being defined is more complex than the tools of analysis can handle.

In 1861, in celebration (as he thought) of the South's trium-

phant establishment of separate nationhood, the South Carolina
poet Henry Timrod sought to depict it in a metaphor:

>   the type
> Whereby we shall be known in every land
> Is that vast gulf which lips our Southern strand,
> And through the cold, untempered ocean pours
> Its genial streams, that far off Arctic shores
> May sometimes catch upon the softened breeze
> Strange tropic warmth and hints of summer seas.
>   ("Ethnogenesis")

A good try, though not altogether specific. Even before Timrod's
day, and many times since, others have attempted to get at it. Poets
have rhymed it, novelists made it fabulous and sometimes monstrous, historians have sought to explain it by deciphering its behavior in time, social scientists have catalogued, analyzed, and
dissected, ad-men have sought to commercialize it ("I wouldn't
trade the Southern life for *anything!*" as one TV life insurance
commercial has it), and politicians to manipulate and exploit it.
The essays in this book represent yet another attempt to understand the South at a time when, as so often in the past, the region
appears to stand at a crossroad. There will be others.

If the South is to survive as an identifiable region, and continue
to provide its citizenry with something tangible in the way of a
community affiliation, apparently it faces lengthy odds—namely,
much of the thrust of late twentieth-century industrial society.
But such odds, one might say, are an old southern habit. Besides,
the South has certain things going for it, including perhaps the
most valuable weapon it could possess at this junction in its affairs: an incorrigible talent at individualizing and humanizing its
experience.

One recent and highly comic example of this skill has gone
largely unremarked, and, though hardly earth-shaking in its implications, it gives an idea of what can sometimes be managed
along this line. If a visitor from a foreign country were to observe
the steady flow of truck and automobile traffic moving along any
of the huge interstate highway arteries that now connect all major points of the region and the nation—say, Interstate 85, between

Richmond, Virginia, and Atlanta, Georgia—he would doubtless see in it the workings, the ravages even, of a vast impersonal industrial process that has converted the region into one immense conveyor belt. What, after all, could seem less individualized, less humane, than the enormous eighteen-tired trailer trucks, all but identical except for the advertisements painted upon them, that grind remorselessly along the monotonous miles between the cities? And if our hypothetical visitor were familiar with the literature of the South, he might well think to contrast such a scene with, say, the image of someone like V. K. Ratliff in Faulkner's *The Hamlet*, with his odd little wagon—a buckboard "drawn by a pair of shaggy ponies" and attached to the reat "a sheet iron box the size and shape of a dog kennel and painted to resemble a house in each painted window of which a painted woman's face simpered above a painted sewing machine"—as Ratliff moved about the Yoknapatawpha County countryside, socializing with the farmers and occasionally selling a sewing machine. Our visitor might indeed see in the contrast the end of the era, the absolute disappearance of an individualistic way of life before the steamrollering conformity of the present age.

What our visitor could not know, however, was that the men who are driving those huge tractor-trailers—southern red-necks for the most part, good ole boys—are not merely boringly watching the multilane road unfold before them. They are busily gossiping away with each other, and with every motorist who comes along and wants to talk. For what they have done is to incorporate another impersonal artifact of the machine age, the citizens-band radio, and put it to work as a socializing medium. Thus, though our visitor could not see it, the air all around him would be alive with amiable conversation as the truckers conversed happily with each other and with motorists in automobiles, using a comic vocabulary invented originally to circumvent the speed regulations by giving warning of the presence of police cars equipped with radar devices. The initial excuse for purchasing the CB radios— sounding the alert when the law put in its appearance—had been made merely the pretext for unlimited individual discourse. Driving along the interstate highway has, in short, been transformed into a social occasion!

I do not want to make too much of this, though I confess that I am rather pleased with it, for it seems a splendid, if minor, example of the way in which the so-called southern life can absorb and humanize even the more recalcitrant and impersonal manifestations of the industrial dispensation. Listen to the red-neck-style CB radio lingo, and compare it with the terse, scientific, abstract jargon of the astronauts—"mission to control tower"—engaged in space exploration, and what is possible to human beings in the grip of supposed technological depersonalization can be glimpsed.

(My own belief is that too much is made of ranch houses and suburban developments, condominiums and supermarkets, television sets and do-it-all appliances, as signifying the standardizing, sterilizing quality of the industrial age. What is left out are the boats and canoes parked in the driveways and carports, the grills in the side yard, the baseball diamonds and basketball courts around the corner at the playground, the family dog snoozing in the sunshine by the front steps, the greenhouses, the home workshops in the basement, the ping-pong table in the corner. *Suburbia* is a dirty word among sociologists and other advanced meditators upon culture; it is not among ghetto dwellers, residents of rundown urban neighborhoods, and so on. In what sense is the ranch house more "depersonalized" than the house in town that the working-class and lower middle-class citizen lived in before he moved out? At least the ranch house offers a little land and space. We forget that people *live* in those rows of ranch houses, and that if they are not insufficiently confirmed in their humanity they will not suffer themselves to be depersonalized merely because they no longer inhabit townhouses, cheap frame bungalows, tenant shacks, and urban slums. And in any event, God knows that the less privileged all over the world would gladly exchange places with them!)

In the 1976 presidential election, the Democratic candidate won because he carried certain key northeastern and midwestern (I almost used the old adjective *industrial*) states and the entire South with the exception of Virginia. What helped him win the electoral votes of the southern states was a combination of white and black votes. As Wilson Carey McWilliams notes, "once assured that Carter's belief in racial equality was genuine, many blacks voted for Carter *because* he was Southern." That is a profoundly true observation, and what it means is that since southern whites and blacks alike have been shaped by the region's historical experience, they share many qualities of outlook and expectation that make for loyalty to a common community, and which, when the old chasm of race has been bridged, are free to assert themselves as never before.

The incredible racial developments since World War II, it seems to me, have provided the potential for immeasurably strengthening the cohesiveness of the southern community, for they have set the most abrasive and divisive force within that community on the way toward extinction, and thus begun to release the full capacities of some millions of very "southern" southerners for community participation. Considering how much impact blacks have had on the patterns of southern life even in their shackled and then segregated status, what they may be able to contribute now that they are on the road to full participation is difficult to overestimate.

Yet notable problems remain. A heritage of two hundred fifty years of separation and mistrust isn't to be wiped out in a single decade or two.

Whether these resisting elements—the enduring power of the community heritage, the aptitude for bringing the most formidable and destructive forces of the industrial age into humane community patterns, the accelerating removal of the most divisive and abrasive element that had led to separateness within the community—can stand up to the continuing and relentless onslaught of mass industrial society upon the life of the so-called Sun Belt remains to be seen. Thus far the issue is very much undecided. This much, however, seems obvious: if the southern community wins out (which is to say, survives and flourishes), it will not be through abstention, through attempts at avoidance of the elements and artifacts of the age of the computer and the mobile home, but through incorporating them—controlling, gentling, and humanizing them. ("We can accept the machine, but create our own attitude toward it," as Stark Young wrote in *I'll Take My Stand*.) This is still the South's best hope, and insofar as the South can by virtue of its community heritage offer example and leadership, it may well be that of others as well. *De te, fabula.*

II

A CHANGING CULTURE

JOHN SHELTON REED

Instant Grits and Plastic-Wrapped Crackers: Southern Culture and Regional Development

In 1928, an unusually far-sighted southerner named Broadus Mitchell pondered the implications of the South's impending modernization, wondering "whether these great industrial developments [to come] will banish the personality of the South . . . or whether the old spirit will actuate the new performance." "Will industrialism produce the same effects here as elsewhere," he mused, "or will it submit to be modified by a persistent Southern temperament?" A half century later, the South has certainly seen its share of industrialization, urbanization, and all the other -ations that sociologists call development and most of us would optimistically call progress, but the answers to Mitchell's questions are still not clear.

When he wrote, a majority of southerners were engaged—unprofitably, for the most part—in agriculture. Only a third lived in the South's towns and cities ("cities," with a couple of exceptions, that didn't amount to much anyway). The South's per-capita income was roughly at the level we use today to distinguish between "developed" and "less developed" countries, and was substantially less than that in the rest of the United States. Since then, both the proportion and the absolute number of southerners working on farms have declined dramatically (fewer than one in twelve does so now, only slightly more than the national figure), and the nature of southern agriculture has changed: the size of the average southern farm has doubled, and it has itself been very largely "industrialized." Per-capita income in the South is now recognizably American and is a good deal closer to the national figure (although a gap still remains). The South has become, like the rest of the United States, an urban society. Two-thirds of its people are now city- or townsfolk, and a half dozen of its cities are grand enough to have teams in the National Football League.

These changes and their correlates are obvious even to the casual visitor, and writing about them has become a staple of American journalism. With monotonous regularity, northern journalists arrive at southern airports, travel interstate highways to Holiday Inns, chat with a few new-style southern politicians or academics, and write that "the South has rejoined the Union," meaning that Yankee culture has finally prevailed, a century after Yankee arms did so.

And, to be fair, the changes of the past fifty years have indeed transformed more than the physical landscape of the South. For better or for worse, Atlanta *is* the model of the "New South" (a hackneyed phrase popularized by an Atlantan a century ago). The benefits of the South's development are clearly evident—in the pay envelopes of southern workers, in public health reports, in the statistics of magazine and newspaper circulation, in state budgets for education and welfare, in nearly all of the eight hundred or so indicators of southern deficiency Howard W. Odum compiled in his 1936 book, *Southern Regions*. Some of the unfortunate consequences of industrial and urban development are almost as obvious. With all this change going on, and nearly all of it tending to make the South look more like the rest of the country, how can the answers to Mitchell's questions still be in doubt?

Certainly there are good theoretical reasons for supposing that economic and demographic convergence between North and South should produce cultural convergence as well, and a good many people who write about the South simply assume that it has—or, anyway, soon will. The French sociologist Frédéric LePlay's formula, "land, work, folk," is a pithy summary of the generalization that, in preindustrial societies, the natural data determine how a living can be made, and how a society makes its living largely determines what kind of society it is. We are how we eat. In the South, conditions favorable to staple crop agriculture led to a plantation economy, which in turn produced a plantation society. Industrialization, however, has weakened the link between "land" and "work," and as the South's economy becomes less distinctive, so, according to this view, should its culture.

But although many of the most dramatic cultural differences between North and South have been decreasing (it could hardly be otherwise), an accumulating body of research suggests that it is easy to overestimate the extent of cultural convergence, and to underestimate the autonomy of southern culture. This research indicates that, in many respects, southerners are still different from other Americans, and that they are as different now as they have been at any time in the recent past. Moreover, these cultural differences cannot be explained in any obvious way by differences in demographic composition or economic circumstances. To paraphrase Irving Babbitt's observation about the Spanish, there seems to be something southern about southerners that causes them to behave in a southern manner.

The disjunction between economy and demography on the one hand and culture on the other, between "work" and "folk," is apparently greater than many of us have assumed. The citizen of the New South may spend forty hours a week at a job indistinguishable from those of other Americans, but nearly twice as many waking hours will be spent in families and communities organized around sentiments and presuppositions somewhat different from those found elsewhere. (Even the hours on the job may be different, of course. Sociologists have rediscovered the primary work group so often that its importance should probably be axiomatic by now.) The educated, urban, factory-working southerner remains a southerner, and that datum often tells us as much about his tastes, habits, and values as any of the others.

Why haven't these "great industrial developments" banished the "personality of the South"? It is tempting to speculate. For example, might importing a "mature" industrial regime—where workers spend more hours off the job than on, and other values compete with short-run efficiency in the managerial calculus—be less culturally disruptive than an indigenous industrial revolution? Possibly, but I suspect the explanation is less subtle than that. I think we may simply have overemphasized the initial dif-

ferences between South and North. After all, southerners have
been Americans, too, of a sort. Whatever the differences between
the cultures of the South and North, they have been more like
each other, surely, than either has been like that of Japan, say, or
the Soviet Union, or the Republic of South Africa. Industrialism
must impose *some* constraints on culture, but the old culture of
the South cannot have been so far out of the range consistent with
urban, industrial society that it could not adapt to it—as the Japa-
nese, Russian, and Boer cultures have adapted.

So the link between work and folk is not without slippage. Nor
is it necessarily one-way. Not only have a variety of national cultures proved to be compatible with modernization, but some of
those cultures have affected the nature of development, if not its
extent. Can the same be said for southern culture? Has development been "modified by a persistent Southern temperament," as
Mitchell put it? Or has southern culture been so "American"—or
so effete—that our region's development is following pretty much
the same course as the Northeast's?

So far, it is not at all obvious that urbanization and industrialization have taken any greatly distinctive turns in response to the
South's culture. There are, here and there, scattered differences
from the North: fewer really big cities and more middle-sized ones;
a larger proportion of "rural non-farm" families, employed in industry but living in the countryside; a residually lower degree of
residential segregation by race (probably reflecting an older belief
that one's help should be close at hand); a higher ratio of blue-
collar to white-collar workers; poverty more prevalent in rural
areas than in urban ones (the reverse of the nonsouthern situation); a significantly lower proportion of workers belonging to labor unions; a somewhat different industrial "mix"; and (primarily
as a result of the last two factors) lower industrial wages. But, by
and large, with regard to things the Census Bureau and the Bureau
of Labor Statistics think to measure, the cities and factories of the
South look pretty much like the cities and factories of the rest of
the country, and what differences exist are more easily explained
by the timing of the South's development than by anything in its
culture.

If there have been inconsistencies between southern culture and the general American pattern of development, as some have argued, culture has had to make way for development. In their eagerness to find a seat for the South at the great American barbeque, southern leaders seem by and large to have adopted the attitude of William Faulkner's character, Jason Compson—"I haven't got much pride. I can't afford it"—and by any standard, southern development so far has been remarkably pell-mell and indiscriminate.

When my hometown in Tennessee turned up on a government list of cities with serious air pollution problems, the newspaper responded with an offended editorial titled "Golden Smudge." When some citizens of Charlotte, North Carolina, complained about the proliferation of "topless" nightclubs in their city, a Chamber of Commerce official replied in defense that the clubs attract "an estimated 5000 people from other towns across the Carolinas and Virginia . . . every day." When I asked a Columbia, South Carolina, banker what he wanted his city to become, he expressed his admiration for—Charlotte. (So much for South Carolina's traditional arrogance.) Charlotte, meanwhile, wants to look like Atlanta; and Atlanta, it seems, wants to look like Tokyo.

This single-minded focus on growth was understandable in the 1930s. Confronted with obvious and insistent problems of poverty, bigotry, ignorance, and disease, most of the South's political, entrepreneurial, and intellectual leadership felt that the evil of the day was sufficient thereto and that they could deal with the problems of industrial society when they had an industrial society to generate them. But now we have one. Although southerners have not "gathered down by the mainstream of American life for baptism by total immersion," as George Tindall put it, the southern economy has certainly been born again. As we begin to enjoy the fruits of that rebirth, is there any reason to suppose we can escape some of its unpleasant consequences? The South's development has not yet gone as far as the Northeast's, and we can still learn from their mistakes. Is there any basis for hoping we shall?

There may be. Southern culture may yet have its impact. Although the broad outlines of the New South are already established (the changes have already taken place), perhaps in the fine tuning some adjustments to a "persistent Southern temperament" may be made, some regional refinements introduced. The South may have some cultural and institutional resources that the North lacked, resources that can help it domesticate and assimilate industrialism and urbanization. In particular, two enduring aspects of southern culture may be useful: the nature and extent of religious belief and practice, and a relatively great attachment to local communities. Both characteristics have been discussed by many students of the South; here I want simply to summarize some of the findings of my own research, and to consider what the persistence of these traits implies for the future of the South.[1]

In this century at least, one of the most striking differences between the South and the rest of the United States has been the nature of the South's religious life. It is no accident that the first southern president in over a century is a Baptist Sunday-school teacher: the South, as Flannery O'Connor observed, is "Christ-haunted," and to understand the region it is necessary to understand the role religion plays in its life.

Public opinion polls reveal that nearly 90 percent of all white southerners identify themselves as protestant, and nearly four out of every five of these are Baptist, Methodist, or Presbyterian. (The homogeneity of southern blacks is even greater.) The fact that the region is uniformly *anything*, that it has never had to adjust to the presence of competing religious groups, may account in part for the prominent part religion plays in the public life of the South. (The fact that it is, to a great extent, uniformly low-church protestant almost certainly has some implications for the nature of re-

1. Most of these data and some of the discussion of them come from my paper, "New Problems, Old Resources: Continuity in Southern Culture," in the mimeographed proceedings of a symposium on "Group Identity in the South: Dialogue between the Technological and the Humanistic," edited by Harold F. Kaufman *et al.* (Mississippi State University, Department of Sociology, 1975); and from my book, *The Enduring South: Subcultural Persistence in Mass Society* (Chapel Hill: University of North Carolina Press, 1974). The data come from surveys conducted by the Gallup Organization (supplied by the Roper Public Opinion Research Center, Williamstown, Massachusetts) and by the Institute for Research in Social Science, University of North Carolina, Chapel Hill.

ligion's role, but that is another, and a complicated, question.)

Poll data also indicate that, regardless of their denomination, southern protestants are more orthodox in their beliefs than non-southern protestants. Despite the fact that southern protestants believe pretty much the same thing, however, there are a number of indications that they take denominational differences more seriously.

Religious institutions play an important role in the social and spiritual life of the South. Southern protestants are nearly twice as likely as nonsouthern protestants to assert that church-going is an essential part of the Christian life, and on any given Sunday they are, in fact, more likely to be found in church. They are less likely than protestants elsewhere to feel that religion is irrelevant to the modern world, and they are more likely to feel that their churches are satisfactory as they are.

The picture of the South that emerges from these data is one of a society that takes religion seriously. Most southerners agree on the fundamentals of religion, which allows them the luxury of disagreement on relatively minor points of faith and practice. They are satisfied with their churches, and they support them accordingly with their time and money.

It can be shown that regional differences in these matters have not become smaller in the recent past, and that there is no reason to expect that they will do so in the near future. Data on trends often show *change*, in the South and elsewhere, but the *differences* between South and non-South are no smaller now than a generation ago, despite the dramatic changes in southern society since then. When statistical controls for education, occupation, and urban or rural residence are applied (to ensure that the regional differences are not due to differences in these factors), nearly all of the differences remain, and a few become even greater. Some regional differences in attitudes more or less related to religion—anti-Semitism, anti-Catholicism, opposition to the sale of alcoholic beverages, and the like—may be decreasing, but the data strongly suggest that the religion of the New South will be as vigorous and distinctive as that of the old.

This prediction is strengthened by a look at patterns of churchgoing within the South. In general, southern protestants are more likely than nonsouthern ones to report that they went to church on any given Sunday. But this difference is smallest for the uneducated farm population—a group that is shrinking rapidly in the South. Many of these people are moving into blue-collar occupations in southern cities, a migration that leads almost everywhere else in the world to a decrease in churchgoing. Outside the South, urban blue-collar workers are among the people least likely to be reached by the churches, but in the South this group is as likely to go to church as its country cousins. Evidently, rural-to-urban migrants in the South take their church with them (and the polity of the Baptist church and similar groups makes it easy for them to do this).

At the top of the status ladder is another interesting difference between the South and the rest of the United States. Outside the South, educated, urban, business and professional people are less likely to be churchgoers than their white-collar employees. In the cities of the South, however, that pattern is reversed: educated business and professional people make up one of the most churchgoing groups in the region. On an average Sunday, more than half are—or at least say they were—in church, a remarkable performance, for protestants, by any standard. Whether these people set the standard for society, as one theory of leadership would have it, or are merely excellent at doing what is expected, it is significant that belonging to a church and actually attending its services are still taken-for-granted parts of upper middle-class life in the South.

A few years ago, I wrote: "The prophet Amos foretold a day when many should 'wander from sea to sea, and from the north even to the east,' seeking the word of the Lord, in vain. In these latter days, the wayfaring stranger would be well-advised to forsake the secular North, abjure the mysterious East, and check out the South. He will find gas station signs like the one in my town, advertising on one side 'REGULAR 29⁹' and on the other, 'WHEN YOU HAVE SINNED/READ PSALM 51.'" This invitation to save and to be saved still stands. The Organization of Petroleum-Exporting

Countries has brought about some drastic changes on one side of the sign, but the other remains—just recently, as it happens, repainted.

Another persisting aspect of southern culture that may have some bearing on how the region adjusts to development is what has been called "localism"—roughly, a tendency to see communities as different from each other, and to prefer one's own. There is more to this, I think, than mere parochialism; the trait seems to be related to the "sense of place" remarked by so many observers of southern life and culture, a sensitivity to the things that make one's community unique and, in particular, the existence of a web of friendship and, often, kinship that would be impossible to reproduce elsewhere.

Once again, we can find outcroppings of this characteristic scattered here and there in American public opinion poll data. For instance, when asked what man "that you have heard or read about, living anywhere in the world today" they most admire, southerners are twice as likely as nonsouthern Americans to name a relative or some local notable. (Nearly a quarter do so, despite the polling organization's obvious attempt to discourage such responses.) When asked where they would live if they could live anywhere they wanted, southerners are more likely—and have been since the question was first asked in 1939—to say "right here." When asked to name the "best American state," southerners name their own; almost 90 percent of North Carolinians do so, for an extreme example, compared to less than half the residents of Massachusetts. Asked where they would like a son to go to college, if expense were no problem, only New Englanders are more likely than southerners to name a school in their own region. (Two-thirds of the southerners did so the last time the question was asked, despite the poor national reputation of southern schools; only 3 percent of nonsoutherners chose southern schools.)

Once again, neither trend data nor statistical controls for the economic and demographic differences between North and South give any reason to suppose that regional differences in localism are decreasing. Although prediction is always a risky business, it may be, in fact, that as conditions in the South became "objectively" more attractive, southerners' affection for their region and their communities will become even greater.

Within the southern population, the degree of localism is lowest among urban groups. Whether this is a genuine effect of urban life or simply reflects the fact that a great many southern urban folk are recent migrants to their cities remains to be seen, but, even so, the people of southern cities are more localistic, by these measures, than their counterparts in northern cities.

How might southerners' religion and their localism help them adjust to the momentous changes their region is undergoing? Obviously, both are useful to individuals undergoing the sometimes wrenching dislocations in their lives that go to make up what we call "social change." Now more than ever, perhaps, southerners need the assurance of personal worth and importance their religion provides; and their taste for rootedness, their sense of community, may help them cope with the disintegrative effects of mass society. (Indeed, the psychic utility of southern culture may have something to do with its persistence.)

But social change threatens more in the South than the mental health of individuals. When pollsters asked a sample of North Carolinians what they liked best about the South, two-thirds mentioned something about the physical environment. The South, it seems, is still a pleasant place to live. But many of the region's amenities—both natural and man-made—are menaced by undiscriminating development. If the towns and cities of the South are not to become examples of southern efficiency and northern charm (to borrow John F. Kennedy's characterization of Washington, D.C.), southerners must have both the will and the ability to make them something else. It is not obvious that they have either, but they may, and if they do I suspect that localism will provide the impetus and southern churches at least some of the means.

Of course, localism is sometimes expressed as boosterism of the crassest sort, but it needn't be. Although several generations of southerners have, for good reason, been mesmerized by the prospect of growth and development, there are signs now of an emerging skepticism. In a recent poll, a third of a sample of North

Carolinians agreed that "much of what is good about the South will disappear if the South gets as much industry as the Northeast" (and another 22 percent were undecided); and 42 percent agreed that "material progress in the South will not be worth it if it means giving up our Southern way of life" (20 percent were undecided). Many southerners, it seems, feel they have seen the future, in the cities of the Northeast, and they're not sure it works. *Their* localism may find expression in a determination to control growth and to preserve the things they value in their communities.

If this happens, we should not be surprised to find the churches of the South involved. Southern churches, black and white, have always responded to a consensus of their members, providing them with everything from leadership in the struggle for civil rights to swimming pools and segregated private schools. In practice, most of the South's churches have been splendidly democratic institutions; in consequence, when they have become politically engaged, they have often done so in ways that strike outsiders as strange, or even downright un-Christian. But—as the ongoing conflict in many states over the sale of liquor demonstrates—the churches have impressive reserves of energy, money, and political power. Although these assets may often have been misdirected and dissipated in the past, I think the South is fortunate indeed to have such mighty institutions dedicated to what is seen as community well-being, and to have a tradition of voluntary and relatively selfless support for those institutions. If southerners' views of community well-being change, we can expect the concerns and activities of their churches to change accordingly.

This essay began with some questions one southerner was asking fifty years ago. At about the same time, another southerner, John Crowe Ransom, advised the South to "accept industrialism, but with a very bad grace, and . . . maintain a good deal of her traditional philosophy." We can see now that Ransom's implied dichotomy was probably a false one. The South has accepted—indeed, sought—industrialism wholeheartedly, but some, at least, of her "traditional philosophy" remains. And these aspects of the region's culture may yet modify and meliorate the development of the South.

WILLIAM C. HAVARD, JR.

Southern Politics:
Old and
New Style

The victory in the 1976 presidential election of James Earl Carter, Jr., (as he was formally styled before the urges of *demos* prompted the exclusive use of the diminutive "Jimmy") had the kind of symbolic meaning that is attached only to epochal beginnings and endings in American politics. The impact was stunning both inside and outside the South. For the first time in over a century, a resident of the undeniably *Deep* South would occupy the White House, which itself had increasingly become both the real and the symbolic center of the active powers of the national government since Franklin Roosevelt had inaugurated what has come to be called—with a somewhat casual attitude toward the conventions of historical chronology—the "modern" presidency.

But this was merely the most obvious element in the symbolic pattern. Carter's nomination and election also abruptly reversed more recent trends in American, and particularly southern, politics. From 1948 onwards the South, in whole or in part, had been in a more or less active state of rebellion against its great symbol of sectional political unity—the Democratic party. From the end of Reconstruction until the 1960 election, the South had consistently furnished the strongest sectional support for the Democratic nominees in presidential elections. But from the latter date onwards, the principal locale of Democratic party strength in national elections shifted to the Northeast, the section which has been aligned against the South more consistently than any other since the early days of the Republic. In the 1968 presidential election, Texas alone among the states of the former Confederacy remained loyal to the party of the southern fathers, and in 1972 the South was "solid" again for the first time since 1944, but it was now solidly for the Republican nominee. In 1976, with a bona fide southerner heading the ticket, the South returned to its traditional place as the regional bastion of Democratic presidential electoral strength, with Virginia as the lone Republican holdout. The margin of popular votes may not have been what it once was, but the feeling of renewal of old and familiar ties could be sensed almost palpably in the reactions to the outcome of the election. With the usual resort to humor to elide the intensity of their sentiments, and with just the appropriate touch of irony about the long relegation by the rest of the country to a status of less than full political equality, at least in potential access to the presidency, old hands at southern politics quickly began to open their conversations about the Carter phenomenon with the gambit, "Won't it be nice to have someone in the White House who doesn't have an accent?"

This reflection of good will through good humor also signaled the apparently successful culmination of the long, and at times seemingly hopeless, effort to eliminate race as the controlling issue of southern politics. One hundred years earlier, the contested Hayes-Tilden election was resolved by the "compromise" that ended Reconstruction in the South in exchange for peaceful acceptance of the special election commission's decision that all of the electoral votes in dispute would be cast for the Republican nominee, Rutherford B. Hayes, thereby securing his election and the long-term dominance of national politics by his party. The South was left to its own devices while the Northeast and Midwest, united into a new multiregional geographic base on which the Republican national majority rested, proceeded to implement the American industrial revolution that was changing a predominantly small town and rural-agrarian society into an urban-industrial, entrepreneurial one. It took the South almost a quarter of a century to consolidate its own "separatist" political position, which involved the removal of blacks from all forms of direct participation in politics, the virtual elimination of the Republican party (the principal symbol of the political forces that defeated

the South in war, emancipated the slaves, and imposed Reconstruction) from the region, and the substitution for two-party com-
petitiveness of the one-party system in which the Democratic
party, in the words of W. J. Cash, institutionalized "the will to
white supremacy."

For more than fifty years, from the completion of the consolidation of the post-Reconstruction victories of the regional Democratic party down to 1948 at least, the pattern of southern politics
that most of us tend to interpret as "usual" prevailed. Although
blacks played little or no direct role in southern politics during
this period (as late as 1944, when the United States Supreme Court
declared the white-only primary party election unconstitutional,
only about five percent of the blacks in the South were even regis-
tered to vote), the complete separation of the races through legal-
ized segregation and the exclusive control of elections and all subsequent political decisions by whites were, with few exceptions,
the tacitly controlling motivations of southern political practice.
The race issue, though surfacing only occasionally during this long
period of "normality," had produced the solid, one-party South
and could easily be dragged up as an ancient talisman around
which white southerners of all classes could rally if racial arrangements were threatened, or if competition over other issues became sufficiently threatening to necessitate a diversion.

During the last thirty years, however, the race issue has not
been merely incipient but, as in the period from 1876 to the turn
of the century, has again been the focal point about which nearly
all of southern politics revolves. By the end of World War II, the
Democratic party had become so strong nationally, and the black
migration from the rural South to the northern metropolitan areas
had added so many black voters to the urban ethnic wing of the
Roosevelt coalition, that the prevailing patterns of racial discrimination in the South began to be challenged openly, especially within
the national circles of the bastion of southern independence, the
Democratic party. By this time, too, the South's loyalty to New
Deal liberalism had produced increasing centers of opposition to
the domination of state and local politics by the Bourbon planters
of the Black Belt areas and their allies, the doctor-lawyer-merchant-

banker county-seat elite (as Jasper Shannon has identified them) and the emerging plutocracy (often absentee) of the new industrial and financial centers such as Birmingham, Atlanta, and Houston. As usual, the South responded defensively to these threats to its "racial integrity," and all of southern politics—from nominations through elections and on into policy determination and implementation—tended to be caught up in the effort to maintain segregation as the first order of public business.

The story of the civil rights struggle is too well known to repeat here. But one must note that, from the Dixiecrat defection in 1948 through the events of the second reconstruction, which began with the decision in *Brown* v. *Board of Education of Topeka* in 1954, in which the United States Supreme Court overruled the 1896 "separate but equal" doctrine by declaring that separate schools for blacks and whites were inherently unequal, through the violence of the late 1950s and early 1960s, and on to the gradual overthrow of de jure (and much de facto) discrimination against blacks through congressional enactment and firm executive and judicial implementation of civil rights acts in the mid-1960s and later, the politics of the South was chaotically reacting to pressures for change from without and to intensive resistance from within.

Southern resistance eroded slowly until, without a clear break, obstruction of black efforts to participate in politics and to influence the course of policy evolved into acceptance and cooperation. Political breakthroughs in the form of voting and election to minor public offices (especially in areas of black majorities) preceded or paralleled social gains among blacks in desegregation of public facilities, schools, transportation, places of accommodation, employment opportunities, and housing. Although the lines of party and factional adherence became confused, and the old patterns of the distribution of votes broke under these pressures, the admission of new black voters to the polls in large numbers changed the rhetoric of the local politicians from blatant demagoguery, or coded statements in support of separation, or mere silence (often accompanied by backroom solicitation of black support) to tacit inclusion, concessions, and open solicitation of black votes and political alliances with black politicians. The election of two black politicians—Barbara Jordan of Houston and Andrew Young of Atlanta—to congressional seats in 1972, and of Maynard Jackson as mayor of Atlanta in 1973, not only brought black candidates to major offices extending beyond the narrow boundaries of counties and the councilmanic districts of towns and small cities, but demonstrated clearly that black and white voters could combine to elect blacks as well as whites to major offices. Politicians can count votes, and southern politicians are no less adept than others at this form of calculation.

The Carter election, then, was in many ways the apotheosis of an improbable dream that had gradually materialized. Not only had southern whites and blacks been brought together under the emblem of a party that had for so long provided the institutional basis for their division (at first as the white man's party, and more recently, in its national majoritarian manifestation, as the main political repository for black aspirations and, in consequence, the dialectical stimulant to white defection and revolt), but they had now been united in support of a white man from the Deep South. It is less important from this perspective that more whites in the South may still have voted for the Republican candidate than that the electoral votes of ten southern states were cast for Jimmy Carter, because *enough* whites joined the nearly unanimous black voters to overcome the white tendency to sustain the race issue as the main focus of southern unity, especially in national elections. It is also less important that the election may have demonstrated that the old Franklin D. Roosevelt coalition, embracing the geographic base of the solid South and the labor and ethnic groups of the great urban centers of the North, could still be revived than that the South again played a critical role in the election of a Democratic president. And going beyond this restoration of regional and party solidarity on a nonracial basis is the fact that southern blacks and whites united in 1976 to overcome the generally accepted national Democratic proscription against nominating southerners for the presidency—a barrier that had still seemed to be in effect (and possibly reinforced) after Lyndon Johnson's rather unusual accession.

These and other implications of the Carter election for a new politics in the South may be most effectively illustrated by an incident that occurred during the campaign. Ironically, this event was not reported through the national media because stories about a Carter statement on financial policy filed at the same time simply displaced the space it might otherwise have occupied. But I am assured by Wesley Pippert, currently the principal White House reporter for United Press International, who told me the story, that it can be fully documented by unreleased written reports, the testimony of the corps of reporters present, and even by a taped record that he thinks is still intact. The mini-drama took place on the Mississippi Gulf Coast. During the course of his speech there, Mr. Carter remarked that the Voting Rights Act of 1965, which provided rigorous federal regulation of registration procedures in designated states and counties and thus nearly doubled the number of qualified black voters in the region, was the best thing that ever happened so far as the South was concerned. To the surprise of some of the reporters, the applause this bold statement evoked was general, so the possibilities of a major story built around it were obvious. Not only that, but the meeting was one that was intended to display the unity of the state Democratic leadership behind the Carter candidacy, so both United States senators from Mississippi—John Stennis and James Eastland—were present, along with a number of other more or less prominent officeholders and party officials. During the question period following the address, a reporter asked Senator Stennis if he agreed with Mr. Carter's judgment on the Voting Rights Act, and he replied almost without hesitation that he did. (Stennis may be held in more respect for integrity by his senatorial colleagues than any other person in that body, despite the opprobrium generally attached by the public outside the South to almost any politician from Mississippi.) The probing reporters then directed the same question to Senator Eastland, who to many is the embodiment of the stereotype of the congressionally powerful, demagogic southern politician whose manipulative skill is both founded on, and used for, the perpetuation of racially oriented politics. Eastland paused briefly before nodding and saying yes, he did agree. Nothing could have signaled the end of an era more dramatically than this simple re-

sponse, which also reflected the general feeling of relief that seems
to have passed through the South as a result of the divestment of
the old burden of racial politics.

Not even the most confirmed optimist would argue that the
problem of race relations in the South is solved, or even that overt
appeal to racial prejudice for political advantage (deriving from
both black and white sources) will not continue to appear from
time to time. But it can be said that, while the race issue will still
influence politics in the South, it probably will not be the major
determinant of political outcomes (either in the direct or the co-
vert sense) that it was for the better part of a century; it will not
be made to work solely in one direction (*i.e.*, to maintain the dominance of white over black); and it will no longer be a uniquely
southern matter because it has been sufficiently diffused to make
it a national rather than a regional problem.

And that brings us to another potential major symbolic feature
in the Carter election, one that is so closely related to those just
discussed that it may ultimately be seen as having enveloped all
the others. I use the term *potential* to emphasize the fact that, for
the time being, the pragmatic basis for considering the Carter
election as a possible symbol of a renewed sense of national unity
is being tentatively explored as a question rather than by way of a
positive hypothesis: did the election actually demonstrate that the
South had rejoined the Union? And the ancillary question, which
is more often implied than articulated clearly is: if the South has
been reunited with the nation, was it readmitted after having been
rehabilitated (or "reconstructed") following its long banishment
on the grounds of moral and political delinquency, or did it, in a
sense, wage a long political war of attrition so successfully that it
forced its way in by eventual domination? These questions may
be too figurative to elicit answers that are themselves anything
more than vague metaphors, but an examination of transition
from the old to the new politics in the South, with due attention
to the relation between the South and the nation before and during that transition, may at least provide some intimations that
could eventually yield something more definitive, if more complex, than the easy explanation of sectional amalgamation through
increasing national homogeneity.

In talking about the transition from the old to the new southern politics, the temptation to resort entirely to sociological explanation is strong, not only because the positivist assumptions of sociology still direct the main tendencies of all the social sciences (and even much of history) towards deterministic explanations, but also because social patterns of race, class, and socioeconomic status do bear clear associational (if not causal) relations to the way politics has been, and is now, carried on in the South. In fact, I have already stressed the fact that race was the controlling factor in the "old" politics of the South, and one can go on to demonstrate (as has been done in a vast literature on the South) how the racial caste system, the economic class system, the rural and agrarian pattern of life and economic structure underpinned the one-party, single-issue politics of the South until the social changes produced by urbanization and industrialization on the one hand, and the civil rights movement on the other, broke up the political system that the old social structures had sustained as a public reinforcement for their own preservation. But neither the old nor the new sociology of the South, even when supplemented by theories of social and political development, fully explain the politics of the region without the need to bring in some further human dimensions, particularly those related to the way general ideas about morals and policies are generated, disseminated, and eventually made effective in helping to shape both society and politics. Unless we allow a considerable scope for the exercise of human influence on social and political events and systemic structures, we are likely to advance tautological arguments in which social phenomena are seen as determining political systems, while the latter are perceived as having reciprocally determined the former. Sociological reductionism has served ideology better than it has explained reality. So without eschewing social explanation altogether, I tend to think that the complexities of the South and its politics can be better revealed if the discussion centers on the uniqueness of some historic events, and on personalities, deep-rooted cultural traits (consciously and unconsciously held), and political typologies, rather than on standard collections of social data.

W. J. Cash noted that the Civil War and Reconstruction turned the South back into a frontier, with the implication that it was thereby reopened for exploitation by human predators from both within and without. The end of Reconstruction meant the abandonment of the former slaves to economic dependence on their former masters, after a period of support that lasted only long enough to confirm southern whites in their resentment against both the Republican ("carpetbagger") reconstructionists and the bids on the part of blacks for political equality, and to intensify the will to restore and maintain white supremacy. Regardless of whether the original picture of Reconstruction as a fiasco of corruption and mismanagement is more or less accurate than the revisionist view that the performance of blacks (and their northern allies) during this period was no more inefficient or corrupt than the regimes that preceded and followed them, the mythical interpretation that prevailed in the South was one of total degradation of the rulers and total humiliation of the subjects at a time when the white males who had been associated with the Confederacy were deprived of all political rights. And the forceful projection of that interpretation gave impetus to the "redemptionist" movements in the southern states that led to the creation between the 1880s and the early years of the twentieth century of the singular political practices characteristic of the old politics of the region.

Ironically, the withdrawal of federal troops and the restoration of citizenship to the former Confederates, which opened the way for the South to create what was in some ways a more constricted version of the political *status quo ante*, also proved a boon to the northern Federalist-Whig types who wanted the Republican party to give less emphasis to the social concerns that had been so important in its origins, and get on with the consolidation of its national power. And that power was used to generate public policies conducive to the growth of large-scale financial and industrial capitalism. If the South wanted to get rid of the Republican party, the northern Republicans could in turn wave the "bloody shirt" of the Civil War to help confine the strength of the Democratic party within the borders of the Confederacy. If southerners wanted to resubjugate blacks, northerners could sublimate their moral concerns over the issue by using the South (where almost 90 percent of the blacks in the country lived prior to the twentieth century) as a scapegoat for this "American dilemma." And if the South developed what Professor T. Harry Williams calls a "garrison state psychology," the North tended to draw a *cordon sanitaire* around the region to isolate it politically, socially, and economically from the rest of the country, and to insulate the other sections against intrusions from the terra incognita of the South. Neither form of closure was completely successful, of course, but each contributed to the way the South practiced its politics and the way the region related to the nation as a whole.

The main configurations of southern politics from the turn of the century until sometime after 1948 are well known. The reduction of the Republican party to a mere token and the elimination of black participation by a combination of legal and extralegal actions (which also substantially reduced white participation) left the Democratic party as the sole mediating political organization in the region. Almost all effective competition for state and local offices took place within the loose frame of the party. Its primary (or nominating) elections were said to be tantamount to real elections, since opposition seldom appeared in general elections other than presidential ones and in a few surviving pockets of mountain Republicanism. Although factional organizations within the Democratic party developed in some states and were more or less successful in controlling both statewide (and some local) offices as well as the party machinery for long periods of time (*e.g.*, the Harry F. Byrd organization in Virginia from the 1920s to the mid-1960s, the Long faction in Louisiana from the late 1920s to the early 1960s, and the Talmadge forces in Georgia in the 1930s and 1940s), most candidates ran individual campaigns, pulled most of their electoral support from the particular section of a state in which they lived, and relied more on personality (and subsequently on incumbency) than on issues in their appeals to the voters. In Florida, the organizational structure was so dispersed that V. O. Key referred to the pattern as "every man for himself." Although interest in politics always seemed to be intense in the South, voter participation tended to be somewhat inverted, with the largest turnouts occurring in the most localized primaries (in wards, towns, and counties) and the lowest in presidential elections, where the outcome was fairly well assured anyway. Since the region remained predominantly rural until after the 1940 census, much of the real political power tended to be exercised at the level of the county seat, where it was also highly personalized.

In national politics, the South's loyalty was critical to the very act of keeping the Democratic party alive in the late nineteenth century, so in many ways the South's role in national politics was, during the period under consideration, an active one. As long as the Republican party was the national majority party, southern Democrats constituted the congressional majority in the minority party. When the Democrats became the majority party after 1932, southerners continued to hold a majority of the Democratic seats in both houses of Congress until the increase in party strength in the rest of the country and their own defections deprived them of this position in the 1960s. This majority enabled the southerners to control elections to congressional party leadership posts in the party caucus and to the House and Senate leadership positions when the Democrats held a majority of seats in those bodies.

Because U.S. senators and congressmen from the southern states tended to hold their seats longer than those from other areas, southerners also came to dominate the powerful committee system of the Congress, which uses seniority for committee assignments and for filling the chairmanships of the committees. Experience and general compatability with elaborate congressional rules and customs have also added to the ability of southerners to maintain a certain preeminence in the Congress. Because the electoral politics of the South bestowed a free mandate on congressional delegations from the South in nearly all matters except the maintenance of the region's peculiar institution of racial segregation, the performance of southerners in congressional politics was far more skillful and deserving of general recognition than has been commonly acknowledged. One may think of Theodore Bilbo, James Eastland, and Strom Thurmond as prototypical, but what of William Bankhead, Joseph Robinson, and Pat Harrison, who served as leaders of Congress during the New Deal days, or of Sam Rayburn and Lyndon Johnson later, of liberals such as Estes Kefauver, Albert Gore, Claude Pepper, Lister Hill, and John Sparkman, or of conservatives of integrity such as Richard Russell of Georgia, John Stennis of Mississippi, and Sam Ervin of North Carolina, of an intellectual such as James Fulbright, or of politicians of the order of Brooks Hays of Arkansas and Frank Smith of Mississippi, both of whom lost their seats because they would not capitulate to the demands of demagogues on the race issue? We seem rarely to have reflected on the irony of the dual functions of the South's congressional delegations in having simultaneously used their skills and formal positions of leadership to protect the region's territorial imperative on race and to advance so many other national policies that seem to fly in the face of the social and economic reaction so often attributed to southerners as a whole. It may be even more ironic that a section of the country that could contribute so much national leadership under considerable adversity failed for so long to find the political resources to put its own house in order.

However, if we look beyond the surface description of the South's old politics, it may be possible to discern more complexity than simplicity in its patterns, as well as some of the underlying sources that contributed to the recent changes in the South, or at least enabled southerners to adapt to those changes as they were imposed on them from the outside. And here it is useful to stress that, despite the limitations on political competition in the one-party solid South, there has always been sufficient diversity of both condition and perspective among southerners to make political opposition and dissent more than incipient. Although the organizational means for generating competition made the political expression of these differences somewhat sporadic, we can discern in a variety of political types different orientations on the fundamental nature of the society and the policy directions that might assist in bringing into reality a particular conception of society.

A broad typology of southern politicians of the older style includes groupings under three main categories—the Bourbons, the Whigs, and the Populists. As with any attempted classification or categorization of political types, each one has to be characterized in the most general terms because it covers a wide variety of subtypes, individuals may be seen as overlapping the categories, and variations appear over time. However, if we try to use some care in attaching labels, a classification scheme does aid comprehension.

The term *Bourbon* actually originated as one of opprobrium, to characterize a post–Civil War, self-designated planter aristocracy that wielded great public power without assuming much public responsibility. Even though the antebellum plantation system reached its apogee only a few years prior to the Civil War, its mythology had developed quickly and intensely in defense of a slavocracy within a republic that rested on classical liberal assumptions of freedom and equality. The myth was reinforced by comparisons with the aristocracies of the ancient world, classical revival architecture, and a particular attachment to the romantic novels of Sir Walter Scott. In the upper South, particularly in Virginia, the cult of the gentleman who owned both his land and his privilege of office by heredity added another dimension to the aristocratic self-conception, which could be spread without too much trouble to the remainder of the South. In the post-Reconstruction South, the romantic legend of the noble Confederate war leaders played its part in helping to consolidate the dominance of Black Belt plantation rule, with a racial caste system replacing the old racially based slavery one. Bourbon political types had no hesitancy in manipulating black votes to beat off the Republican and Populist threats to their political dominance, particularly in the 1880s and 1890s, and then promptly mobilized the whites of all classes to remove blacks from the voting rolls. It is the Bourbons who have given the South its reputation for extreme conservatism, and it was their dominating presence in the Democratic party circles in the South that made it possible for the Black Belt, with a steadily declining proportion of the white vote, to continue to control the politics of the region so effectively.

The Bourbon planters have frequently entered into alignments with merchants and bankers of the southern cities and small towns. In Louisiana, particularly, the upstate planters were allied with a New Orleans political machine from the 1890s until Huey Long's incursion in 1928 broke up the machine, only to reconstitute it for Long's own use in organizing a new majority in the state.

In Virginia, the Byrd organization dominated state politics for forty years through a quiet process of rule by gentlemen based on a small electorate in which most of the support came from conservative upper-middle and upper-class voters in Richmond and the rural and small-town whites in Southside Virginia.

The element of *noblesse oblige* has not been entirely lacking among representatives of this particular political type. Probably the finest expression of true paternalistic quality among the planters is to be found in William Alexander Percy's lyrical autobiography, *Lanterns on the Levee*, in which he tells the story of his father's defeat for the United States Senate by the demagogic populist, James K. Vardaman, in an election that was one of the early manifestations of the internal struggle in Mississippi between the planters of the delta and the plain folk of the hills. Senator William Fulbright of Arkansas and Senator Richard Russell of Georgia may be considered among the more responsible Bourbon types of recent vintage (especially when it is considered that the South was the most international-minded section of the country until quite recently), while persons such as Strom Thurmond of South Carolina and Governor Fielding Wright of Mississippi, who were the Dixiecrat candidates for president and vice-president, respectively, in 1948, represent a more inflexible embodiment of Bourbon political views.

The Whig category derives from an obvious source, the American Whig party, which was the direct heir to the Federalists from the 1830s until it broke up under the strain of the antislavery issue and yielded its major party status to the Republican insurgents in the North after 1856. Although the Jacksonian Democrats had a substantial edge on the Whigs in the South during this competitive period, the latter did provide a real alternative before finally being absorbed into the southern Democratic party as one of the continuing influences on its internal differentiation. Many old Whigs in the South were planters, but the party's main directions were set by the merchants, bankers, and emerging industrialists.

The Whig designation, then, relates mainly to those politicians in the South who have been associated with the development of

trade and industry, and whose politics is primarily business oriented. In this respect, the ideological range that might be covered
by the main characteristics of such politicians is fairly broad. One
thinks of the Whigs as being in the vanguard of the "New South"
movement or, more properly speaking, movements, because practically every generation since Henry W. Grady of Georgia first
enunciated the creed in the 1880s has had its enthusiastic Whig
boosters, with platforms aimed at diversifying the South's economy by attracting capital and industry to the region, stimulating
the growth of its cities, advertising the features of the respective
states that make them attractive to investors, and maintaining
tax and other incentives to stimulate both internal and external
sources to expand the total economy.

In many states, the Whigs have been in alliance with the Bourbons, but some of them have also been mildly progressive because
they see in public education programs and public works (especially parks, highways, recreation facilities, and municipal services) amenities that not only enhance their own environment,
but are essential to efforts to attract outsiders to the South. As the
rift in the Democratic party between its conservative adherents
to the regionally based wing and those who remained loyal to the
national organization (including the "new" black voters) widened
from 1948 onwards, many of the Whig types moved into the Republican party, thereby strengthening suburban Republicanism to
the point of making it an alternative in some places to the badly
divided (and often demoralized) Democratic party.

By no means social reformers, the Whigs did contribute indirectly to the amelioration of the race issue, not only by their contributions to the urbanization of the region, but also by their refusal to allow industrial growth to be halted or slowed down by
the several impediments placed in its way by the Dixiecrats and
their epigone. In many ways, the Whig type was instrumental in
creating the economic thrust after World War II that has gradually
brought the South into line with the rest of the country in produc-
tivity, personal income, and levels of urbanization.

At his most extreme, the Whig has been a throwback to the age
of McKinley; but in general, the increasingly bland sophistication

of southern politics has been a product of the internal movement toward a pattern that is (on a statewide basis, and especially in the office of governor) almost indistinguishable from the Midwest. In their study of *The Transformation of Southern Politics*, Jack Bass and Walter De Vries illustrate this point well in a report on an interview with David Broder of the *Washington Post*, who found the attitudes of state leaders throughout the country similar, with the southerners being "perhaps" a bit more progressive.

The Populist is probably the most interesting of the southern political types. Although his historical roots may have been in Jacksonian democracy, the name derives from the Populist or People's party movement of the 1890s. The actual movement may have originated in the Midwest, but in retrospect its activities are noted as having been more intense and having had a longer-range effect on the southern and border states than elsewhere. It represented the culmination of a succession of third-party movements in the late nineteenth century that were directed, in many respects, against the political consequences of the 1876 Compromise. Its strongest appeal everywhere was to the small farmer as victim of a system of taxation, credit, transportation, and marketing that, in the main, served the interests of finance and corporate capitalism at the expense of the "little" man. In the South, it so threatened the recently established Bourbon dominance of the Democratic party that the latter group resorted to the extreme measures described earlier to defeat the Populists and then consolidated their control by severely limiting the right to vote. Although the Populists enjoyed only sporadic success at the time (and later for that matter), they demonstrated beyond any doubt that, beneath the apparent unity of the Democratic party in the South, social and economic discontent was widespread, and means for relief by way of a competitive politics that was capable of being responsive to all strata of society did not exist. The spirit of populism since that time has been so persistent that almost every effort to open southern politics to real competition in the twentieth century has had a populist tendency in it, and has been met by a Bourbon counterreaction.

The terms *populist* and *populism* have been applied to so many politicians and so many factional movements that Professor George Tindall has argued that we ought to place a moratorium on them for being meaningless. While it is true that these words have come to be used more often ascriptively than descriptively, they do have some currency because much of the color and variety of southern politics have been displayed in populist (or apparently populist) circles. And one of the reasons populist politics has been colorful is that it has had at least two sides, one being its radical (mainly agrarian and individualistic) dissent against big, entrenched power structures of both a private and public nature, and the other is its reflection of features characteristic of twentieth-century mass movements, in which ideology is effectively used to manipulate large collectivities without much respect for rational behavior in either the selection of ends or the use of means.

The classic case of a "spoiled" populist was Tom Watson of Georgia. In his (and populism's) early days, Watson attempted to use his considerable powers of political persuasion to bring black and white laborers and small farmers into a coalition to dethrone the Bourbon Democrats. Whether from frustration over his lack of success at the polls or for other reasons, Watson turned to race-baiting as a means of advancing his personal political ambitions, which culminated in his election to the U.S. Senate, but with all of his radical idealism in sad disarray. One is reminded of how much the career of the latter-day populist, George Wallace, followed the pattern set by Watson, and of how Orval Faubus of Arkansas also turned from a style and program that resembled Jacksonian democracy to one in which he relied on his stand on segregation to return him to term after term in the governorship. The most interesting of the southern neo-populists in the twentieth century was Huey Long of Louisiana, who did not revert to racism to solidify his hold on power or to divert attention from failure to implement reform programs, but who did mold his following into a dedicated mass that proved itself ready to support him in the exercise of unlimited personal power.

Although populist labels have been placed on such traditional New Deal liberals as Senators Estes Kefauver and Albert Gore of Tennessee and Lister Hill and John Sparkman of Alabama, it is not easy to point to examples of genuine populists in southern politics today. For one thing, the populist idea and image was rooted in the red clay soil of the hill country of the rural South, so the personalized style and rustic rhetoric of the old populists were radically different from the media-based, carefully orchestrated and standardized campaigns characteristic of contemporary politicians, including those in the South. George Wallace, of course, is still around, as is Lester Maddox of Georgia. But Earl Long, Huey's younger brother, who called himself "the last of the red hot papas" and practiced an old-fashioned, stump-worming, barnyard image oratory, and took a race-free and generally liberal stand on issues, may have been the last survivor (he died in 1960) of the authentic tradition in which race was subordinate to a stubborn moral stand on predominantly economic issues. Henry Howell of Virginia is effective in using some elements of the style (especially in the mountain areas) and talks about "keeping the big boys honest," but his urban sophistication and University of Virginia law school background show through as he puts together a new coalition of white labor and blacks to challenge the long-standing dominance of respectable conservatism in the Commonwealth. Yesterday's populist is in many ways today's straightforward southern liberal, who is similar to liberals everywhere else, but who may retain a few distinctive local traits.

What these brief profiles of southern political types are meant to suggest is the survival, but in substantially changed form, of some of the human elements and their relation to persisting issues in the politics of the South. Since the region is still in political transition, it is not possible to say whether the constrictive one-party politics of the past will eventually evolve into a two-party system or some other arrangement for the coalescence of interests into effectively organized means of competing for public offices through which policies are formulated. But if we return to our point of departure—the symbolic effects of Jimmy Carter's elevation to the presidency—it is possible to discern some of the practical ways in which this phenomenon contributed, at least temporarily, to the stabilization of a politics that had ranged from fluidity to near-chaos for almost thirty years.

Carter's capacity to unite disparate groups into an improbable coalition—thereby exerting an annealing influence on the South's near-anomic divisiveness, as well as producing a reconciliatory effect on the politics of the South in relation to the nation at large —is partly a result of the representative reflection in his personal style of all three of the major types in southern politics. Whether this is natural or contrived is by no means clear. Nor is it at all certain that, as President, Carter can hold his coalition intact as he tries to translate a hazy mandate on campaign "themes" into policies that assist in resolving the specific issues confronting his administration. But he does seem to unite in his person elements of paternalism, whiggery, and populism.

As a planter Mr. Carter is far from being one of the "cotton snob" Bourbons of the Black Belt, but his "peanut farm" is on a scale that requires many dependents, his sense of place and extended family are strong, he is well educated, and he has had the appropriate connections with the military tradition of the South. His manner and speech, too, are often those of the liberal paternalist, if not quite those of the pure Bourbon. On the other hand, when Mr. Carter emphasizes his background as a nuclear scientist and stresses the development and implementation of programs through the utilization of techniques derived from scientific, military, bureaucratic, and business skills, he seems to be the epitome of the deliberate, rationally calculating, and somewhat progressive Whig, for whom efficiency and economy are the hallmarks of successful administration in either business or government. Above all, though, Mr. Carter seems most at home in his populist role. Here his plain farmer image, fundamentalist religious background, and compassion for the dispossessed, coupled with moral indignation over the perceived causes of their plight, lend plausibility to his appeal as a social and political reformer who values simplicity over complexity, moral substance over either style or efficiency, and small- over large-scale associations of all types. It may be this combination of the three main types of southern politicians in the one man that has caused so many observers to be puzzled over efforts to categorize the President as a liberal, radical, conservative, or middle-of-the-roader. His capacity for unification has depended on being all of them in succession, and at times even simultaneously, because the old identifications in pure form tend to be more divisive than integrative. His very independence and appearance of indirection are themselves southern traits that have contributed to the sense that a new politics is coming into being in the South and in the nation as Mr. Carter has emerged from obscurity and moved relentlessly toward the pinnacle.

Behind this appearance of being all things to all people, however, is a partially obscured restorative function that helps explain the combination of traditionalism with change (or mixture of conservation and innovation) in the altered style of southern politics that Carter exemplifies in its most extended form. During the long period of southern exile, the region remained closer to the social foundations and, in many instances, the moral and political conceptions underlying the origins of the Republic than the rest of the country, despite its aberrant racial policies and the stigma it bore for maintaining them. While the country went through great changes by means of geographical expansiveness, alteration of the composition of its population through immigration, and urban-industrial development, the South remained sequestered, its ethnic makeup (and therefore its social structures) largely fixed, and its main socioeconomic characteristics (predominately rural-agricultural, with set class and caste structures) only gradually and partially modified. In brief, the South retained something of the cast of a preindustrial society throughout the American transition into a massive, technocratically organized industrial power, and it still brings something of those qualities with it as it merges its politics with that of the nation in the so-called postindustrial era.

Some, if not most, of Carter's appeal outside the South must be attributed to the way in which his style evokes a partly sublimated nostalgia for a more self-assured society predicated on simple virtues, in preference to the complex and uneasy arrangements under which the nation has come to exist. The features of the South that make it different, and the extent to which the differences persist over time, have been sources of extended controversy on the part of intellectuals. Among the most obvious special attributes of the region (other than accent) are personalism, an awareness of history (as recognition of the influence of the past on the present), an attachment to place, an emphasis on family and local community, a commitment to religion (mainly Protestant Christianity), and a preference for the concrete and individual over the abstract and collective. In *The Enduring South*, John Shelton Reed notes that "two institutions, the family and the church," are more powerful in the South than in any other region, and others have stressed the continued dominance of a folk culture in the South that has resisted the encroachment of the mass culture of urban-industrial America. Professor Charles Roland has perhaps summarized this whole range of effects as well as anyone in his perceptive volume, *The Improbable Era*, which surveys the thirty years of dramatic change through which the South has just passed: "Despite a persistent malaise from their heritage of slavery, secession, defeat, and poverty, southerners looked upon themselves as defenders of the ancient American virtues."

The point is that Jimmy Carter personified many of these characteristics of his region at a time when the country had passed through an era of domestic unrest and international turmoil that had shaken the confidence of the society in its leadership, its institutions, its moral reinforcements, and its capacity to deal with problems that threatened the possibilities of leading decent private or public lives. While George Wallace had been able to touch some responsive chords in the ordinary citizenry through resort to some of the aforementioned southern attributes, his efforts were too tinged with racial implications to make these responses general. But Jimmy Carter managed to hold out the promise of these sources of individual and community virtue without the taint of the old racial politics that for so long had such debilitating effects on the South and its relations with the rest of the country.

The South's politics may still be far from having undergone a complete transformation, but enough of its old difficulties have been overcome to permit some of its underlying potential values to surface. The promises the southern political style offers for national leadership based on a revival of tradition that can still adapt successfully to change are now being tested in the difficult arena of practical politics, and the outcome will be no less important to the nation as a whole than to the southern region.

Growing Up in the Deep South:
A Conversation with
Eudora Welty, Shelby Foote,
and Louis D. Rubin, Jr.

RUBIN: I was reading something about George W. Cable, the New Orleans novelist, the other day, and there was a funny remark about Cable by the Scottish writer James M. Barrie. He said, "Don't visit New Orleans. Go into the boiler room and read George W. Cable." I was just thinking that here in Jackson, Mississippi, where the temperature today is about 95 degrees, you could almost say the same thing: "Don't visit Mississippi. Go into the furnace room and read Eudora Welty or Shelby Foote."

I want to ask you to bear with me for a minute while I read a quotation from Ring Lardner, who, as you know, was not from the South. This is from a piece called "Christmas Suggestions"—presents to give one's children. This is "Age 17 and Over":

> When a boy gets to be 17 it is high time he had a good mouth organ. This will not only bring him unlimited pleasure but will be a blessing to his friends, male and female.
>
> If he is subject to smallpox, a prettily put -up box of vaccine will make his Christmas a merry one.
>
> He will be overjoyed with a dog house, particularly if he has a dog.

I think that passage is extremely funny, and I think Ring Lardner is extremely funny, but you could pick that paragraph up and you would know at once it was not written by a southerner and was probably written by someone from the Midwest. I wonder why?

FOOTE: Well, it has no southern speech pattern to it. It has no rhythm to it, to my ear, and that's why no southerner would write it.

RUBIN: It doesn't have the rhythm. I hadn't thought of that. But it also has no sense of rhetoric, really, or of the sound of words, or language, or anything like that. The cadences aren't regular. There isn't any of that rhetorical sense. Now why do southern writers not write like Lardner?

WELTY: We don't talk that way. I think Lardner's ear is marvelous, but I think in that case the content even more than the cadences makes it seem nonsouthern. Nobody needs a mouth organ at the age of seventeen. In the South, they've been playing since they were two. All those things wouldn't be thought funny by the children, you know.

FOOTE: There's another thing nonsouthern about it: he's not telling a story. I've never known southerners do anything *but* tell stories.

WELTY: Even in that short a space, I imagine.

FOOTE: "I remember the boy down the block," or something.

RUBIN: We are doing this broadcast in the State of Mississippi, which is sort of headquarters for storytelling, I guess. Here is where the biggest storyteller of all comes from, right up the road about ninety miles, in the town of Oxford. That passage from Lardner reminds me just a little of the Jason section in Faulkner's *The Sound and the Fury*. He has Jason talking a good bit like that. He's deliberately making Jason talk in that unlovely naturalistic way in order to show that that's the sort of person Jason is.

FOOTE: An outlander in the land. Characteristic southern writing, though, does something that Miss Welty calls attention to just by the use of a word. I saw a quotation from her recently in which she spoke of the scene of a novel as being a "gathering-place," which is the best possible description you could give of a scene for a novel. That's what the scene in a novel is—a gathering-place for characters, where something's going to happen. I think that's characteristically southern, the notion of it.

WELTY: I do, too, and not only the notion but the technique of it, from the novelist's point of view—you use it to gather in every-thing you want to deal with, all of your threads.

RUBIN: It's a gathering *place*; not just any old place but a particu-lar place.

WELTY: It's where it's happened before and where it may happen again; that's the place.

RUBIN: It seems to me that Ring Lardner's stories, for example, could happen almost anywhere. This isn't to say that Faulkner's stories aren't universal, because they are, but I get no feeling of any real sense of place in Lardner—any more than I do in Hem-ingway, unless he's deliberately setting out to describe a place, such as Paris or a particular spot in Spain, or something like that.

WELTY: I think Lardner located his stories within the realms of sa-tire or sports or something; he had a style that was his circle that he put things inside. His style was the circumference of where these things happened. And he wasn't interested, as you said, in the place as a place, as I think perhaps we are. Shelby, don't you agree?

FOOTE: Yes, I do. Another thing about Lardner: he had a marvel-ous ear, but he had an ear for the quirky, the strange, in everyday speech. He would speak of someone's girl friend's boy friend. He liked the sound of things like that. It had very little to do with the natural rhythms of speech, which I don't think interested him much.

WELTY: That's why he was so wonderful also in the letters he wrote, which are ten thousand miles removed from speech, but on purpose, because his people were writing letters to sound dif-ferent from the way they talked.

FOOTE: And they were satire, especially a story told by a middle-aged Illinois businessman on vacation, who calls his wife "Mother."

RUBIN: If you were going to draw up a literary map of Mississippi, it would be a series of places—you would have northern Missis-sippi where Faulkner grew up, and you would have Oxford, Greenville, and the Delta, where you, Shelby, and Walker Percy grew up, and Elizabeth Spencer in nearby Carrollton, and here in Jackson would be Eudora Welty, and in Natchez, Richard Wright. And where did Tennessee Williams live in Mississippi?

WELTY: Columbus.

RUBIN: That's quite a collection, you know. You could legitimately work up a book and call it *Mississippi Writers*, and you wouldn't be dealing with any little provincial reputations at all; you'd be dealing with major currents of twentieth-century American literature.

FOOTE: One of the characteristics of Mississippi is that there are at least seven very distinct areas, all different from the other six. I suspect most states are like that; I know Tennessee is. But Mississippi does seem to me to have diversity. And it's not because part of it is mountains and part of it is flat, because there aren't any mountains in Mississippi. The Gulf Coast is the Gulf Coast because it is, and the Delta is the Delta because it is; the Jackson area is the capital of the state; Faulkner's area is in the hills. But there's not a huge geographical distance, the way there is in Arkansas, for instance. It goes back to history. The Black Prairie region was settled by a certain kind of people in a certain way at a certain date, and the same with other parts of the state, especially Natchez and the Delta.

RUBIN: Mississippi has the most wonderful [place] names. I really don't know any other state that has names like Senatobia.

FOOTE: There again you get that enormous variety. There are Indian names, there are German names, there are French names, there are Anglo-Saxon names. It's not like Pennsylvania, where half of them are Dutch, or something. There's just everything in the world in Mississippi.

RUBIN: They all seem to be created, too. I get the feeling that places in Mississippi were all consciously named. I mean, they didn't just say "Let's call this place 'Brown's Corner,'" or something like that. It's as if someone went out and said, "I'm going to call this place 'Senatobia.'"

WELTY: Or "Midnight," or "Coffeeville," for a good reason. Of course those are extreme.

FOOTE: There's a funny story about names. There's a British cricket player and a man who didn't know cricket. There was a certain kind of fly ball that you catch and it was called a "ruger," and the man asked the cricket player, "Why is that called a 'ruger'?" The player took his cap off and scratched his head and said, "I honestly don't see what else you could call it."

RUBIN: Shelby, you grew up in Greenville, and Walker Percy was a close friend of yours when you were in high school together, and Walker's uncle was Will Percy, who as a literary figure is not well remembered now, although I think most people remember *Lanterns on the Levee*, the book of memoirs he published in the 1940s. Eudora, did you know Will Percy?

WELTY: I never did get to meet him. I wish I could have.

RUBIN: He was a remarkable man. You knew him, of course, Shelby.

FOOTE: I knew him very well indeed. I was over at Walker's house about as often as I was over at my house. Will Percy single-handedly is responsible for anything literary that came out of Greenville. Not by having a literary coterie or anything like that. He did it by example and by a sort of teaching that you didn't know was going on. He was a man who had traveled widely throughout the world. He had good music in his house, which very few of us had. He had a formidable library—just the fact that it was there—plus the fact that he published books of poetry, actually published books. It was quite a thing to be close to. I guess there are at least fifteen published writers from Greenville, and practically all of them are due to the presence of Will Percy. Not a direct influence, just his presence.

RUBIN: There is usually somebody like that, or else a school teacher. Have you noticed that there will be a particularly good high school teacher somewhere, and for this reason there will be a group of writers in that place?

WELTY: Absolutely.

FOOTE: Well, Percy was there for that reason. Carrie Stern, a teacher there at home, was the one who fostered Will Percy when he was a boy.

WELTY: I'm so glad you said what you did about Will Percy, because I think those things need to be said, and I was awfully glad. Louis, did you read the new preface that Walker Percy wrote for *Lanterns on the Levee*, for the LSU Press? I thought it was a marvelous thing for him to have done, because it's sort of a translation for people who couldn't perhaps comprehend the exact background or the measure of what Will Percy did.

FOOTE: Walker spoke in there of something that's very true—about how Will Percy was one of the greatest teachers he had ever known. Simply by the way he presented what he wanted you to know, he made it attractive, in the way a great teacher can, and didn't detract from it by boasting about it or leaning on it too heavy, or anything. He really knew how to do it.

RUBIN: Eudora, did you have a teacher, a particular teacher, whom you found when you were in grammer school or in high school?

WELTY: Oh, sure. We were talking about that the other day—about my particular high school class. It wasn't in high school, it was in grammar school—the principal of the grammar school was Miss Lorena Duling. We were trying to wonder why nearly every one of our little class (it was the year that they added a year on, so it was a very small graduating class, sixty people) mangaged to do something kind of special in whatever he chose. And we all said it was Miss Duling. I think she was from Kentucky.

FOOTE: It could well be true.

WELTY: It could really be. I remember there was one Sunday when there were seven people from Jackson represented as reviewers in the *New York Times Book Review*. They weren't all still living there, but we'd all grown up under Miss Duling. It was very funny. One was Bill Hamilton, from Duke; they were scattered about.

FOOTE: It's a real talent, and you find it everywhere. Thank God, you do.

RUBIN: You usually have a teacher in every one of your books, Eudora, one way or the other.

WELTY: I'm sure I do, because it meant a lot to me. Also, my mother was such a teacher, although she didn't teach me, but I heard her tales of schoolteaching in the mountains of West Virginia. She was the same kind of soul that these other teachers were.

RUBIN: I guess Faulkner didn't have a teacher like that, did he? I guess he had Phil Stone.

FOOTE: I'd be willing to bet anything he did. I never knew anybody who didn't.

WELTY: I never knew anybody who didn't.

RUBIN: I know I had one, a Latin teacher, even though I flunked finally.

WELTY: Yes, it doesn't matter about the subject so much.

FOOTE: I had an English teacher. Her name was Lelia Hawkins— Miss Hawkins. I think teachers in those days made about eighty dollars a month, and what they got was the respect of the community, which they certainly deserved. Miss Hawkins never gave me a high grade—oh, it would be a great day or month when she would give me a B, because she would always tell me, "You can do much better than this; I am not going to give you anything over a C."

RUBIN: I remember distinguishing myself with my Latin teacher in South Carolina my senior year in high school by turning in a paper which came back with a 17 on it. He went through the answers in class, and I found he had failed to give me credit for one correct answer, so I brought the paper up at the end of the class and he changed the 17 to a 19 and said, "That makes a great deal of difference, doesn't it, Rubin?" He was a fine person and one of the greatest teachers I ever had. He taught me a great deal, a sort of respect for learning, as this sort of person always does. It's not just what he teaches, but how he or she makes you think that there's something fine about knowing things.

WELTY: About learning, and that it's in the *thing*—not to beat somebody, but *it*.

RUBIN: The dignity of it, as such.

FOOTE: I've found the common characteristic of all the good teachers I ever had was that they could communicate to you their enthusiasm for their subject. They did it in many different ways, but that was always what it came down to. And others gave you an example of a life well lived, that the values that she (usually) lived by were indeed worth living by because you saw the result of them in her life. If I were ever able to do it I would write about Miss Hawkins, for instance, who lived what you might call an empty, lonely life, but it was one of the best lives I've ever seen—a great life, and everyone knew it, too.

WELTY: I think children are very much aware of integrity. When they see it, they know it, though they wouldn't know the word.

RUBIN: Well, this certainly has been one of the things you've written so much about. I was just thinking of Miss Eckhart in "June Recital," and the teacher in *Losing Battles*, and then you have a teacher in *The Optimist's Daughter*.

WELTY: It always takes me aback to realize that I repeat myself this way; I don't realize it, I just don't know that I do it. But I think we all do this kind of thing—there are patterns in our minds.

RUBIN: The teacher in *Losing Battles* is Miss Julia Mortimer, and at the end of the story when Gloria and Ralph go to the graveyard where she's been buried, Gloria says, "Miss Julia Mortimer, she didn't want anybody left in the dark, not about anything. She wanted everything brought out in the wide open, to see and be known." But Ralph says, "People don't want to be read like books." I guess it's that kind of tension between the need to know and the instinct, almost the animal instinct, I guess, to hide, that is one way of representing the human condition, or something like that.

And writing about a teacher is an awfully good way of showing that.

FOOTE: I've thought back about Miss Hawkins, and it's a wonder any of us ever reads Shakespeare again after being exposed to him in high school; and now that I look back on it with my vast wisdom, I can see that Miss Hawkins didn't know a great deal about Shakespeare, either, but she loved Shakespeare and that is what came across. And it was up to us to get from it what she had somehow managed to get. It was a very real communication.

RUBIN: This sort of person is like the outside world coming into the community. Here's the community with all its patterns and its doings and its own values . . .

FOOTE: Will Percy did that, and in a good way. He had been to Japan, he'd been all over South America, he knew Europe quite well, and to hear him speak of these as real places was quite different from reading about them in a book or hearing some tourist tell about the day he or she went to Brussels and Paris all in one day, or something. It was a real experience to hear somebody speak of it the way he did.

WELTY: You know another thing about what Louis was saying, about the pattern in the South of the teacher, is that it also applies to the way we all lived in those days, of not moving around much in the South, so that teacher knew the generations and the generations knew her. And that made another web.

FOOTE: That could really be extended. There was a woman named Miss Lee who taught my mother in the first grade, she taught me in the first grade, and she taught my daughter in the first grade. That's three generations she taught in the first grade.

RUBIN: I remember in 1931 or 1932, we moved to the town of Summerville, right outside of Charleston, for a couple of months—my father was ill—and I went to the public school there. I must have been in about the second grade, or maybe the third grade. I'd never seen the teacher before, but she returned a book that my aunt had lent her twenty-five years before!

FOOTE: I was interested in reading Dan Young's biography of John Crowe Ransom, *Gentleman in a Dustcoat*. To think of Ransom teaching in a little Mississippi town. He spent two years there, in some little country town, living over the stable or boarding in somebody's house. He was so young when he finished at Oxford, and this was between Vanderbilt and Oxford, wasn't it? Or was it between years at Vanderbilt, because he didn't have enough money to go back? He was only about seventeen or eighteen years old. He finished high school when he was only about fifteen, and was in college at sixteen, and then took two years off to make some money.

RUBIN: They commonly did that—went to school for a couple of years and then went off to teach. And of course, in the rural South most of the teachers were not college graduates.

WELTY: You were trying to get to be one; that's why you were teaching.

FOOTE: It's so strange to think of Ransom going off to teach, to make some money. He was probably making about eighteen dollars a month teaching.

RUBIN: And probably saving twelve dollars of it.

FOOTE: Right. There was nothing to spend it on.

RUBIN: We were talking about Will Percy, and of course Will Percy was a planter and the son of a U.S. senator and the grandson of another senator, wasn't he?

FOOTE: Of a Confederate colonel.

RUBIN: And he was a person who had been all over the world, highly sophisticated, and so forth. And a figure like Will Percy meant a great deal for the town, as you say. But when you read Will Percy's poetry—and for some reason I've been acquainted with Will Percy's poetry since I was about twelve years old; I just happened to have come across it—although this man was living through a great deal of the most interesting events and periods and so forth in southern history, when he wrote poetry almost none of this ever appears. There's almost no attempt on his part to describe Mississippi, or to show his time and his place, in his poetry. His poetry tends to be sort of world-weary, end-of-century-ish, like Dowson and the *Rubaiyat*, languorous subjects, the death of the gods, and things like that. It's as if his cosmopolitanism and his generation's cosmopolitanism, in terms of literature at least, wasn't turned into any real scrutiny of their own time and place. This wasn't true at all of the next generation of southern writers.

FOOTE: Well, they had what I consider a bad misconception, that there were certain areas of experience that were fit for poetry, and certain areas that were not. Will Percy did write some regional poems, of course.

WELTY: Remember the one called "Home"? In that one he said he was sick of the rest of the world, and he described the levee and the river at Greenville.

RUBIN: Did he write about the levee and the river as if they were at Greenville, in terms of the actual levee at Greenville, or did he make it seem as if it were a levee of the Nile, or something?

FOOTE: Only in his lyrics did he write about his home. Any time he sat down to do some serious writing, he took it to Greece or the Children's Crusade, or as far away as he could get. But he did write local lyrics. Probably his best-known poem is about a flowering bush that's only down there. He wrote a nice poem to his dog, "To Rip Who Died Mad"; that's a good poem. But Will Percy was not a poet, he was just somebody who wrote poetry. I don't think he ever came to grips with his art, so far as being a poet went. That's why he was never truly good at it. *Lanterns on the Levee* is a lot better than his poetry.

RUBIN: Do you think this has anything to do—I'm trying to use Will Percy representatively, of course, rather than just as Will Percy—with his time and place?

FOOTE: Yes, almost everything to do with it. When I mentioned definitions of fit subjects for poetry, I meant that the group subscribed to that notion. But Mr. Will was cut off from what happened to poetry in a direction that he was not taking. He didn't like Ransom's poetry, for instance. He thought that "Bells for John Whiteside's Daughter" was rather silly and inaccurate, and he said, "Geese don't move like that; that's not real." I didn't know what to make of his not liking Ransom. I didn't see how anybody could not like Ransom, but he didn't. He had no use for Eliot. Faulkner he didn't like because Faulkner came down there and played tennis once and got drunk on the court and wouldn't take the game seriously. He objected very much to that.

RUBIN: Faulkner tried to write Percy's kind of poetry; Faulkner's early poetry was very much like that. Eudora, did you ever write poetry?

WELTY: No.

RUBIN: Not at all, not even as a young girl?

WELTY: Well, I wrote some in high school, but not since I've grown up.

RUBIN: It's a lot harder to deal with the texture of everyday experience, to document the world around you, in poetry than it is in prose, don't you think?

FOOTE: I don't think anything's harder than prose.

WELTY: I don't, either.

FOOTE: Nor as satisfying. I envy poets sometimes. I began, like every writer I ever knew, as a poet, but it really didn't satisfy me. I couldn't spreadeagle enough in it. It held me in ways I didn't want to be held and didn't turn me loose in ways I wanted to be turned loose.

WELTY: When was this?

FOOTE: At the very beginning, in high school. I haven't written a poem in thirty years or more.

RUBIN: When I studied poetry in high school in the South—I don't know about you-all in Mississippi; I was in South Carolina—the poems that were taught to me were things like "The Building of the Ship."

FOOTE: That's when the New Englanders dominated poetry.

RUBIN: I mean, nobody would have thought to teach me anything about a poet as recent even as Carl Sandburg.

WELTY: Oh, no, never.

FOOTE: By the time I came along in Greenville, the American literature textbooks had poems by Eliot and Sandburg at the back of them.

WELTY: Well, you're that much younger.

FOOTE: They were taught, too. Miss Hawkins taught it to us. She pointed out to us that it was very sensitive poetry, not coarse, crude stuff, especially Eliot's. It was good to come in contact with. And Sandburg came by and gave a reading once. Vachel Lindsay came by and ranted and raved for two days.

WELTY: I think he came by home, too. I didn't realize that was poetry, I guess.

FOOTE: The school was where it was available. There was another quality to it. I grew up in a town that in my boyhood went from a population of about ten thousand to fourteen thousand, somewhere in there. (Greenville is now about fifty-five or sixty thousand.) There was one high school. I have to correct that by saying there was one *white* high school. In any case, every white person in that town between the ages of fourteen and eighteen was in that one building five or six hours a day. And we all got to know each other in a way that it's not possible to know somebody by any other method. So that in Greenville, Mississippi, in those days when nobody left and nobody moved in, everybody in that town knew each other in a way very different from the way you would have known each other in a larger town.

RUBIN: How big was Jackson when you were growing up, Eudora?

WELTY: About the same size, from fifteen to twenty-five thousand.

RUBIN: One high school for whites and one for blacks, or were there more than one?

WELTY: There was one senior high school for whites and two junior highs.

RUBIN: You were much more advanced than we were in Charleston. We didn't have any junior high schools. We just had grammar schools and high schools.

WELTY: I don't mean junior high schools. We had junior high schools, but our class didn't go to them. There was one in West Jackson and one in North Jackson. There's West Jackson and North Jackson just because Jackson is made that way—two extreme ends. There was only one high school where everybody had to go, and one black high school, I guess. It's awful that people my age didn't even really know the conditions of the black schools. We knew the black colleges, where they all were.

RUBIN: Well, we had in Charleston, which was a city of 62,265 (we all had to memorize the 1930 census), one white high school for boys and then one white high school for girls . . .

FOOTE: There's segregation!

RUBIN: . . . and then a black high school. I don't think the black high school was segregated, though it may have been.

WELTY: Ours wasn't segregated, I mean sexually.

FOOTE: My son is fifteen now and he's never been to school with girls, and I don't see how he's ever going to learn to respect them the way I did because they were all smarter than we were, and he won't know that.

WELTY: Miss Duling, of whom I was speaking, had a girls' side and a boys' side to the recess yard, just as there were two different basements and toilet facilities. We watched each other play, but a sidewalk went down the middle.

RUBIN: You didn't play together?

WELTY: Well, supervised play we did, you know, physical training or whatever it's called, but at recess we clustered each in our own yard, but in full view of the others.

FOOTE: We did that too, Eudora, and one time there was a boy who kept wandering over on the girls' side, and three girls caught him and put a dress on him one day, and when they turned him loose he tore the dress all to pieces and ran back to the boys' side, and he never went over there again.

RUBIN: You say in Jackson there was a west end and a north end of Jackson. Did this carry social distinctions, too?

WELTY: Maybe I was just so dumb, but I didn't know that it did. We found that *they* had a chip on their shoulders when we were forced to meet for that one little class I told you about. There were thirty from each selected to graduate, and we were all furious. We wanted to keep our own group—they wanted theirs, we wanted ours. It didn't last more than a month once we were mixed up in the classes, which was done on purpose, and that's all it took. There wasn't any sense of "across the tracks," or that kind of thing that you read about.

FOOTE: There was in Greenville, because the grammar schools were regional, and there were people who lived near the gypsum mill and their folks worked in the gypsum mill, which was a dreadful thing to do—working in the mill.

WELTY: Well, we didn't have any of those.

FOOTE: It was a bad situation, but quickly corrected when they all got together in high school.

WELTY: Exactly. The children corrected it, and that's all it needed.

FOOTE: The good thing about that grouping was that, of your two best friends, one might be the son of the garbage collector, and the other the son of the president of the bank, and you were very close friends, the way you are in high school. Education is in pretty bad shape today. They're all shaken around, teachers are not used to new methods, and the schools are pretty bad in Memphis, for example. It's a powerful argument for a boy going off to a good prep school where he will get a good formal education. He can still get Latin, and even Greek if he wants it, and so on, which you can't in Memphis. But I can't face up to my son not spending his adolescence in his home town. It just seems horrible to me to grow up in a cubicle in a prep school. I see the advantages, and not only the educational advantages, but still it just seems terrible to me for a boy not to experience his fifteenth, sixteenth, and seventeenth years milling around. And sometimes, too, get up and have a bacon and tomato sandwich and a Coca-Cola for breakfast. That's a great breakfast.

RUBIN: You've been talking about Greenville, with a population of twelve to fifteen thousand when you were growing up there, and Jackson, with about twenty-five thousand. I grew up in Charleston, South Carolina, and the population there was, as I say, about sixty-two thousand, and that was within four thousand of the population of Charleston at the time of the Civil War. I suspect that the population of Jackson was probably no more than twice as large as it was at the time of the Civil War.

WELTY: Oh, heavens, no. And it's the only city in the state, you know.

FOOTE: There was a time, I'm sure, when other places probably made the same claim, but I remember hearing in the forties sometime that Jackson was the fastest growing city in the United States, and it was doubling and doubling and re-doubling.

WELTY: I know it. Meridian and Vicksburg used to claim with us, who was going to win out, and so on. And of course, it's just a pure matter of circumstances. But Mississippi is really, as I'm sure Shelby will agree, a rural state with small courthouse city-towns, like Greenville. That's its structure. We didn't really need a city like Jackson. I wish we'd stayed like we were.

FOOTE: And Greenville, too. Greenville's sixty thousand now, and it used to be I knew every dog in town, not only every person.

WELTY: You did, and everybody's car, too.

RUBIN: You know the old joke about the two largest cities in Mississippi being New Orleans and Memphis.

WELTY: That's true, and Jackson was half-way between.

RUBIN: What I was getting around to was this: these places—these southern towns and southern cities in which you grew up—were still rather small communities in which there was a considerable amount of defined stratification. You knew who everybody was and everybody knew who you were, and all this sort of thing. I'm not talking now about caste and class, I'm just talking about a sense of a very tightly knit social community, for good or for evil. These school teachers we were talking about were, in a sense, the harbingers of the change of all that. They were bringing in that outside world.

FOOTE: They were exempt from any notion of class. They were outside it, like the third or fourth estate or something. But I'll tell you something interesting—about the Delta, in any case. Nobody could afford to look down on anybody else, and nobody needed to look up at anybody else, because everybody had been up and down so fast with that easy credit in the Delta. I don't know of anybody, friends of mine, who didn't have somebody of considerable consequence in his immediate ancestry, no matter how poor they were now. And no matter how rich they were now, you'd know they were apt to be broke within a couple of years. All it took was a bad crop. But the glorious thing, Louis, the really glorious thing about growing up in a Mississippi town, is what you got from it that you could use as a writer. I'm in the egocentric predicament of looking at it from that direction. When you are thoroughly aware of the ins and outs and vicissitudes of the family who lived two doors down the street, what their grandfather had done (and everybody knew perfectly well he had done it, and shame on him for doing it) and then the tragedy that came on his children and then the glorious recovery of what the oldest boy managed to do when he opened the Buick agency, and so on—those things are of enormous value to a writer and I do not see anything that could take their place. I wouldn't swap it for anything.

WELTY: I wouldn't, either. And it's what gives you a sense of narrative and a sense of the drama of life. Everything has a consequence, and everything has a root.

RUBIN: You know where everybody comes from. I can remember all the new people that came into my class when I was a child.

WELTY: Sure, I can, too.

RUBIN: And where they came from.

WELTY: Absolutely. I can remember the first Yankee that came into my class. We were in the fourth grade and he was from Indiana and he said "cor-dju-roy." We used to say, "Say 'corduroy.'" Can't you remember *every*thing about them?

RUBIN: I used to go up to visit my relatives in Virginia, and that seemed like I was going to the North. I really thought I was going North, going to Richmond. And they used to make me repeat words. They used to make me say "late date at eight," and I'd say "let debt at et." You know, I still had that deep Charleston pronunciation, which I've almost completely lost. But these teachers that we were talking about sort of stood for that outside world, and they were telling you all, "Listen, right out beyond the city limits is not where the world ends."

FOOTE: They didn't necessarily know the geographical outside world, but they were certainly aware of the world of art in a way that other people were not.

RUBIN: I was thinking of things like history, and geography, or anything you want. And the way you look at things, in the sense that you don't judge everything by the people involved in it, because there's another world out there. And that's what these teachers represented, in a sense. They had been out there in the world, if only to the normal school, to learn to teach.

FOOTE: Or one quick trip to Europe when they were young. And they lived on it forever, remembering.

RUBIN: The outside was breaking in, then, and now you look around there and you say, "Greenville is gone. It used to be fifteen thousand and now it's sixty thousand." Of course, I think part of that is just a basic sort of nostalgia.

FOOTE: It's pretty heavy to look out where you used to go bird-hunting and see subdivisions and what looks like miles and miles of little houses. You can't think it's good, and it's not good. It's a vitiation of what was a good thing.

WELTY: The road on which we drove out to this radio station, which I had to find the same as you did, was our old blackberry-picking road when I was a child. And right next door down here—it's called "Hanging Moss Road"; it used to be just called the "Pocahontas Road," its real name—there are trees with hanging moss on them, and one little lot that they haven't torn down. I guess they left it to interest real estate people. That's the way this whole country used to look. And the sight of it just gripped me. I thought it's like a slice out of the past looking at me, just one block long. As for all the rest of it, you could be anywhere in this state, or Indiana, or anywhere else.

FOOTE: A Wisconsin historian named William Appleman Williams summed it up in a good way. He said, "Better highways don't make better picnics."

WELTY: Absolutely.

RUBIN: Well, on the other hand, you can still find in Jackson neighborhoods that are just like the neighborhoods where you grew up, can't you?

WELTY: Not exactly.

RUBIN: Pretty close to it?

WELTY: No, they've torn everything down. We've been ruthless here.

FOOTE: What's left is in tatters, you see. If for some reason it got overlooked, boy, did it get overlooked! You can find somebody's estate which they've still got the money to keep up, but it would be a very tight enclosed thing and what was going on around it would not be good. No, it's gone.

WELTY: It's really gone.

FOOTE: In a lot of ways it deserved to be gone, but I'm talking about for my purposes and my pleasure, not making a judgment as to whether it justified its existence or not except for my use.

WELTY: Not just because it's old, but the first things they got when they began tearing up old neighborhoods were the most worthy. Now there are petitions to save such-and-such, which nobody really wants, because they think they should have saved something.

FOOTE: They grabbed the best first, like when they tore down the old depot in Memphis. That was the thing they really should have saved. And when it was gone everybody said, "My god, we must save, we must save," because it was gone.

RUBIN: And they try to hold on to it, but all they're really holding on to is a façade, isn't it?

FOOTE: They have some very strange ideas. They've come up now with the idea that when you put on something it has to have a theme. In Memphis now the old fairgrounds is Liberty Land, and there are Walt Disney characters wandering around in costumes and everything. It's not near as much fun.

WELTY: It's so unreal.

FOOTE: Right. They're going to restore Beale Street and they're going to do something down on the riverfront, finally, but they've got to call it "The Mark Twain," and they're going to have imitation steamboat runs, and things like that, and it won't work. What they really ought to do is what they did at the start. Get the very best architects you can afford and tell them to do the very best job they can, and see what you come up with. But they'll never do that.

WELTY: The sad thing is that when they call something "The Mark Twain," the young people will grow up thinking, "Is that all it was?"

FOOTE: That's right.

RUBIN: In Charleston harbor there's an old boat which is made into a restaurant. I think they built on the façades for the paddle wheels, and in large letters on the side it says, "The Scarlett O'Hara." With all the historical things that went on in Charleston, they have to sell a restaurant by calling it "The Scarlett O'Hara," and I don't think Scarlett ever put a foot in Charleston. They could at least have called it "The Rhett Butler"—Rhett Butler came from there.

FOOTE: I remember Faulkner telling me once—we were driving through one of those subdivisions and they all had picture windows and what they were looking at was each other right across the street there—and he'd look at one of those picture windows and not know what to make of it. And he said, "I know what it needs. It needs a *Gone with the Wind* lamp in it."

RUBIN: How much of your literature is built on just that sense of all this changing, though? I don't mean in terms of subject matter, but in terms of your relationship to it.

FOOTE: I'm sure a great deal, but I wouldn't be able to analyze that. I write mainly about what it was before it changed, because I liked it before it changed.

RUBIN: Would you be writing it, though, if it hadn't changed?

FOOTE: Maybe not. It's just like you don't ever know your homeland until you get away from it.

RUBIN: Don't you think that what, on the surface, on the obvious level, is nostalgia in a good deal of southern writing gets below that level of nostalgia and looks at the pros and cons, and that it's out of the tension between those two that a good deal of the impulse to write about it comes?

WELTY: I don't think nostalgia in itself is a very serious reason for art. It means something, but it's sentimental, I guess, in essence, when it comes to material for art or to conceiving it. But I think, if I understood what you meant, that's true of all we do when we write, isn't it, to try to get the fountainheads of these things— why things change?

FOOTE: I think that when something *has* changed and you believe you have seen the end of something, then you're able to assess it, because you're aware of its beginnings and you have seen its end, and therefore you can deal with it. So in that sense, yes.

RUBIN: But we all always see the end of things in that sense. I'm not saying that all times are relative, because I don't think they are. And I do think that a good deal of what southern literature is today is built on a particular time and place and a particular change. But nevertheless a sense of change. One of the most beautiful passages I know is in a writer that I know you admire a great deal, Shelby, and you do too, Eudora—Marcel Proust. It's the passage close to the end of *Swann's Way* when Marcel tells about going back to the Bois de Boulogne and he sees the people in their fashions, the fashions of the 1910s, and he thinks, these people don't know what beauty is. If they'd seen Mme Swann come along here, the way she was dressed with a different kind of hat. . . . Then he says that what he is really looking for is not a *place* at all but a *time*. Nostalgia, which seems to be memory of a place, is really memory of a time. But how much *had* the Bois de Boulogne changed? All of us have this built in us, don't we, in a sense?

FOOTE: Well, he began by looking at the automobiles and the women's clothes, and his reaction was, specifically, "Oh, horrible!" And then he says regret for a particular place is regret for a particular moment, just as you say.

RUBIN: And when you've got this particular moment built into the change from a small town to a much more eclectic cosmopolitan modern society, then you've got a powerful looking-back involvement, haven't you? It seems to me that our first reaction to anything like that is this sort of nostalgia: isn't it nice to look at these old photographs and think about these days and remember this and remember that? But when we get to thinking about it more, there's something real about that that doesn't seem real, imaginatively, about contemporary experience. That is, we sort of anchor it.

FOOTE: I was looking last week at some photographs Eudora took during the thirties . . .

RUBIN: *One Time, One Place.*

FOOTE: Yes. And I was saying how differently these same eyes see those pictures thirty years later from how these eyes saw those pictures then. They seemed perfectly pictures of things that were happening; now they've taken on an oddness, they are encrusted by time. It's very strange what time can do to things. That's what happens, what Stendhal called an encrustation has built up on them—a crystalization.

WELTY: And that's what gives the pictures any value, I think. That's why I thought they could be published after all this time—because now we look at them through that knowledge of what's happened between then and now.

RUBIN: Let me ask you this. When you took those pictures in 1935 or 1936, did you have the sense at the time that you were preserving something?

WELTY: Oh, no, indeed not. I took them because something appealed to me in the form that a story or an anecdote might have—to capture something. I just did it for the moment.

RUBIN: You didn't have any sense of being a recorder?

WELTY: Oh, no. I think that attitude probably would have ruined everything. They were utterly unself-conscious.

FOOTE: It's not only that you look at them with a more knowing eye, later on, but that mystery gathers. It's not only knowledge, but it's un-knowledge. They get an added mystery. Someone said once that you could take a pretty junky doll and bury it in damp ground for a couple of weeks and dig it up and you'd have an authentic mysterious object because of what had happened to it in the ground there. It would be very strange looking. And some of that gathers, too; as well as the knowledge, the mystery gathers. Somebody's arm being in a particular position can be very strange in a photograph.

RUBIN: To me, one of the most mysterious things about old photographs, when they involve things that I knew, is what was right off the edge of the photograph that didn't get in.

FOOTE: Nobody did that better than Vermeer, a long time ago.

WELTY: That also is connected with the storytellers—the sense of what is impending, what is threatening.

FOOTE: That's what Vermeer could do. He would never tell a story in a picture, and yet the picture is surrounded by story, but not on the picture itself. Nobody's sighing over anybody or anything.

WELTY: No painting can afford to tell a story.

FOOTE: Very bad ones have.

WELTY: And I don't know that my photographs tell a story. It's just that I felt the story possibilities . . .

FOOTE: All around the frame.

RUBIN: Did you travel up and down the state doing those, or just around Jackson?

WELTY: All around the state. It was the first time I'd ever seen it up close; I'd just seen Jackson.

RUBIN: Did you print your own pictures and everything?

WELTY: Yes, in the kitchen. But I did not develop the negatives. I couldn't do that. I should have.

FOOTE: What picture taking I did, I did the same thing. I'd send the negatives off and make the prints.

WELTY: And then enlarge them and play with them.

FOOTE: Have fun with them. Print them very dark or very light.

RUBIN: When you have the picture, though—here's a photograph of two people sitting on a bench, say, and this photograph was taken twenty-five or thirty years before. Now you remember when you took that photograph that your car was parked over here, and let's say it was a 1932 Ford V-8, the first Ford V-8, for example. But that's long since gone. Now, you know your car was over there. If you could somehow open the picture frame up . . . that's the strange kind of sense I get about pictures, old photographs—the frozen time involved in it and the way that by freezing it in time you liberate the place and everything around it and so forth.

FOOTE: I have a sort of postcard picture of me at the age of two standing by a cart to which a billy goat was hitched, and I'm required to hold the thing, and I'm terrified of the billy goat, looking at me with his yellow eyes. It's a very spooky picture of a kid holding a billy goat.

RUBIN: How much of this that we've been talking about would have been true if, instead of you and I and Eudora sitting here, Richard Wright, a black Mississippian, had been sitting here?

WELTY: I can't think there would be any sense of inhibition or something; I don't think so. That isn't probably what you meant. Do you mean subject matter?

RUBIN: No, I mean talking about the good old days and how things were so much better when they were smaller.

FOOTE: I think he would share every good old thing we remember. He would remember some horrible injustices—how could he not —but he would have some of the same feelings that we have, I'm quite sure.

WELTY: I've talked to other people of his age and color, and it is exactly that. You share many things. I've had letters from people—I had a letter from a black friend of mine when something had happened to me, and she said, "I don't know if you remember me, but my mother was your mother's wash-lady, and I used to come to your house on the express wagon"—this would have been when the children were six or seven years old—"and we used to play together." It was when my mother died; she had seen it in the paper. And she said, "She was a nice lady and you were a nice little girl. And my daughter and I think of you." She said she was now the wife of a professor at a college somewhere, but she often thought of those days. Now this was completely spontaneous on her part. But that's what you remember. She shared something when she read that about my mother. She thought, "We have memories in common."

RUBIN: That's what I was hoping you'd say, because that's the feeling I have. I think one of the difficulties in dealing with black American literature and black southern literature is that so few white critics think of the black community as having its own complete life, and the black community in the South, even in the worst of time, as not being defined by its relationship to the white people at all, but having its *own* integrity, its own identity. And that experience—however in this area or that area, politically, socially, or economically, it may have been very much underprivileged—was real. And the relationship of the writer to it is not just in terms of political issues or things like that.

FOOTE: I know the Negroes had integrity under those circumstances, and some of it was pretty militant, too. If I went back in the kitchen and got in the cook's way, I was committing a very serious offense and I'd get run out of there fast, maybe with the flat of the bread knife.

RUBIN: Well, I would say that what you've both been talking about —for the past forty-five minutes we've been going all around Robin Hood's barn—but what you are finally getting down to, really, is that you've lived in a time and a place that have a very palpable kind of identity, and that you wouldn't be what you are as a writer without that particular time and place.

FOOTE: No, indeed.

WELTY: Absolutely.

FOOTE: It has to be understood, about these things that we're talking about, that everybody's integrity was well understood to be not only important but precious, and people respected it. I'm talking about from this level down to that level, or from that level up to this level. Everybody knew perfectly well that everybody else had his integrity and it wasn't to be sneered at or fooled with. There could be serious consequences of doing that, including getting shot off a horse some day out of a bush, and you didn't do that. The broader the social separation, like plantation owner and sharecropper, the more formal the relationship was. It was as if everyone perfectly well understood that this thing is not to be shaken around by any heavy-handed person. There were people who did it, and it was disastrous. They had no tenants. Nobody would put up with it. And you couldn't put up with it. You were finished in your own eyes if you did. So nobody required you to put up with it. There was a great deal of very real courtesy in relationships between people.

RUBIN: In towns and cities?

FOOTE: Just as much in towns and cities as in the country. There was a quite formal relationship between my aunt, for example, and her cook. They were close friends, but it was perfectly well understood that each had to treat the other with a certain kind of respect as part of that friendship, and it was a very real thing. Now, it's true the cook was making $7.50 a week.

RUBIN: That would have been pretty good wages in Charleston.

FOOTE: It was pretty good wages there, but it was an outrageous wage, and that was one of the things that was wrong with it. But that's been corrected now, with a vengeance. You see, she was making $7.50, and she was worth about $40. Now she's making $60, and she's worth about $40.

RUBIN: So the more it changes, the more it remains the same.

FOOTE: Something like that. I'm really joking about that, I hope you know.

RUBIN: Of course. We'll make sure your cook doesn't see this transcript. I think we should say something noble and interesting that would end this conversation, but I can't think of anything noble and interesting. You've done exactly what I wanted you to do, which is to talk about everyday Mississippi. I didn't want you to have a literary discussion, because we can read those by the dozen.

FOOTE: I think that was a good ending.

MARY E. MEBANE

Black Folk of
the American South:
Two Portraits

I often fantasize what would happen if American blacks should, like the ancient Etruscans, disappear, leaving behind only their writings and their art. What would the verdict be about these people? Could some archaeologist in the year 5000 A.D. successfully reconstruct what life was like for them and write a fairly accurate history? Or would there be serious gaps and distortions in the picture that emerged? I think the latter would be the case, and the reason, I feel, is that there are many problems inherent in writing about black folk and that no one so far has successfully solved them all. These problems exist whether the writer is black or non-black, and whether his fiction is set in the past or the present, although, oddly enough, some of the problems are greater in the post-1960s' climate of the South than they were in the hundred years after the Civil War.

The two main problems confronting the writer who would concern himself with the black folk in the South are the problems of stasis and what, for want of a better term, I call "the margin of difference." James Agee's phrase "the timeless land, the chosen people," which he used to describe southern rural life, is as appropriate for southern blacks as it is for southern whites, although the word *chosen* is particularly ironic when used to describe southern blacks. Indeed, life in the South, for nearly a century after the Civil War, was static, unchanging. A black could be born, live his allotted number of years, and die, and have virtually nothing happen to him during his life. The social, political, and economic system of the South planned it that way. For, by the end of the nineteenth century, segregation laws in the South had fixed the black man and woman at the bottom of the social order—the planners hoped—forever. So change of any kind was not only undesirable; it was threatening, for it implied a total blow to the system as it was then instituted.

Life became a cycle, a ritual—birth, existence, death. One worked for subsistence wages, or below, partied on Saturday night to relieve the harshness and monotony of daily existence, and on Sunday prepared his soul to die. That was black life in the South, and there were only two escapes: North and Heaven. Both, as it turned out, were more fantasy than reality.

Stasis becomes a problem for the writer when change, no matter how slight, is introduced into the picture. First, should he record it? Second, how much significance does it have in the way he sees black folk and in the way black folk see themselves, the world, and their role in it? It is as though the subject of a photograph suddenly moves ever so slightly just as his picture is being taken. That shift, though slight, will cause the picture to blur.

The problem of stasis in writing fiction about southern blacks is seen clearly in the works of Richard Wright (1908–1960), a native of Natchez, Mississippi, who first came to national prominence in 1938 when a collection of his short stories won a national prize. These four stories, titled *Uncle Tom's Children*, are set in the Deep South, presumably Mississippi, and all have as their protagonists southern blacks, peasants for the most part, and all, with one exception, are starkly realistic portrayals of what life was like for the black folk of the region. In these stories, time does not move, nothing changes. What is, was and always will be. It does not matter, therefore, what time it is, because the lives of these characters would be the same whether the calendar says 1900, 1915, 1930—generation after generation.

The one story, "Fire and Cloud," that shows some change is atypical in that in it—as in his later story "Bright and Morning Star"—Richard Wright tries to show how things might be changed through radical politics. He moves his story from the fields to the town and introduces two outsiders, political radicals, who have come to show the black folk—and the white folk, too—a new and better way, a possible solution to their problems. In tone, "Fire and Cloud" differs a great deal from the other stories in the collection; it is didactic and shifts from telling what the lives of the black folk are like to the promulgation of a political ideology, with some blunt punches at another ideology that has a strong hold on southern blacks—Christianity.

Wright's handling of religion in "Fire and Cloud" is interesting in that it reveals one of the difficulties in writing about the lives of black folk. During the time of this story, religion was a major force in black communities all over the South, yet the overwhelming majority of black intellectuals—and this includes writers— very much disliked Christianity, feeling that it was indeed the opiate of the people. The fictional treatment of religion was thus a problem for black writers. The solution they most often came up with was either to discount or ridicule it, or, as in "Fire and Cloud," to attack its effectiveness as a solution to social problems. This is the real purpose of the scene where the white mob forces the black minister to repeat the Lord's Prayer as it beats him. To discount, ridicule, or attack religion satisfied the intellectual needs of the black writer, but the question remains whether such a stance accurately portrayed the world view of the black folk themselves? The answer seems to be that it did not, that after this important facet of the lives of the folk was filtered through the prism of the minds of the black intellectuals, what emerged was something very different from reality.

Black artists in other media, such as choreographer Alvin Ailey, are more at ease and less defensive in presenting various facets of the black experience without rage or apology. In his masterpiece "Revelations," Ailey presents a hauntingly beautiful view of the black religious experience. He shapes the material, but he does not do violence to its basic concepts.

Although the publication of *Uncle Tom's Children* established Richard Wright as the premier writer about the black folk of the South (Jean Toomer was an anomaly), he did not use the South again as a setting for a major piece of fiction until many years later, long after he had become a resident of France. Then he wrote *The Long Dream* (1958), a novel set in Mississippi. The novel is striking in that it includes no black folk—that is, rural peasants—although Wright does show some change in the racial climate. The protagonist is a young, middle-class black who in the end forms an alliance of sorts with a white liberal to try to change some of the unjust conditions in his town. The absence of rural black folk in the novel makes for interesting speculation. Perhaps Wright felt that he had already exhausted the subject and thus had nothing more to add, or perhaps time and distance prevented his perceiving that soon the black folk themselves would begin making an effective protest about the conditions under which they had to live. In other words, a static situation had become fluid.

It is precisely in this area of change, in the time when the picture blurs ever so slightly before the new position is fixed, that a truly significant body of literature can be written. What writers in the United States—and particularly in the South—witnessed in the decade from 1954 to 1964/65 (from the Supreme Court decision outlawing segregation in the public schools to the Public Accommodations and Voting Rights Acts) was a breakup in the social order so vast and pervasive that the consequences of it may be even greater than those following the Civil War.

Those black writers still present and remaining in the South are thus in an excellent position to record the most minute of the continuing changes in the ways the black folk see themselves, and in the way they relate to the world around them and to the people in it. A word, a gesture, personal relationships, professional relationships, the slightest change in the way of speaking, in posture and stance should be noted and commented on, for they are significant. They are records of a change in the social order and, as records, are valuable. What better person to describe these changes than the black writer who, coming from the same environment, is more observant and has a keener eye? What he writes about it will last.

The characters in *Uncle Tom's Children* are without the "margin of difference" that I mentioned earlier as another of the problems facing the writer who concerns himself with southern blacks. They and the parts they play in these stories are, for the most part, interchangeable. Big Boy, the protagonist of "Big Boy Leaves Home," has no feelings, thoughts, or ways of looking at the world that differ in any way from those of his buddies as they move to encounter their destiny on a white man's farm. Nor is Big Boy's response to the danger he encounters and tries to escape any different from that of his pal—who does not escape but dies at the hands of the mob. Had Big Boy been the victim and his pal the one hidden on the hillside, the story would have been the same. Big Boy is not a person; he stands for a type, a model for the role played by millions of black boys in the rural South.

This "margin of difference" proved to be most troublesome for black writers who dealt with southern black folk. Here the writer's purpose can most often be misinterpreted or distorted. Consequently, most writers steered away from instances of individual adaptations.

Most of them felt that the socioeconomic and political conditions under which black folk of the American South lived were so horrendous that their primary function as writers was to tell about and protest those conditions. Thus, their goal was to show the usual, the typical, rather than any individual variations. That aim was understandable—and a necessary and right response, then and now. But should it be the *exclusive* function of the writer? Black folk produced the spiritual, the gospel song, jazz, the blues, the sermon, "the dozens," "fine talk," prison "toasts." The black folk by definition are not writers, and those who write about them have not thus far articulated as wide a range of black experience as they themselves have expressed.

Many writers were also disturbed by an underlying fear that racists would seize on examples of less dehumanizing adaptations to life as proof that the social, economic, and political conditions under which southern blacks lived were not so bad after all, if they could produce such fine people. They feared that if they wrote about successful or happy characters they would be open to charges of racism, political naïveté, or worse. This attitude had a great deal of validity, of course. However, one cannot help but wonder whether great literature can be produced if its writers are forever on the defensive, wondering how will this or that sound, or who may or may not read this or that into their work. If a literature is to mature, it seems to me that eventually the writers are going to have to feel secure enough about themselves and their work to say, "This is life as I have observed it. There are other writers who have observed the same facets or different facets than I have, and they may or may not share my feelings or beliefs about them. That is as it should be. But this is the way *I* see it. Make of my work what you will."

In my own writing, I find interesting the lives of black folk and what happens to them—what stays the same, what changes, how they adjust, how they fail to adjust, what moves them, what leaves them unmoved. I most often find it enough just to record, without commenting, although I have sometimes found it necessary to comment, primarily because it is expected of me and because it is possible that some people who read my work won't know the historical background or will fail to see the implications of certain things. A full and complete record is what I seek. Since no one writer can tell everything, not even about a small bit of time or place, there should be many, many black writers recording things that they remember, things that were told to them, and things that they observe, for these things are the stuff of art.

To illustrate my contention, I want to offer two sketches of two different black women—"case histories," as it were—that depict the life and spirit of two human beings who are black. "Roxcine Brimmage," the first sketch, represents the marvelous triumph of the human spirit, without which no people can survive.

Shortly after Christmas, 1973, after a bright sun came out and burned away the heavy rain clouds that had lain over the state for more than a week, I left Orangeburg, South Carolina, and drove into the low country to a place called St. Stephen. Turning off Interstate 95, I followed a secondary road through mile after mile of drab winter countryside, brightened incongruously in places with strips of newly sprouted wheat and oats, glistening like green artificial grass. Here and there on church doors, Christmas wreaths still hung. They seemed out of place, somehow, in the warm sunshine.

My route took me through Eutawville, Eutaw Springs, and Pine-hills and was unmarked by any memorable landmarks, except for a metal drawbridge over a diversionary canal near Eutawville and a tall lookout tower in Pinehills. What most impressed me were the trees laden with Spanish moss, so thick in places that they sometimes obscured the sunshine, giving me the feeling that I was driving under a canopy.

I was going to St. Stephen to visit a remarkable lady named Mrs. Roxcine Brimmage. I had wanted to meet her as soon as I saw the walls of the library at South Carolina State College come alive with the colors and designs of her quilts and rugs. At eighty, Rox-cine Brimmage was having her first one-woman show.

When I arrived in St. Stephen, I inquired at the Exxon station about Mrs. Brimmage, "a lady who makes quilts and rugs," but they had never heard of her. I mentioned that she lived near the railroad tracks—a railroad bisects the town—and they told me how to find her. Near the tracks, I stopped a black man and asked if he could help me locate somebody. "Lady," he said, "I'm just home for Christmas. I haven't been in St. Stephens in twenty years." But when I told him that I was looking for a lady who made quilts and rugs, he pointed down the street, indicating that I should follow the tracks for a long way, then turn off on a little road. I was skeptical about taking directions from someone who hadn't been in the town in twenty years, so I asked him, "Is she an eld-erly lady?" "She ought to be," he said, "I've known her since I was a child, and I'm forty-three now myself." A little New York City humor in the South Carolina sunshine.

I followed his directions, and soon my car began hitting some really rough places in the road. It was the beginning of the black neighborhood, and the pavement had ended.

I arrived at 10:10 A.M. Mrs. Brimmage was waiting for me and called out in a strong voice for me to come on in and not pay any attention to the dogs. I had parked some distance away because the road to her house looked too rutted for my car to make it and I was scared of the barking dogs.

Mrs. Brimmage greeted me with a kiss. At eighty years of age, her caramel-colored skin was smooth, her eyes bright, and she had a wonderfully wistful, childlike smile. She told me that I was just in time, because she always "gave witness" at 10:30. I thought she meant that she listened to religious music or to a church service on the radio; but she said no, she had a platform outside, and she talked from that. The platform was a board nailed across two posts on the front porch; it served her as a pulpit, and there she gave her introductory testimony, then announced her subject. On the day of my visit, it was "Jesus and the Woman at the Well," and she talked on the significance of that encounter for twenty minutes or so. Then she sang a song, and the morning service was over.

Roxcine Brimmage was a missionary, and her work was a vital part of her life. She "gave witness" every day, most of the time by herself, not waiting until Sunday or until she was invited to speak at one of the churches in the area, in Goose Creek, or even in Charleston.

But Roxcine was neither an eccentric nor a religious fanatic. She liked to hear "the preacher's daughter who can sing so good. What's her name? Teresa?" "Do you mean Aretha [Franklin]?" I asked. "Oh, yes," she said. "Aretha. She can sing so good. I like to hear her sing." I remembered this conversation later when Dr. Twiggs, the art historian at South Carolina State College who arranged the exhibition of her quilts, told me of his meeting with Roxcine Brimmage when he went to persuade her to let him show her work. She was very skeptical at first, because people had told her that he would probably take her things up to Orangeburg and she would never see them again. But Dr. Twiggs persisted, and she finally agreed. On the day he went to get the quilts and rugs, Roxcine was so pleased that he was honoring her that she asked him to share a glass of wine. He agreed, thinking that she would bring him the traditional homemade wine. But she didn't. Roxcine reached up on the shelf over the refrigerator and brought down a bottle of Mogen David.

Roxcine liked to reminisce about her visits to two of America's great cities. When she first arrived in New York, she went to a holiness church at the foot of the subway. They were having a rally that day, but when she explained that she didn't have anything to contribute because she had just arrived in the city and had no work, the pastor immediately asked the sisters to give her some of their "day's work." Three hands shot into the air: "I will! I will! I will!" They raised twenty-five dollars to help her out until she got started. When she got home, her grandchildren asked, "Babalou, what kind of game have you been in? Here we gamble every night and never win. Most of the time we come home broke, and you just got here and come home with twenty-five dollars!" Roxcine laughed and said, "I've been in God's game!"

Once when she was visiting her daughter on L Street in Washington, one of the churches asked her to prophesy. She told them that Washington was another Babylon, a wicked city, and that even at that very moment God was going to and fro in the city seeking just one righteous man. If He found him, He wouldn't destroy the city.

It was while Roxcine Brimmage was visiting her relatives in cold northern cities that she started making quilts to keep them warm. Even today she still views her work as purely functional. She had her own quilts and rugs on her beds and on the floor, although the people she sold them to told her that they kept her quilts to take out and show to people. She made no profit on her work, but she said that if she could have bought fresh, high-quality materials without having to pay such high prices, she could have made some money.

Roxcine Brimmage shied away from talking about her economic conditions. She did admit, however, that she wished she had running water in her house. Instead, her great-grandchildren brought her water from some distance away because the well in her yard was contaminated. Some time before I met her, she received a letter from the government in Charleston [HEW] saying that she might be eligible for more benefits (about $20.00 a month), but they wanted her to sign papers about her property and people told her not to answer the letter. She showed it to me, and a cursory glance showed that all of the questions did indeed concern property: Did she have any? Was the title in her name? And so on. She looked at me questioningly, and I told her that I agreed with those people who said that it was best for her not to bother; she might lose what she had. But even a casual glance at Mrs. Brimmage's surroundings showed that she was living just barely at a subsistence level.

At night Mrs. Brimmage sat on a sofa sewing under a naked light bulb. She had been widowed twice, and her children were far away, although some grandchildren lived in a house within calling distance. She still thought with pain of the young man she had raised—her sister's son—who got hurt bad inside in the service and came home only to die. And underneath her fingers, colorful "designs" formed.

I left wondering what Mrs. Brimmage's life would have been like had she been given the opportunity to get an adequate education—she could neither read nor write—and if hard economic necessity had not forced her to spend most of her time struggling just to survive in what is often described as one of the world's most affluent societies. And I wondered about the many hundreds of her contemporaries who died unknown, their potentials undeveloped.

"The Tenant on Ocean Avenue" is another black southerner, and her situation exemplifies the absolute stasis under which millions of blacks still live. Her story could be set in any time—1945, 1955, 1965—and it would make little difference, for she is caught in an unchanging cycle of poverty and ignorance.

Ocean Avenue is really a lane. It is narrow, paved, with no sidewalks or curbing, and is located between the main shopping district and the pride of Orangeburg—the beautiful Edisto Gardens down by the Edisto River. The houses, which are on only one side of the street, face the river, but the inhabitants can't see it. Instead, they look out on the blank sides of mercantile buildings or the uncut vegetation of empty lots.

The houses on Ocean Avenue are nearly all of the style known as "shotgun"—two or three rooms placed directly behind each other, so that if a gun were fired through the front door the bullet would travel through the house and exit at the back door. Many of them have tin roofs, and they are unpainted and crowded close together—a small fire out of control would quickly burn up four or five houses. There is no grass in the sandbox-sized yards. Because there is little room inside the houses, the tenants have to improvise storage, often hanging clothes across the porches. One family has its washing machine on the front porch.

Mildred Graham lives on Ocean Avenue. Her husband left her years ago with six small children. He went off one day, saying that he was going North to find work and that after he got settled he was going to write and send for them. Since then, she's heard nothing from him. She doesn't know if he's living or dead. His folks, who live on a nearby street, say that they haven't heard from him either. She doesn't know, but that is what they say.

For a long time, she made it without any help, cooking at night in a cafe. But the children were so small that she didn't want to leave them alone at night, and she didn't have time to do all the washing and ironing needed to keep their clothes nice for going to school. Now she gets a monthly check from the welfare. Her oldest child, a daughter, is twenty-five now, and the baby is sixteen. In the ancient way of life in black communities, Mildred Graham keeps three of her grandchildren with her. Two of them stay with her all of the time; another grandchild sometimes lives with her and sometimes with his mother. None of her other children finished high school, but she hopes that the baby will. He is in the tenth grade at Orangeburg-Wilkinson High School, and he says that he is going to finish. She worries about him—she knows how kids are if they get to running with the wrong crowd. But she hopes that he'll finish.

She never got much schooling herself. After her father died, her mother often had to keep the children out of school to work. Mildred Graham stripped sugar cane, dug sweet potatoes, picked cotton when the crop was so bad she'd have to walk thirty or forty minutes to find a boll, picked redpeas. She tells her children that they're having it easy now, that she came up hard.

Mrs. Graham, her three grandchildren, and her son—the one who is sixteen—live in two rooms, one right behind the other. The front room has no sofa or chairs, just four beds—one on either side of the narrow walkway, a smaller one jammed against the inside wall, and a folding cot. Her son, a dark, slight, wiry boy, is lying across one of the beds in this room he shares with three other children. I wonder where he can sit to read a book or write a paper. There is no space, and even worse, no quiet. How can he finish school? The factors in his life weigh against him. There is a wood stove in the center of the floor, and clothes lie in little bundles in various nooks and crannies of the room. One gets the sense of being overwhelmingly suffocated in this cramped space. A stray spark would cause utter devastation.

The kitchen is smaller. Food is cooking on the wood stove in the middle of the floor. Less than a foot away is a large double bed. Mrs. Graham sleeps there. In the heat of the summer, the kitchen is unbearable. Within arms' length of the bed is the refrigerator, the only modern appliance in the house. The bathroom is really just a little enclosure jutting off the side of the house. The tub tilts crazily at an angle and is stacked with wood. Obviously it has not been used for bathing for some time. The toilet is broken. The landlord says that he is coming to fix it, but he hasn't gotten around to it yet. There is a fist-sized hole in the floor, through which I could see daylight. The weight of one of the grandchildren could easily cause the whole floor to give way.

Mildred Graham went to school for a while, along with other people on welfare, but the program was discontinued. She studied history and math and learned how to cook fancy, the way they didn't know to cook when she came up. She doesn't make any of those fancy dishes for her family because her cook stove has given out and she doesn't have the money to buy another one. There is a hole in the oven through which cinders drop, so she can't use it for baking. She buys light bread sometimes, but it costs forty cents a loaf, so she makes most of her bread, cooking it on top of the stove.

Mrs. Graham has no telephone and cannot afford to subscribe to a newspaper. She doesn't have a television set, but she listens to the radio. She's heard that gas is going to be short this winter and wonders what is going to happen to people who burn gas. I asked her some questions about current events.

"What about the [Spiro] Agnew case?" I asked.

"That's something, isn't it? What do you think about it?" she answered.

"Well, I just don't know."

"Reckon he did for the best? You think so?" she said.

I didn't respond to that, because I had seen the pattern. It was the wary peasant, talking very carefully when matters of importance involving people in high places were mentioned. A person could get into trouble talking that way. So I let that subject drop, and we talked about other things for a while, until she discovered that I wasn't trying to solicit an answer from her. Then she said, "They've got another man in his place, haven't they? What's his name?" She looked inquiringly at me, as though she couldn't remember the name.

"Ford," I said.

"What about the Watergate?" she continued, seemingly interested in what I thought. I hazarded an opinion that it was quite a case, wasn't it? and she shook her head "yes" it was.

"Did you vote in the last election?" I asked.

"No," she said, "I didn't."

"Have you ever voted?"

"Yes, I voted for the Kennedys," she said. "Both of them. Since then I haven't bothered with it."

"Did you vote for Johnson?" I asked.

"Oh, yes," she said. "And I voted for the Kennedys. I was going to vote for the baby brother, but he backed down, didn't he."

"You mean Senator Ted Kennedy?"

"Yes, he's the one. I was going to vote for him. But he backed down. I don't blame him. I didn't see how he could—with two brothers dead like that," she said.

"Did you vote for Mr. McGovern?" I asked.

"No, since the Kennedys, I don't bother with it."

"He ran against Mr. Nixon," I said.

Mildred Graham has never been out of South Carolina. She has been to Charleston, to Bamberg, and to Bowman, where she was born. She has lived on Ocean Avenue for six years. She volunteered the information that she had never been to New York. I asked her about Georgia (Augusta is just seventy miles away). But she said no, she had never been to Georgia. I asked her about North Carolina—she had mainly stayed right around Orangeburg all of her life. I asked her how old she was, and she said that she was fifty or forty-nine; she looked ten years older. I noticed this oddity of speech—that is, putting the larger of two numbers first. When she told me about the death of one of her sons, she said that he got killed between 10 and 9:30 at night.

I asked her what she did for pleasure. She said that she went to church sometimes, but that she hadn't been in a long time. She had been to the movies twice in her life, one was a cowboy picture; she didn't remember what the other one was about, but the children wanted to go when they were small, so she went with them.

Her children are grown now and "living around." She was not specific about where, but when pinned down she said that they are living around Orangeburg. She raised six, but one got killed in a car wreck last year. He was twenty-three. Last year was a time of troubles for her. Six months after her son was killed, her mother died—she had a bad heart. Then her brother-in-law died—he had a bad heart, too. Then his brother died—some say he let his sugar get up too high. At the time of my visit, she had a cousin in the funeral home, but so far she hadn't got a chance to go see her, and she didn't think she'd be able to go to the funeral, either.

It was Saturday night, and so far she didn't know what she was going to cook for Sunday dinner. Last Sunday, she had neckbones. She said she was not like some people who can stockpile food or who have freezers—she had to buy from day to day. In a few minutes, she was going to walk out to the Big Star and see what she could find. She got sixty dollars worth of food stamps each month, but with meat so high that didn't go far. She just did the best she could.

Feeding her family is doubly difficult because her children refused to take the same lunch to school that she had carried as a child—a boiled sweet potato and a biscuit with molasses on it. She can afford to give them that, but they won't have it. So she has to try to give them things that they won't be ashamed of. They eat a lot of beans and peas, and she makes a lot of pancakes, which she gives to the children along with sugar water to drink. When she mentioned sugar water, I thought of the man who died because his sugar got too high.

As I was leaving, I wondered what time it was. She had a clock, but it was broken. "It look about six o'clock, don't you think?" she said.

BLYDEN JACKSON

Growing Up Black in the Old South and the New: or, Mr. Wheat Goes with the Wind

When I am thinking about race in America at the submerged level in my mind that literary critics might well call "stream of consciousness"—that uncensored level at which I have no secrets from myself and where a single fleeting word or phrase can signify to me a whole, sometimes terribly long and all too intricately involved train of though—I occasionally recall Mr. Wheat and, for myself, I need do no more to summarize my subject.

Mr. Wheat was a white man whom I got to know, although more or less at a distance, while I was growing up and working as a young man in Louisville, Kentucky, my home town. Considering his age, I suspect he died some ten or perhaps fifteen years ago. I might have known him better had I ever been a Boy Scout. Mr. Wheat, whatever his title, headed the Negro Boy Scouts in Louisville.

Rumor whispered that Mr. Wheat had been, in the dim, shadowy white world from which he had, in a manner of speaking, stealthily emerged, a minister of the gospel who lacked the gifts he should have had to be effective with his white parishioners. He had friends, apparently, who felt that a job had to be found for him. That, it seems, is how he ended up really a sort of proconsul, junior-grade, for white-supremacist America. On the evidence I can recall, I believe Mr. Wheat was not a bad Scout executive. And he lives in my memory as a rather likable person who certainly did not go around lording it over his Negroes. Yet things happened which suggested that an unofficial, undeclared adjunct responsibility of Mr. Wheat's job was surveillance. Principalships of public schools, for example, to a people with very limited rewards available to them, were prizes of great distinction in Negro Louisville as it was then. And they clearly always went to "safe" recipients, apparently on the basis of "inside" evidence of the kind conveyed to the proper ears (although not necessarily without corroboration from "Uncle Toms") by Mr. Wheat. In exchange, that is, for the patronage Mr. Wheat had received (I rather think none of this was ever put into words), he was expected by his patrons, the influential whites who "ran things" in Louisville (and surely could determine who got jobs like Mr. Wheat's), to keep an eye for them, and so for all of Louisville's whites, on Louisville's blacks.

Ever since the latter part of the seventeenth century, there must have been in every southern generation hundreds, if not thousands (by Mr. Wheat's generation the thousands seems more likely) of Mr. Wheats. They were part of an industry that began around 1660, with slavery (although actually, to be precise, shortly before), survived the end of slavery and Reconstruction, and, from the so-called "Redemption" until within the last ten or fifteen years, clearly was the South's major employer and concern. For, although, on the one hand, only twenty years have passed since the paratroopers helped to desegregate Central High School in Little Rock and, on the other, emotions still can turn into white heat over "forced" busing, the double-barreled fact remains that today's southern youth, white and black, who are less than college age, cannot, except in unreliably abstract terms, know what their South was like in the years before they were born into it and that the reason they must eternally remain actually unable even to suspect the true nature of a past reality is the dismantling, to the sweeping degree already accomplished (a lesson in miracles to members of my generation), of the industry that accounted for Mr. Wheat.

That industry, of course, was the keeping of Negroes in their place, and for a long, long time, southern whites, with some exceptions, worked hard at it, whether they were paid to do so or not. Indeed, even the southern whites who did not work at it, and did not want to do so, often must have found it difficult not to contribute, however unwittingly, to a system as pervasive and compulsive as the southern system which ensured that blacks knew who they were and the things they had better not do, or even try to do. In much of the South, the system flouted the Fifteenth Amendment. Blacks did vote in Louisville, but in Mississippi, or Alabama, or Georgia, or Louisiana, for example, an attempt to exercise his constitutional right of suffrage might well have cost a Negro his life, especially if he was too intractable in his attempts to enjoy a privilege guaranteed him by the supreme law of the land he rightfully called his own. There was no part of the South, with its separate schools and its plethora of taboos in the use of public accommodations, governmentally controlled and private, that did not make a bitter mockery of the Fourteenth Amendment (the North did a considerable amount of sinning in this regard also). And there were some scattered local practices in the South, such as peonage, of which it could be soberly asserted that they, in effect, repealed the Thirteenth Amendment.

The South that had spawned Mr. Wheat was capable of resorting to savagery of the most revolting kind in maintaining its system unimpaired. It lynched more than three thousand Negroes between 1885 and 1915. But systems do not endure on terroristic violence. Indeed, inherently systems and terroristic violence are incompatible. The function of the first essentially is the establishment and maintenance of order; of the latter, the abrupt disruption of tranquillity. And so the system that constituted the southern way of life which long ago, for its proponents, became traditional and sanctified, depended fundamentally on measures far more universal in their application than terroristic violence. Those measures tended toward the habitual, the familiar, and the relatively easy to execute. Any child could learn them. Old people could remember them and continue until they died to do their best to maintain them. Lynchings, night ridings, floggings, after all, did not happen every day. The discipline that Mr. Wheat represented did. It was a constant, a vade mecum. It was, in the South, ubiquitous. It was what one meant when one spoke of southern customs. God surely had ordained it. For a southern white to transgress it was a sacrilege, a trampling on a foreparent's grave.

Let us turn the clock back fifty-two years and spend an imaginary day with one Ernest Ellis—a real friend, once, of mine—in Louisville on the upper border of the South. Ernest lives eleven blocks from the "colored" Central High School where he is a senior. In the morning, Ernest walks these eleven blocks straight up Chestnut Street to school. All the homes he passes are occupied by Negroes. Ernest has never been in a white home. His family is middle class. If he had not been so middle class, if his father had not been an agent for a Negro insurance company, he might have had some white acquaintances, perhaps the white family, or families, for whom his parent, or his parents, worked. In such a case, he might well have seen inside a white home, or some white homes, from the back, of course, and under restraints that would make, and keep, it clear to him that, in the South, there were two worlds, one white, the other black, with all the advantages between the two reserved for whites. But not only has Ernest never seen inside a white home, no white has ever seen inside Ernest's home, at least not as a guest. It is possible that some white salesman or bill collector may have actually gotten across the threshold of the Ellis' front door. But it is not probable. Part of the unwritten code of Negroes like Ernest's parents was that whites on business should be given no excuse to penetrate the privacy of any Negro's dwelling. So Ernest's day is a day in which all the whites he sees—and they are few, when not altogether nonexistent—tend to be physical spectacles only and, as persons, no more than figments of his imagination. He knows that somewhere in Louisville there are whites of his own age who are doing substantially what he does. He stays in school until mid-afternoon. He comes home, loitering along the way with schoolmates who are his friends. He eats an evening meal and studies. He may even, for a while, drop in on a friend of his before he retires for the night. But everything he does is in a world that is of his own peculiar breed. All his life is segregated, by choice when not by force.

Any transaction with a white, then, on Ernest's part becomes abnormal, not a part of an average day. And the abnormality of such a transaction is increased, for Ernest at least, because he knows that throughout the duration of that transaction he must deal with some form or other of Mr. Wheat. Ernest, for example, cannot avoid shopping on some occasions in Louisville's so-called "downtown," where all the stores, and all the clerks who sell, are white. He must obtain, if nothing else, commodities he cannot do without, like clothes. To purchase them he must enter the world of the whites on—as much as the whites can manage it—the whites' own terms. Let us say he needs a new suit. He goes to a department store or to one of the two or three largest haber-dashers in Louisville, emporia occupying buildings two, three, or four stories tall. He will hardly venture into a small store, on the theory that the larger the store the more impersonal may well be its atmosphere. In great likelihood, his father will accompany him. In greater likelihood, his mother will not. For Mr. Wheat's South attached great importance to the way in which Negroes were ad-dressed. They must, obviously, never be granted a title of courtesy like "Mr." or "Mrs." Ideally they should be called, as pointedly and often as possible, by their first names. And it is the mission of Ernest's father (who will, presumably, have a cooler, wiser head than Ernest), as well as of Ernest himself (who is now reaching the age where he must assume a man's responsibility), to keep to a minimum, if not to eliminate entirely, any opportunities for the clerk who waits on Ernest to indulge in the South's formula for addressing Negroes. Indeed, every excursion into a white store for Ernest, alone or otherwise, is an ordeal, a test of his ability to con-fine within tolerable limits petty assaults upon his own self-esteem by whites whom circumstances have put into situations where they can callously combine commercial acts with blatant social discourtesies.

But in almost all of Ernest's activities, as we have seen, he is not making excursions into white stores or doing anything that brings him into direct contact with whites. Sometimes he rides the streetcars in Louisville, which are not segregated as they would always be farther south. If he cannot sit down alone in them or be-side another black, his custom is to stand. One of the things he knows is that in white stores or any of Louisville's public build-ings, including the courthouse and the city hall, blacks are not welcome in the rest rooms, unless there are separate accommo-

dations, and Louisville, which tends to mute overt signs of its racial discrimination, might just as often have unmarked rest rooms
intended for whites only as rest rooms in dark, out-of-the-way
corners obviously meant for people as inconsequential as Negroes.
Below Louisville in the South, Ernest, in a sense, would not have
had a problem with rest rooms. For, generally, Mr. Wheat's South
was a land of signs (Mr. Wheat was something of a sign, himself).
On public carriers such as trains, streetcars, (and, later, buses), in
railroad and interurban stations, state, county, and municipal
buildings, stores (even some restaurants with carry-out windows
in the back), and shops, such as those, for instance, where things
could be repaired, Mr. Wheat's South was a posted area with its
signs for "Whites" and its various designations for its Negro citizens. The time, effort, and inconvenience that Mr. Wheat's South
invested in segregation may astound today's young southerner.
To Ernest, young as he was, it seemed pathological. Surely the
best that can be said about it is that it is a form of pathology no
longer in evidence in the South.

Perhaps, if any single incident marks the beginning of our present time when such pathology is not in evidence, that incident
would be the sudden, unpremeditated decision of Rosa Parks in
Montgomery, Alabama, on the evening of December, 1955, not to
surrender her seat on a cross-town bus to a white man. Montgomery buses were segregated then according to a plan that illustrates
not only the offensiveness of segregation as a social policy but
also the Alice-in-Wonderland character of some of the ways a particular prescription for segregation could be designed. All of the
passengers on a Montgomery bus entered from the front in 1955.
White passengers were supposed to seat themselves in the front.
Black passengers sat anywhere behind the white passenger far-
thest back. Thus, if a new white passenger entered a bus on which
all the seats were occupied, a sort of rolling readjustment was
supposed to occur. The black seat immediately behind the last
white seat was supposed to be vacated for the new white passenger. Mrs. Parks, who lives now in Detroit (but who would now be
called Mrs. Parks in Montgomery), refused to vacate. She was ar-
rested. Montgomery's black community rallied to her support.

The Montgomery Improvement Association was formed, with Martin Luther King at its head. The Montgomery buses were boycotted. Eventually, complying with a verdict from the Supreme Court of the United States, they were desegregated. Elsewhere in the South, as well as in Montgomery, civil rights activism, joined in by blacks and whites, with youth strongly represented, from the North as well as the South, precipitated demonstration after demonstration against segregated facilities of all kinds. The rising wind of which Walter White had spoken in the 1940s—the wind of the have-nots' expectations—after a long winter had found a spring. It swept away the southern segregation and the signs. In so doing, it swept away Mr. Wheat.

A young man in Montgomery now of the same age Ernest Ellis was fifty-two years ago will still know whether he is white or black, but not because some sign on a public corner or in a building tells him so. In Montgomery the airport, like many American airports, has recently been improved. It has men's rest rooms and ladies' rest rooms, a restaurant, ticket counters, a waiting room, and departure lounges. Everybody sits anywhere. There are no signs for whites and blacks. The sky caps in the airport are black. But so is one of the two agents selling tickets at the Eastern Airlines desk.

About forty miles east of Montgomery lies the campus of Tuskegee Institute, surrounded by the small town of Tuskegee and the cotton acreage of Macon County. It will soon be a century since Booker T. Washington, young, tall, and light-skinned, came there, an unknown protégé of General Samuel C. Armstrong, the white founder of Hampton Institute, whom young Washington worshipped. From the west a left turn at a traffic light leads into the Institute, scarcely a hundred yards away from Tuskegee's famed guest house, Dorothy Hall, named after Dorothy Lamb Woodbridge, of Connecticut, born in 1745 and dead in 1791. A memorial plaque on the wall in her hall tells about her and announces that her building was given to Tuskegee, in her name, by the families of the Phelps and the Stokes. Dorothy Hall was dedicated in 1901.

There is a circle in front of Dorothy Hall. On the side of the cir-

cle away from the hall is the statue of Booker Washington standing over a kneeling former slave and lifting, it was probably the
sculptor's intent, a veil from the former slave's eyes. But when
Ralph Ellison, a student at Tuskegee, took a good look at the statue he could not tell, as he testifies in *Invisible Man*, whether
Washington was lifting the veil or replacing it. Not more than
fifty yards from the circle, the statue, and Dorothy Hall, is the
new Tuskegee chapel, quite literally one of the most beautiful
buildings on any campus (or off, for that matter) in the world.

It was not in this chapel, but in another one on this same site,
that Ellison heard a Tuskegee choir sing both Bach and Negro
spirituals. Six years before the dedication of Dorothy Hall, Washington made the speech in Atlanta as a result of which, it can be
argued, in the judgment of the white power structure, he established himself as the leading American Negro of his day. This was
the speech in which he enjoined southern Negroes to "let down
their buckets where they were" while, in his next breath, as it
were, he issued what could be interpreted as an assurance to southern whites that southern Negroes, realizing the cultural and economic gaps they still had to bridge between themselves and other
Americans, would concentrate on bridging those gaps rather than
on immediately seeking social equality and the vote. But it is easy
to oversimplify Washington, to forget how little he started with
at Tuskegee, how intimately he knew the South he wanted to
help, and how astute he often was in distinguishing between what
he perceived as an apparently necessary temporary expedient and
an ultimate objective.

In 1977 a goodly number of teachers at Tuskegee are white. A
few of the students are. One may say, then, with warrant, that
Tuskegee is not yet integrated. The very same remark may be
made, too, with warrant about the South in 1977. But, naturally,
nothing is ever simple in this world. As one may oversimplify
Washington, so one may oversimplify, either too positively or
negatively, both the South in which Tuskegee was founded and
the present South in which Tuskegee remains vigorously alive.
Some of the buildings at Tuskegee are made from brick which
Washington learned to fire and his students to lay. They speak of

the Tuskegee of Washington's era, when both, in all America, handicrafts had not been so totally superseded by technology as they are now, and, in the South, the vocational ceiling for Negroes was dishearteningly low. But today, on the outskirts of the town of Tuskegee just off Interstate 85, there is a Holiday Inn, franchised to the black partnership that operates it. The bar in this Holiday Inn is called the Tiger Lounge. Tuskegee Institute's athletic teams are named the Tigers. The bar opens daily in the late afternoon. Customers, some white, some black, drift in and out as the hours pass. One of them who comes in on an autumn day is a young black man, a resident of Tuskegee, with a white companion. The two are working together, promoting a benefit sponsored by the local Optimists club. Someone makes a pleasant remark to the black young man about his brother, who is a few years younger than he, has finished Tuskegee, and is, at present, commuting for further study to Auburn University, an easy ride of twenty or twenty-five minutes from Tuskegee.

The conversation about the absent brother is quiet and casual, yet interspersed with significant revelations. Whatever the absent brother wants to do (apparently to get a start in the world of business), he has had some flattering offers to come North. But he firmly intends to live and work in the South, to let down his bucket where he is. The skill which he is developing he believes can be used as much to his advantage in the South as in the North. Moreover, his personal life will be more comfortable in the South. He does not have to specify all the things that account for his preferences. One knows what they are—the changes, the alterations in a way of life, that have ended the South of Mr. Wheat.

Religion, the Bible Belt, and the Modern South

Most of that part of the United States now referred to as the Deep South or the Bible Belt passed from frontier to civilized society between about 1790 and 1830. Three of those states closest to the lower Mississippi River and the Gulf of Mexico were admitted to the Union between 1812 and 1821, and Arkansas became a state in 1836. (The Louisiana Purchase by which most of this land was acquired from France was not formally ratified until December, 1803.) As the people who settled this region made their way down from Virginia, the Carolinas, Kentucky, Maryland, and the states farther up the eastern seaboard, they brought with them only the barest necessities—food, work animals and milch cows, their long rifles to supply meat for the table. Almost all of them also brought along their Bibles, the divinely inspired word of God upon which their religious faith was firmly established. Most of these early settlers belonged to the more fundamental Protestant sects, although there were a few Episcopalians among them.

As soon as a settlement was founded—as Faulkner says of Habersham, the original name of Jefferson, the county seat of his mythical Yoknapatawpha County—a church was built and an ordained minister employed. But many of the early settlers lived considerable distances from these settlements and sometimes miles from their nearest neighbors. For them, church services were held wherever they could be accommodated, often by persons whose only qualification for this position of honor and influence was that they had received a special call from God to serve Him. These lay ministers were supplemented by circuit riders who, because they were ordained ministers, could administer the sacraments of the church—marriage, the Lord's Supper—and officiate at Christian funerals and the few other rituals that the believers insisted upon. The circuit rider also preached, of course, but his territory was so large that he could be expected to visit a particular location only four or five times a year. Between his visits, a lay leader held the congregation together.

Often he was able to secure the services of a professional evangelist, who ordinarily was not an ordained minister and was therefore unable to administer the sacraments. His sole purpose or function was to bring lost souls to God, to fill the spirits of sinners with the redeeming grace of Jesus Christ. If there was no meetinghouse in the community large enough to hold the vast crowds the evangelists attracted, the "protracted meeting" was held under a brush arbor built especially for the occasion. Some of the newly built churches, like one in south Mississippi, prepared for these most important events in an unusual way. Afraid that sinners would destroy the pews when they "were seized by the Holy Ghost" and began "shouting and proclaiming" in the "unknown tongue," the churchleaders appointed a special committee to take any member they found in this "delicious condition" outside and fasten him or her to a pine stump until the mood passed. After the meeting—and the worth of the evangelist was always determined by the number of souls he saved—there was always a baptismal service in which those who had "found Jesus" and, consequently, were "born again" were immersed in the water of a nearby stream.

One specific result of these conditions was to emphasize "preaching" and deemphasize other elements of the service—music, liturgy, and the sacraments. Ralph Gabriel once called this kind of evangelical religion "Romantic Christianity," a creed that emphasized the individual and his emotions, "a gospel of love which cleansed the world." In the literature of the time, one will find it most often as the butt of a joke in the writings of the humorists of the old Southwest—Johnson Jones Hooper, Joseph Glover Baldwin, and George Washington Harris. Sut Lovingood, one of Harris' characters, says, "One holesum quiltin' am wuth three old pray'r-meetins on the poperlashum pint." Sut lists his principal hates as "a circuit rider, a nigger, and a shotgun." One of Hooper's funniest stories is his explanation of how Simon Suggs, the protagonist of most of his yarns, outwits the Reverend Mr. Bela Bugg and walks off from the camp meeting with the collection plate and all the money it contains. Mark Twain describes another camp meeting in *The Adventures of Huckleberry Finn*:

> There was sheds made out of poles and roofed over with branches, where they had lemonade and gingerbread to sell, and piles of watermelons and green corn and such like truck.
>
> The preaching was going on under the same kind of sheds, only they was bigger and held crowds of people. The benches was made out of slabs of logs, with holes bored in the round side to drive sticks into for legs. They didn't have no backs. The preachers had high platforms to stand on, at one end of the sheds.

When Huck and the "King" arrived at the meeting, the congregation was singing hymns.

> The people woke up more and more, and sung louder; and towards the end, some begun to groan, and some begun to shout. Then the preacher begun to preach; and begun in earnest too, and went weaving first to one side of the platform and then to the other, and then a leaning down over the front of it, with his arms and his body going all the time, and shouting his words out with all his might; and every now and then he would hold up his Bible and spread it open and kind of pass it around this way and that, shouting, "It's the brazen serpent in the wilderness! Look upon it and live!" And people would shout out "Glory!—*A-a-men*!" And so he went on, and the people groaning and crying and saying amen:
>
> "Oh, come to the mourners' bench! come, black with sin! (*Amen*!) Come, sick and sore! (*Amen*!) come, lame and halt, and blind! (*Amen*!) come, pore and needy, sunk in shame! (*A-a-men*!) come all that's worn, and soiled, and suffering!—come with a broken spirit! come with a contrite heart! come in your rags and sin and dirt! The waters that cleanse is free—the door of heaven stands open—oh, enter it and be at rest!" (*A-a-men*! Glory, glory hallelujah!)

Thousands of such emotional appeals filled the mourners' benches in hundreds of churches, meetinghouses, and brush arbors, and swelled the rolls of those who had seen the light, had been born again, and were determined to follow God's leadership, as the hymn says, "every day and in every way." These backwoods

evangelists were the forerunners of their twentieth-century counterparts, Billy Sunday, Oral Roberts, and Billy Graham—to name
only a few of the best known.

The image of the South as a region dominated by evangelical-
ism persisted into the period following the Civil War. If one takes
into account the common practices of the predominantly Protestant churches of the section, not to mention the dozens of traveling evangelists moving across the countryside from Maryland to
Florida to Texas, such a view seems neither distorted nor exaggerated. Soon after the war Walter Hines Page, editor of the *Raleigh
State Chronicle* and the *Atlantic Monthly* and one of the founders of the publishing firm of Doubleday, Page, and Company, proclaimed that the South would never enjoy the material prosperity
of the Northeast until it brought its maniacal religious fervor under control.

The strong evangelical flavor of southern religious practices
came forward into the twentieth century, nevertheless, as is demonstrated by an experience related by Richard Wright in *Black
Boy* (1945). On the last night of a revival meeting, the minister
asked all of the congregation who were members of the church to
stand. Wright was one of the few who remained sitting. Then, after each of those "living in darkness" had been spoken to privately
by a deacon in a room adjacent to the sanctuary, they were brought
back and a prayer was offered for them by members of the congregation. Then the preacher asked, "Would any man in this room
dare fling no into God's face?" All the sinners were placed in the
front row while the congregation began to sing softly, "This may
be the last time, I don't know" and "It ain't my brother, but it's
me, oh, Lord, / Standing in the need of prayer." Next the minister
asked the mothers of the young sinners to bring them forward for
baptism if they wanted their sons to be saved. As Wright points
out, this matter of "saving souls knows no ethics; every area of
human relationships was shamelessly exploited."

Even if one discounts Wright's account, allowing for the well-
known anti-Christian sentiments expressed in his later works, it
is obvious that certain Christian practices have not changed much
in the South. Writing in nineteenth-century Mississippi, William

Hall used a similar incident in a vastly different manner. At the close of his sermon, the minister gives an invitation for those living outside the church to join the fellowship. "All of you," he says, "who want to go to Heaven, please rise." Everyone stands except one man. "John Hawkins," the preacher says in dismay, "don't you want to go to Heaven?" "Oh, sure," John responds, "but I thought you were trying to get up a load for tonight."

Readers of William Faulkner's *The Sound and the Fury* will remember the sermon that the Reverend Mr. Shegog, a visiting minister from St. Louis, delivered in the black Baptist church on Easter Sunday, April 8, 1928.

> When the visitor rose to speak he sounded like a white man. His voice was level and cold. . . . They began to watch him as they would a man on a tight rope. They even forgot his insignificant appearance in the virtuosity with which he ran and poised and swooped upon the cold inflectionless wire of his voice, so that at last, when with a sort of swooping glide he came to rest again beside the reading desk with one arm restng upon it at shoulder height and his monkey body as reft of all motion as a mummy or an emptied vessel, the congregation sighed as if it waked from a collective dream and moved a little in its seats. . . .
>
> Then the voice said, "Brethren" . . . the voice died in sonorous echoes between the walls. It was as different as day and dark from his former tone, with a sad, timbrous quality like an alto horn, sinking into their hearts and speaking there again when it had ceased in fading and cumulate echoes.

Then the Reverend Mr. Shegog began to walk around the raised platform, first murmuring then gradually raising his voice until he was almost shouting: "I got the recollection and the blood of the Lamb!" The congregation watched and listened until the minister "was nothing and they were nothing and there was not even a voice but instead their hearts were speaking to one another in chanting measures beyond the need for words." After a few seconds from the crowded church there came a "long moaning expulsion of breath" and a single soprano voice, "Yes, Jesus!" Then the minister, with everyone in the church devouring his every word, rapidly reached the climax of his sermon, the point to which he had led them as carefully and as surely as if he were conducting a symphony orchestra and his congregation, the members of this orchestra, were following a musical score: "I sees hit, breddren! I sees hit! Sees de blastin blinding sight! I sees Calvary, wid de sacred trees, sees de thief en de murderer en de least of dese; I hears de boasting en de braggin: Ef you be Jesus, lif up yo tree en walk! I hears de wailing of women en de evenin lamentations; I hears de weepin en de cryin en de turnt-away face of God: dey done kilt Jesus; dey done kilt my Son!" And the congregation responds: "Mmmmmmmmmmmmmm: Jesus! I sees, O Jesus!" During this entire performance Dilsey, the black servant of the Compsons who has brought Benjy Compson, a thirty-three-year-old idiot, with her to church, "sat bolt upright . . . crying rigidly and quietly in the annealment and the blood of the remembered Lamb."

Not only is Faulkner previewing here the basic patterns and rhythms of many well-known sermons—including the Reverend Dr. Martin Luther King's "I Have a Dream"—but with minimum allowance for differing details, he is describing the experience that occurs in churches of dozens of fundamentalist sects all over the South every Sunday. The members of some of these churches demonstrate the genuineness of their faith by handling poisonous snakes or taking lethal doses of strychnine and refusing the services of a physician. Members of other congregations vividly proclaim their awareness of the "blood of the remembered Lamb" through physical seizures—called the "shakes"—and shouting in an "unknown tongue." No formal religious denomination, none of which I am aware, would agree with Jed Tewksbury, the intellectually sophisticated protagonist of Robert Penn Warren's latest novel, A Place to Come To (1977), that to accept the dogma of any organized church is to "fly in the face of the whole intellectual history of the Western world since the renaissance." Few, if any, I suspect, would accept John Crowe Ransom's statement in The World's Body (1938) that "religion is an institution existing for the sake of its ritual, rather than, as I have heard, for the sake of its doctrines." But all churches in the South are not fundamentalist, few of the Methodists shout any longer, and most of the Protestant sects recognize the importance of ritual and tradition in making their doctrines more palatable to their membership.

One of the most gifted modern southern writers, Flannery O'Connor of Georgia, insisted, however, in the words of Pascal, that she believed "in the 'God of Abraham, Isaac, and Jacob and not of the philosophers and scholars.' This is an unlimited God and one who has revealed himself specifically. It was one who became man and rose from the dead." Although President Jimmy Carter is a Baptist and O'Connor was a Catholic, I suspect he would find this statement of her religious views compatible with his own; her "unlimited God who reveals himself specifically" is the one responsible for Carter's being "born again." Although some of O'Connor's best-known stories—and she is widely read all over America—are rooted in orthodox Christian dogma, her ingenious handling of her material prevents her stories from being didactic. Few writers of her generation anywhere have created a more arresting group of characters than she—a garrulous old grandmother who reaches her greatest moment in the face of death, a thirty-year-old Ph.D. who attempts to seduce a supposedly naïve Bible salesman little more half her age, a one-armed itinerant handyman who marries and abandons a nearly blind deaf-mute in order to gain possession of a twenty-year-old car. Only the closest reading of the stories in which these characters appear—and many of her other excellent stories as well—reveals the Christian message they contain. But it's there, concealed behind some of the most polished and sophisticated writing done in America in the twentieth century. Once, when asked why she filled her stories with such freaks as those described above, or placed these unusual human beings in such grotesque settings and situations, Flannery O'Connor responded: "When you can assume that your audience holds the same beliefs you do, you can relax a little and use normal means of talking to it; when you have to assume it does not, then you have to make your vision apparent by shock—to the hard of hearing you shout, and for the almost blind you draw large and startling figures." As O'Connor suggests, her use of warped and grotesque characters as well as horrible and frightening incidents in her stories is not an end in itself but merely a means of showing man's perilous voyage through this world. Beneath this weird surface, her work is unrelenting in its insistence on imperfect men living in a world that reflects their imperfection. Man's only means of salvation is through the redeeming grace of Jesus Christ.

This kind of creed has persisted in the South, for Protestant and Catholic alike, and has resulted in the section's being referred to as the "Bible Belt." This is the region that produced Jimmy Carter, who would believe, with Flannery O'Connor, that man's lost innocence is available to him only through the redemption accessible by belief in a slain and risen Christ.

JAMES SEAY

The Southern Outdoors: Bass Boats and Bear Hunts

The traditional concept of the southerner as one possessing a strong attachment to the land—and, by extension, a predilection for outdoor sports, especially hunting and fishing—has not diminished appreciably, to judge from the current raft of assessments of the southern character attending Jimmy Carter's transfiguration from peanut farmer to president. In fact, Mr. Carter himself has shrewdly played on this image (and in turn reinforced it even further in the public imagination), inviting journalists and photographers to walk the fields with him or observe as he demonstrates how to catch fish from his farm pond.

The tenacity of this concept of the southerner's inherent sense of the land is understandable, of course, for it has long since been a given in any enumeration of the essential characteristics of the southern psyche. Owing to the agrarian traditions of the South, the average southerner has always had a more than casual association with the outdoors. Or at least this was so in the past. Until recent times, the probability was almost certain that a southern family either itself owned and farmed land or had relatives or neighbors who did, and, as W. J. Cash points out in *The Mind of the South*, the natural inclination was to hunt, fish, race horses, or what have you on those lands. Cash accounts for this inclination as follows, speaking of the typical male citizen in the Old South: "In his youth and often into late manhood, he ran spontaneous and unpremeditated foot-races, wrestled, drank Gargantuan quantities of raw whiskey, let off wild yells, and hunted the possum: because the thing was already in his mores when he emerged from the backwoods, because on the frontier it was the obvious thing to do, because he was a hot, stout fellow, full of blood and reared to outdoor activity, because of a primitive and naïve zest for the pursuit in hand."

There are still woods and uncrowded spaces in the South suitable for the outdoor life—and even a fair number of retrograde cases who fit the character description above, though not as many of either as some writers and film-makers would have us believe. I am not suggesting in these opening comments that this aspect of southern experience will vanish in the predictable future (assuming that it continues to be possible to discern a distinct southern character). But it should be obvious to the most superficial observer that in the contemporary South the frequency and quality of the outdoor experience have, like most other traditions, changed radically.

The forces behind this change should also be obvious, for they are in no way unique to the South or the contemporary period. The naturalist John James Audubon, for example, observed the same thing happening a century and a half ago along the Ohio River between Pennsylvania and Kentucky. In his essay "The Ohio," he comments on the changes he has witnessed along that river since the time of one of his journeys from Pennsylvania in the early 1800s, some twenty years earlier:

> When I think of these times, and call back to my mind the grandeur and beauty of those almost uninhabited shores; when I picture to myself the dense and lofty summits of the forest, that everywhere spread along the hills, and overhung the margins of the stream, unmolested by the axe of the settler; when I know how dearly purchased the safe navigation of that river has been by the blood of many worthy Virginians; when I see that no longer any Aborigines are to be found there, and that the vast herds of elks, deer and buffaloes which once pastured on these hills and in these valleys, making for themselves great roads to the several salt springs, have ceased to exist; when I reflect that all this grand portion of our Union, instead of being in a state of nature, is now more or less covered with villages, farms, and towns, where the din of hammers and machinery is constantly heard; that the woods are fast disappearing under the axe by day, and the fire by night . . . when I remember that these extraordinary changes have all taken place in the short period of twenty years, I pause, wonder, and, although I know all to be fact, can scarcely believe its reality.

There is an interesting coincidence here with regard to the present topic. Audubon's odyssey from Pennsylvania eventually led him into the Deep South and, on one brief occasion, into the very area that another artist, though not a painter, would a century later use as his model for a fictional landscape within whose boundaries would be rendered the same changes that Audubon had described. I refer to William Faulkner and the hunting stories contained in *Go Down, Moses*, most notably "The Bear." Audubon's acquaintance with this specific part of Mississippi—which Faulkner would later use as his geographic model for the hunting lands of "The Bear"—was the result of an unexpected meeting with a squatter who so fascinated the painter with his talk of the local wildlife that Audubon stayed on as his guest for a few days, during the course of which he joined the squatter in a hunt for a panther that had been ravaging the squatter's livestock. Reading Audubon's enthusiastic account of this experience in his essay "The Cougar," one comes to realize how close to actual fact is Faulkner's depiction of the unspoiled quality of the wilderness that was once there. Audubon was so impressed with the natural state of this region and the abundance of wildlife it supported that he was inspired to make its existence known to other naturalists and give explicit directions to its location: "This tedious account of the situation of the Swamp, is given with the view of pointing it out to all students of nature who may chance to go that way, and whom I would earnestly urge to visit its interior, as it abounds in rare and interesting productions: birds, quadrupeds and reptiles, as well as molluscous animals, many of which, I am persuaded, have never been described."

Whether other students of nature followed and described those "rare and interesting productions" I do not know, but it is clear that Faulkner, a century later and despite its greatly altered state, responded deeply to what he envisioned of the "Swamp's" past. What is more, he gave us a narrative that posits special meaning in the relationship between those changes in the landscape and the characters whose dramas he centered there. The feeling of loss that Isaac McCaslin experiences when he sees the material and equipment for the projected expansion of the lumber mill in "The Bear" is rendered all the more intense for the reader by Faulkner's success in having created a sense of the sustaining energies generated within the primal depths of the wilderness and the possibility that human beings might connect with those energies. It is indeed one of Faulkner's most resonant and richly textured pieces of fiction, and one that presents a vision that Audubon himself would perhaps have appreciated, considering the hope he expresses at the end of his essay "The Ohio," with regard to the changes he has noted along the river:

> Whether these changes are for the better or for the worse, I shall not pretend to say; but in whatever way my conclusions may incline, I feel with regret that there are on record no satisfactory accounts of the state of that portion of the country, from the time when our people first settled in it. This has not been because no one in America is able to accomplish such an undertaking. Our Irvings and our Coopers have proved themselves fully competent for the task. It has more probably been because the changes have succeeded each other with such rapidity, as almost to rival the movements of their pen. However, it is not too late yet . . . Yes; I hope to read, ere I close my earthly career, accounts from those delightful writers of the progress of civilization in our western country. They will speak of the Clarks, the Croghans, the Boons, and many other men of great and daring enterprise. They will analyze, as it were, into each component part, the country as it once existed, and will render the picture, as it ought to be, immortal.

The Boon to whom Audubon refers is, of course, Daniel Boone. Faulkner, although probably unaware of Audubon's expressed hope, created his share of fictional characters who would qualify for such a list. In addition, he unwittingly did the Irvings and Coopers whom Audubon had in mind one better by writing of a Boon of considerably less than great and daring enterprise—a fictional Boon whose character is nonetheless as unique and interesting as any historical figure's, and as permanently fixed in our literature. I refer to the inept and reckless Boon Hogganbeck of "The Bear." At the same time he is unique, however, Faulkner's Boon is also representative of those countless anonymous individuals who took the southern wilderness for granted and, independently or as agents of various commercial interests, used it as though its resources were inexhaustible. The picture would not be complete without him and his kind lined up alongside the more renowned figures of historical fact.

For reasons of his own Audubon chooses in the above passage to withhold explicit judgment on those aspects of "the progress of civilization" that he was witness to. His vision led him to make inquiries and judgments of a different sort, and it would hardly be fair of us to ask for more than that, considering the richness of his gift to us.

The nature of Faulkner's vision, on the other hand, was such that he was led to point up the moral implications of those particular aspects of change that involved the wilderness and the characters whose lives were in some measure defined by their experiences within its diminishing boundaries. A reader will be disappointed, however, if he expects a clear-cut and neatly outlined indictment, because Faulkner makes it difficult and pointless to regard his judgment in terms of familiar and simplistic oppositions such as the Old and Good versus the New and Evil. Such a scheme mistakenly assumes that a natural apposition exists within the individual pairings. That assumption presents a problem if one considers, for example, that in "The Bear" the lumber interests are accommodated in significant ways by one of the paragons of the old order. Major de Spain, we learn toward the end of the story, sold the lumber company the land on which the company's loading platforms and commissary store were subsequently built. And after the old bear is killed, the major sells the timber rights to his hunting lands to an out-of-state lumber company. Thus the old order shares culpability for the destruction of the wilderness. It is a further measure of Faulkner's sense of the difficulty of attaching specific blame for this destruction that he accomplishes Old Ben's symbolic death through the agency of Boon, who is allied with both the old order and the new.

At the end of "The Bear," Faulkner makes it clear that the way of the future lies in the direction of Hoke's, the lumber mill camp town where Boon has acquired the position of town-marshal. It is to this lumber mill that the timber from the immediate area is brought for milling. The narrow-gauge railroad train that the hunters sometimes used for transportation has been bringing the cut timber to Hoke's for twenty years, going regularly in and out of the woods within earshot of Major de Spain's hunting camp, and yet the hunters have been oblivious to the inevitable—or else they have chosen either to ignore it or remain silent. Ike McCaslin finally comprehends the ramifications of all this when, a year and a half after the old bear's death, he passes through Hoke's on what will be his last trip to the hunting camp and sees the new planing mill under construction and the preparations for further expansion into the logging grounds. Faulkner expects the reader to share Ike's shock and grief at the realization that the wilderness as he once knew it is vanishing. Ike's response, however, is the exception; Boon's, the rule—for Boon's is rather a lack of response. In Boon's particular economy, the job at Hoke's, if he ever gave it a second thought, would involve no more complicity in the destruction of the wilderness than would, say, saddling a horse or going to Memphis for bonded whiskey.

If I have tended to dwell on *Go Down, Moses*, it is because the events and patterns within it are emblematic of the actual history of most of the virgin forests in the South, and it thus affords one an ideal model for examining the changes in the southern landscape and the forces behind those changes. For one thing, Faulkner's fictional chronology is consonant with historical fact. The expansion of the fictional Hoke's around 1885, for example, coincides with a historically verifiable increase of activity by lumber companies in Mississippi and other southern states during the late 1880s. During that time, word was getting around that the southern forests could be had at relatively low prices, for most of the farmers regarded the timber as an obstacle. An additional attraction was the fact that these forests were much closer to the lumber consumers than were those of the Pacific Northwest, and hence shipping was cheaper. Speculators, usually from outside the South, came with a fury to buy up large tracts of timber. In Mississippi, for instance, the number of sawmills doubled in the twenty years between 1880 and 1900, and by 1909 the figure had more than doubled again, with a total of 1,761 sawmills in operation. By 1942 all the best hardwood timber had been cut from the forests of the Mississippi Delta. Much of what is at the heart of *Go Down, Moses* is contained in those statistics. In "Delta Autumn," which is set around 1940, we find that Ike McCaslin, now in his seventies, and the younger generation of hunters have been forced to go deeper and deeper into the Delta to find suitable hunting. Lumber companies such as Hoke's have denuded most of the land, and large cotton plantations occupy the space where virgin forests once stood, "the land across which there came now no scream of panther but instead the long hooting of locomotives."

It is easy to assume a tone of righteousness when dealing with all of this, but one needs to remember that the lumbermen who cut the timber and the farmers who cleared the land were serving a public need for lumber, food, and textiles. Faulkner himself recognized the complexity of the problem and had this to say about it in answer to a question put to him at the University of Virginia:

> Change if it is not controlled by wise people destroys sometimes more than it brings. That unless some wise person comes along in the middle of the change and takes charge of it, change can destroy what is irreplaceable. If the reason for the change is base in motive—that is, to clear the wilderness just to make cotton land, to raise cotton on an agrarian economy of peonage, slavery, is base because it's not as good as the wilderness which it replaces. But if in the end that makes more education for more people, and more food for more people, more of the good things of life—I mean by that to give man leisure to use what's up here instead of just leisure to ride around in automobiles, then the [sic]—it was worth destroying the wilderness. But if all the destruction of the wilderness does is to give more people more automobiles just to ride around in, then the wilderness was better.

What Faulkner could have added is that much of the guilt lies in the fact that selective cutting and reforestation were not practiced, and that not enough was done to ensure that portions of the virgin forests were set aside for conservation and recreational purposes. It is ironic that today many of the large lumber companies are among our best conservationists, albeit for economic survival and good public relations. In addition, some of these companies, for nominal fees, open their woodlands to hunters, many of whom would not otherwise have access to hunting lands.

A situation that is almost as ironic as the lumber companies' *volte-face* is the recent overpopulation of deer in some farming areas in the South as a result of game conservation laws and the abundance of crops such as corn and soybeans, which deer find highly edible. In fact, some farmers have applied for special permits to kill deer out of season, claiming a necessity to reduce crop damage. This overpopulation owes also to the reduced number of predators such as wildcats—or, as they are sometimes called, panthers—that formerly preyed heavily on fawns and does.

Except in the densely wooded and remote terrain of mountains and swamps, larger animals such as wildcats and bears now are a rarity in the South. In some of the game sanctuaries and government parks where hunting is prohibited, there are active programs directed at increasing the populations of these animals. But the animals are not necessarily safe even in those places, the fact notwithstanding that they are threatened or greatly diminished species. A case in point is the recent report that poachers in the last few years have allegedly taken an estimated one hundred bears a year from the Great Smoky Mountains National Park in Tennessee and North Carolina, where the bear population is estimated to be only around six hundred. Further, it is reported that some of these poachers hire radio-equipped guides who smuggle the guns and equipment into the park before the hunt and out again afterwards, along with the carcasses of any bears taken, while the hunter slips out in the guise of a hiker.

This kind of exploitative attitude exists among some lumber companies as well, despite the advances of colleagues more mindful of conservation needs. There are woodcutters in the South (and elsewhere) who continue to practice clear-cutting—or a relatively new method known as strip harvesting—on land not suited to these types of logging. In strip harvesting, large machines are used to level a given area of timber. For spots within the site inaccessible to the huge machines, poison is sprayed by airplanes. After the timber is removed, the site is burned, crudely rowed, and replanted in trees, usually pines or cottonwoods for the pulp or paper market. One problem in this method is that the sites, if they are in hilly terrain, become extremely susceptible to erosion, which eventually clogs nearby valley lands and streams with sterile silt. If the pines or cottonwoods that replace the former growth are not indigenous, there is also the loss of the natural mixture of tree species as well as the ground cover and wildlife hosted by the indigenous forests, although some wildlife tends to return if proper ground cover grows back and there is an adequate food supply.

As we have learned from the arguments between conservation groups and businesses engaged in activities posing threats to the environment, the issues are complicated and difficult, if not impossible, to resolve under the present terms. Obviously, the South will be forced to continue making environmental compromises as long as the nation—the South included—continues to consume large quantities of products requiring cellulose fiber, fossil fuels, and other natural resources available in the South and as long as there are those willing to provide these resources, not to mention those working to promote the introduction of new industries into the region. The dilemma becomes acute when one realizes that the problems in some instances are associated with the production of basic necessities. In some of the coastal areas of the South, for example, where vast tracts of land have been completely cleared of woodland and converted into what are known as "superfarms," it has been discovered that the fishing in adjacent coastal sounds and estuaries has been adversely affected by contamination from water run-off containing poisons, pesticides, and fertilizers. Initially, the effects are felt only by commercial and sport fishermen, but the problems ramify far beyond.

Any drastic and sweeping improvements in technology to protect the environment seem many decades away. One has only to consider what Audubon observed along the Ohio in a mere twenty years or what Faulkner witnessed in a like span of time—or, for that matter, what one finds missing in one's own lifetime—and the full challenge of the future becomes apparent.

One of the major changes in outdoor recreation, especially fishing and boating, in the South has been brought about by the creation of a number of large impoundments of water—which, incidentally, are themselves the subject of controversy because they involve the damming of rivers and streams. Typical of these impoundments is the one that covers a portion of the area where Faulkner hunted and fished. In a magazine article in 1954, he had this to

say of it, speaking of himself in the third person: "They who altered the swamps and forests of his youth, have now altered the
face of the earth itself; what he remembered as dense river bottom jungle and rich farm land, is now an artificial lake twenty-
five miles long: a flood control project for the cotton fields below
the huge earth dam, with a few more outboard-powered fishing
skiffs on it each year."

Faulkner saw only the beginning. The dazzling flotillas of fi-
berglass bass boats arrayed with electronic depth recorders, fish-
finders, water temperature gauges, oxygen meters, and the like
that skim around on these lakes all across the South today would
elicit a mixed reaction from him, I suspect. One cannot help but
be amused by the armament these fishermen have raised against
the wily bass, especially since it is quite easy to go out thus arrayed and still come back to the dock with an empty creel. On the
whole, however, they catch their share of fish. Almost all of these
lakes are regularly restocked with fish by the state game commis-
sions, and it does not seem likely that the black bass will appear
on the endangered species list in the near future.

The black bear, of course, is a different story. If you were to visit
the area that Faulkner hunted and fished and rode horses over and
wrote about, you would be hard put to find a bear. A small portion
of it (Faulkner exaggerated a bit) is under the water of the Corps of
Engineers reservoir, and most of the rest is under soybeans, cotton,
and pasture cover. But fishing is good, and so too, because of the
abundant soybeans and adequate woodland and ground cover, are
the dove and quail hunting. The same conditions obtain throughout the South, more or less.

I have turned to the Faulkner country for the bulk of my illustrations because it is the most widely known and also, if I may
introduce a personal note, because the Mississippi hunting camp
that Faulkner came to as a young man and that served as his model
in the hunting stories happens to be in my home county. As it
turns out, the hunting lodge itself is still standing, and of all the
images I could possibly conceive of, it affords the best emblem of
the situation we have been examining. It is in the middle of a big
soybean field. And in any direction you turn are silos, John Deere

tractors, and more fields under cultivation. Except for a big water oak that has been left standing beside the lodge, the only thing that would suggest there was ever a wilderness here is a line of trees that forms a horizon along the Tallahatchie River about a mile away. In the other direction, about a half-mile across the field, is a paved road that was formerly the bed of the narrow-gauge railroad that ran between a nearby lumber camp and a sawmill in the town of Batesville, some thirteen miles distant. If you take that road into town, you will notice that interspersed among the old tenant houses and farm buildings along the way are new mobile homes. And on trailers beside most of them are shiny bass boats, waiting, we can assume, to take their owners out after the legendary old bass that has eluded them for years and has probably even earned a name for himself in the land.

SYLVIA WILKINSON

Red-Necks on Wheels: The Stock Car Culture

At the turn of the century, the grandfather in William Faulkner's novel *The Reivers* had a "nightmare vision of our nation's vast and boundless future in which the basic unit of its economy and prosperity would be a small mass-produced cubicle containing four wheels and an engine." With false hope, he dreamed that "the motor vehicle was an insolvent phenomenon like last night's toadstool and, like the fungus, would vanish with tomorrow's sun." Grandfather's nightmare has been realized, as Faulkner knew very well, and where politics, religion, and entertainment have failed, this four-wheeled, motor-driven cubicle has welded the prince and the pauper into one society.

In a recent country music hit, Johnny Cash sings, "One piece at a time, and it didn't cost me a dime," the saga of a Detroit factory worker who removes one part a day from the factory where he works until he has enough to assemble a car. When the mines gave out in Appalachia, the hillbillies left their mountains, half-starved and without skills, and stumbled into the big cities looking for work. Detroit collected them into its auto assembly lines.

Back home in the hills, yards were spotted with the rusting hulks of automobiles, grass growing around their flat tires. The sign of prosperity was grass pressed down behind two inflated rear wheels. That meant the auto had moved recently, moved and taken the dirty fingernailed man who bent under the hood of his backyard spaceship to the open road, to freedom. As Jerry Bledsoe writes in his history of stock car racing: "In the wake of Watergate and the energy crisis, James Reston was complaining in the New York *Times* about how much more riled folks in this country got about gasoline being in short supply than they did about Watergate. You could tamper with an American's freedom, he concluded, but don't dare mess with his car. And there was Reston missing the whole point. Freedom wasn't some abstract thing being watched over in Washington. Hell, freedom *was* the car."

The country man who stayed home coaxing his automobile to more life than the mild versions off the assembly lines in Detroit could muster has found his place in southern history. The big city man from Detroit came to the country man making deals. He wanted this corn liquor-drinking, rough and burly fighting man to serve as the cornerstone for the biggest advertising scheme in American automobile history—stock car racing. Starting with a contradiction in terms—it is hard to find anything stock about these race cars—the auto-making factories poured millions into developing the living legend of the stock car racing hero and the automobile that gave him his power. Why did this strange marriage between red-neck and executive take place? Because a Detroit statistician noticed that when a Ford won a race on Sunday afternoon, sales boomed the next week. Unlike Grand Prix or Indianapolis racing, the spectator at a stock car race identifies directly with the car as well as the driver; the driver is a good old boy from his home state and a small town like Level Cross or Timmonsville, and the car can be bought from a local dealer.

Darlington. The stock car event of·the year, the granddaddy of them all, takes place in this South Carolina town. Yet the first showing in 1950 received almost no press, and most of the major papers stubbornly dwarfed the results under the weekend baseball scores. But the people came to Darlington, that first time. They came in droves. Twenty thousand spectators came and liked what they saw, and unknown at the time, baseball players all over the South were about to have their diamonds yanked from under them. A new day had come.

Stock car racing had an image problem from the start, a hard hat, blue-collar association that made it a one-class attraction. Bledsoe says: "'Respectable' people didn't think much of stock car racing at the time. Stock car racers were looked down on much as motorcycle gang members are today. Roughnecks. A wild bunch banging around on those dirt tracks, drinking, gambling, fighting—always fighting. 'I think they liked to fight about as good as race,' says Junior Johnson. 'Just as soon fight as drive. They fought all the time. They'd stop the race and fight.'" Junior himself once made an unscheduled pit stop to arm himself with a pop bottle for an infield fight with a competitor.

After World War II, more cars were sold in the South than in any other region of the United States. The South was emerging from the backwoods into an urban and industrial society, and men were confronted with the complexity of the machine. In *The Reivers*, Faulkner recorded the impact of this change:

> "He's ruined it!" Boon said. "He's done took it all to pieces just to see what was inside! He wont never get it all back together again!"
> But Buffaloe did. He stood, mild and grease-stained and gently dreaming . . . and a year later Buffaloe had made one of his own, engine, gears and all, into a rubber-tired buggy; that afternoon, stinking noisily and sedately and not at all fast across the Square, he frightened Colonel Sartoris's matched carriage horses into bolting with the luckily empty surry and more or less destroying it; by the next night there was formally recorded into the archives of Jefferson a city ordinance against the operation of any mechanically propelled vehicle inside the corporate limits.

Cars replaced horses, tractors and trucks replaced mules, but in the South the automobile never took on the impersonality of a machine. Like mules and horses, they were named: Old Bess, Smokey, Chantilly Lace, the Midnight Creeper. Each of their parts was lovingly caressed and cared for. When they died, they went to automobile graveyards where their corpses were dismantled to keep their successors on the move until their remains turned to dust and rust. Not rare in the South is the spectacle of a spit-shined car parked in front of an unpainted house in a garbage-littered yard. During the fuel crisis, the good old boys waited for the government to say it wasn't so. The race organizers armed themselves with statistics, such as the data showing that one jet flight to take the Rams football team from Los Angeles to New York used as much fuel as an entire season of auto racing. The automobile was to be protected, defended. Southerners look upon demolition derbies, a popular northern and western event where cars are demolished with the last survivor emerging as the winner, with the disgust awarded a Neronian atrocity. Only the worst kind of "trash" would do that to a car, as Dude demonstrates in Erskine Caldwell's *Tobacco Road*.

Stock car racing is without doubt a sport for red-necks, not the southern gentility. Speed has gone from horse racing in kid gloves to the bare-knuckled driving of heavy cars. Recently a driver at Daytona was burned severely on the hands because he wore no gloves, a lack of protection unheard-of in modern European road racing, but still a southern holdover from the past when it was considered "sissy" to wear gloves. Automobiles get your hands dirty. The good old boys were by nature more attracted to the insides of cars than the rich. For every fifty-thousand-dollar Ferrari, there has to be a mechanic wise to its complexity; the elite live in dependence on these mechanics. The working class, however, sneers at the helpless dude who doesn't know a dead battery from a busted fuel pump.

Jack Burden, in Robert Penn Warren's novel *All the King's Men*, speaks of riding in a Cadillac with Willie Stark's chauffeur, Sugar-Boy:

> Sugar-Boy was driving the Cadillac, and it was a pleasure to watch him. Or it would have been if you could detach your imagination from the picture of what near a couple of tons of expensive mechanism looks like after it's turned turtle three times at eighty and could give your undivided attention to the exhibition of muscular co-ordination, satanic humor, and split-second timing which was Sugar-Boy's when he whipped around a hay wagon in the face of an oncoming gasoline truck and went through the rapidly diminishing aperture close enough to give the truck driver heart failure with one rear fender and wipe the snot off a mule's nose with the other. . . . Sugar-Boy couldn't talk, but he could express himself when he got his foot on the accelerator.

In the automobile, the working class had found a way to express itself.

The truth is if the car roaring around the super speedway at Darlington or Talladega really was "stock," stock as the car Joe Average drives to work, it would blow its tires, turn over, and fall apart before five laps were up. In the first stock car race at Daytona Beach, the cars were so ill-suited to racing conditions that the competitors got stuck in the sand and the race was called before it was meant to end. The sport was doomed to failure unless the tracks and cars were made for racing competition. From the stands, the stock car of today looks like a brightly painted version of Joe Average's Plymouth minus bumpers and headlights. Up close, it is revealed the doors are welded shut and the shiny object that appears to be a door handle is only tape; the insides are gone and replaced by a special racing seat that wedges the driver in position like a vice. Joe Average in his heart knows his own car is different, but he still buys all the performance parts he can tack on so that he can continue the charade.

It *is* fiction that the cars are stock, but putting them to the test of racing does build a better mousetrap. Anyone who has witnessed a super speedway crash knows the safety built into the stock car. Shoulder harnesses and rearview mirrors were in use in racing before they were standard in street cars; all race drivers wear their seat belts without being prompted by a government-ordered buzzer. It is more than sport; it is the progression of the machine age.

Actually, Detroit and Madison Avenue weren't the ones who thought of stock car racing in the first place. Appropriately the whole thing was conceived by a man named Bill France from Horse Pasture, Virginia. France, now the czar of stock car racing and a crucial endorsement for every southern politician, went as a driver to that first Daytona Beach race, where for the first time cars went in a circle rather than a straight line. France got his car mired up in the sand with the rest of the contenders and decided that this had the makings of something big. In 1949 he staged the first "new" car race in Charlotte, North Carolina—Henry Js, Hudsons, Nashes, Studebakers, Packards—and the first winning "stock" car was a Lincoln. World War II had dampened the sporting spirits of the whole country, but what emerged at the end of it all was not the familiar baseball that used to cop all the headlines. With the prosperity at war's end, even poor country boys could have cars. Politicians rushed to ride in the pace car; tossing out the first ball was passé. No more men hitting at a ball with a bat, kid stuff. These country boys could handle cars better than anyone. Why? Because they learned how to use them to the limits in the family business—moonshine whiskey running.

The "illegal" races when these backwoods men and their cars delivered their goods at night were not unlike the open road races such as the Monte Carlo Rally that took place in Europe. They sped over country roads to carry their processed corn to market, knowing they had to have the fastest car and be the fastest driver to stay out of jail. In reality the men never thought of what they did as illegal; making liquor was an old family business, and a far easier way to get the corn they raised to the market than carrying it in bushel baskets. They figured the government was trying to horn in on their profits and they aimed to keep them from doing it. The quality of the driving was awesome; Junior Johnson and Curtis Turner could reverse the direction of their speeding cars— the bootleg turn—at the drop of a pin and the sight of a roadblock. Undeniably there is an attraction to breaking the law and getting away with it. Johnson said, "I always think someday I'm gonna look in my mirror on the race track and see a flashing blue light." Johnson, who was one of the greatest moonshine runners turned stock car racers, says proudly, "I got caught at the still. I never got caught on the road."

As the law cracked down on more and more moonshiners, stock car racing grew. The likelihood and reality of serving time in prison cooled the passion of the bootleggers. As late as 1971 a stock car racer was caught by the law moonlighting at moonshining, but the legend has run its course. When the first races at the track got underway in the late 1930s, legend has it that the best races took place on the way to the track. More money was bet on those jaunts than the drivers could hope to win as a race purse, a purse that often was stolen by the promoters before the event was over. From the first there was enormous pride in the cars. Just like the whiskey that was "copper licker," not car radiator poison, these cars were developed and constructed with precision.

Dead now are three legendary heroes: Fireball Roberts, who earned his nickname throwing a fast baseball and died of injuries

from a fiery crash; Little Joe Weatherly, killed in Turn 6 at Riverside; and Curtis Turner, the greatest character of them all, dead in
the mysterious crash of his plane that he could land on a barn roof.
Curtis and Little Joe would get drunk and race *after* the race, one
night leaving a car in a motel swimming pool. Living is the fourth
legend, Junior Johnson, a quiet man who served time in prison for
his role in the family moonshine business, who now manages a
major stock car team, and who amassed a fortune in a nationwide
chicken business. The joke used to be that when Junior won another race, he bought another hundred chickens. Junior laughed
all the way to the bank.

The driver legends vanished alongside the romance of the backyard mechanic with grease up to his elbows. The facility of a modern stock car racing winner is a hospital operation room for machines—specialized, efficient, and *clean*. The new stock car man
is less flamboyant than his predecessors, more of a businessman.
Much of the special color is gone forever. Yet the southern stock
car racing hero is still known to his fans by his first name—Rich-
are, Cale, David. Richard Petty is called "King Richard" because
he has won more Grand Nationals than any man in history—185
at this writing. Representative of the new generation of drivers,
he didn't learn his trade in a family moonshine business but a
family racing business: his father was a great driver—Richard's
now famous Number 43 was chosen because his father, Lee, ran
Number 42—his brother and cousin handle the mechanics. Richard is tired of hearing about moonshiners; his father vehemently
denies that his former trucking business ever had liquor as its
cargo.

There's a joke in racing circles. A driver dies and goes to heaven,
finding to his delight that they race up there for amusement. Entered in the Heavenly City 500, he is doing quite well until he
looks in his mirror and sees a driver approaching with "Petty" on
his helmet. The befuddled driver crashes. He attributes his accident to shock; he didn't know that Richard Petty was dead. "He
isn't," the driver is told. "That's God. He just *thinks* he's Richard
Petty."

Unlike European racing, stock car racing is a sport for seasoned men. When a driver nears retirement age in Europe (late thirties, early forties), he is in his prime in southern stock car racing. The stock car driver is a business man, not just an athlete. Petty has ulcers, Pearson is called the "Silver Fox" for his graying temples and slyness, Cale Yarborough is a politician.

No women are allowed in the pits; this is male country that is shamelessly protected. This writer was told recently by a male sports writer that a plan was in the works to allow certain women an hour visit to the hallowed pits each race weekend. This bit of news was supposed to fill me with gratitude and excitement. Superstition still prevails about the bad luck brought by female presence, although I have never been told there was any truth to the myth about the bobby pin in the carburetor. While walking among the race cars in the paddock, a girl asked her usually affectionate boyfriend why he walked away from her when they were around race cars, refusing to hold her hand. "It's like holding hands in church," he replied piously.

Although it might be disputed by the participants, one of the attractions for the racing spectator is violence. Americans of the 1970s respond to passive entertainment. Television sets overpower books. An average viewer can see several dozen violent deaths in one evening's entertainment, violence that moves at a rapid pace. The tension of baseball is left for the older generation. One set of statistics places baseball viewers at an average age of forty-five, while the under-thirty—and the prime buying group—packs the race tracks. Baseball allows tension between the action, racing is constant tension merged with action. In the delay while a person waits for the baseball pitch, he knows the most that he can anticipate is a hit, a miss, or a refusal. In racing the only wait occurs before the flag drops or after an accident. Racing is dramatic in the direct sense, a gut reaction.

The equipment for racing is expensive; whereas with a ball, a bat, and an open field you have a baseball game. Stock car racing reflects the prosperity of the times. Like drag racing, it was organized to get the participants off the open road and legitimized. Although the preparation for the sport is vastly complex, the rules and performance are simple. No advance knowledge is required to spectate. The driver who gets the checkered flag first wins, and every time he drives onto the track, not only his reputation but his life is at stake. It offers no less tension than the bull ring.

The rules are supposed to be adhered to literally, but not in spirit. If a baseball player uses spit to throw a curve that breaks sharply, in complete violation of the rule and the spirit of the rule, the crowd isn't indignant. Only the opponent is indignant—the crowd thinks how clever the pitcher is. Stock car racers have their own laws. Richard Petty said of David Pearson's now famous dirty trick to win a race—he slowed suddenly in front of Richard and forced him to hit his brakes—"It was smart, I suppose, but it wasn't right. We have unwritten rules we live by, and he broke one of them and could have killed us both." Of his long time feud with fellow competitor Bobby Allison, Petty said, "We whopped one another in races from time to time, but I swear I never hit his car until he hit me first. . . . you can bend fenders in stock car racing without killing one another . . . I'm no saint and never pretended to be. . . . A bunch of times I've come up behind somebody I've lapped maybe 10 or 15 times, and deliberately tapped him or maybe run him down off the track because he didn't belong out there racing." And the fans cheered him on.

I've heard stock car drivers say they wanted to beat cheating drivers with a legal engine of their own, rather than get them disqualified and beat them with the rules. I've heard crowds cheer when they saw a driver shove another driver into the wall for committing some offence they felt was retaliatory. I've heard drivers say everyone is cheating, just some more than others, and the cheating has only to be kept under control. In football, a crowd will boo if they feel a player gets away with an illegality. At a recent college game, I felt the men were so strapped down by rules that the game was too technical to enjoy. In basketball, men with whistles keep stopping the action. The only thing that stops the action in racing is a pileup that blocks the track. Then, until the debris is cleared, a special caution flag goes up that draws the competitors back into a pack and cancels the lead the leader might have built up.

Bobby Allison, one of Richard's and David's close competitors for overall victories, describes a fender-bending episode with Richard: "I don't think it was supposed to be tap-tap-tap; it was supposed to be a cah-LUNK. So, after that I didn't hesitate to cah-LUNK him when the opportunity arose." The fans loved it, but the economics of this ruckus finally brought the feud to a close. "Maybe you do that with $5,000 Sportsman-category cars," Richard Petty says, "but not with $40,000 Grand National cars." It *is* an expensive sport. A team can't consider a season without $200,000. It is the most impure of all professional sports, the most directly commercially related. A baseball player might have his sponsor's name on his uniform and endorse a shaving lotion, but a race car is a rolling billboard. An exhausted driver will crawl from a car and say to the first microphone shoved in his face, "I couldn't have won without my Firestone tires and my STP and my Valvoline, and I couldn't wait 'till the race was over to smoke a Viceroy."

And when it is over, they don't go home to their chalets in Switzerland, but to the house that racing built, which is rarely more than a few miles from where the driver grew up. While most European racers come from or aspire to the upper class, times used to be hard for many of the southern stock car men. For most, indoor plumbing and a guaranteed meal were luxuries at one time in their lives. Success didn't spoil Richard Petty, who has the largest fan club membership of any professional athlete. Success didn't spoil the others either. Richard still goes to the fence to sign autographs for the kids, a fancy, careful autograph that he learned in a handwriting course, just to do something special for his fans. The step-up from blue collar to middle class was made behind the wheel.

What does the automobile mean to the South? When a boy gets a car, he can escape. He can leave the farm. Richard worked in the tobacco fields for a dollar a day; he knew he needed more than his feet to change his station in life. The bright boys leave the farm because they're smart enough to get a car and keep it running. A car is the first big step up from adolescence. A comedian once joked that they ought to combine the driver's education and the sex education classes in the high schools; teenage marriages started for years in the backseats of cars at drive-in picture shows. To have a car is the assertion of a boy's masculinity. To race a car and win—that makes him a king.

Robert Penn Warren says in his introduction to *All the King's Men*:

> I picked up a hitchhiker. He was a country man, the kind called a red-neck or a wool-hat, aging, aimless, nondescript, beat-up by life and hard times and bad luck, clearly tooth-broke and probably gut-shot, standing beside the road in an attitude that spoke of infinite patience and considerable fortitude, holding in his hand a parcel wrapped in old newspaper and tied with binder twine, waiting for a car to come along. He was, though at the moment I did not sense it, a mythological fig-ure. . . . The roads, he said, was shore better now. A man could git to market, he said. A man could jist git up and git, if'n a notion come on him.

Whether with outstretched thumb or in his own mass-produced cubicle, Faulkner's grandfather's nightmare is a reality, a reality so powerful that food would be taken from a baby's mouth if a man thought his Ford could run on it. This is a place where "a man can jist git up and git, if'n a notion come on him." As Mr. Shiflet remarks in Flannery O'Connor's short story, "The Life You Save May Be Your Own," "Lady, a man is divided into two parts, body and spirit. . . . The body, lady, is like a house: it don't go anywhere: but the spirit, lady, is like a automobile: always on the move, always."

KATIE LETCHER LYLE

Southern
Country Music:
A Brief Eulogy

Until recently, nobody took country music very seriously. Since 1925 a lot of people have listened to the Grand Ole Opry on Saturday nights, and there have always been some cultural highbrows who liked the southern country sounds even though they knew they were listening to trash. To its detractors, the music was and still is monotonous, sentimental, obvious, musically inferior, and lyrically substandard. Even to the initiated, the addicted, country music often recalls too clearly a past deprived of class, culture, and comfort. And the people who cherished it were not usually inclined to be analytical about it.

In 1928 Victor Records held its first recording session in Nashville, Tennessee, but that was a false start. Only about one-half of the cuttings were released. No further country music records of any importance were made in Nashville until well after World War II, when the modern recording industry began in earnest.

But starting at about the end of the folk renaissance in American music in the early 1960s, the bigger world began to take notice of Nashville, and a lot of things about the country music industry began to change. Elvis Presley helped, with his "rockabilly" sound. Glamour and glitter came to country music, and old-timers Wilma Lee and Stoney Cooper began to look shabby next to newcomers Dolly Parton and Marty Robbins with their fancy hairdos and sequined suits. Roy Acuff, once dubbed the "King of the Hillbillies," changed his title to the "King of Country Music." Electrified instruments made the older Dobro guitars look positively primitive, and echo chambers replaced or enhanced the harmonious part singing of the Jordanaires, a quartet of gospel singers. A growing number of women began to appear on the Opry stage where previously a typical Saturday night saw only Kitty Wells and Minnie Pearl, modestly, even dowdily, clad, performing beside all the men. Bob Dylan, a singer of protest songs, cut a record in Nashville.

And yet I believe that the changes have been largely superficial. Country music, like the South that it represents, is conservative, and more significant by far than gold guitars and big-band backups is the fact that country music, underneath, is much the same now as it has been for half a century. The lyrics and tunes of country songs portray an aspect of the American scene that appears to be fairly constant in a world where few things endure unchanged for long.

To write an essay about country music is to face the problem of definition, and even the problem of naming the music. For it goes by many names, none connoting precisely the same thing, all overlapping in meaning. When I was growing up in the forties and early fifties, we called it all *hillbilly*, even when Margaret Whiting and Jimmy Wakely sang "Slippin' Around." Today this seems pejorative, condescending; the term *hillbilly* now implies backward, feuding, moonshine-dazed southern mountaineers singing about their darling Cory in deliberately nasal tones. *Bluegrass* denotes a rather specific area within a larger whole, a mandolin accompaniment, a Kentucky origin, and a certain kind of close harmony. It also implies a somewhat narrower set of themes than country music in general: most specifically, songs of homesick rural southerners who have moved to the city. Wilma Lee Cooper, widow and partner of Stoney Cooper, stated recently, "Bluegrass is now what we called country or hillbilly music as a kid." The confusion proliferates. *Country-western* lumps together two disparate types, the cowboy and the rural southerner, whose costumes may be similar but whose themes and concerns and lifestyles are a world apart. The cowboy—from "Home on the Range" to "Desperado"—is strong, silent, without parents, democratic, reverent but never conventionally religious, a killer, valuing male companionship, eschewing women as sweethearts or wives, avoiding urban existence, and pressing ever beyond the borders of civilization. The rural southerner, as we shall see, is nearly his opposite. *Nashville music* covers everything produced today in that city: "pop country," "mellow country," folk, and gospel, as well as the more traditional bluegrass and country. Today, Nashville music obviously is no longer confined to the traditional instruments of country music or its themes; social protest music, popular music, and country lyrics in front of big-band instrumental accompaniments roll off the record presses at a confusing rate. It's hard to tell what's what any more: "Country Charlie" Pride is a Negro; Chet Atkins has gone classical after years of playing backup guitar for country music; and Freddy Fender sings parts of his songs in, of all things, Spanish.

Probably the term *country music* best suits the purposes of this essay. By it I mean the music of the rural southern Bible Belt that evolved generally from the folk music of the English-speaking settlers in the area, and that celebrates the land, the values, and the people of the area. There is nothing particularly new in this process. Beethoven and Brahms utilized folk music of their times; Italian opera developed from folk music; and in our own place and time, Aaron Copland has made extensive use of folk music.

In general, popular music in this country portrays romantic relationships between unmarried people, be it "Muzak" (the bland sounds piped into all sorts of public places), rock, soul, jazz, blues, or any other kind of popular music with lyrics. Of course there are many individual exceptions, but this is generally so. The people portrayed in popular songs are for the most part young, celebrating the concerns of youth—sex, love, yearning.

Country music stands in sharp contrast to the other sorts of popular music in this country. We may wonder to what extent it reflects the actual lives of rural white southerners. Is the music wish-fulfillment for boring lives? A reflection of reality? A mere convention, like courtly love or sonnet-writing in the sixteenth and seventeenth centuries? Is its conservatism justified?

As early as 1939 the state of Georgia was concerned about migration out of the state because of boll weevils, reduction of cotton uses, farm mechanization, and better job opportunities in the

North. In the 1940-1950 decade alone, the farm population in the South declined by one-fourth; in the last quarter century two and a half million farms have disappeared, and three million people in the South have left the land. During the years between 1942 and 1962, the South lost another 20 percent of its farm population, according to Alvin Bertrand and Floyd Carty. Significantly, one of the most prevalent themes of county music is the country boy leaving the farm to go to the city to improve his opportunities.

Perhaps the singers choose the themes or perhaps the themes are tailored to the singers. At any rate, country singers on the average are older than other popular singers, and so are the people they sing about. And yet—if we may believe the songs—age does not offer the key to happiness. One may infer a too sudden leap from childhood to adulthood, which may well be at the root of at least some of the marital problems that the songs discuss at such length. Statistically, public figures—including country singers—have more than average marital problems.

In the *Billboard* Top Hundred Songs for one week in the early months of 1977, a quick rundown reveals the conservatism of country music. Twelve of the hundred were at least ten years old; five of the top fourteen were ten years old or more. Twenty-nine of the songs were sung by women, or women with men, by which we may infer that the field is today roughly three-fourths male. One song had a religious theme; and of the remaining ninety-nine, only fifteen were about something other than love. That leaves eighty-four. Thirty-six of those, or about 43 percent, were about marital infidelity, which is, in general, portrayed as secret and unideal in the long run. Adultery is referred to with less delicacy than it used to be, and with more explicitness (from "Slippin' Around to Have Your Company" to "Slide off of your satin sheets . . . , 'cause I know what you're crying for"), but infidelity still leads to unhappiness, as it always has in country music, and isn't generally portrayed as fulfilling.

J. Richard Udry has discovered that divorce is most common on the lower rungs of the economic status ladder, and that disruption in marriage decreases as the educational level rises. It is probably true in the South that poverty and dearth of opportunity have forced extremely young marriages (marriages of convenience, really) in rural areas, so that by the time they are in their early twenties the wife or husband, bored by the responsibilities of children and home, seeks new relationships.

Country songs lyrically portray—and always have—a very consistent sort of man. He is vocal, self-pitying, true to the memory of mother, childhood, and home. He is sober, conventional, married and monogamous, dreams of life in the big city and its successes, is self-righteous and fundamentally religious, but weak when abandoned by the woman who molds him, makes him, and breaks him—a woman gone wrong. He is the extreme opposite of the cowboy hero. They pass each other somewhere on their journeys, as the cowboy leaves the city to seek new wide-open spaces and the hero of country music heads for the glamour and glitter of the city, leaving behind him his unromantic and unproductive rural past.

The hero of country music is a Puritan-descended American of paltry means: white, southern, Protestant, conservative, undemocratic, uncomplicated, agrarian rather than metropolitan, uneducated and unsophisticated, and proud of it. He sentimentalizes children; his thinking is very old-fashioned. For example, large families were considered virtuous by the rural society of an underpopulated country a generation or two ago; in general they still are in country music. The rural southerner has much thought in common with the Nashville Agrarians of the 1930s. Alvin Bertrand states, "In the United States, a close and powerful association between land, family and home . . . developed, carrying a definite sentimental overtone. . . . Both the respect for ownership and the sentimentality persist in the present rural family."

The rural population of the South is almost entirely Protestant. Eighty percent of southern rural adults are affiliated with some church, and Baptist and Methodist groups predominate. According to Robert Sherrill, the fundamental southern Christian "believes in every word of the Constitution, but he's his own lawyer. He believes every word of the Bible, but he's his own Pope to interpret it as he pleases. Not even all the literalists agree. . . . Through all the diversity, though, there is one central theme—the lost soul and a forgiving God." He further comments that "next to Catholicism . . . [the] chief foe . . . is modernism." Religious songs make up one of the largest categories of country music, which is not true of other sorts of popular music.

The names of the singers and the names that appear in the songs suggest an exclusive Anglo-American monopoly on the music. (A single exception is Charlie Pride, the only successful black hillbilly singer to date. But his popularity has come at the expense of his racial identity; he has cultivated a white, country voice, and there is nothing Negro in his "sound" or in his themes. Nor, we note, has he renamed himself Muhammad Something-or-other.)

Today's country music has a motley heritage strengthened by miscegenation. Its strongest ancestor is the music the white settlers brought with them when they came to America, lyrics that were generally tragic. The lyrics fared better than the ballads, providing a basis for much of our popular music today. Many very old lyrics still survive in America virtually unchanged. "Pop Goes the Weasel" and "London Bridge" are two; and "La Cucaracha," still sung partly in Spanish, is traceable to sixteenth-century Spain. Occupational lyrics, such as sailors' chanteys and lumberjack lyrics, are still widely sung in near-original form. Rounds, such as "Row, Row, Row Your Boat," were popular among our ancestors. In seventeenth- and eighteenth-century England, no one of any education whatever was ignorant of music, and most people played an instrument, so the English settlers here, though perhaps having a smaller choice of instruments for accompaniment, brought with them a natural inclination to music. In fact, the early Calvinist tunes were so gay they were dubbed "Geneva jigs," until the American Puritans decided they were too much fun not to be a sin.

Ballads brought from the Old World tended to disintegrate into lyrics. Some ballads of the British Isles, it is true, remained popular here into the twentieth century, but for some reason the most popular ones were the least violent. "Lord Randall" merely implies that a lady has poisoned her beloved; "Barbara Allen," easily the most popular of the Scottish and English ballads in America

(101 versions were found in Virginia alone during the early years of the twentieth century), is perhaps the gentlest of all the tragic ballads. The girl, although cruel, does not do violence to her lover; she allows him to die of a broken heart. There was probably little impetus to remember the ballads well and to pass them on—they were part of another world. But why the ballads that were remembered were the least violent is a matter for speculation; at any rate country music is absolutely nonviolent, as we shall see.

Many early American lyrics were refrains or segments of English or Scottish ballads from which the story had disappeared. "The Lass of Roch Royal" is only one example of many. Child Ballad No. 76, this is the story of a girl going by boat with her baby to seek her true love who has exchanged tokens with her and promised to marry her. All that remains of this dramatic story in American folksong are Annie's sad words as she is driven away at the start of a storm and the mother-in-law's reply. These stanzas appear in various versions in scores, perhaps hundreds, of American songs:

> Then who will shoe my pretty foot,
> And who will glove my hand?
> And who will kiss my ruby lips,
> And who will be my man?

And the mother-in-law's reply:

> Your father will shoe your pretty foot,
> Your mother will glove your hand,
> Sister will kiss your red red lips,
> And you don't need no man.

Other ballads that met a similar fate are "Jamie Douglass," "Twa Sisters," and "Riddles Wisely Expounded." In the last, the Devil and a virgin have a debate which she wins only because she is innocent. This ballad and others like it may originally have had a kinship with morality plays, but in this country they were fragmented into nonsense songs, such as "I Gave My Love a Cherry."

Traditional British ballads also served as the prototypes for outlaw stories retold in a familiar form that probably evolved into the western branch of country-western music. Ballads were sung about many occupational groups besides outlaws, of course—cowboys, miners, lumberjacks, sailors. These ballads, with their lonely men struggling in their lonely existences, produced the portrait of the most popular type of American hero: the absolutely self-sufficient man who conquered the wilderness.

Following the Civil War, cities all over the South absorbed large numbers of freed slaves and their music. Work songs, spirituals, game songs—all with heavy emphasis on rhythm and repetition—evolved into the kind of folk music that we came to call the blues. Black spirituals, basically African music adapted to Christianity, tended to be developed in the form of a couplet plus refrain, which is the form the blues later took.

Part singing of ballads, lyrics, and spirituals developed from the part songs popular in sixteenth-century England; singing schools in this country perpetuated part singing well into the twentieth century. Unquestionably, modern bluegrass owes much to part singing, as does the harmony singing of a great deal of gospel music. Around 1900 songsters, cheap songbooks of lyrics without melodies, became popular in this country. The songs in them tended to be vulgar and whining. *Hit Parade* and other magazines like it published lyrics without music for more than twenty years in the forties, fifties, and sixties, and in doing so helped cement the popularity of the songs they published.

If we may believe the evidence of early commercial country music, it was the marriage of two strains of music, white and black, that produced the progeny out of which modern southern country music, now an extremely commercial enterprise, developed. Jimmie Rodgers, the Singing Brakeman, wrote his own songs, a mixture of cowboy songs, railroad songs, and blues. Although he was preceded by other well-known singers such as Vernon Dalhart and Riley Puckett, he is perhaps the first "great" in country music. He sang folk songs like "Frankie and Johnny" and "Muleskinner Blues"; railroad songs like "The Hobo's Lullaby" and "The Wreck of Number 9"; at least a dozen songs adapted from the blues to which he gave titles like "Blue Yodel No. 4" or "Blue Yodel No. ll"; ballads like "The Drunkard's Child"; and love songs like "T. for Thelma."

The early Carter Family songs, recorded in the late 1920s and early 1930s, are folksy, lyrical, bluesy; there is a heavy religious emphasis and a hint of the violence of old ballads that is virtually gone from today's country music. In the list of more than twenty-five years of the hundred *Billboard* top hits, I believe there are only two songs in which the jealous lover kills his beloved: "Miller's Cave" and "The Cold Hard Facts of Life." National crime statistics show that the urban male is, in fact, less inhibited in aggression and violence than his rural counterpart.

"Gathering Flowers from the Hillside," an early piece attributed to A. P. Carter, seems to be halfway between the high tragedy of traditional ballads and the passive nonviolence of today's country music. In this transitional song, recorded on May 7, 1935, the first two lines of Stanza 1 are a familiar fragment found in many folk and blues songs; A. P. Carter is firmly in the folk tradition with his frequent use of already-extant lines. Notice the strongly lyrical—as opposed to narrative—quality, the partially dropped story, and the repetition so typical of blues, work songs, and spirituals.

GATHERING FLOWERS FROM THE HILLSIDE

Refrain: I been gathering flowers from the hillside
To wreathe around your brow
But you've kept me awaitin' so long, dear
The flowers have all withered now.

1. I know that you have seen troubles
But never hang down your head,
Your love for me is like the flowers,
Your love for me is dead.

2. It was on one bright June morning,
The roses were in bloom,
I shot and killed my darling,
And what will be my doom?

3. Closed eyes cannot see these roses,
Closed hands cannot hold them, you know,
And these lips that still cannot kiss me,
Have gone from me forevermore.

Most of our major cities today, in the North and West as well as the South, have radio stations that play hillbilly music around the clock. Mike Seeger was recently quoted as saying, "Country music is headed more and more where we're headed: toward greater urbanization all the time." "Country Music is Here to Stay" was the title of a hit from 1958. Hillbilly music is undoubtedly heard by as many city people now as country people. It has even made its way to Japan; a *Newsweek* article in March of 1968 describes the popularity of Flatt and Scruggs in that country. The migration from farm to city is a central fact of life among the hillbillies as well as a central theme of their music. Given the circumstances of southern rural life—the social, cultural, and educational deprivations; the juvenile marriages; the attraction of the city and its apparent opportunities for new and better lives; the lack of job skills among the migrants; their perplexity in the face of computerization and city lights; their nostalgia for home—the themes of hillbilly music are fairly predictable as reflections of reality.

Is the portrait that so consistently emerges out of country music spontaneous or is it the conscious result of Nashville song writers' success formulae? Bruno Nettl, in *Folk and Traditional Music of the Western Continents*, notes that "the singing of folk songs on radio and television has evidently also affected the rural folk tradition, where instrumental accompaniment, part-singing, the hillbilly style, and strict adherence to meter seem to have increased since the 1940's." Certain fads in the music have been born, grown old, and died in the years since 1949—boogies, bounces, rags, and rockabilly are some of them—and the music being sung now has of course developed from earlier music. However, the essential qualities of country music persist and are still enthusiastically accepted (in 1961 the Grand Ole Opry was chosen America's most popular musical radio program; it has run continuously since 1925 and on a single Friday or Saturday night may draw visitors from as many as forty states).

That the themes remain unchanged seems the most amazing single fact about country music. A great part of the appeal of the music is in its unique and yet familiar sound; indeed, the tunes are so simple and so similar that an average musician can *play* many more songs than he can sing the words to. Perhaps the very repetitiveness of both tune *and* theme suggests the traumatic quality of the deepest emotional preoccuptions.

What *kinds* of communities preserve old songs? Surely it is the ones where the discipline of communal taste prevails, where the culture is single: one economy, one religion, essentially one class. This situation has always existed more in the South than in the North, and certainly more in rural areas than metropolitan. Although oral traditions have been largely destroyed by printing and mass media, an economic principle of selection is still at work, censoring by the most effective method of all—money—what it does not like or trust. As audience values and morality change, so will the music. Louise Pound believed in individual origins but a sort of "group ownership" of folk music. This is clearly how Nashville music must be viewed. Old songs are reissued by new singers with new arrangements all the time, and themes and plots and even stereotyped phrases are stolen shamelessly even when the songs aren't.

Country songs tell stories, and they tend to tell the same story again and again. Moreover, the protagonists of the stories are a great deal alike. The usual country song protagonist is a grown man. At least half the time he is married; his marriage or his romance provides the impetus for his story. But his crown has already become his cross, and the curtain rises on his misery, upon which he is relieved to expound. The country hero is not in all ways admirable. A democratic spirit is not his forte; he is suspicious of those who live differently from him, especially those in more fortunate situations, as songs like "Satisfied Mind" show. The song states flatly that a man with riches can't have a satisfied mind. The hero of country songs is often sentimental and weak, complains "Excuse Me, I Think I've Got a Heartache." He knowingly allows himself to be cuckolded, sadly inquiring of his wife, "Does My Ring Hurt Your Finger (when you go out at night)?" or following his wife into the bar where she has gone to solicit, and telling her in front of a customer, "It's a fine time to leave me, Lucille, with four hungry children and a crop in the field."

But there is also a great deal to admire in the hero of country songs. Love is the foundation of his creation, the central fact of his life, and worth everything. He has simple and total faith in it, which makes its subsequent destruction the more devastating. In his later loneliness, his errant wife takes on the aspect of a "Fallen Angel." His response to the injustice dealt him is restraint and fortitude ("I'll Sail My Ship Alone"), sentiment and tears ("Through the ages I'll remember / Blue eyes crying in the rain"). His sexual tastes are completely conventional; no deviations of any sort (*i.e.*, miscegenation or homosexuality) have found their way into country music.

There are many more songs about marital infidelity than about fidelity ("I Heard the Jukebox Playing When You Called Me On the Phone"). In fact, infidelity is the single most frequent theme of country music. It occurs in well over half the hit songs of the last quarter century. The first and most frequent reason for unfaithfulness is that another person has stolen away the beloved, although the partner herself is more often blamed than her new lover. For every happy marriage, roughly seven unhappy ones are described. Perhaps because female singers, and consequently the female point of view, are more scarce—though less so now than previously—it appears to be most often the women who leave home. Because so many of the love songs involve married people, we may infer that marriage is considered the only proper setting for a good life. (It is patently true of American thinking in general that a bad marriage is better than no marriage at all.) So, although marriage appears to be sacrosanct, love is held, as it is in all our popular music and literature, at an even higher premium. In country music, middle-class morality endures, but true love prevails. "Walk On By" is a good example in which the man, unable to curb his illicit desires, admits that he'll continue to see his paramour in the nighttime world although he cannot acknowledge her by day. Infidelity occurs only under cover of darkness, in the songs in which a time of day is mentioned at all. What is important is that the lover loves faithfully. When the singer is the one left behind, money or a rival or a combination of the two is given as the usual motive for his abandonment; when the protagonist is the one leaving, love is the sole motive. According to the abandoned one, the new relationship will lead to no good, because material goods cause spiritual corruption, and adultery is against God's laws. According to the one who abandons, on the other hand, the only possibility for his happiness and salvation lies in the new relationship.

The second type of infidelity depicted in the songs often blends with the first. This group includes songs in which one partner has been lured away by city life and has fallen prey to its attendant evils: drunkenness, haughtiness, and either the threat or the actual occurrence of a fall. The city is a symbolic hell to which sinners seem to be condemned. The southern hillbilly's view of the city links it to the woman, but to the wrong sort of woman—the evil, conniving, emasculating female. There has been an increase in this view over the years. Women (and men) who choose the life of pleasure and reject socially sanctioned ethical married life come to no good end, as songs like "Mansion on the Hill" tell us. In this song the girl has rejected her country lover for a life of riches, and now she is lonely and loveless. Rising in the world and accruing material goods are synonymous with mortal sin and loss of honorable values. "Pick Me Up on Your Way Down," a man confidently sings to his girl-turned-glamour-girl. In fact, there is considerable justification for this rejection of urban life and its values. In cities the birth rate does decrease; with families living closer to other families, there is less familial interdependence and more peer-group identity. Sheridan T. Maitland and Stanley M. Knebel offer evidence indicating that migrants from rural backgrounds have lower incomes, fewer skilled jobs, less "involvement in the community"—and therefore, less satisfaction—than those raised in cities.

These persistently popular love songs have a sameness of theme and similarity of tune. They are saved from monotony by a peculiar tendency to clever phrasing, by *mots justes* of a whimsical sort, certain apt metaphors, some fractured familiar phrases that, corny though they may strike us, are catchy. This tendency to tricky phrasing manifests itself primarily in the love songs, since the problem of originality is obviously much greater here. Country music, like all literature, is seeking new ways of saying the eternal things: "Silver Threads and Golden Needles" ("cannot mend this heart of mine"), "There's an Unwanted Sign Upon Your

Heart," and "My Shoes Keep Walking Back to You." In some cases the language is gimmicky: "I've Enjoyed as Much of This as I Can Stand" and "The Last Word in Lonesome Is Me." Sometimes the images become downright grotesque: "Our Hearts Are Holding Hands Across the Miles," and "My Tears Have Washed 'I Love You' from the Blackboard of My Heart." In 1952 a hopeful lover was "Waiting in the Lobby of Your Heart." In 1968, keeping up with the times, the situation is repeated, only this time Buck Owens is "Waiting in Your Welfare Line." Country love lyrics are freer now than previously, partially in keeping with the sexual liberation of our society as a whole.

The country music hero is usually unchanged by suffering. There are no epiphanies in his life, because there is no introspection. The causes for broken marriages are of the most basic sort: jealousy, boredom, or the novelty of someone new. Rarely are there social or religious differences or money problems between marriage partners.

Instead of revenge, the country hero tends to seek the comforts of alcohol, as in "I'm Gonna Tie One On Tonight." Drinking and drunkenness have become increasingly common factors over the years. Conservative to the point of reactionism, the southern Bible-Belt ethic may allow open drinking only at the point where the middle-class elements of society have begun doing something even worse. The use of drugs has indeed seemed by comparison to render drinking less sinful than it used to be: "I've got swingin' doors, a jukebox, and a barstool / My new home has a flashin' neon sign . . . / You can come to see me anytime you want to / Cause I'm always here at home 'til closin' time." The country hero also frequently seeks relief in tears, which in his world are not considered unmanly. It seems paradoxical that in tragic ballads, where the action is violent, the characteristic tone is one of restraint; the country hero characteristically indulges in unrestrained grief over much less. He is "Born to Lose." "Amanda, light of my life, fate should have made you a gentleman's wife," he grieves, merely because he's now "crowding thirty and still wearing jeans."

In country songs drinking is condemned as a recreation but is accepted as a solace for grief. It seems fair to conclude that drinking is a sin only if it induces happiness or pleasure. "There stands the glass/fill it up to the brim,/ It will ease all my pain,/ It's my first one today," sings a man full of self-pity as he prepares to drink himself into oblivion. As the unhappy hero drinks, he listens to the juke-box play songs about other unhappy heroes who are drinking and listening to country songs.

When the thwarted lover turns to drink, there is usually the suggestion that the alcohol isn't effective. Alcohol cannot, of course, be viewed as a satisfactory remedy in a society that disapproves of its use on moral and religious grounds. The songs make it clear that the hero has been driven to this extremity and is not responsible for his sorrows or his subsequent behavior. Although he may be philosophical about his loss, he is never a psychologist. Reality is easier to handle when it is simplified. The country music hero cannot accept unconscious motives; his reaction to the world is emotional, not intellectual.

There is another solace besides alcohol, and once again two themes frequently blend. The hero is often sustained by his faith in God. Even when he drinks, it is with the certainty that God will forgive him. He may have the moral responsibility for his own actions that Calvinism has ingrained in him, but even as he blames himself for his sad fate, he can still see himself as victimized, innocent, childlike, cruelly wronged. When the lonely hillbilly lover chooses religion as his comfort, it is with the self-righteous assurance that God is on his side and will duly punish his fallen wife. In "The Wild Side of Life" he accusingly sings, "I didn't know God made honky-tonk angels." However, man in his free will can and apparently does corrupt God's creations, because his wife replies, also accusingly,

> It wasn't God who made honky-tonk angels,
> As you wrote in the words of your song,
> Too many times married men think they're still single,
> Which has caused many a good girl to go wrong.

In "City Lights," the hero claims that God made the stars but that man made the corrupting lights of the city.

Typically, in an effort to compete with the glamour of the world that has stolen the thing he loves most, the southern hillbilly hero —whose sole and pure motive is that of recovering his wife or keeping his family together—is forced to leave his failing farm and make an odyssey to the city, where he believes job opportunities are better. The man's migration is fraught with disillusionment and evil; and so the city becomes a testing ground, a purgatory that will teach the hero a lesson he could not have learned in any other way. In "Detroit City" the hero "makes the cars" by day and "makes the bars" by night, and always longs for home.

The city most maligned in country music is Detroit, for the obvious reason that it is more accessible to Kentucky, Tennessee, and other southern Appalachian areas than many of the other northern or midwestern cities, and it has had innumerable opportunities for unskilled industrial workers, although Baltimore, Chicago, and New York are also mentioned in the songs. "The boy next door don't know it,/But come June he's gonna gain himself a wife,/Mr. Walker, it's all over,/I don't like the New York secretary's life" is a typical sentiment. It should come as no surprise that these are the same cities where some of the worst riots occurred in the late sixties, for here are hotbeds of disappointment, unfulfilled promises, and frustration—for whites and blacks alike.

The vision of the city as evil is hardly unique. The nineteenth-century sectional feelings in this country apparently remain a factor in the unsophisticated southern mind: city life is northern, or Yankee. Thus chicanery is expected, and all of industrialism's evils looked for. Southern American folklore has traditionally contrasted the unscrupulous Yankee "hare" with the slow but wise "tortoise" of the rural South. The country bumpkin in "Little Ole Wine-Drinking Me," thought he'd "find a home here in the city, but in Chicago a broken heart is still the same." In fact, studies have shown the immigrants' adjustments to city life to be slow and painful; the songs apparently both reflect and ease their situation.

When city life turns out to be empty of satisfactions, the country music hero wants to go home to the rural South. Ironically, although he has fled the unproductive country life with good reason, what he finds in the city is so much worse that nostalgia tricks his mind into false memories of home. In "The Grass is Greener" the man remembers that everything was better in the mountains: the grass, the sky, the air, the girls. Songs of homesickness are very common.

An interesting psychological effect becomes evident here. Although the man, when seen prior to his journey, is going to the city for better opportunities, which in turn (he hopes) will make his wife or sweetheart more accessible to him, in most of the songs in which homesickness is a factor, it is the mother, not the wife or sweetheart, who is remembered. The father rarely appears. This suggests a strong degree of parental authority and filial regard; no other kind of American music depicts so close a family relationship. The hillbilly's attachment appears to be an oedipal one: his mother is regarded as a symbol of all that is good in women, whereas his wife is not so highly valued. (This attitude has not changed in fifty years, at least two generations.) Mother is "Sweeter Than the Flowers." Occasionally, the parents are mentioned as a unit. In "Mom and Dad's Waltz," the son will "fight in wars" and "do all the chores" for his parents.

Given the nostalgia, so prevalent in the songs, that grows grass on eroded land and turns shacks into palaces, one might expect other memories of home to be as revealingly selective. Perhaps the father's absence indicates he is killed in memory. Is this why the country music hero so seldom succeeds as a husband? In truth, he does not appear to want to progress; his desire is to remain innocent. The ungrown boy-hero is America's most typical folk figure; certainly the dream of innocence (rural life) that society (city life) corrupts haunts American literature. Happiness is, time and time again, associated with a nostalgic sense of youth, the past, rural life, and close family ties. The breakdown of the country boy's marriage heralds the death of the old way of life, and is thus all the more tragic. It is a major paradox of American literature in general that although this nation is vaunted as the land of youth and opportunity, opportunity is nevertheless feared because it leads to progress, progress is synonymous with change, and change threatens those qualities of life previously held valuable.

On the infrequent occasions when children appear in the songs, they are depicted as victims, as in "My Daddy is Only a Picture," or as deprived: "Will Santa Come to Shanty Town?" They are used as lures to make wandering parents return. Children lose their illusions early in these songs and often die untimely deaths that become occasions for moralizing, because the parents are invariably beset with guilt after the child is dead. When a child is the narrator, he describes a pathetic situation of financial or emotional deprivation in which he is either forced early to work for a living, or is striving vainly to keep mother and father together. Compare this to the country music hero's adult recollections of home: never does the adult narrator remember a deprived childhood, except in a financial sense—the sentimental memories blot out the realistic ones. It is interesting to note that, although *wives* roam, and must, therefore, neglect their offspring, the *mother* in memory is invariably loving, faithful, hardworking, and self-denying.

So loyal is the hillbilly to his southern roots that he is suspicious of any change in intellectual status. In keeping with the American heroic myth, intellectuality is not seen as a virtue, and formal education, on the rare occasions when it is mentioned, is denigrated. Anti-intellectualism triumphs in a large number of southern rural jokes: Q: "What's a intellect-yew-all?" A: "A intellectual is someone who can read without movin' his lips." "Okie from Muskogee" is a good example of this intellectual conservatism that also makes a virtue of noninvolvement. Along with an anti-intellectual stance goes a naïve bumper-sticker patriotism: *America: Love It or Leave It.* Proud reference is made to "red neck, white socks, and Blue Ribbon beer." No country songs about the wars in Vietnam or Korea, for instance, failed to support unquestioningly the policies of our government there. The men who died were heroes and their cause is never disputed.

Except in the few cases of patriotic songs, most of which appeared between 1959 and 1963 and were about the Vietnam War, there are no social problems discussed in country music, only individual ones. Unlike so many contemporary folk and rock songs, this music contains virtually no elements of social rebellion. Racial problems, for instance, are not mentioned. Attention to civil rights in country music has not increased a bit since 1954; it wasn't mentioned before and hasn't been since. Negroes are apparently not seen at all; they are neither a danger nor a challenge, although the hillbilly's country has been the scene for much racial tension in the last quarter century.

The country hero's faith in God is infinite, sentimental, emotional, and fundamental. He is at God's mercy, and God is responsible for creating honky-tonk angels and taking people away by death. God sometimes appears to need more angels in Heaven—"The White Dove" says this. The hillbilly hero is naïvely convinced of a palpable heaven, with streets of pure gold, a Lord who keeps a record, bands of angels, eternal sweethearts, and other tangible accouterments. The hillbilly's metaphor, sometimes awkward but often poignant, gives us insight into his religious beliefs. Death is portrayed as an angel who gathers flowers (souls) for the Master's bouquet. The song, "Life's Railway to Heaven" is an extended simile; it describes life as a mountain railroad, with a brave engineer who will guide the train on a trestle over Jordan toward a meeting at the end with the railroad superintendent, God. In the song, the listener is exhorted to keep "your hand upon the throttle, and your eye upon the rail." "The Great Speckled Bird" employs a huge bird as a symbol for the Church of God, and the metaphorical vehicle upon which true believers will be carried up to Heaven. The reliance on a better world after this one reflects the typical Christian philosophy of reversal: the rich in this world become the poor in the next and vice versa—further reason not to lay up treasures upon earth.

Country boys occasionally break out of the mold and exert themselves to more liberated lives, which they brag about. Eddie Arnold, rejecting married life nearly thirty years ago, sang "I'm a Ladies' Man." (Recently, even a woman may brag, without, one presumes, seeming unfeminine, as in "You Ain't Woman Enough To Take My Man.") A variation on the bragging theme is found in songs in which a man celebrates his own meanness. "It Ain't Me, Babe," warns a girl that if she wants love, kindness, and tenderness, she had better look elsewhere.

These liberated country rogues come to full flower in the songs about truck drivers: their hero is a southern picaro who leaves broken hearts in every truck stop across the nation. He is a twentieth-century tall-tale hero; he brags that he has more women, can drink more coffee, and can drive his rig longer and better than anyone else. He's "King of the Road." In "Truck-drivin' Son of a Gun" the narrator has so many women across the country that in the case of one he "forgets her name, but not her figure." A man of this sort offers a subtle threat to a society based, at least in theory, on monogamy. So he is often portrayed as lonely. What he needs is a wife.

A need to moralize runs through many of the songs in all the categories, reminiscent of our Puritan ancestors who believed literature could be justified only if it were didactic. There are few work songs and even fewer prison songs, most of them generally adapted from folk music. There are some dance and fiddle songs with nonsense rhymes that echo tall tales, like the song about Uncle Pen, who "combed his hair with a wagon wheel." There are a few songs that describe that hungover, miserable aura known as the blues; several moralistic but not religious songs, like "Satisfied Mind" and "Detour"; and a few songs that make fun of some of the less savory aspects of country living, like feuds, primitive plumbing, and having to "Take an Old Cold Tater and Wait."

It seems fair to infer that country songs present a near-truthful portrayal of the type of southerner they describe, and not merely the fulfillment of vicarious dreams of adultery or literary conventions, although such stock metaphors as weeping and feeling blue indicate that literary conventions obviously do prevail. As an example, the pathetic fallacy is common in the songs; nature often reflects the hero's moods. The sorrows of early marriage, migration to the city, a strong and naïve faith in God, and adulation of the mother are the major themes of the lyrics.

Perhaps country music is more important to the South than anyone has yet seen, is not merely a frivolous tacky pastime for indigent southerners but rather a powerful impetus for good or evil, for stability or change. Country music may indeed be shaping minds and pointing directions. Certainly country singers who keep singing develop loyal lifetime followers no matter how old or bad they get. The fact that southern country music continues to speak for and to so many southerners—even though they are city-dwellers now—and that the coming of urbanization appears to have altered neither its forms nor its values very much, seems to indicate a social and cultural continuity that remains tenacious amid change. Whether we choose to praise country music or condemn it, we had better not ignore it.

GEORGE B. TINDALL

The Resurgence
of Southern
Identity

When the phenomenon of Jimmy Carter surfaced in the bicentennial year, it was suddenly time to rediscover the South all over again. The craze for things southern began to mushroom like skyscrapers in Atlanta or mellow accents in Washington. The two supreme cultural events of the television season that followed—the revival of *Gone with the Wind* and the dramatization of Alex Haley's *Roots*—further quickened interest. On a slow day in the world of media hype, all one had to do was to reach for the nearest bag of peanut jokes, pick up one of the half-baked books on how to talk "red-neck," and—presto!—one had a feature, a column, an editorial, a cartoon, a skit. Best of all, perhaps, was to do an interview with Jimmy Carter's beer-drinking brother Billy, who suddenly became the chief guru of the red-neck mystique. Once the perpetual outsiders in American culture, southerners suddenly found themselves very "in."

For a while, "Southern Fried Chic" was served up by the box or the bucketful. It came plain or barbecued, and sometimes downright crispy. But a lot of it was still awfully high in grease and cholesterol. The result was what Louis Rubin called a "hoked-up diet of cliché and truism being mass-produced to commemorate the accession of Carter to the White House."

The chefs who prepared this zestful menu, of course, had ingredients to spare. For few parts of the modern world have bred so great a variety of styles or so diverse a cast of character types as the American South. Southerners, Jonathan Daniels once said, are "a mythological people, created half out of dream and half out of slander, who live in a still legendary land." What he had reference to was the fact that the main burden of southern mythology still rests on those compelling categories ordained by the sectional conflict of the nineteenth century: the romantic plantation myth of gentility on the one hand and the obverse, if in many ways similar, abolitionist plantation myth of barbarity on the other. The Sunny South versus the Benighted South, as it were. Or to cite the cultural events of an earlier day that served to fix them in the public mind: *The Birth of a Nation* versus *Uncle Tom's Cabin*, or, more recently, *Gone with the Wind* versus *Roots*.

Old habits of thought die hard, and old stereotypes abound. Conventional wisdom (Yankee style) is still touched by a lingering view of the South as Uncle Sam's Other Province, a strange land and a peculiar people. The image of the Benighted South is too deeply etched in the American mind. It haunted our last southern president, long before he fell prey to worse problems. "I did not believe . . . that the nation would unite indefinitely behind any Southerner," Lyndon Johnson wrote in his memoirs. "My experience in office had confirmed this reaction. I was not thinking just of the derisive articles about my style, my clothes, my manner, my accent, and my family. . . . I was also thinking of a more deep-seated and far-reaching attitude—a disdain for the South that seems to be woven into the fabric of Northern experience. . . . To my mind, these attitudes represent an automatic reflex, unconscious or deliberate, on the part of opinion holders of the North and East in the press and television."

It's odd how these habits persist. Shortly before the inauguration of President Carter, cartoonist Oliphant supplied an updated version of the Johnson ordeal when he rendered the White House as Tobacco Road, littered with a deposit of stereotypes: a broken-down car, a pickup truck, old tires scattered about, a mangy hound dog, an outdoor privy with the inevitable crescent in the door. The point, of course, was that southerners tend to be tacky—just a bit dowdy and unfashionable.

About the same time Betty Beale, who writes a newspaper column on Washington society, found her sensibilities offended by the new dispensation. "The pictures of Jimmy Carter carrying his own luggage are beginning to gall Americans," she wrote. "When the subject came up at an embassy party recently there wasn't anyone who thought it looked right." All of which seems to put Mr. Carter in the rather distinguished company of some other southern-born presidents. One is put in mind of a Virginian named Thomas Jefferson, who mortified the British minister by wearing a dressing gown and carpet slippers to receive him. Or one remembers a rail-splitter from Kentucky by way of Illinois, Abraham Lincoln, whom the cognoscenti of the capital found more than a little unrefined.

Northern reporters who encountered Jimmy Carter's religious conviction experienced a sudden education in the obvious. In the final decades of the second millenium, they noted with astonishment, there still existed a faith called Christianity! And a sect called Baptists who believed one could be born again! Call the same experience an identity crisis and the same reporters would likely salivate by automatic reflex. But the astonishment at southern Protestantism bears out in a convincing way historian Samuel S. Hill's observation that the southern church is unique in its single-minded focus on salvation, its sense of assurance, and its rejection or simple unawareness of other versions of Christian experience. The unawareness seems to run both ways.

A lot of nonsoutherners, nevertheless, show a willingness to learn. In fact they have been learning for some time, often unwittingly. For more than a century the South has been a seedbed of population and cultural styles for the rest of the country. Southern styles have threatened to conquer the fields of literature and pop culture. The journalist Robert Sherrill has remarked that southern writers like William Faulkner and Thomas Wolfe "got inside the non-Southern head and near about unplugged all the synapses." Yankees—and in fact people around the world—all along have been taking up cavalier romances, bourbon whiskey, Coca-Cola, *Gone with the Wind*, spirituals, and southern cuisine in the guise of "soul food," among other things. More recently they have been picking up country music, stock car racing, CB slang, and *Roots*. So Jimmy Carter is not the first southerner who saw what was coming before the rest of the country caught on.

The intensity of the new rage for things southern evinces more than just a taste for the exotic. Lurking near the surface there seems to be a haunting suspicion that the South harbors some ancient virtues down home. One of the reasons people have seized on things southern and chosen a southern president, says poet and novelist James Dickey, is "because they feel that the South has preserved . . . individuality of region as well as person and has not been homogenized to quite the extent of the rest of the nation. People want those differences."

It is not that the South has escaped change. It has in the past been engulfed in the crosscurrents of change, the most conspicuous being those of the mid-nineteenth-century Civil War and Reconstruction. Since 1945 the region has experienced what historian Charles P. Roland calls an "improbable era" of new things, the consequence of the civil rights movements, the breakup of the one-party system, and the emergence to economic maturity. In the 1970s it has become fashionable to speak of a burgeoning "Sunbelt" along the southern rim of the United States. Although the vision of a region rolling in riches remains false to the facts so long as individual income remains below the national average, there is no question that the gap has been significantly narrowed.

But contrary to the supposition that social and economic change would quickly obliterate the ethnic and regional differences in American life, southern cultural differences have stubbornly reasserted themselves. Jimmy Carter's experience has been like that of many southerners in the present generation who have been taken out of the traditional culture either by travel or education and have returned to see it in a new perspective. Carter went off to Georgia Tech, then to Annapolis, and traveled widely around the world in the navy, but at the same time he was rooted in the older culture of the South. One of the reasons he was elected president is the sense that in a society that feels the need for roots, Carter has retained a sense of roots. In that respect he is a characteristic southerner of the present day. It may be that, having had to cope with such sweeping change in recent years, southerners are in a good position to deal with it in a broader theater of action.

Once we get a little more perspective on the phenomenon of

North-South myths and cultural cross-pollination, we may see in the 1970s a significant crossing of the ways. Clearly a breakthrough has occurred when the nation is ready to accept for the first time since 1849 a president from the Deep South, and for the first time ever, one who was born and bred in that particular brier patch. As editor Brandt Ayers wrote in the Anniston, Alabama, *Star*: "It is time to say that our nation has finally come into full historical maturity with the recognition that neither original sin nor God's truth is the exclusive property of any American tribe."

As for southerners, it is time to say that they sense a coming release from the curse of what British historian Denis Brogan called the *damnosa hereditas* of the South, and suspect that they have begun to lay down what C. Vann Woodward has called the burden of southern history: the poverty, the habits of defeat and failure, the guilt of racial oppression that bound white and black in a common tragedy. This is not to say that any people can escape history. We may at least hope that from its chastening experience the South has distilled a wisdom born of suffering.

And maybe the South has something else to offer. "I think that the South is pointing the way to some new kind of future for this country," James Dickey says, "and I think . . . that it will be a good thing for the South to lead, at least for a while, and maybe for good; to set the trends and furnish the leading politicians and the leading writers and the leading artists. We've got plenty of them down here. This is the most fertile literary region that has ever existed in this country."

The hopefulness displayed by Dickey is a trait more endemic to the South than is usually recognized, according to historian F. Nash Boney. In an article entitled "The South's Peculiar Intuition," published in *Louisiana Studies*, Boney suggests that, in the long catalogs of southern traits, the quality of optimism, usually omitted, belongs at the top of the list. "This vibrant optimism, absent from so many cultures in history, was always present in America and was especially obvious in the South." It was present in the beginning, from the time of Elizabethan swashbucklers like Sir Walter Raleigh. "The first transplanted Englishmen who dared and died along the banks of the James River," Boney writes, "were possessed of a peculiar intuition that everything would work out well despite almost hopeless odds. . . . Virginia was founded not on a cloud of tobacco smoke but on a vague but vigorous confidence in the future." Time and again this spirit of optimism manifested itself: when Jefferson "shook the world with his call not only for life and liberty but also, incredibly, for the pursuit of happiness"; in the drive to the West; in the burst of nationalism that followed the War of 1812, with the young John C. Calhoun at the forefront. "Young Calhoun," Boney says, "was pure Southerner; he saw no real limits to his own and his nation's destiny." But with his ambitions frustrated and his region's future clouded, Calhoun became, by American standards, a thoroughgoing pessimist.

In fact the whole white South followed Calhoun's negative example after the burst of emotional optimism at the birth of the Confederacy ended in the holocaust of the Civil War. At the same time those other true southerners, the black freedmen, responded to emancipation with a burst of passionate, even desperate optimism. But as the victors wearied of the Reconstruction crusade, they too were soon gone with the wind, leaving southerners both white and black united only by the experience of high hopes utterly frustrated.

But out of the ashes there arose, like a phoenix, the old spirit of optimism, this time under the banner of the "New South." It is not necessary to spin out all the examples that Boney presents. But he does invoke something deeply embedded in the culture when he describes "the stubborn optimism of the normally inarticulate Southern masses." For some vibrant examples one might turn to the early novels of Erskine Caldwell with their poor white characters who pursued even the most hopeless projects with fanatical purpose and dauntless optimism.

At the conclusion Boney presents a perhaps prophetic vision:

> Yet just beneath the gloomy surface of contemporary America, the old optimism still lives in the Southern heartland. Almost unnoticed in the fashionable fatalism of contemporary culture, the Southern masses are on the move again. At a time when the nation stumbles uncertainly and wavers before new challenges, the South is stirring again

with a sense of purpose and motion, generating the kind of confidence the whole nation must regain if it is to remain great. Once again history can be frozen for a split second as Southerners mass for another assault up Cemetery Ridge. They are already swarming forward with the old élan, this time as an unarmed mob of every race, sex, and previous condition of servitude. This time the enemy, nebulous but real, is a jumble of obsolete customs and traditions from a past era. The struggle rages quietly in the schools and factories and homes and churches and indeed every nook and cranny of Southern life, and the outcome will remain uncertain for many years to come. But at the present time of national despondency and inertia, the important thing is that an energetic, optimistic effort is being made. Haunted by a peculiar intuition which has driven them through a long and sometimes frustrating history, Southerners are once again the confident shock troops for the nation they have so powerfully and permanently influenced from the very beginning.

A column by journalist Richard Reeves echoed Professor Boney's observation: "The nation needs the zeal of the new Southerners— even though some of it, I am sure, will be misguided. There is more to energy than oil, and the United States has to look to new sources—Italians, blacks, women, all the spiritual outsiders. . . . The most striking contrast between the early Carter campaign and Washington, or Harvard for that matter, was the sheer energy of the Southerners—the ambitions, the resentments, the aliveness."

Meanwhile, back home the South has surmounted a host of troubles, but one of the everlasting ironies of history is that in solving problems people encounter new problems. Rupert Vance, the eminent sociologist, in one of his last essays, "Beyond the Fleshpots: The Coming Culture Crisis in the South," pronounced the Mason-Dixon line "no longer . . . an iron curtain against the Affluent Society" but expressed worry about the subtler aspects of the South's quality of life. He summoned his native region to "turn from preoccupation with its peculiar navel—the Southern way of life—to the pursuit of high culture."

In the title of Vance's article are summarized the South's present problems and its potential: "Beyond the Fleshpots." With the genius to seize the day, this generation in the South can exploit a chance that comes to few generations. Racial and regional reconciliation are not out of reach, the land remains relatively unspoiled, the political system is more open and unrestricted than ever before. It may be something of a cliché, but it is also a self-evident truth, that a region so late in developing has a chance to learn from the mistakes of others. What Lewis Mumford said on a visit to North Carolina twenty-five years ago remains almost as true today as it was then: "Most of the measures that must be taken in the South may be of a positive rather than a remedial nature; they are matters of preserving a balance that still exists, rather than of re-establishing a balance that has been almost utterly destroyed."

Clearly the drive to develop is here, along with the energy, the ambition, the aliveness, as Richard Reeves put it—and the quality of optimism that Nash Boney reminds us is perennially born again. The supreme problem, and the supreme opportunity, now facing the region is how to reconcile economic development with the quality of life, whether we can avoid the kind of progress that will turn one of nature's masterpieces, the South, into a modern wasteland. We are already too far along the way.

In his celebration of the southerners' hopefulness, Professor Boney added a cautionary note: a reminder of how easily a vibrant optimism can turn sour. Writing of Calhoun, he said: "This dramatic shift from one extreme to another is always a possibility when a single characteristic, especially one as volatile as optimism, is too exaggerated, and more than one talented Southern leader has suddenly abandoned the traditional high road which leads onward and upward somewhere or other and detoured down the twisting trail to despair and usually oblivion." This referred to Calhoun, but other examples flood the mind. Secessionists, reconstructionists, populists, Wilsonians, Lyndon Johnson, the civil rights leaders, all tended to turn sour when they failed to produce the instant millenium—with some noteworthy exceptions, to be sure.

So if southerners have a chance now to learn from the mistakes of others, they have a chance also to learn from their own. As the South begins to cast off the burden of southern history, it will do well to contemplate the memory and—in its headlong rush to the future—not to forget that a heedless optimism can nurture the seeds of tragedy.

III

LITERARY
IMAGES

The Crisis in Culture
as Reflected in
Southern Literature

In an essay entitled "Romanticism Re-examined," René Wellek has described the common endeavor of the great romantic poets of England, Germany, and France as an attempt "to overcome the split between subject and object, the self and the world, the conscious and the unconscious." Such has also been the endeavor of later generations of literary artists, including some of the most distinguished writers of our present century. The crisis in culture to which the title of my essay refers is precisely the split described,

Some of the twentieth-century writers would not, to be sure, be thought of as romantics. They are usually called symbolists or modernists, and at least one of them has called himself a classicist. But the cultural situation with which they have been concerned is essentially that encountered by the great romantics of the nineteenth century.

William Wordsworth had seen the problem as primarily having arisen from man's alienation from nature. He became gravely concerned over the distance that had opened up between the poet's way of perceiving reality and the way in which the scientist or the man of affairs perceived it. The heart found itself more and more in conflict with the head. In one of his sonnets Wordsworth mourns that "Little we see in Nature that is ours" and insists that men have given their hearts away. His brother poet, Samuel Taylor Coleridge, urged that it was necessary to keep the heart alive in the head. Let me hasten to say that the rift between heart and head was becoming visible long before the date of Wordsworth's birth. But it is not my purpose here to go back as far as René Descartes, who, someone has said, had cut the throat of poetry by limiting the poet's exercise to a purely subjective realm, whereas the scientist took over the great outside world of objective fact.

Nor am I here particularly concerned with what happened after the time of Wordsworth and Coleridge—with such figures as Charles Darwin, T. H. Huxley, John Ruskin, John Henry Newman, and Matthew Arnold. In this essay I shall be concerned with some of the more special forms that the problem has taken in the twentieth century and with how the twentieth-century writers of the southern states have addressed themselves to it.

Yet, before turning to the southern writers we might consider briefly how some of the writers of the first third of our century have responded to the situation. William Butler Yeats reacted sharply against what he saw as an increasingly secularized and industrialized world. Ireland had remained agrarian and traditional well into the twentieth century, and, in spite of an official Roman Catholicism, somehow pre-Christian—at least Yeats wished to think that the legends of ancient Ireland had not been utterly forgotten. He brought the ancient gods of Ireland into his poetry; he retold Irish fairy tales; and he involved himself in astrology, Hermetic lore, and spiritualism. The impact of applied science and its effect on human beings worried Yeats quite as much as the influence of theoretical science. He carried on a lifelong quarrel with the bourgeoisie; the country gentleman, the peasant, the saint, and the artist possessed, in their rather different ways, the virtues that he admired.

D. H. Lawrence's reaction was nearly as extravagant as Yeats's, though it attached itself to a different sort of primitivism and developed a different mythology, one dominated by the dark gods of the blood.

T. S. Eliot very early faced up to the contemporary world and addressed himself to writing poems based on life in the modern city. But the cultural crisis underlies nearly every one of his earlier poems, and his way of coping with the problem fairly soon became a restatement of the orthodox Christian "solution."

The influence of Eliot on the writers of the twentieth-century South has been profound, but even writers on whom he early made a sharp impact devised their own responses to the cultural situation in which they found themselves. After all, they had deep commitments to a cultural province that had its own special history, customs, and even, to a limited degree, language.

John Crowe Ransom of Tennessee early became concerned with the fissure that had opened between man's inner and outer life. Just how early, one does not know, but a poem written by 1926 has as its theme the plight of such a fragmented man. Ransom, however, states the problem not as one of fragmentation but of loss of orientation; for he has titled his poem "Man Without Sense of Direction."

This creature of modernity is, as Man should be, a microcosm, a little world, but in this particular world "There is no moon . . . that draws / His flood of being." He does not lack abilities and potentialities; what he lacks are purposes to be achieved. Without "direction" he is simply a mechanism, and Ransom describes him so:

> He flails his arms, he moves his lips:
> "Rage have I none, cause, time, nor country"
> . . . .
> So he stands muttering; and rushes
> Back to the tender thing in his charge
> With clamoring tongue and taste of ashes
> And a small passion to feign large.

He cannot give himself totally to a loved one any more than he can give himself to a cause. One further line in the poem summarizes his total situation: he is a creature "Who cannot fathom nor perform his nature." In an earlier day, man did have some sense of what he was and so could fulfill himself. But this typical man of our age cannot do so.

A poem written in the same general period, "Persistent Explorer," suggests why he cannot. The world that he inhabits has become strange and unknown. Nature, in short, has been neutralized, and the sensitive observer feels somehow betrayed by that fact. Thus, when Ransom's explorer comes upon a mighty waterfall, the sight leaves him unsatisfied. He notes that "Water is falling—it fell—

therefore it roared. / But he cried, That is more than water I hear."
In an earlier age the great cataract might have seen the proper setting for a theophany, its "cloud of froth" a fit vesture for a goddess
revealing herself to some mountain shepherd. But to the explorer
in question, no goddess appears and he must remind himself that
such beings as "fierce faun" and "timid" water nymphs do not exist—must remind himself that the descending substance is only
"water—the insipid chemical H_2O."

Neither the poet nor his explorer reproaches the scientist for his
nonanimistic account of the situation. Ransom has moved far, far
beyond Wordsworth's taunting reference to the "fingering slave"
who would "peep and botanize/Upon his mother's grave." It is folly
to dismiss as false the scientific description of nature. Nevertheless, the explorer refuses to accept as a valid account of reality the
neutralized nature that the modern scientist has described and
analyzed. This "persistent explorer" means to go beyond such a
world in the hope of finding one that will satisfy the human spirit.
But no one, least of all the poet, can promise that even the most
persistent exploration will reveal another more meaningful world.

So much for the cause of the modern disease—Arnold's "sick
hurry and divided aims"—and its typical effects on the human being, whose life in a reduced and de-animated world loses purpose
and direction. Ransom's most brilliant account of the division
within modern man is to be found in his sonnet sequence "Two
Gentlemen in Bonds." The gentlemen in question are twin brothers between whom man's full being is divided. Their dead father,
speaking from the grave in the final sonnet, puts matters in this
wise: "My manhood halved and squandered, two heads, two hearts,/
Each partial son despising the other's parts."

The paired opposites, clearly, cannot be neatly tagged as "heart"
and "head." They are more properly seen as the "intellectual"
man, who tries to live by abstractions, and the sensual man, who
revels in his appetites. Paul is the sensual, pragmatic man-in-the-
street; Abbot is the intellectual and idealist—though these definitions are not wholly satisfactory, either. Abbot, for instance,
has something of the sour ascetic in his nature. He scorns the flesh:

Vainglorious he may have been, stiff-necked;
His stars conspired together to deject
Him from conspicuous glories; he lived on air
And would not taste earth's sweetness; great and spare
And pale, his ghost still haunted the slight girl
Who, husbanded now with her fair lord the churl. . . .

Ransom tries to be impartial in describing these opposed half-men: Paul is frankly the churl, though successful in love and fortune, and Abbot's pride—"he clung to his cold and poverty and night / And leaned in the rain"—is essentially a self-destructive folly. The last phrase is not too strong.

Ransom is an artist, and the artist always allies himself with the whole man—man as a total and harmonious being. Art rests upon the life of the senses. This point comes clear in Ransom's fine late poem "Painted Head." "Beauty is of body," the poet insists. The "head" needs all of the help that the body can give it.

One might observe that neither Paul nor Abbot represents the poet. Neither of these half men is capable of writing a poem: Paul is too deeply immersed in the flesh to be able to rise above it; Abbot despises the flesh too much to give it its due regard. For Ransom, as for Wordsworth, one suspects, the poet must succeed in holding in fruitful tension both body and mind.

Duality is thus at the core of Ransom's aesthetics. In 1927 he wrote to his fellow southern poet Allen Tate: "Give us Dualism, or we'll give you no Art." In the same letter he told Tate that it was necessary for the artist to accomplish three things: to "find the Experience that is in the Common Actuals," to have "this experience" carry as its precious freight "the dearest possible values to which we have attached ourselves," and finally "to face the disintegration or nullification of these values as calmly and religiously as possible." His program is as ambitious as it is austere.

I assume that the disintegration of which Ransom writes here is the inevitable erosion of "our dearest possible values" as we become distracted or forgetful or tired and old, and that he is making no special reference to the breakdown of values in our contemporary civilization. But in either case, Ransom's recommendation would surely be the same. His *God Without Thunder* spells out these issues in detail with special reference to those who have been brought up in the Christian values. But small wonder that few Christians could accept his transformation of Christianity into the kind of nature religion that *God Without Thunder* essentially sought to effect.

Though Ransom joined his friends in an Agrarian Manifesto, *I'll Take My Stand* (1930), and seemed for a time to take seriously the formation of a practical program for an agrarian economy, in his later years he wrote that he had come to feel that Agrarianism was a diet too rich for his blood. Yet his attitude toward man's plight remained basically unchanged: to face the disintegration of these (and even dearer) values "as calmly and religiously as possible."

Such quiet detachment reminds one of the philosopher George Santayana's attitude toward Christian and traditional values generally, though of course there was nothing of Santayana's Mediterranean Catholicism in Ransom's personal background. In this general connection, I remember Ransom's once saying to me that the younger men, confident of building a new and better civilization, would, of course, fail to achieve their aims. Nevertheless, one had to allow them to make their attempt. The tone of the remark was not bitter or cynical; it was spoken with what I can only call a rather kindly detachment.

The reader will find a somewhat early stage of Ransom's personal religion spelled out in his *God Without Thunder*. Again, it reminds one of Santayana's position with reference to religion. The poet Robert Lowell referred to Santayana as that "free-thinking Catholic infidel." He would never have applied these terms to his old mentor John Crowe Ransom. He would have felt, if not seen, important differences, but I am confident that there are resemblances, too.

To face the loss of our traditional values "as calmly and religiously as possible" did not and does not appeal to Allen Tate. Yet the difference between Tate and Ransom was only in part a matter of temperament and personality. Basically, it amounted to their differing interpretations of religion. Ransom's was an attitude of acceptance of the natural world, and was, in the deepest and least frivolous sense of the word, "aesthetic." He had shorn away from Christianity its supernatural elements and preferred to stress the nurture, through liturgy and meditation, of the life of the spirit. His set of values deserves to be called a "religion," if we take seriously the etymology—a "binding back" of the individual to nature and to past history. But it was a religion that was nondogmatic, without any of the accouterments of ecclesiastical organization or acceptance of supernatural beliefs.

I have said that Ransom's position would not have appealed to Allen Tate, who had very early—and long before he came to accept orthodox doctrinal Christianity as embodied in Roman Catholicism—rejected as wholly inadequate the naturalistic account of man. But his essential diagnosis of the distemper of modern man may have close affinities with Ransom's own. Both men agreed that man required more than a purely scientific account of reality. Otherwise, values and facts become detached from each other, the realms of ends and means are without relation, and as a consequence man is not a whole being but becomes a fragmented creature.

Tate's essays record the developing stages of his philosophical and religious position even more thoroughly and in more detail than do Ransom's, but to sense the special timbre of alarm and concern in Tate's observations, one has to turn to his poetry. Perhaps the classic example is his celebrated "Last Days of Alice." Like the little heroine of *Alice in Wonderland* and *Alice Through the Looking Glass*, modern man finds himself in a strange and perplexing world in which objects that had for generations past been regarded as stable and solid have become "empty as the bodiless flesh of fire." Man himself, a creature of flesh and blood, turns out to be no more than a "mathematical shroud," being "all infinite, function depth and mass / Without figure," something that can be accurately described only in mathematical terms. Modern man is "blessèd without sin," not because his sins have been forgiven, but because the concept of sin has been explained away.

The desperate man who speaks the poem is in no way comforted by such a state of blessedness. Indeed, at the end he calls upon the

"God of our flesh" to return man to His wrath. To be damned is somehow better than being immersed in antiseptic nihilism, and in his desperation the speaker even begs to be evil. But in the context of the total poem, his meaning becomes plain: better to fail morally in a world of good and evil than to inhabit a realm where the terms *good* and *evil* are meaningless. Baudelaire would have had no trouble in making out what the speaker is praying for. (My reference to Baudelaire is probably apposite: as a very young man Tate was attempting translations of some of Baudelaire's poems.)

In his novel, *The Fathers*, Tate refers the malaise that he has earlier treated only in general terms to a historical context, that of the Old South on the verge of the War Between the States. The character in this novel who represents modern man is a disoriented southerner. He is the attractive young George Posey, who marries into an extremely conservative Virginia family. Posey turns out to be Ransom's "man without sense of direction." He fits such a description in almost precise detail; for he has neither "cause, time, nor country." "Rage," too, he lacks: for he is thoroughly detached, an almost entirely cold-blooded character. True, under stress, he is capable of shooting his brother-in-law; but he acts on sudden impulse, almost automatically, for Posey is a spasmodic man. Lacking any coherent code of conduct and ill at ease in any ritual designed to confirm such a code, he is at the mercy of whim and impulse. The manners and morals that are instinctive to the life of his father-in-law, Major Buchan, turn into absurdities under Posey's skeptical gaze. Indeed, an unwary reader, himself a man of the twentieth century, may come to think of Posey as the one "rational" character in the novel. But Posey's skepticism is simply an instrument for debunking any claims that the older tradition may make upon him. It has no positive force. Posey clearly does not lead Santayana's recommended life of reason.

By choosing as the setting for *The Fathers* the area around Washington, D.C., at the time of the outbreak of the War Between the States, Tate has adopted the perfect historical setting for his purpose. In these critical years men living on the uppermost borders of the Confederacy are driven back upon their most deeply held political beliefs and their ultimate loyalties. Posey, a citizen of

Georgetown, Maryland, married to a Virginia girl, finds it impossible to decide what his true country is. He has difficulty in associating himself with either cause. Actually, he ends up by working for both sides, buying war supplies from the Union forces in order to get them through the lines into the Confederacy. He tells himself that he is actually aiding his Virginia friends and relatives, but the result of his endeavors is that he makes a great deal of money for himself. It is appropriate that this should be so, for money is the one commodity that knows no country.

Tate has been very shrewd in his accounting for Posey's disabilities. Posey had grown up in a family that had lost any sense of community. His cantankerous father had died early. His uncle was an eccentric freak, his mode of living much like that of Edgar Allan Poe's Roderick Usher. He isolates himself in the upper room of the ancestral house, completely absorbed in the fancies and aberrations of his own mind. George Posey's mother and his aunt were "peculiar ladies," as self-absorbed and self-indulgent as was their brother. Any sense of genuine family relationships has completely disappeared—perhaps it had never made an appearance throughout George's childhood.

George's wife, Susan Buchan, on the other hand, had grown up in a family that was, if anything, too cohesive, too tightly bound to one another. The transplantation of Susan from the family world of Pleasant Hill in Virginia to the Posey establishment in Georgetown eventually brings her to madness: she succumbs to what for her has become a radically disordered world.

Tate, however, does not set forth the virtues of the good and honorable "southern" Buchans against the wrong-headed, neurotic, and "Yankeefied" Poseys. In the first place, the Poseys are by birth and breeding southerners, too. Of course, merely being southern guarantees nothing. If the Buchans do typify some of the virtues and pieties that we associate with the Old South, they also suggest the dangerous rigidities of a traditional society. The head of the family, Major Buchan, is almost absurdly set in his ways and utterly unable to imagine a world different from the one he knows. He has his own form of hubris. He reposes so much confidence in his inherited code of family virtue and honor and is so sure that he himself embodies them that he is blind to the issues that are pulling the country apart. He self-righteously repudiates his own son for enlisting in the Confederate army. It takes the wreck of his family and the destruction of Pleasant Hill by Union soldiers to bring him to a realization of his folly. The realization is too much: he hangs himself.

Major Buchan is not, then, the perfect foil for his son-in-law, answering each of George Posey's defects with an antithetical virtue. Good drama does not allow such neat polarities; nor does human history. As depicted in *The Fathers*, the Buchans are too much immersed in their own immediate and parochial customs and habits to "see" what they are. for one has to be aware of other modes of living to become fully conscious of one's own. But, of course, to learn that one's own values are not necessarily the only or even the best values may begin the process of finally disowning them.

Ransom had very pertinently said: "Give us Dualism or we'll give you no Art," and Tate would surely agree. The art appreciated by the Buchans, one judges, must have been a very unsophisticated kind of art, and so, historically, was that which appealed to the men and women of the Old South. Why this was so and why a great southern literature had to wait until the third decade of the twentieth century for its creation would, years later, become the subject matter of Tate's great definitive essay, "A Southern Mode of the Imagination." For southerners had to see the old virtues threatened with loss before they could come—in literature, at least—to realize fully what those virtues were. How can one know the dancer from the dance? It may be even more difficult for the dancer herself, caught up as she is in the dance, to "see" herself dancing.

Before leaving the subject of *The Fathers*, we ought to consider one other aspect of the author's judgment on the "modernity" of George Posey. Tate finds—a thoroughly "southern" thing to do—an analogy for Posey in the past, and specifically in ancient Greek legend. As the youngest of the Buchans, Lacy, the narrator of the novel, walks back to Pleasant Hill, grievously ill, pretty much out of his head, his dead grandfather appears to him and, in an attempt to help Lacy understand George Posey, tells Lacy the story of Jason, who with the other Argonauts sought the Golden Fleece.

The ghost of Lacy's grandfather begins by describing George as the typical alienated man of our own times. The grandfather, of course, does not use this newfangled term. What he actually says is: "My son, in my day we were never alone as your brother-in-law is alone." To translate into our present-day terms, George Posey lacked the sense of community, of beliefs and values unquestioningly shared, that in an earlier day bound men together.

Like Jason, George had tried to master "certain rituals" that the King of Colchis (Major Buchan) had insisted Jason, now that he had come to Colchis, should learn. But Jason found it impossible to learn them. He fell in love with the king's daughter, Medea, "a high-spirited girl of a more primitive society than that from which the arrogant Jason came." (Tate, one notes, is willing to allow that the Buchans were more primitive than the Poseys. Elsewhere in the novel the Buchans are stated to be more civilized than the Poseys, though less refined. In the contexts in which the words are used here, *primitive* and *civilized* are compatible, for an arrogant sophistication is antithetical to both states of society.)

The grandfather goes on to say that it was Jason's misfortune to "care only for the Golden Fleece . . . while at the same time getting himself involved with the humanity of others, which it was not his intention but rather of his very nature to betray. . . . He was a noble fellow in whom the patriarchal and familial loyalties had become meaningless." What counts here is not the soundness of the grandfather's interpretation of the Greek legend about Jason, but that a spokesman for the old southern society would be likely to impose such an interpretation on the situation in question—that, and the significant fact that it was the habit of such southerners to discover in the myths and histories of the past analogies for their own manners and morals.

I have dwelt at this length on *The Fathers* because it is not only a fine and still undervalued novel, but because it dramatizes very forcefully theories about the culture of the South that appear in Tate's several essays on that culture. Even if those theories are not always shared by other southern writers, the interpretation of southern culture that is embodied in *The Fathers* will provide a useful model against which to measure divergent interpretations. The argument that I shall develop is that in the main there is agreement.

A dominant theme in Robert Penn Warren's fiction is the partial man's attempt to regain his wholeness. Characteristically, Warren's heroes suffer in their alienation and struggle toward the knowledge that will bring their powers back into harmony with each other and with the world in which they live.

In what is probably Warren's most widely read novel, *All the King's Men*, Willie Stark, the idealist turned into a power-hungry demagogue, and Adam Stanton, the idealistic young scientist and physician, are frankly described as men who were destined to destroy each other because "each was doomed to use the other and to yearn toward and try to become the other, because each was incomplete with the terrible division of their age."

It may be significant that the characters in Warren's fiction who are least afflicted by self-division are people like the old buffalo hunter in *Nightrider* or, in *Heaven's Gate*, Ashby Windham, the hillbilly who experienced conversion and found a Christian vocation. Both are men who come out of a more primitive culture. Modern civilization makes fragmentation almost inevitable, but Warren, of course, never countenances the attempt to relapse into an innocent arcadianism. His heroes must strive for a "new innocence," a mature reintegration of the self.

Warren has somewhere described the process by which this reintegration is achieved as "experience redeemed into knowledge." His poetry as well as his fiction makes it plain what kind of knowledge is involved: not an aggregation of facts or the refinements of scholarship, but a knowledge of reality that involves self-discipline. The old term for it, of course, is wisdom. The quest of all Warren's protagonists is the acquisition of wisdom.

Though his fiction and his poetry reflect the same basic interests and concerns, it is in his poetry that Warren's concern with what I have called the cultural crisis is revealed most nakedly. A rather late poem entitled "Stargazing" presents in almost ultimate purity the split that rends apart man's experience and alienates him from nature. The speaker begins by declaring that "The stars are only a backdrop for / The human condition." But as the poem develops, we learn that he once saw them otherwise. For in answer to his companion's remark that he does not look at the stars, he concedes the point and states why he no longer looks at them. He knows

> That if I look at the stars, I
>
> Will have to live over all I have lived
> In the years I looked at stars and
> Cried out, "O reality!"

Now he knows better, for if reality encompasses the human condition, then the stars have no part in that reality. Nature and man's inner life seem to be separate realms of being. Though he has to think of nature as a nurturing force ("The stars / Love me"), and though nature is lovely to contemplate ("I love [the stars]"), the stars do not love God. Nonsense? Or if the statement does make sense, then what is that sense?

It is this: the world of purpose, meaning, piety, and aspiration lies outside the self-subsistent, self-authenticating system by which a star or a starfish lives and moves and has its being. In this context the Christian God is anthropomorphic indeed; not merely an idea shaped by man, but an image of man himself. The God of Genesis who created the universe has shrunk to an idea within the human skull. But if the reader concludes that the speaker is content with this situation, I think he has underestimated the poignance of the last lines of the poem: "I wish [the stars] / Loved God, too. I truly wish that." A poem of this sort is moving, but as an intellectual structure it is deeply searching, too. The dramatic situation on which it focuses is the fact of the Cartesian division.

A whole group of Warren's latest poems show his fascination with religion. "A Way to Love God," "Answer to Prayer," "Trying to Tell You Something," "Old Nigger on One-Mule Cart Encountered . . . in the Back Country"—these are only a few of Warren's poems of the 1970s that exhibit a search for absolute truth that is ultimately religious in its nature. It would be rash, however, to claim that these poems are Christian, even though in some important respects they may be compatible with Christianity. In any case, their relation to Christian orthodoxy is not the issue here. My point is simply that Warren takes seriously the tragicomic situation of man, that creature whose consciousness allows him to respond to the majestic or poignant or terrifying beauty of the universe about him, but yet who is barred from the blind and insensate life of this universe by his very ability to respond. The general theme, of course, is not new. It is essentially that of Keats's "Ode to a Nightingale." But Warren has used the context of contemporary civilization to bring the same theme home to us.

Can it be said that William Faulkner also is concerned with this split within man, this contest between heart and head? Yes, emphatically so; but in much of Faulkner's work the theme is so deeply embedded in the drama of the novel or story that a superficial reading may miss it altogether. Is it, for example, to be found in a novel such as *Sanctuary*? I would unhesitatingly answer yes. But since this essay has limited space for illustrations from Faulkner, I shall refer only to some of the clearest instances in his work.

Perhaps the most obvious is "The Bear," which relates the story of the young Isaac McCaslin's initiation into the wilderness. Through his tutor, the old hunter Sam Fathers, Isaac comes to know the power and the beauty of nature and yearns toward its unwearied immortality, for throughout its myriad seasonal changes it remains itself. Isaac learns to respect the very creatures that as a hunter he kills, for Sam Fathers has taught him that he must not kill wantonly and that nature itself is to be loved and revered, not only as the necessary resource for man's very life, but as a model of the harmony and unself-conscious delight that man should seek in his own life.

Isaac is profoundly moved by his vision of nature as, for example, when he visits the graves of the great hunting dog Lion and Sam Fathers. Though all creatures must suffer death, in a larger sense there is no death. Nature takes her creatures back into herself and she herself cannot die. Yet Isaac McCaslin knows better than to try to make his own life the instinctive life of a natural creature. He cannot be an arcadian. He is not the unfallen Adam, innocent of fire. He is a fallen man who must assume the burden of consciousness, who is condemned to experience guilt, self-doubt, and responsibility.

"Natural" man, however, fascinated Faulkner from the very beginning of his literary career. There are to be found among his characters a number of faunlike men. Donald Mahon acts on impulse and lives a fresh, instinctive life; Benjy Compson and Ike Snopes, two of Faulkner's famous idiots, are so deeply merged in nature that they are just barely human. Faulkner uses these innocents as foils to point up the vicious inhumanity of the Jason Compsons and the Flem Snopeses of our human world, or else to point up the heavy burden necessarily assumed by men who aspire to be fully human. His fauns cannot serve as the heroes of his novels; that role can belong only to the person who possesses a heart in conflict with itself, the contest that Faulkner declared to be the only one worth writing about. Thus, in spite of the great celebrations of nature that we find in his novels and stories, it is history that is the domain of the human being, the domain in which that being's necessary and inevitable struggles, not only with others but with himself, take place.

Does the contemporary world offer an area in which human beings can demonstrate what they are? I suppose that Faulkner would have to admit that it does. Virtue is not confined to past ages; grace is not a matter of chronology. Yet it is plain that there were elements in the contemporary world that, in Faulkner's opinion, tended to limit man's possibilities for heroism and even for attaining a complete humanity. The increasing abstraction and complexity of political, social, and economic life in modern America tended to depersonalize one's relationship with his fellows, as did the mechanization of work and man's deeper involvement with the machine. The erosion of the community and of the family and the breakdown of traditional manners and morals were other aspects of the process. So also was the power of the mass media and the shameless exploitation of whatever was sensational. Faulkner's essay "On Privacy" makes quite plain his deeply held feelings about the invasion of his own privacy, but clearly more than personal pique was involved. The willingness to violate a person's private life simply to make money thereby was for Faulkner a betrayal of the Founding Fathers' proclamation of liberty for every citizen.

The best evidence of Faulkner's attitude toward the modern world, however, is to be found in his fiction. There is his acid description of life as lived by the rich in southern California ("Golden Land"), or his sardonic indictment of the motor age in *Pylon*, or his rage at the military bureaucracy in *A Fable*, or his various attacks on American respectability, of which *The Wild Palms* will provide a good example. True, the passages just referred to are spoken by characters who do not necessarily express Faulkner's own sentiments. Yet the evidence of Faulkner's distaste for, and active reprehension of, twentieth-century American life—including the peculiar faults of his native region—is overwhelming. This is clear whether the criticisms are implied in his fiction or are delivered to the public as from himself.

With reference to the heroic periods in American history and the nonheroic and too slavishly respectable present age, there is an interesting passage in a letter in which Faulkner is commenting on Warren's *All the King's Men*, to which a friend had called his attention. Faulkner had been much taken with the tale of Cass Mastern. Mastern had betrayed a friend and caused indirectly a slave girl to be sold down the river, probably to a New Orleans brothel-keeper. In remorse for what he had done, he accepts responsibility for his sin and attempts to expiate it, seeking his death as a private serving in the Confederate army, deliberately exposing himself but taking care not to fire a shot against the enemy. Young Jack Burden finds great difficulty in understanding Cass Mastern's story, though he does come to do so before the novel closes.

Faulkner wrote in the letter to his friend: "there has been little in this country since [1860–1870] good enough to make good literature. . . . since then we have gradually become a nation of bragging sentimental not too courageous liars. We seem to be losing all confidence not only in our national character but in man's integrity too. The fact that we blow so hard so much about both of them is to me the symptom."

I shall not urge the reader to take this judgment with absolute seriousness; I don't know myself precisely how much weight to give it. Yet taken in the context in which Faulkner made it, the remark can tell us a good deal about his scheme of values. The stress of a war within a nation—whether you call it a Civil War or a War Between the States—was one which indeed tried men's souls. It made the most severe demands upon one's sense of principle and courage, one's virtues and resources of character. Faulkner has certainly not been the only American who has regarded the mid-nineteenth century as America's truly heroic age.

The crisis in culture that we have been examining in this essay is of another order entirely: it has to do with a division not within a nation or a community, but within the individual soul, the fruits of which are listlessness and lack of purpose, or an indifference to principle that comes from the individual's basic confusion as to who he is. To illustrate from one of Faulkner's novels, *Flags in the Dust*, Miss Jenny DuPre and Old Bayard Sartoris, both of whom had lived through the Civil War, know who they are and know what they believe. But neither Young Bayard, a fighter pilot in World War I, nor his fellow townsman, Horace Benbow, with his "sick nervous face," who had served as a YMCA secretary, knows. Now that they have come home, they have no clear conviction as to what they want to do. Both are deracinated—Horace, the would-be poet and ineffectual dreamer, quite as much as Bayard, the violent man of action, who can now find no meaningful action in which to fulfill himself.

With Faulkner, the division within modern man is of the first importance, but it never emerges as a preachment or even as an articulated abstract idea. So also with Warren, though in novels such as *All the King's Men*, or *Flood*, or *Band of Angels*, a specific theme does approach formulation in explicit terms. Of course both Faulkner and Warren deal with particular characters in a particular cultural climate, or else they would not be true artists at all.

The novelist Walker Percy tends to be more directly "philosophical" in his handling of the climate of ideas. He goes further in describing the peculiar malaise of characters like Binx Bolling or Will Barrett. That is to say, Percy concentrates on the symptoms of what he regards as the special sickness of the modern world. He provides a somewhat detailed diagnosis and, though he is properly cautious and undogmatic, he does suggest a remedy that may possibly cure it. Such a strategy risks turning the fiction in question into a novel of ideas, risks making it prescriptive rather than descriptive, and Percy's last two novels have been impugned for just such faults. I believe, however, that if *Love in the Ruins* and *Lancelot* are read perceptively, it will be seen that the author has provided more qualifications of the intellectual issues and more hedges against simplistic applications than most of the reviewers have succeeded in finding.

Be this as it may, my concern here is simply to draw attention to the fact that the crisis in culture achieves full magnification in this writer's work. Percy knows his Kierkegaard; as a convert to Roman Catholicism, he knows his Christian theology; and as a serious student of linguistics, hermeneutics, and symbolism, he is not under the rhetorical limitation of having to use an old-fashioned vocabulary.

To approach matters from a different angle, Walker Percy makes direct contact with the national and even international stream in his attempt to avoid writing the "southern novel." This maneuver has been quite conscious on his part, as some of his remarks in published interviews make plain. Yet I know of no present novelist who is more "southern" in every sort of way than is Walker Percy. Perhaps he would claim that his basic attitude is that of a modern Roman Catholic intellectual, and the claim is fully vindicated in his fiction. Yet as an observer of the southern scene, he can scarcely be bettered as he describes the sights, smells, and sounds of the French Quarter in New Orleans; or the chatter and posturings of a concourse of automobile sales in Birmingham; or the precise differences in manner and accent between a damsel from Winchester, Virginia, a girl from Fort Worth, and a big, strapping drum majorette from Alabama. Whether or not Percy fancies himself as a writer of the southern novel, his southern heritage has stood him in good stead as he deals with his chosen theme, the alienation within man's soul. One can say the same of Ransom, Tate, Warren, and Faulkner.

Here, one might ask: do other southern writers deal with the theme of the terrible division of the age; and if so, do they also benefit from their southern experience and heritage? In the cases of Flannery O'Connor, Caroline Gordon, and Andrew Lytle, the answer is clearly yes to both questions. With such writers as Eudora Welty, Katherine Anne Porter, and Marion Montgomery, all of whom draw on a southern background, the concern for man's psychic disorientation is demonstrably there, though it is less easily abstracted as an articulate theme.

What advantages does the southern writer have in dealing with what I have been calling the crisis in our culture? His first advantage is that the South is still the least "modern" part of the country in its values, habits, and associations. It has been less riven by the severing of ends from means, techniques from values. Whatever the sins and deficiencies of the South, there has been less abstraction and intellectual confusion. There is still some personal connection with the past, some sense of history, and the stabilizing effect of traditional moralities. Whether or not religion can be said to flourish in the South, it still remains a force. The sense of community has not been totally lost. There is still a folk culture in being.

Change has come—and of course is still coming—but the questioning of old attitudes and values is a powerful stimulant to observation, memory, and cogitation. If the loss of the old provokes in some no more than the irritation at being disturbed, it sends others back to an examination of their first principles. If the new constitutes a challenge to the old ways, in the philosopher and the poet the old may offer a counter challenge to the new.

LOUIS D. RUBIN, JR.

Mark Twain's South:
Tom
and Huck

Of all the creations of American authors, no others have so entered world literature as have Mark Twain's Tom Sawyer and Huckleberry Finn. One need only exhibit a portrait of two barefoot boys toting fishing poles, and with one of them wearing a straw hat with frayed brim, and Tom and Huck will be instantly identified. As literary figures they have become as familiar as Cervantes' lean knight on bony steed, Shakespeare's grave-visaged young man pondering Yorick's skull, Goethe's fabulous alchemist-doktor—icons of the imagination, images whose lineaments are identifiable not merely by scholars and intellectuals, whose business it is to know them, but by general readers of whatever nationality, ideology, race, or pigmentation.

Literature, as is well known, grows out of a culture. Tom and Huck, off for a day's fishing expedition in the summertime—how much of our national past, not so much as it was but as we wished it to be, is caught up in that image! For the image is of innocence, freedom in nature. It is not the frontier or the wilderness—that is another kind of freedom and innocence entirely—but the town, close by the river, where the fish are available for the taking and it is summertime and there is no need to wear shoes and get all ensnared in the expectations and requirements of a complex social organization. It is Eden Retold, and also the simple, classless, democratic society of the New World, where corruption, evil, privilege, and original sin were not to be permitted to establish themselves, kept out by three thousand miles of ocean and a written constitution.

Nor is that all there is to the image. For as Mark Twain wrote in his Preface to *The Adventures of Tom Sawyer*, one of the book's functions is "to pleasantly remind adults of what they once were themselves, and of how they felt and thought and talked, and what queer enterprises they sometimes engaged in." In other words, nostalgia, to be savored by adults caught in the toils of ambition, desire, moneymaking, social reform, status seeking, adulthood in general, whose lives are beset with complexity and who yearn for the vanished simplicity of an earlier day. "Saturday morning was come, and all the summer world was bright and fresh, and brimming with life. There was a song in every heart; and if the heart was young the music issued at the lips." Thus a day in the little town along the river, before the Fall of Vicksburg, the Dow-Jones Average, and Man.

It has been said that because history in America has happened so swiftly and tumultuously, from virgin wilderness to agricultural republic to industrial behemoth to world power, within so brief a span of time, our national past seems farther away, more removed in time and meaning, than for most countries, and that therefore we tend to be more concerned about it. This may well be true; in any event, nostalgia is one of our most powerful and pervasive commodities, and we have long since learned to market it much as we do automobiles, household appliances, and life insurance. In coming up with Tom Sawyer and Huck Finn, Mark Twain was by no means the first American author to capitalize upon such sentiments, but he did it so well that since then his performance has been the criterion against which others have been measured. Moreover, the worldwide acceptance of Tom and Huck clearly indicates that although nostalgia for a simpler past is powerfully American in its application, it is by no means peculiarly or exclusively so. And indeed, it may be that the nation which has become supposedly the most industrialized and most "advanced" of all nations is thereby the best suited for dramatizing the nostalgia for the past, because it has seemingly done so thorough a job of emerging from its simpler, agrarian origins.

It was in the mid-1860s that Samuel Langhorne Clemens, for whom the pen name "Mark Twain" served both as a protective disguise and a sally port for attacking the enemy, appeared upon the American literary scene in the role of a platform funny-man from the Pacific Slope, and not until he had been accepted as a popular humorist and had installed himself in a fashionable suburb in New England did he begin, however cautiously, to reveal his true origins. For Sam Clemens was no wild westerner, but a partially reformed southerner, with a strong sense for order and decorum as well as a gift for irreverence. As James M. Cox and others have pointed out, in the 1860s and the 1870s, just after the American Civil War, it was not at all fashionable to be a southerner, even from a border state like Missouri. For a popular humorist whose fortune and self-esteem depended so much upon public approbation, Clemens' suspect background was, one might say, no laughing matter, and he knew it very well. One would never have guessed, from the public pose he struck in the 1860s and early 1870s, that he came from a slave-owning family in a southern-sympathizing community, and that when the Civil War broke out he had enlisted in a Confederate volunteer unit. Later, when he got around to admitting it, he attempted to pass the latter escapade off as a lark, as if it had happened to a callow youth in his teens instead of to a twenty-six-year-old man who had been holding down a well-paid piloting job on the Mississippi River for several years.

The ruse worked—worked so well that even though Clemens later confessed all, and even took to strolling about New York City dressed in white suits and puffing on long cigars just like the old-time planters he described in his books, nobody really believed it. "He was the most desouthernized Southerner I ever knew," his friend and fellow author William Dean Howells wrote of him after his death, by which Howells, who knew him well, meant that Clemens had repudiated the customary southern view on slavery, white supremacy, and sectional defense, as indeed he had. But this son of a Virginia gentleman and a Kentucky lady of Virginian ancestry not only retained but even intensified his taste for southern ostentation and show, his relish for rhetorical excess and tall talk, and his gentlemanly scorn of mere money-grubbing (even while getting all he could whenever he could). He set his greatest, most imaginative, most deeply felt writings in the time and place of his boyhood and youth—a small town in a slaveholding, southern-leaning community, and the river that flows between St. Louis and New Orleans—and his finest novel is written on what for the southerner has always been Topic A: race relations.

Constantly and eloquently, he berated the South for its backwardness, its penchant for romance and theatricality, its racial intolerance—just as most of the better southern authors such as William Faulkner, Robert Penn Warren, Allen Tate, William Styron, and Walker Percy were to do in the generations after Clemens. For it wasn't that as a writer he was the less southern for his criticisms of southern failings, but only that he was a literary generation ahead of his time.

To understand Clemens' intense, if often oblique, relationship to the South, we need only examine the progression inherent in his best writings, beginning with his much-heralded "discovery" of the river and his experiences there, as a "virgin subject to hurl into a magazine," as his friend Joe Twitchell put it. Mark Twain had one of those imaginations in which actual facts played only an emblematic role; he could move them around at will when he wanted to adjust his account of the past. "When I was younger I could remember anything, whether it happened or not," he declared once, "but I am getting old, and soon I shall remember only the latter." Thus on the celebrated occasion when he and Twitchell went walking, and Twitchell suggested that his piloting adventures should be written and published—whereupon Clemens went home and began writing "Old Times on the Mississippi"— Clemens ignored the fact that he had several times expressed his intention of writing about his days on the river, and was already working on a novel about two boys who lived in a town along that river. In any event, in 1875, with "Old Times on the Mississippi," he published the first installment of his recreation of that portion of his experience that had happened *before* he became a journalist and writer. Such experience, as he later remarked, constituted his literary capital; but it was a while before he learned how best to use it.

"Old Times on the Mississippi" is almost exclusively concerned with the river. Except for the first memorable paragraphs beginning "when I was a boy," in which Mark Twain described the town of Hannibal and the twice-daily arrivals of the steamboats, the only other treatment of life ashore is the passage about the inhabitants of the flooded areas of the river, for whom the high water gives them almost their only opportunity to do and see something different in their otherwise squalid lives.

"Old Times" is supposedly memoir, not fiction. As such it presumably takes its form from what actually happened, not from any kind of fictional ordering of experience. But it is hardly straight reportage; the autobiographical cub pilot whose initiation into responsibility is chronicled in this work is shaped to the demands of the initiation process. For one thing, the cub is quite a few years younger than Sam Clemens actually had been when he took up piloting: a naïve, callow youth makes a much better innocent afloat than a man in his twenties who had previously worked as a journeyman compositer in Keokuk, St. Louis, Cincinnati, Philadelphia, and New York City. We know relatively little of Clemens' years on the river, but clearly they are not adequately summarized in the adventures of the cub pilot.

The opening paragraphs of "Old Times" are significant, for as critics have pointed out, they include much of the "Matter of Hannibal," both in terms of characters to be developed in the later fiction and of hints of the author's complex attitude toward his past. As a community the town is left unexamined, even though in those paragraphs are, in embryo, images that will later be developed for portrayal of such themes as slavery and freedom, Pap Finn and unregenerate evil, the quest for status, squalor, and cultural and emotional starvation, all of which will figure mightily in subsequent and more critical depictions of Clemens' prewar situation.

Of course the village is only the starting place, a setting for the beginning of the cub pilot's initiation; but that is precisely the point. The desire of the boy to escape from the tedium of the tranquil village and find adventure, fame, and fortune upon the river is what is stressed. "Old Times" is a disquisition not only upon river piloting but upon the nature of status and fame. In the opening chapter the boy looks at the captain and crew of the packet boat and envies their grandeur. A little later he becomes a passenger on a riverboat; now *he* can lounge along the railing during a stop for fuel, and let the innocents along the shore envy *him*. Yet he knows that among the professionals on the boat—the captain, the pilot, the mates, the crew—he has no status whatever, since he is only a paying guest. He decides to become a pilot, for the lofty status of a Mississippi River pilot is pure and unalloyed.

No sooner does he commence his apprenticeship, however, than he discovers that such status is not bestowed, but earned; it is the recognition of the pilot's mastery of the river. Acquiring that mastery will be a painful and lengthy process, with many ups and downs. It requires courage, but not foolhardiness, for the courage is based upon knowledge of the river as well as a quality of spirit. The pilot Horace Bixby can take what seem to be long chances, can run the shoaling bar of Hat Island when his fellow pilots are apprehensive, because he knows his boat and the river so thoroughly that his nerve is backed by absolute knowledge. The cub envies the man who can calmly maneuver an expensive steamboat, loaded with passengers and cargo, right up alongside an unseen landing in darkest night, meanwhile singing "Father in heaven, the day is declining" as he handles the wheel.

Such confidence, which confers its own "rank and dignity" and requires no verification from the public, is very different from the burning desire for status and renown that the boys of the town exhibit at the beginning of "Old Times." And if the pilot's mastery of the river is in any way comparable to a writer's mastery of his art, as is repeatedly suggested in "Old Times," we begin to see what the "rank and dignity of piloting" symbolized for Mark Twain. The relationship between the two may be characterized in the double meaning of the word "craft": the pilot steers his craft, the writer masters his craft. Clemens develops it at length. He likens the cub pilot's learning the river to the reading of a book; "throughout the long twelve hundred miles there was never a page that was void of interest, never one that you could leave without loss, never one that you would want to skip, thinking you could find higher enjoyment in some other thing. There never was so wonderful a book written by man, never one whose interest was so absorbing, so unflagging, so sparkingly renewed with every re-perusal." He describes the signs that the pilot sees in the river in terms of typography, and then says that when he had mastered every detail of the river there was loss as well as gain. For now he could no longer see it as aesthetically beautiful, as had been possible before he had learned to read it properly in terms of navigating it.

Learning the river in terms of its use, he says, destroyed it as an object of aesthetic contemplation. But the passage in which he describes how the pilot reads the river, as contrasted with the innocent passenger's conventional rhapsodizing, is not at all flat and utilitarian, but every bit as aesthetically wrought as the other. It is merely not abstract, empty, self-consciously poetic, conventionally stylized.

Clemens must have recognized the superiority, as a piece of writing, of the supposedly utilitarian passage to the conventionally rhapsodic scenic effusion. Yet it is as if he didn't quite believe it, wasn't entirely convinced of the literary quality of his own prose. As a man of letters he lacked the kind of confidence in his writing talents that as a river pilot Horace Bixby exhibited, and despite all his artistic triumphs, he never outgrew the need to have his status as author and public figure verified from the outside. At all stages in his career as writer, he seems to have craved recognition by the keepers of the accepted and conventional literary modes of his day—the aesthetics of the genteel tradition of the late nineteenth century—to confirm his literary merit, his mastery of the craft of writing. Mere popular acclaim, though essential, wasn't sufficient for him.

So it isn't surprising that from beginning to end "Old Times" is filled with the thoughts of status, the consciousness of the rank and dignity that a pilot could command. Nor is it in any way strange that *The Adventures of Tom Sawyer*, which Clemens had begun writing before "Old Times" and which he concluded shortly afterward and published in 1876, is infused with the same motif. For Clemens' memories of Hannibal, Missouri, which he renamed St. Petersburg and later Dawson's Landing, seem to have been laden with the sense of caste and class, rank and renown. Though, as he once wrote, it was a democratic village, the class lines were drawn socially, and the aristocratic taint was there. His own father, John Marshall Clemens, Virginian and Whig gentleman, was a man of dignity and probity, respected by his fellow citizens. As his son wrote of Judge York Leicester Driscoll in *Pudd'nhead Wilson*, a figure modeled upon his father, "in Missouri a recognized superiority attached to any person who hailed from Old Virginia; and this superiority was exalted to supremacy when a person of such nativity could also prove descent from the First Families of that great commonwealth." It followed that such a Virginian "must keep his honor spotless . . . Honor stood first." But John Marshall Clemens turned out to be no businessman, and when a partner without any such gentlemanly scruples outmaneuvered him, he lost everything; at the time of his death the Clemens family was living upstairs over a friend's drug store. Maintaining the rank and dignity due the children of gentry without the wealth to confirm it must have been rather difficult for the young Sam Clemens, especially when shortly after his father's death he had to go to work as a printer's devil. In any event, for Tom Sawyer life in St. Petersburg is a never-slackening quest for fame and fortune, and its ending completes an American success story along the approved Horatio Alger-Henry Ford-Thomas Alva Edison pattern. At the outset Tom is an ambitious nobody who burns for glory and excitement. By the time the novel is done, he has succeeded in turning the humdrum village life into an affair of pirates, buried treasure, hairbreadth escapes, and has won the esteem of the populace—with his share of the treasure invested at 6 percent interest. For the cub pilot in "Old Times," reputation, respect, and a princely income as pilot are harder to come by, but of course "Old Times" is supposedly factual, while *Tom Sawyer* is written as fiction, in which such things can be managed more handily.

The trouble with the South old and new, Mark Twain wrote in *Life on the Mississippi*, the book-length extension of "Old Times," is that it has suffered from an overdose of Sir Walter Scott's romances and romanticism, so that it lives in the past, goes in for gaudy extravagance, "the duel, the inflated speech, and the jejune romanticism of an absurd past that is dead, and out of charity ought to be buried." Scott it was who "created rank and caste down there, and also reverence for rank and caste, and pride and pleasure in them." But all men kill the thing they love, as a poet once said, and surely Sam Clemens was criticizing not merely the South but a part of himself as well, for Tom Sawyer—in so many ways his most autobiographical character—is the youthful incarnation of Sir Walterism, with his love of storied romance, his ability to visualize "A-rabs and elephants" when his friend Huck can see only a Sunday school picnic, his penchant for converting every activity into an adventure involving literary heroes and heroines, his desire to show off and be admired. Mark Twain says that as a character, Tom is of "the composite order of architecture"; but though he may have given Tom adventures that his own childhood friends such as the Bowen boys underwent, there can be little doubt that the way that Tom talks, thinks, dreams, and schemes is a fairly accurate reconstruction of Mark Twain's memories of the ways of Sam Clemens when young.

The fact that "Old Times on the Mississippi" is ostensibly autobiography, however fictionalized, while *Tom Sawyer* is ostensibly fiction, however drawn from life, has an important bearing upon the depth that their author was able to go beneath the surface of nostalgic memory and into its meanings. By writing avowed "fiction," with its logic based not upon what actually happened but upon what was appropriate to character and situation, Mark Twain was able in the novel to recreate a childhood world that, however gentled by the presence of an adult narrator, involved a considerable amount of violence, terror, awe, superstition, and confrontation with evil. The late Bernard DeVoto has made the point that Clemens' memories of his childhood were strongly marked by the presence of slavery and constant association with slaves during his Hannibal years: "The slave's world was dominated by the terror of death. No sunlit landscape lacked its oppression of unseen malevolence. The air vibrated with the will of ghosts and witches to do evil to the luckless race of men. It was a world that stank of death and shuddered with its terror. The mind was spellbound, obsessed, conditioned by the presences of corpses, their will to evil, and their power. Till a child could not venture beyond candlelight without dreading the touch of clammy hands." A bit strong, perhaps, but a less excitable scholar, Dixon Wecter, has demonstrated that the Hannibal that Clemens grew up in was no tranquil village paradise, snoozing in the antediluvian heat, but crowded with tumult, acts of violence, change.

The point is that the nostalgic picture of a carefree Tom and Huck setting off for a day's fishing at the riverside is *not* what happens in *Tom Sawyer*, and it is Clemens' imaginative fidelity to the truth of the experience lying beneath the genteel nostalgia that accounts for the superiority of *Tom Sawyer* to most books written about childhood. Imitations such as Booth Tarkington's Penrod books sidestep the dread; they leave out graverobbers, halfbreeds who talk of slitting women's nostrils and notching their ears, children lost in caves, corpses by moonlight, innocent old drunks sentenced to die for murder, and the like. Paradoxically, the fact that *Tom Sawyer* is fiction, not memoir, enabled Mark Twain to let his imagination work on the story, and thus to achieve greater authenticity than was possible otherwise. Because it wasn't literally true, it could be psychologically true. If such a diet of violence and dread were served up in unmediated form, of course, *Tom Sawyer* would not be the nostalgic symbol for boyhood that it is; but the presence at all times of the adult narrator, making jokes, assuring us that this is only a tale of childhood, that it all happened in the past—that, indeed, the implied evidence that *he* is alive and present to chronicle the tale is assurance that evil will not finally triumph and that all will turn out happily in the end—is what makes the violence in the novel emotionally bearable. (For though it is fiction, it is autobiographical fiction in the way that it is told; the reader senses that.)

Slavery. DeVoto was astute in recognizing the importance of slavery for Clemens' imagination, and this not so much as a matter of guilt for past acquiescence in the ownership of human beings, as of his constant association with blacks as a child. Yet neither in *Tom Sawyer* nor in "Old Times" is any criticism made of the recently outlawed Peculiar Institution, any suggestion that the problem of moral right and wrong that it posed is of concern to anyone. Clemens' views on slavery, as Arthur Pettit has shown in *Mark Twain and the South*, changed decisively from uncritical acceptance to violent hostility, and the change coincided with, or more properly followed closely upon, a change in his attitude toward the South and to his past. Thus by the 1880s, when he completed *Life on the Mississippi* and wrote most of *The Adventures of Huckleberry Finn*, the community of his origins ceased to be a white town drowsing in the summer sunshine, and became an emotional and cultural wasteland of starved intellects, cruel slaveholders, and squalid country folk.

It is Pettit's idea that the trip he made down the river to New Orleans in 1882 was instrumental in changing his mind, so that after making it, "Mark Twain's vision of an antebellum Arcadia clashed so harshly with the mechanized and polluted postbellum South that he began to make a sharp distinction between the two, a distinction that grew sharper as the years passed." Though I think Pettit makes too much of this particular expedition—the entries in Clemens' notebooks do not justify the importance placed upon them by Pettit—his observations make considerable sense and constitute the best analysis of Clemens' lifelong love/hate relationship with the South.

One might wonder why it is that "Old Times" and *Tom Sawyer* contain almost nothing derogatory to slavery or the South, whereas the added portions of *Life on the Mississippi* and *Huckleberry Finn*, as well as subsequent novels such as *Pudd'nhead Wilson* and (by inference) *A Connecticut Yankee in King Arthur's Court*, are full of such material. It cannot be ascribed merely to the return trip of 1882, for the opening portion of *Huckleberry Finn* had already been composed by then, and though not as savage as the later chapters it contains considerable incendiary commentary on Hannibal, its citizenry, and slavery. It is difficult to see a difference of anything other than degree between the pre-1882 and post-1882 attitudes toward the South. By the time that he wrote *Tom Sawyer* and "Old Times," he had taken up the matter of slavery and race in other, minor writings.

I think the answer lies, in part at least, in what happened within Clemens' imagination during the writing of *Tom Sawyer* and, to a lesser degree, of "Old Times." We have seen how the novel, begun as a nostalgic idyl, took on the dimensions of violence, terror, and pain that gave the book so much of its psychological authenticity. Clemens had originally planned for the book to describe a happy, innocent childhood, then take its characters into manhood and old age, and to end in a commentary on the sad ravages of time. He got no further, however, than boyhood, and for a very good reason. My guess is that once he got to the recreation of the "Matter of Hannibal" the deepening inquiry, though muted by the nostalgia of the genteel adult narrator, turned up the areas of symbolic meaning that he had not foreseen and which gave the reminiscences of childhood along the river a more somber turn. And when Tom Sawyer, having undergone peril and dread, wins through to fame and wealth, instead of the result being joy, it comes closer to sadness. For where is Tom going to go? And what is he going to do? The good times are over. There is no way that he can continue to live in St. Petersburg; he has already pretty much exhausted its possibilities.

Moreover, Clemens was forced to confront the fact that the community that Tom and Huck inhabited, as recreated in the process of rediscovery through memory, had been no arcadian paradise, and that it was only Tom's (which is to say, the youthful Sam Clemens') unawareness of its moral and ethical failings that had made it seem so. For though Tom was autobiographical, the adult author could not help but see many things about his childhood situation that Tom could not be made to see—because when Clemens had been a youth in Hannibal *he* had not perceived them. And it is when, three-fourths of the way through the story, he began to recognize the possibilities inherent in the viewpoint of Huck Finn that he discovered the way to deal with the moral and social shortcomings of that childhood community—by using a different, nonautobiographical character who, because of his lowly circumstance, has far less reason to be blind to the evils of slavery, the distortions of evangelical religion, the cultural deprivation, and the social squalor that were present in the little town and the antebellum South.

Huck Finn, to repeat, is not an autobiographical character in

the sense that Tom Sawyer is—which is to say that the author did
not seek to shape him and his attitudes and sensibilities in accor-
dance with what he remembered of himself when a boy. Rather,
Huck represents the views and sensibilities of the *adult* Mark
Twain. His role in *Huckleberry Finn* is to search out the moral
dimensions of the community of Sam Clemens' rearing. In that
sense, Huck is an anachronism: his insights are those of a sophisticated adult of the 1870s and 1880s. To have a book centered on
Tom Sawyer become an exposé of the social and moral flaws of
antebellum Hannibal and the society of the river would not be
right: for Tom, though he exhibited some of those shortcomings,
couldn't help it, having been schooled like his author not to see
them as wrong. It was when Huck came along, with his much
greater freedom and his lack of stake in the community, and offered the possibility of a far keener critique, that Clemens could
get on with the dissection. But it was only through the development of Tom's characterization in *Tom Sawyer* that Clemens
had been able to reach the stage at which he was prepared to take
advantage of Huck Finn's possibilities.

We see this beginning to happen late in *Tom Sawyer*, when
Huck apologizes to Tom for having eaten meals with Uncle Jake,
the Rogers family slave: "He likes me, becuz I don't ever act as if I
was above him. Sometimes I've set right down and *eat* with him.
But you needn't tell that. A body's got to do things when he's awful hungry he wouldn't want to do as a steady thing." From that
point on, the characterization of Huck Finn assumes dimensions
that involve truth-seeing and freedom. And when Mark Twain
completed *Tom Sawyer* he set out at once to write the new novel.

"Old Times on the Mississippi," though it had preceded most of
Tom Sawyer in composition, had also led, though much more
tentatively, in the same direction. For what had begun as a reminiscence of the way that a young man learns to be a river pilot
ends not with the satisfaction of apprenticeship concluded and
the rank and dignity of pilot attained, but with a discourse on the
commercialization of the piloting profession, first with the formation of a pilot's association to keep salaries high, then with a
loss of trade to railroads and tow boats, and the end of the pilot-

ing era of achievement and importance. When late in the 1870s Clemens set out to develop "Old Times" into a book, he added several more chapters about his apprenticeship, then described the death of his brother Henry in a steamboat explosion—a death for which he blamed himself. But that is all about piloting days; he does nothing with the several years during which he was not an apprentice but a full-fledged pilot, and apparently a good one.

Instead he resumes with the return visit of the adult Mark Twain, now a prosperous and famous author and businessman, to the scene of his apprenticeship, and he proceeds, in his own right, to castigate the postwar South for jejune romanticism, racial injustice, violence, barbarism, viciousness, boorishness, rhetorical excess, and just about everything else. He also approves of the commercial and industrial progress along the river, laments the decline of steamboating, and as he gets farther and farther northward on the return trip upstream, becomes more and more enthralled with industrial development. It is skin-deep boosterism in the best late nineteenth-century style, for it was written to pad out a book so that it would be hefty enough for sale by house-to-house subscription canvassing.

The point is that in omitting the piloting years, supposedly the most happy of his life, and jumping from apprenticeship to middle age, he omits any portrayal of himself as an adult in the antebellum South, even though surely the criticisms he directs at the postwar South were not only equally valid but if anything even more appropriate to the South of the Peculiar Institution. Why the omission? Again, because the cub pilot was autobiographical, and the Sam Clemens of those years, who lived high and handsomely aboard the riverboats and in New Orleans, Memphis, and St. Louis, had been without the perspective to identify the moral and social failings of his society. To portray him as enjoying himself, participating in the goings-on, would make him appear callous, irresponsible, even wicked, when he couldn't help it at the time. To make him far more aware and critical and indignant than he had been during those years would be to falsify what he had been. How, after all, could a man stay up there in the pilothouse and enjoy working the river, and live happily and sumptuously on the best fare of the dining saloon, when out on the deck, next to the baled cotton, there were black men, women, and children, chained to each other, being sold down the river like animals? But a man *had* seen such things, and yet gone right on enjoying the life of a river pilot.

But Huck Finn is another matter. As we have seen, Huck does not have the status or the involvement in the community to encourage him to be uncritical. Huck not only can break bread with a black man, but join up with him and abet his flight to avoid being sold down the river. Through his distance from the values of the community he can perceive the falseness, tawdriness, sham, and cruelty of the life along the shore, and can remain on the raft with Jim and, for a time at least, avoid the unpleasantness and evil by living on the river in a state of natural freedom. Thus as the raft drifts downstream the critique of the society along the banks past which the river flows becomes ever more severe. Instead of St. Petersburg drowsing in the sunlight we get Bricksville, with its squalor, frustration, cruelty, sentimentality, emotional and moral suffocation.

Every item of the Bricksville scene has its symbolic counterpart in the portrait of the sleeping town at the beginning of "Old Times"; but now the full potentiality for disgust, disdain, and despair is foremost in the author's mind. Finally comes Phelps Farm, when Huck Finn, having decided to go against his conscience and rescue a slave from captivity, reaches Tom Sawyer's uncle's farm, and Tom shows up, and we have the great "evasion" in which Jim is rescued and Tom gloriously wounded, and a story that had given signs of incipient tragedy is jerked back into comedy, at the expense of changing Jim into a minstrel darkey again instead of the man Huck had discovered him to be. Why need it end that way? Because the freedom of the river had to come to an end: they could not drift downstream forever, and so life on the shore was unavoidable. Thus the only way to close it out was to convert the story back into Tom Sawyer's comedy of escape through imaginative extravagance, and let Huck plan to light out for the territories, the still-unsettled regions of the nation where the hypocrisy and falseness of society might be avoided for a few years longer yet.

Thus the creative zeal of the adult Mark Twain, remembering the old times on the river, caught up in the marvellous opportunities for freedom and moral honesty that had been there if only he had been able to perceive them—the American classic, *Adventures of Huckleberry Finn*. Which, however, had to end, because when he had been a child there he had not been Huck but Tom, or rather, more *like* Tom than Huck. The territories would not suffice for him, since they too were being rapidly civilized and spoiled by the greed and materialism of fallen human beings. So the only possible escape from the guilt and disappointment was through the imagination, the "let's pretend" of Tom Sawyer. Let's pretend that the young Sam Clemens had been able to recognize the meanings as well as the amusements, the truth as well as the beauty— let's pretend that Sam Clemens was Huck Finn.

This is why he was, as Allen Tate has said, the first modern southern writer. His was the first important literary inner duel with his own memory and conscience, in which rhetorical defense became dialectical self-examination, and love and anger were forced to confront one another. Through the accident of geography and history he had been dislodged from the time and place of his early community allegiance, and his genius and his honesty (if these can be separated) had forced him into exploring what he had become in terms of where he had come from and what he had once been. What he found was Tom, and then Huck—and, through Huck, Jim.

ROBERT D. JACOBS

Tobacco Road: Lowlife and the Comic Tradition

Gaunt, racked with ague, dull-eyed and hollow-cheeked, he has been with us in fiction for more than two hundred years. Until recently travelers through the South could see his real-life counterpart leaning against the doorframe of a paintless, screenless shack on the edge of a cotton field in Georgia, South Carolina, or Mississippi, or sitting on the porch of a perilous hillside shanty in eastern Kentucky with tin cans and the rusted hulks of abandoned cars in his grassless yard. In the more than two centuries of his literary history, the southern poor white has been called shiftless, depraved, degenerate, vicious, sadistic, and abysmally, unbelievably ignorant. No one has ever called him sanitary. In the early nineteenth century, critics from the North pointed to him as an inevitable product of the South's peculiar institution, chattel slavery; literary comedians, usually from the South, had great fun with his appearance, language, and behavior. When he squatted on the borders of broad plantations in the Tidewater, he was an object of derision even to black slaves, who called him "po' Buckra" or "po' white trash." When he lived in isolated groups in the southern swamps and sandhills, his gene pool became impoverished, and inbreeding, together with his usual diseases—malaria, hookworm, trichinosis, and pellagra—made him a distinct physiological type that erroneously became identified with his entire class and persisted in some minds up into the twentieth century. Yet when he had energy enough to leave the Tidewater and move westward to the frontier, he was turned by legend and the literary comedians into an outlandish folk hero, "half horse, half alligator," whose rifle never missed and whose bullet-hard thumbs could gouge out the eyes of any opponent—man, bear, or panther. On the frontier he could hunt and fish—he was never much of a farmer, anyway—and he could pursue the one career open to him in an agricultural economy where the good land was owned by his betters: he could go into politics.

An Eighteenth-Century View

The southern poor white—the central figure in any representation of lowlife in the South—appeared in the full panoply of his forlorn appearance and disgraceful habits in an early eighteenth-century account by William Byrd II, a baronial Virginian who in 1728 headed a commission to survey the boundary between the colonies of North Carolina and Virginia. Byrd's *History of the Dividing Line* was not published until 1841, but there is evidence that he had intended to publish it, and it probably circulated in manuscript among his friends. No ignorant colonial, Byrd had been educated at the Middle Temple in London and included among his friends the playwrights William Wycherley and William Congreve and a literary nobleman, Charles Boyle, fourth earl of Orrery. Byrd himself became a corresponding member of the Royal Society and displayed in his *History of the Dividing Line* a virtuoso's interest in the flora and fauna of the backcountry of Virginia and North Carolina. Not the least interesting of the fauna was the creature he named a "lubber"—the poor white of the swamps and backwoods of North Carolina.

Like the Indian, the lubber of North Carolina lay slugabed while his poor wife scratched the virgin soil and scattered a few seeds of Indian corn, which grew so profusely that little cultivation was needed. The necessary protein for the lubber family came from lean hogs that gobbled the "mast" from pine trees and oaks and required no attention until butchering time. Yet too exclusive a diet of pork, Byrd tells us, gave the lubber a disease called the "country distemper," which, untreated, was likely to produce "yaws" (great lesions of the bones and skin). One should say here that Byrd's medical knowledge is suspect. The "country distemper" was probably trichinosis, caused by tiny parasites (trichinae)

that infested the intestines and can be acquired by eating insufficiently cooked pork from an infected hog; whereas yaws, like
syphilis, is caused by spirochetes. Be that as it may, Byrd's account of the lubber disease simply lays the groundwork for his
rather brutal joke about the North Carolinians. The yaws, Byrd
claims,

> seizes the throat, next the palate, and lastly shows its spite to the poor
> nose, of which 'tis apt in a small time treacherously to undermine the
> foundation. This calamity is so common and familiar here that it ceases
> to be a scandal, and in the disputes that happen about beauty the noses
> have in some companies much ado to carry it. Nay, 'tis said that once,
> after three good pork years, a motion had like to have been made in the
> House of Burgesses that a man with a nose should be incapable of hold-
> ing any place of profit in the province; which extraordinary motion
> could never have been intended without some hopes of a majority.

Whatever the verity of Byrd's callous jest, an excessive appetite
for pork has been attributed to southerners from his day to ours.

Regional humor has flourished in the United States, usually on
the basis of stock figures developed from provincial characteristics and exaggerated for comic purposes. In Byrd's *History of the
Dividing Line* we have the first appearance of a stock figure, the
southern poor white. If we were to believe William Byrd, we would
see the entire colony of North Carolina as populated by escaped
debtors, ne'er-do-wells, and the chronically lazy, who relied on a
mild climate and the abundance of nature for survival. Byrd's lubbers, literary ancestors of the red-neck, were not only lazy but dis-
solute. Their slatternly women were always available for a tumble
on the straw bed or the dirt floor, provided that one could tolerate
their filth and scabs. Many poor-white couples cohabited without
benefit of clergy, and nearly all drank a villainous rum distilled in
New England and locally called "kill-devil."

Byrd did notice that the lubbers were often afflicted with a disease endemic to the lowlands of the South—malaria: "They are
devoured by musketas all summer and have Agues every Spring
and Fall, which corrupt all the Juices of their Bodies, give them a
cadaverous complexion, and besides a lazy, creeping habit, which
they never get rid of." Here Byrd spoke the literal truth. The ca-

daverous complexion, caused by the malaria parasite, and the "lazy creeping habit," a result of physical debility, were attributed to the poor whites of the lowlands until modern insecticides controlled the anopheles mosquito that carried the parasites. Never mind that the mosquito was no respecter of persons, that the twentieth-century poet John Crowe Ransom's "lady of beauty and high degree" died of chills and fever just as quickly as a tacky from the swamps; malaria was considered a disease of the poor whites along with their other characteristic maladies. Byrd's physical and moral characterization of the poor white became a convention, not because of his literary influence—after all, his book was not available until 1841—but because the type he called the lubber did in fact exist. The poor white was despised and sometimes feared in the plantation South, and he was laughed at *because* he was despised and feared. The moral and physical defects pointed out by Byrd became reference points for the entire class of poor whites. Throughout the nineteenth century and into the twentieth, the poor white's diseases, instead of arousing compassion, have been paraded as evidence of his degeneracy. Further, he has been considered lazy beyond belief and as amoral as an animal.

Only the naïve expect a literary text to correspond to verifiable reality, but the poor whites of the South have been used as bad examples so often that the person who has never known them begins to believe that they are indeed a special breed, genetic freaks instead of simply less-capable cousins of their economic betters. We shall see in a moment how closely Byrd's prototypical poor whites matched nineteenth-century accounts. Only the name changed. In later years the poor white was called clay-eater, tacky, wool-hat, sandhiller, hillbilly, mountain grill, red-neck, and other unflattering names based upon his appearance, his locale, or his supposed habits. Today the name "red-neck," with or without the hyphen, is applied indiscriminately to rural and small town southerners, and it has gained in respectability to the extent that the younger brother of the president of the United States was photographed recently wearing a T-shirt that bore the legend, "Redneck Power." But in the early nineteenth century, the poor white, by whatever name, was a despicable comic object.

The Nineteenth-Century Version

About a century after Byrd made his memorable excursion into North Carolina, the lubber reappeared, this time as a clay-eater, in the fiction of Augustus Baldwin Longstreet, who had traveled through the backwoods settlements of Georgia in performing his duties as a circuit judge. Longstreet—lawyer, minister, and sometimes president of four different colleges—let it be known distinctly that he was of the gentry and that he was recording the lowlife of the backwoods only as a historian. The Judge framed his tales in literary English, while his backwoods characters spoke a comic dialect eventually considered as typically southern by everyone except southerners. Moral distance from these backwoods tackies was established by the Judge's expression of dismay at their uncouth language and brutal behavior.

Lowlife in Georgia in the first quarter of the nineteenth century, according to Judge Longstreet's tales, was made up of such events as swapping horses (not only a business deal but also a popular diversion), fights (another popular diversion), gander pullings (contests in which men on horseback attempted to pull off the greased heads of suspended ganders), fox hunts, and shooting matches. Usually Longstreet's characters were drawn from the "plain folk," whom some historians prefer to distinguish from the poor white primarily on the basis of character and energy; but in one tale, "The Fight," there is a classic portrait of a Georgia clay-eater:

> [Ransy Sniffle] in his earlier days had fed copiously upon red clay and blackberries. This diet had given to Ransy a complexion that a corpse would disdain to own, and an abdominal rotundity that was quite unprepossessing. Long spells of fever and ague, too, in Ransy's youth, had conspired with clay and blackberries to throw him quite out of the order of nature. His shoulders were fleshless and elevated; his head large and flat; his neck slim and translucent; and his arms, hands, fingers and feet were lengthened out of all proportion to the rest of his frame. His joints were large and his limbs small; and as for flesh, he could not, with propriety, be said to have any. . . . His height was just five feet nothing, and his average weight, in blackberry season, ninety-five [pounds].

Sniffle—note the satirical name—should have been too listless to move, had the Judge taken seriously the symptoms of malaria and malnutrition he recorded; but instead he endows the clay-eater with remarkable energy when sufficiently motivated: "There was nothing on this earth which delighted Ransy so much as a fight. He never seemed fairly alive, except when he was witnessing, fomenting, or talking about a fight. Then, indeed, his deep sunken grey eye assumed something of a living fire; and his tongue acquired a volubility that bordered on eloquence." In Longstreet's story Ransy is stirred into frenetic activity by the prospect of fomenting a fight between two local champions, who, in contrast to Ransy, are magnificent physical specimens named Robert Durham and William Stallings. After Ransy reports to Durham that Billy Stallings had insulted his wife, these two heroes stage a frontier fight, complete with biting and gouging. After the fight, mutilated by the loss of a nose, ears, and a finger or so, the young fighters take to their beds for several weeks and then become reconciled in manly fashion, while Ransy Sniffle, the clay-eater, basks in his reflected glory. Judge Longstreet carefully separates these backwoods rowdies from southern civilization with his concluding pieties: "Thanks to the Christian religion, to schools, colleges, and benevolent associations, such scenes of barbarism and cruelty as that which I have been just describing are now of rare occurrence, though they may still be occasionally met with in some of the new counties."

Curiously, Ransy Sniffle, with his patently comic name, is the only true clay-eater among Judge Longstreet's backwoodsmen, and the type appears infrequently in other humorous tales of the southwestern frontier. When he does appear as a comic figure, the clay-eater is often treated with contempt by the other poor whites. Tales concerning Captain Simon Suggs, a poor white turned confidence man and rogue, were published in the 1840s by Johnson Jones Hooper, a newspaper editor. In one tale, Simon Suggs, who professes to be an experienced Indian fighter, raises a volunteer company when there is a report (erroneous) that the Indians are on the warpath. Simon appoints himself captain of the company with half-concealed bragging about his own qualifications. The only voice raised to challenge him is that of "a diminutive, yellow-faced spindle-legged young man," whom Simon kicks in the rump, addressing him as follows: "Take *that* along, and next time keep your jaw, you slink, or I'll kick more clay outen you in a minute, than you can eat again in a month, you durned, little dirt-eatin' deer-face."

Even among the lower classes, then, the clay-eater was considered a contemptible creature, and his eating of dirt was thought to be a "morbid appetite" rather than the result of malnutrition. That the physiological type actually existed is beyond question. Travel writers as well as literary comedians recorded his appearance. A British traveler, James Silk Buckingham, observed the type in the wet ricelands not far from Charleston, South Carolina, in 1838:

> We saw some young white boys of fourteen or fifteen years of age, children of poor overseers, born and bred in this region, and more ghastly and cadaverous complexions I never remember to have seen. One of our fellow-passengers, a resident of Charleston, said, that the deathlike and livid paleness of complexion was greatly augmented by the practice of eating a sweetish kind of clay, which he represented to be quite general among the poor whites here. . . . The Americans here do not take the sweet clay as a substitute for food, since they are never without abundant supplies of the kinds in use by them; but they contract an artificial and vitiated taste for it, as for tobacco, and then find it difficult to leave it off; so powerfully do the morbid appetites enslave a large portion of mankind. . . .

William Byrd II had known better. The cadaverous complexion came from malarial anemia and malnutrition. The children of the overseers probably also suffered from hookworms, an intestinal parasite brought from Africa by the slaves. But no one in those days cared to know *why* the poor white might be a physical degenerate; most writers preferred to make a moral example of him, or, as did Frederick Law Olmsted, well-known New York architect and travel writer, serve him up as an illustration of what happened to poor whites when the economy was dominated by wealthy slaveowners. Olmsted traveled through the South just prior to the Civil War, paying much more attention to the inhabitants of the backcountry than had Buckingham. He records the universal diet of bacon and cornbread, which alone should have been enough to send children to the clay bank; but he professed to find degenerate poor whites only in the slave districts, whereas poor whites in the mountains, where slaves were few, were hospitable, well fed, and, astonishingly, quite well read. To prove his point that chattel slavery was as harmful to the white race as it was to the black, Olmsted borrowed a passage from a book by Dr. John Davy, an English physician who had described poor whites in Barbados, to reinforce his own argument. As a medical man Davy had been much interested in the physical degeneracy of poor whites. He noted their pallid complexions, which resembled the albino's more than the ruddy Englishman's, and he also commented on their pale eyes and sparse light hair, their feebleness and lack of muscular development. "In brief their general appearance denotes degeneracy of corporeal frame." Nor did Davy neglect making a moral judgment, as had Byrd, Longstreet, and Buckingham: "In character, morally and intellectually, they show marks also of degeneracy, not less than physically. They are generally indolent and idle, ignorant and improvident, and often intemperate. Is it surprising then, that they are poor, and objects of contempt? What they are they have been made by circumstances, and this is in the course of a few generations."

Instead of describing the poor whites as he had observed them, Olmsted claims that Davy's description of the Barbadians applied perfectly to the appearance and condition of the class of nonslaveowners in the plantation districts of the American South.

Olmsted was no abolitionist, for he feared the result of political interference with the southern institution, but he did advocate gradual emancipation, voicing the hope that the white population of the South could be "sufficiently christianized, and civilized, and properly educated" to understand that both self-interest and moral obligation demanded emancipation of the slaves. Judge Longstreet had thought that Christianity and education would eliminate the brutality of the poor whites in the backwoods, whereas Olmsted had faith that these same two agencies of benevolence would reform the slaveowning class, of which Longstreet was a member. That Olmsted is only interested in supporting his argument that slavery was more damaging to the whites than to the blacks is quite clear. Accordingly, the whites of the "plantation districts," slaveowners or poor whites, are seen as uncivilized and ignorant, and the slaveless whites of the mountains are praised as competent husbandmen who keep books in their homes and read aloud to their children.

Other northern writers, also using poor whites as an illustration of the evil of slaveholding, were less kind than the gradualist Olmsted. In 1836 Richard Hildreth, a novelist and historian, described the poor whites as follows:

> They are idle, dissipated, and vicious; with all that vulgar brutality of vice, which poverty and ignorance render so conspicuous and disgusting. Without land, or at best, possessing some little tract of barren and exhausted soil, which they have neither the skill nor the industry to render productive; without any trade or handicraft art, and looking upon manual labor as degrading to the freemen, and fit only for a state of servitude,—these poor white men have become the jest of the slaves, and are at once feared and hated by the select aristocracy of rich planters.

Historians of the past quarter century have pointed out the inaccuracy of considering the population of the antebellum South as composed only of rich planters, slaves, and poor whites, ignoring the millions of small farmers who did their own work or owned at most ten slaves. Hildreth, however, was writing propaganda, and both novelists and propagandists sometimes find it inconvenient to be veracious.

Some twenty years later James R. Gilmore, an abolitionist who had gained his knowledge of southern poor whites by traveling about the South for sixteen years doing business with planters and merchants, gave a description of the moral condition of the tackies more damning than any other account since William Byrd's description of the lubbers of North Carolina. "They are totally destitute of morals and religion," he wrote, "and live in open violation of almost all laws, human and divine. Fathers cohabit with daughters, brothers with sisters, and husbands sell or barter away their wives, just as they would their jack knives or their rusty rifles."

Here an even more sinister charge is laid to the account of the poor white—incest. This is hardly matter to be considered in a comic light, but it surfaced again in the twentieth century in a crude joke once rather widely circulated: that a Tennessee virgin was a twelve-year-old girl who could outrun her brother. It also appears in Thomas Wolfe's brief but vicious description in *Look Homeward, Angel* of "Loney Shytle, who left a stale sharp odor as she passed, her dirty dun hair covered in a wide plumed hat, her heels out of her dirty white stockings. She had caused incestuous rivalry between her father and her brother, she bore the scar of her mother's razor in her neck, and she walked, in her rundown shoes, with the wide stiff-legged hobble of disease."

We can see in the antebellum northern writers a significant change toward the poor white's alleged depravity. Southerners Byrd and Longstreet recognized the animalistic tendencies likely to be displayed in a state of nature, and both were aware that diseases could be the cause of the poor white's lassitude. The northern writers, however, held that slavery was responsible for both the moral and physical degeneracy. The poor white lived on worn-out land that he had no skill to rehabilitate; he considered labor beneath the dignity of a free man; and, clustering in the sterile sand hills without benefit of either church or school, he became a creature of vile and lawless appetite.

If the sandhillers and tackies of the plantation country were objects of contempt for both North and South, it remained for those backwoods saga spinners, the southwestern humorists, to present comic portraits of poor whites who were neither corpse-colored nor feeble; in fact some of them were mighty men, folk heroes of strength and cunning. In southwestern humor the poor white as frontier demigod was typified by Davy Crockett. Fantastic feats were attributed to him. He could burn the bark off a tree trunk by grinning at it, put a rifle ball through the moon, wring the tail off a comet, and leap astraddle of the lightning. He could even outwit the shrewdest of folk characters—a "gander-shanked Yankee." In the tales about Crockett a stock character emerges, the redoubtable Kentuckian, although Crockett himself was from Tennessee. This was a genuine American folk hero with little if any trace of

European origin, unless his precombat bragging derived from the boast of the medieval Anglo-Saxon warrior. Yet he was also a comic hero. His speech habits were atrocious, his manners abominable, his disposition ferocious; but his courage was beyond question and, quite unlike the poor white of the plantation country, he was credited with a rude chivalry. In one of the exploits associated with Davy Crockett, a shooting match with Mike Fink (legendary keelboatman), Davy loses the match when he refuses to shoot a comb from the hair of Mike's wife, a target that Mike himself had selected: "Davy Crockett's hand would be sure to shake," proclaims the hero, "if his iron war pointed within a hundred mile of a shemale."

Out of place among the great plantations of the Tidewater, diseased and undernourished in the swamps and sandhills of the Piedmont, the poor white found a proper home on the frontiers of the South, a step ahead of the planters with their wagonloads of slaves. David Crockett (1786–1836) was in real life a poor white who fulfilled himself in the backwoods of Tennessee by hunting, fighting Indians, and being elected to public office. Returning from the Indian wars a hero, he became a justice of the peace, a colonel in the state militia, a member of the state legislature, and a congressman of the United States. By dying magnificently at the defense of the Alamo in 1836, Crockett became a national hero, still renowned in the twentieth century.

No doubt such celebrations of the common man were needed in America. The European type of gentleman-as-hero, although he flourished in southern plantation fiction longer than elsewhere, was not viable in a self-consciously democratic society. The frontiersman, though a lawless squatter, an indifferent farmer, a drunkard, and a brawler, could be turned into a democratic myth glorifying the plain folk of the South. His faults were mitigated by the comic mode, while the elasticity of comedy permitted exaggeration of his virtues without the requirement of verisimilitude that would have obtained in serious fiction.

After the 1830s the comic frontiersman began gradually to disappear from the popular literature. Mark Twain did revive him satirically around 1880 for a chapter of *Huckleberry Finn* that was not used in the published version of the novel. In this chapter Huck, concealed on a Mississippi log raft, observes two raftsmen who strut and brag, frontier-fashion, about their prowess until both are thrashed by a smaller man of deeds, not words. By this time the comedy of America's heroic age was obsolete, however, and Mark Twain knew it.

With the virtual disappearance of the mighty Kentuckian from the comic literature of the frontier, a less savory type of poor white was featured—the rogue. Simon Suggs, who has already been mentioned in this essay as the creation of Johnson Jones Hooper, is a classic example. If Davy Crockett could cheat a "gander-shanked Yankee" out of ten quarts of rum for his backwoods Tennessee constituents by trading the same coonskin cap (not infrequently used in place of currency) over and over, Simon Suggs could cheat anyone out of anything.

Suggs spent his early life in a poor white district near Augusta, Georgia. He began to live by his wits when he was not yet seventeen, after he swindled his father out of a horse and moved to the backwoods of Alabama. There he pursued a career of trickery unparalleled in the literature of southern lowlife until William Faulkner's Flem Snopes appeared a century later. One of Suggs's most imaginative tricks is his persuasion of the congregation at a religious camp meeting that he has been converted. His piety is so ostentatious that the congregation takes up a collection for Suggs to found a church in his own godless neighborhood. Once the money has been collected, Suggs announces that he must sanctify it in solitary prayer. He retreats to the swamp, where he has tied his horse, and gleefully gallops away.

This tale, "The Captain Attends a Camp-Meeting," presents an aspect of poor-white life in the South that had previously been rather neglected by the literary comedians—frontier religion. In Hooper's tale, however, there are actions and implications that were to become elements of the comic tradition: the group exhortation in comic dialect by self-appointed ministers, the "holy shakes" and the laugh of religious hysteria, the suggestions of sexual arousal, and the intimation that the ministers were more interested in profit than prayer. Mark Twain drew upon this story for one of the episodes of *Huckleberry Finn*, in which the rogue who calls himself the Dauphin swindles a congregation in a similar way. Then in the twentieth century Erskine Caldwell devotes an entire novel, *Journeyman* (1935), to the exploits of Semon Dye, a rogue turned evangelist without relinquishing his roguery. Lecher, con man, gambler, and brawler, this "man of God" swoops hawk-like on a community of poor whites and blacks, seduces their wives, cheats them out of their money, and exhorts them to confess their sins! Always ready to fight with fists or pistols, Semon Dye combined the pugnacity of the frontiersman with the amorality of the itinerant rogue, making victims of his own class.

If Simon Suggs was the prince of rogues in the Alabama backwoods of the 1840s, surely the king of tricksters in the Tennessee mountains during the 1850s was Sut Lovingood, a character invented by George Washington Harris. Stories about Sut appeared first in newspapers and were published in collected form in 1867.

Although he does not have the physical lassitude of the clay-eater, Sut resembles the type. The mountaineer is a "queer looking, long legged, short bodied, small headed, white haired, hog eyed, funny sort of a genius." His dialect, composed both of colloquial expressions and of comic misspellings, is almost unreadable today: "Wo! Wo! Tarpoke, yu cussed infunnel fidety hide full ove hell faire, can't yu stan' still an listen while I'se a polishin yer karacter off es a mortul hoss tu these yere durned fools?" The trick, of course, is to read it aloud.

The poverty of the Lovingood family matched that of the poor white of literary tradition, although it is evident that some of the families in the mountains were quite well off. In the first tale of the series, "Sut Lovingood's Daddy, Acting Horse," the huge family, composed of the parents and some fifteen children, is living in a mountain cabin. "Daddy" is a farmer of sorts, but he has no horse to pull his plow. The prospect appears dismal, a situation like that of the Lesters in Caldwell's *Tobacco Road* or the Armstids in Faulkner's *The Hamlet*; but Harris' mountaineers are tough. Sut's Daddy vows that he will "act the horse" and pull the plow himself. Undertaking the role with fire and fury, he behaves like a real horse, champing the bit, kicking, and pulling the plow at alarming speed through "sprowts an' bushes same as a rale horse." Daddy is unstoppable until he dashes into a hornet's nest, runs away with the hornets after him, and dives, plow and all, into a creek. Of course no living man could have such prodigious strength, but extraordinary feats had already been established in the comic tradition of the frontier, and the Lovingood tales are in that tradition.

In other Lovingood episodes, Sut puts a bag full of lizards in a country parson's breeches, breaks up a wedding, and destroys Mrs. Yardley's quilting party by tying a rope with quilts attached to a nervous horse and then whacking the horse with a board. Mrs. Yardley herself is fatally injured when the horse runs over her, but Sut swears she died from grief over the loss of her "nine dimunt [diamond] quilt." Incapable of remorse, Sut attempts to seduce Mrs. Yardley's fat daughter immediately after her injured mother is carried into the house, and he would have succeeded if Mr. Yardley had not happened upon them and planted one of his heavy boots between Sut's coattails.

Although Sut Lovingood as a character is a composite of the types of poor whites previously discussed in this essay, his social role is original. Knowing his own weaknesses, Sut chooses his victims from those who are superior in status but morally no better than he is. They are the hypocrites, the lechers, and the "durned fools"—a large category. Relishing food, whiskey, and sex, Sut is quick to doubt any paragons of puritanical virtue; and thus he becomes something unprecedented among the fictional poor whites, an indirect moral agent. The Sut Lovingood tales are a masterpiece of the comic tradition of lowlife in the South. They differ from the earlier tales in that the poor white is neither despised nor made into a folk hero. Instead, his very shortcomings serve as a standard by which to measure those who consider themselves his moral superiors. Since George Washington Harris as author virtually disappears in most of these tales, Sut Lovingood is allowed to speak for himself. At last the poor white is given a voice, and his message is, "Air yu any bettern I am?"

Between the end of the Civil War in 1865 and the beginning of the Great Depression of the 1930s, the poor white of the South was presented in modes too mixed to summarize. John W. De Forest, a pioneer realist from the North, wrote of the "low-down people" in much the same spirit as had Richard Hildreth and James R. Gilmore before the war. Mark Twain, although of southern origin, looked at the shabby villages along the lower Mississippi River in 1882 with eyes conditioned by several years' residence in Hartford, Connecticut. His account of "Pap" Finn, Huckleberry Finn's father, is as damning as anything in the literature; and the poor whites of Bricksville, Arkansas, as depicted in *Huckleberry Finn* (1884), are as dirty and shiftless as Byrd's North Carolina lubbers. When southern regional writers of the 1880s and 1890s came to write of the poor whites, however, the backwoods tackies were frequently transformed into hardworking "plain folk" or sturdy, self-reliant mountaineers. In the fiction of this period there was an attempt to catch what was called local color, and the inhabitants of the southern mountains who were both poor and white were considered the most colorful of all. Regionalists like Mary Noailles Murfree, Sherwood Bonner, Joel Chandler Harris, and John Fox, Jr. succeeded quite well in making the mountaineer into something of a romantic outlaw. Proud and independent, he had a code of honor that governed his behavior, even in his conflicts with the federal officers who attempted to destroy his illicit stills. This transformation of the poor white does not concern us here; rather, we must turn to the twentieth century to see him revived as a comic object.

The Twentieth Century

It was Erskine Caldwell's Jeeter Lester of *Tobacco Road* (1932) who gave a character to the southern poor white that he had not borne since the days of antebellum southwestern humor. The enormous popularity of this novel made the name Jeeter Lester synonymous with the southern red-neck. This was unfortunate, because Caldwell's purpose was not to disparage the poor white but to account for his degeneracy on economic grounds and to drive the lesson home through comic exaggeration. Taken seriously, the novel describes a deplorable situation in the South of the early depression years; farmers live in virtual starvation on the land with no means to farm it. Once again in his long history the poor white is made to serve a polemical purpose. In an emotional preface to the novel, Caldwell claims to have seen people like the Lesters, hungry and ragged, walking the roads in winter. These people, says Caldwell, had "such faith in nature, in the earth, and in the plants that grew in the earth, that they could not understand how the earth could fail them." Throughout the novel a plea for understanding is reiterated, chiefly in the author's voice, but frequently in Jeeter's. Few readers, however, are likely to find Jeeter's voice reliable, for the character, like those who preceded him in southwestern humor, is a comic exaggeration, a caricature.

It would be a mistake to assume that Caldwell considered the Lesters representative, in spite of his prefatory claim to have seen such people; for this family has lost the knowledge that for generations had kept the poor whites alive—the knowledge of how to live off the land. The fish of the streams, the squirrels, rabbits, and opossums of the woods, the half-wild pigs and chickens that took care of themselves, pokeweed, ramp, and dandelion greens— all are denied the Lesters, and the family is starving. The point is fairly obvious. Jeeter Lester is eager to work the land, but he has been conditioned to raise money crops—tobacco and cotton. Without money he is unable to buy the cottonseed to plant, the nitrate to make the cotton grow, and the mules to pull his plows. Formerly, all these had been supplied by his landlord under the sharecropping system, through which the landless farmer obtained tools and provisions from the landlord at a ruinous rate of interest; but Jeeter's landlord has given up farming as economically unsound, and Jeeter has neither money nor credit. Had Jeeter been able to use the traditional resources of the poor white, Caldwell's indictment of the system would have been diminished. Actually few small farmers, share-croppers or landowners, had any money during the depression, but unlike the Lesters they were rarely hungry.

If Jeeter Lester's plight is atypical, his behavior is stereotypical of the poor whites of tradition. Father of seventeen children by his wife, Ada, and of others by his neighbors' wives, Jeeter arouses memories of Sut Lovingood and of the licentious squatters described by northern novelists before the Civil War. Accused by Sister Bessie of having incestuous desire for his own daughter,

Jeeter resembles the depraved sandhillers of James R. Gilmore. In *Tobacco Road* sexuality is exaggerated to the point of low comedy. All of the Lesters are interested in sexual intercourse. They watch as the harelipped daughter, Ellie May, rapes Jeeter's son-in-law Lov, to whom Jeeter had earlier traded his twelve-year-old daughter Pearl for quilts, a gallon of motor oil, and seven dollars. Sister Bessie, a self-styled evangelist, appropriates Jeeter's sixteen-year-old son Dude and "marries" him in a ceremony of her own invention. After the ceremony, Sister Bessie drags Dude to bed in the Lester cabin, and Jeeter pulls a ladder to the window, hoping to see them in sexual congress. When Dude and Bessie take a wedding trip to Augusta, they rent a room in a brothel, thinking it a hotel. All night Sister Bessie is shunted from one room to another by various customers, and she has never had such a glorious time. The whole episode is a bawdy variation on the old comic convention of the countryman-come-to-town, a stock situation in American humor.

Equally in the comic tradition is the Lesters' callousness. Like Ransy Sniffle, Simon Suggs, or Sut Lovingood, they are indifferent to the suffering of others. Dude and Bessie drive their automobile into a wagon and leave a Negro man unconscious and dying. When they carelessly back their car over the old Lester grandmother, no one pays her any attention until they presume she is dead; then they throw her into a shallow grave. To survey these monstrous people outside of the comic tradition is to regard them with horror, but their dialect and their behavior had been prepared for by two hundred years of literary treatment.

Unfortunately, the enormous popularity of Caldwell's early novels derived from his comic handling of sex and violence, not from an aroused compassion for his characters. Although he attempted to force the conscience of the nation to take cognizance of the predicament of the poor white of the South during the transition between an agrarian and an industrial economy, his broadly comic approach prevented any sympathetic identification with his characters.

During the same period a greater writer, William Faulkner of Mississippi, also included the poor whites in his cultural panorama of the South. Faulkner's poor whites appeared as principals first in his novel, *As I Lay Dying* (1930), but the characters of the tale, except for Anse Bundren, owe little to the comic tradition. Anse, incompetent as a farmer, cuckolded as a husband, and ineffectual as a father, does resemble the comic stereotype; but Faulkner's technique distinguishes this novel from any of its predecessors. The story is told through interior monologues, enabling the reader to know the consciousness of the many characters, to understand their desires and their frustrations. Faulkner succeeded in making the poor white a comprehensible being, neither an object for comic caricature nor a shabby argument for political and economic reform.

In 1941 Faulkner published a novel about poor whites living during the period when the southern land was beginning to be owned, not by farmers but by businessmen. In this novel, *The Hamlet*, an infamous clan named Snopes moves into comic focus, but the comedy is as grim as a tornado warning. Faulkner does draw heavily upon the comic tradition for some of the characters. Ab Snopes, patriarch of the clan, had previously appeared in some of Faulkner's short stories and in his Civil War novel, *The Unvanquished*. Ab, like the antebellum sandhiller, is regarded contemptuously by the planters. During the Civil War he joined neither Rebels nor Yankees but stole horses from both, selling them to the highest bidder. In later years Ab became a sharecropper who fancied himself a horse trader whenever he could swap his landlord's fencing wire and farm tools for a horse. As a horse trader Ab is most obviously of the comic tradition, suggesting the characters of Augustus Baldwin Longstreet's story, "The Horse Swap." It is Ab's ambition to outswap the most redoubtable trader of them all, Pat Stamper. Outwitted by Stamper, Ab grows sour and resentful, eventually becoming the most despised of his class, a dangerous malcontent likely to express resentment by burning his landlord's barns. Ab is given no effective voice in the novel, but he is interpreted by another character, V. K. Ratliff, whom Faulkner develops as a reliable witness. Through Ratliff we see Ab at first as a conventional comic type derived from southwestern humor; but later Ab's sullen hatred of the landlords who "fur-

nish in six-bit dollars" (charge him 25 percent interest for supplies) is expressed in barn burning. He is given a fierce though
degraded pride that exacts revenge for humiliation even when he
precipitates the humiliating situation; in this Ab emerges from
the comic convention and becomes a character instead of a caricature.

Much less representative—more a symbol than a person—Ab's
son Flem bears the external signs of the nineteenth-century poor
white. He is short, like Ransy Sniffle, but squat rather than attenuated. He has a complexion reminiscent of the corpse-colored
clay-eaters of earlier times, but his nose is a tiny beak like that of
a bird of prey, and his eyes are the color of stagnant water. These
characteristics are chosen for symbolic rather than representational value. Like Simon Suggs, Flem Snopes is a trickster, but
if Suggs could cheat a backcountry church out of its collection
money, Flem Snopes could cheat the Devil himself. Ratliff illustrates this with a tall tale about Flem's pledging his soul, so small
that it fits into a matchbox, to the Devil. When Flem arrives in
Hell to redeem his soul, the Devil finds the matchbox empty, and
Flem takes over Hell. Thus his cunning becomes legendary, as if
he were a debased version of Davy Crockett.

One element of the poor-white type is missing from his character, however—the element that Erskine Caldwell exploited to the
fullest in *Tobacco Road*. Flem not only lacks the sexual appetite
of a Sut Lovingood or a Jeeter Lester; he is without passion of any
kind, unless it is avarice. Eventually (in another book) we learn
that he is impotent, thus fulfilling his symbolic role as the commercial spirit. Flem will own the farmer's land; in time he will
move from the hamlet to the town and own the bank; later he
will be murdered by his own kin. Loveless, sterile, and alone, he
arouses our compassion by his very lack of human qualities, but
he threatens us as the soulless incarnation of a commercial civilization.

Although one Snopes is an idiot who performs sodomy with a
cow while his cousin sells viewing rights to the yokels who watch
the act through holes in the barn wall, Faulkner does not commit
himself to unrelieved caricature. The idiot's love for the cow is

rendered in a long lyrical passage that makes the episode seem like a nature myth. Mink Snopes, another member of the ubiquitous clan, is a murderer who shoots from ambush, but it is possible to perceive him as if he were one of the proud mountaineers of regional legend who could no longer bear the insults of the gentry. Other poor whites in *The Hamlet* are presented with such understanding that it is not easy to recognize any stock attributes. Henry Armstid, one of the poorest whites in Frenchman's Bend, is thought by Ratliff to be typically lazy, but Armstid's neighbors say that he is merely unfortunate. When one of the Armstid mules dies, Henry and his wife have to plow their land working alternately in the harness with the other mule. In the novel such an anecdote explains the desperation with which Armstid spends the last of his wife's money (five dollars intended for children's shoes) for an untamable Texas horse put up for sale by Flem Snopes. The origin of this anecdote is Sut Lovingood's tale of his daddy's "acting horse," but Faulkner changes a grotesque comic situation into an act of necessity. His humor, always more thoughtful than that of the comic tradition, reveals the passionate need behind the absurdity or even the viciousness of behavior.

Of the major twentieth-century writers only Faulkner has given us insight into the behavior of the poor whites without relinquishing humor or explaining their nature simplistically in terms of economics; and Faulkner may well be the last major writer to make the poor white his subject, for the class has lost its historic identity. During World War II the sons and daughters of the poor whites were sent throughout the world, and when they returned they were able to obtain higher education at public expense. Most of them left the land for employment in the towns and cities, and many of them joined the professional classes. The marginal lands of the South were no longer operated under the sharecropping system but, with government assistance, were often planted with trees. The better land was farmed with machinery. The old opprobrious term, red-neck (so called because he worked his land under a burning sun) began to lose its bite with its broader application to almost anyone who spoke with a southern intonation and lived in the rural regions of the South. In the past few years the red-neck has even achieved a commercial success. His music, called "country" music, has been broadcast for nearly half a century from Nashville, Tennessee; and it has appealed to an ever-wider audience, first through radio broadcasts, then through television. The redneck's alleged fondness for pork, hominy grits, and turnip greens, and his preference for jeans over business suits and small trucks over cars are now elements of the "red-neck chic" that American newspapers claim is spreading in Washington under the Carter administration.

Here and there one may still find fictional descendents of the traditional poor white. Occasionally vicious red-necks who hate blacks and outlanders will be depicted in movies, sometimes in comic terms, more often as villains. In a contemporary comic strip entitled "Snuffy Smith," a lazy, illiterate mountaineer lives with his family in a cabin as dilapidated as those of William Byrd's lubbers. Snuffy, of course, is anachronistic. Like Byrd's eighteenth-century North Carolinians, he leaves all labor to his wife; and like the degenerate poor white trash of the nineteenth century he makes illegal whiskey and steals chickens from his neighbors.

Legends die slowly, and that of the degenerate poor white of the South has lingered long in the land; but out of this once despised social class has come a new democratic culture-hero. Born in a two-room shack in a small Mississippi town, he achieved sudden fame like Davy Crockett, but he carried a guitar instead of a long rifle. Gifted with an extraordinary voice, he sang songs that appealed to the masses. He translated poor white sexuality into symbolic gesture and tone, and he united the sensuous sorrow of Negro blues with the hypnotic rhythm of what is called rock and roll. When he died recently, some of his incredibly devoted followers spoke of him with the reverence that an ancient Greek might have felt for Dionysus. In the late Elvis Presley, the southern poor white achieved apotheosis. After Presley's virtual coronation, it is certain that the comic poor white of tradition will soon join the shanty Irishman, the Chinese laundryman, and the minstrel show Negro in the oblivion reserved for cruel humor that is directed at an unfortunate class of society.

LEWIS P. SIMPSON

William Faulkner
of
Yoknapatawpha

Like Thomas Hardy's Wessex, William Faulkner's Yoknapatawpha County originated in the imagination of a young writer reared in a provincial community. In both instances a youthful mind, endowed with literary genius, discovered that the small, remote world of his nativity embodied the major experience of modern Western civilization: the world historical differentiation of a novel society of history and science from a sacramental order of myth and tradition. In either case a youthful writer entered into the knowledge of this phenomenon through an unacademic but intense and sustained process of reading in varied literary and philosophical works; and in either case, during the struggles of his self-education, a youthful writer began to conceive of himself as a member of the cosmopolitan realm of poets and literary prophets that for five hundred years or more has sought to give moral and spiritual guidance to the long process of societal differentiation in Western civilization. Foreshadowed by Petrarch and Chaucer, clearly represented by Shakespeare and Cervantes, this realm has been perpetuated by myriad literary figures, great and small, to the present day—when it may be that the process of differentiation has become so attenuated that the vocation of the writer is failing for lack of an assumed rationale. But in the first half of the twentieth century the literary vocation was still a basic cultural assumption wherever appreciable reading and writing skills extended. A Faulkner in Lafayette County, Mississippi, or a Hardy in Dorsetshire, England—no less than a Thomas Mann, a James Joyce, or a T. S. Eliot, who were early associated with the great metropolitan centers of letters—defined his interest in literature (with more difficulty and less certainty of course than the metropolitan writer) in terms of the continuing mission of the Western writer. He thought of himself as being at once literary artist and "clerk," storyteller and prophetic voice in a vast historical transaction involving every aspect of past, present, and future.

Although the literary vocation had suffered a severe constriction in the American South during the years dominated by the slavery issue, and by the Southern War for Independence and its aftermath, a writer in the twentieth-century South stood in relation to such cosmopolitan figures of his own region as Thomas Jefferson (the poet-philosopher-prophet who wrote the Declaration of Independence), Edgar Allan Poe (who had a larger influence in Europe than in America), and Mark Twain (who walked on the world stage for at least half his career). In his own time he stood, or would come to stand, in relation to a panoply of writers associated with the sophisticated twentieth-century southern literary movement—including John Crowe Ransom, Allen Tate, Donald Davidson, Andrew Lytle, Robert Penn Warren, Katherine Anne Porter, and Eudora Welty. Indeed, by virtue of a civilized commitment to letters that was still taken for granted, the twentieth-century southern writer stood in a relation to all modern Western writers—writers, that is, from the time of Shakespeare on. He shared in the large body of writing, imaginative and critical, which for five centuries has recorded the drama of differentiation—the conquest of the older community by the modern order—and which in so doing has come to constitute a large, many-faceted secular myth, the literary myth of modern history. The modern writer participates in this myth both as its author and (in various guises of alienation from modernity) as actor in it. The literary myth of modern history is in an important sense a myth of the modern literary vocation. Faulkner's involvement in this myth as demonstrated by his efforts to express and define it in his early writings and by his complex realization of it in the creation and peopling of Yoknapatawpha County, Mississippi (a more audacious undertaking than Hardy's creation and peopling of Wessex), is the major aspect of his career.

The quality of Faulkner's initial experience of the drama of cultural differentiation in Western civilization may be deduced in part from what we know specifically about his voluminous reading. At the age of twelve or thirteen, for example, he evidently began a lifelong devotion to *Moby-Dick*, of all nineteenth-century American novels the largest and most complicated treatment of the disjunction of the sacramental world of medieval Christendom from the modern world. But the influence of Melville on the early Faulkner was less powerful than direct and comparatively simple visions of cultural transformation: those implicit, on the one hand, in A. E. Housman's ironic, Stoic pastoralism and, on the other, in Swinburne's lush, despairing farewell to the Greco-Roman gods. Young Faulkner was also strongly drawn to the earlier nineteenth-century poets, especially Shelley and Keats. Keats became a crucial influence on him, a permanent, shaping force, who helped Faulkner to understand his own imaginative capacity and his growing compulsion to literary expression by serving as a prime model not only of literary attainment but also of literary apprenticeship.

Remarkably like the aspiring Keats, Faulkner grasped the problem of the imagination in the time between boyhood and manhood. "The imagination of a boy is healthy, and the mature imagination of a man is healthy," Keats says in the Preface to "Endymion," his first long poem, "but there is a space of life between, in which the soul is in ferment, character undecided, the way of life uncertain, the ambition thick-sighted." Even as he lived and worked in it, Faulkner endeavored to comprehend the nature of the "space between." In fact, he cultivated its possibilities more assiduously and in more complicated ways than Keats, projecting into it a series of figures, or figurations, of the poet seeking his identity. All symbolic figurations of the young Faulkner himself, these included the image of the poet as dispossessed faun in *The Marble Faun*, sighing for "Things I know, yet cannot know, / 'Twixt sky above and earth below." More significantly, they included the oblique image of the poet presented in the remarkable twinned exemplars of modern sexual narcissism, Pierrot and Marietta, the chief characters in *Marionettes* (the early play by Faulkner only recently published). "I desire—What do I desire?" Marietta asks, and in his seduction of her the vain Pierrot echoes the same futile question. In both *The Marble Faun* and *Marionettes* the formal garden setting suggests that the poetic spirit has become confined in history or, more widely, that the literary imagination in general is imprisoned in a world in which all the mythic and traditionalist—the sacramental—attitudes toward human existence are becoming historicized. But in the figures of the poet represented by Pierrot and Marietta, Faulkner began to see in the historicizing of sexuality—in the differentiation and specialization of sex—a major symbol of modernity.

His preoccupation with this symbol and its bearing on the role of the poet (a preoccupation increased and enlarged by his reading of Freud, it would seem) is evident in various other poems written in the early years of his career and collected in 1933 in *A Green Bough*. A short poem entitled "Eros and After" in one typescript and "And After" in another (published as poem number XXVI in *A Green Bough*), depicts the withdrawal of Selene, Greek goddess of the moon, from the world.

> Still, and look down, look down:
> Thy curious withdrawn hand
> Unprobes, now spirit and sense unblend, undrown,
> Knit by a word and sundered by a tense
> Like this: Is: Was: and Not. Nor caught between
> Spent beaches and the annealed insatiate sea
> Dost myriad lie, cold and intact Selene,
> On secret strand or old disasterous lee
> Behind the fading mistral of the sense.

Whether this poem simply symbolizes sexual experience or is a symbolic deliberation upon the Cartesian crisis, its portrayal of the sundering of sense and spirit brings it within the ambience of the prevalent rendering of the modern psychic condition. In particular it focuses the tensions in Faulkner's imagination that proceeded from his recognition of the historicizing of time. These tensions include his awareness of the remorseless demarcation of *is* from *was*; of being-in-time from not-being—of the abyss of historical cessation that opens before the spirit in modernity. The tensions also include the impulse to restore the sense of cyclical wholeness—of mythic or cosmic time which the historicizing process so relentlessly destroys. Such tensions are ironically made more complex when they are brought into connection with another poem in *A Green Bough* (number XLII). This is a sonnet about the consequence of Eve's seduction by Satan.

> Beneath the apple tree Eve's tortured shape
> Glittered in the Snake's, her riven breast
> Sloped his coils and took the sun's escape
> To augur black her sin from east to west.
> In winter's night man may keep him warm
> Regretting olden sins he did omit;
> With fetiches the whip of blood to charm,
> Forgetting that with breath he's heir to it.
>
> But old gods fall away, the ancient Snake
> Is throned and crowned instead, and has for minion
> That golden apple which will never slake
> But ever feeds man's crumb of fire, when plover
> And swallow and shrill northing birds whip over
> Nazarene and Roman and Virginian.

Although the imagery of this poem is awkward, it conveys the concept of the absolute primacy of the Hebraic-Christian blood knowledge of man's beginning and continuity through original guilt. However it may be charmed by dreams of pagan license, the "whip of blood" quickens with the "northing birds." In the historical progression of empire and knowledge, usually depicted as an advance of order and enlightenment from east and west, the rule of the dark historicism of man's blood is a force that admits of no alleviation. The question of the discrimination between myth and history, the relation of *was* and *is* to *not* in the structure of human existence, is resolved in a bleak puritanical determinism.

The most direct vision of the situation of the poet in Faulkner's early writings occurs in a poem he entitled "Twilight" when he wrote it (poem number X in *A Green Bough*). Obviously written under the influence of Keats's "Ode to a Grecian Urn," a poem which always served Faulkner as an emblem of the vocation to art, "Twilight" is about a precociously self-conscious youth who, forced to strive "with earth for bread" in the day, upon the approach of night forgets "his father, Death" and "Derision, His mother" and yields himself to the "dream that hurt him."

> Nymphs and faun in this dusk might riot
> Beyond all oceaned Time's cold greenish bar
> To shrilling pipes, to cymbals' hissing
> Beneath a single icy star
>
> Where he, to his own compulsion
> —A terrific figure on an urn—
> Is caught between his two horizons,
> Forgetting that he cant return.

Although naïvely expressed, Faulkner's vision of the poet caught between his self-imagined horizons of myth and history reminds us that each major writer since the end of the sixteenth century has had to situate himself with reference to these two horizons. Writing his poems (and, it should be added, several prose sketches not discussed here) in the first half of the 1920s, Faulkner recapitulated in his own experience the often-repeated literary experience of the differentiation of the historical from the traditionalist-mythic, or sacramental, mode of consciousness.

The initial, or poetic, phase of his career cogently represents the literary myth of modern history: the story of the self trying through the power of the literary art to cope with its irresistible identification with history. But the young Faulkner's recapitulation of the drama of differentiation would not be completed until he took the path of Cervantes rather than the one of Shakespeare. Whereas the poets, like Shakespeare and Donne, conceived the most intense initial versions of an alienated self emerging out of a disappearing world of sacramental unity, novelists have verily been created by the loss of the unified society. Beginning with Cervantes, they have exhaustively explored each successive stage of the movement out of the old society into the new, projecting endless images of the historical self in quest of its meaning. Although Faulkner says that he gave up being a poet because he found that his basic proficiency in poetic techniques seemed too limited, the inner reason would seem to be his discovery that the myth he was living—the drama of self and history, the story of the Knight of the Pale Countenance in quest of his historical identity—im-

plied the shift from poet to novelist. The creation of Yoknapatawpha County, and of the Faulkner of Yoknapatawpha, had nothing
to do with Faulkner's fundamental motive in writing his novels.
Nor, for that matter, is the transformation of the Yocona River
country with its red clay hills and fertile bottomlands into Yoknapatawpha County to be construed as his basic novelistic subject.

In 1944, when Malcolm Cowley became engaged in editing *The
Portable Faulkner* and decided to represent the Yoknapatawpha
stories as comprising the legend of the South, Faulkner agreed
with the editorial concept but observed in a letter to Cowley:

> As regards any specific book, I'm trying primarily to tell a story, in the
> most effective way I can think of, the most moving, the most exhaus-
> tive. But I think even that is incidental to what I am trying to do, tak-
> ing my output (the course of it) as a whole. I am telling the same story
> over and over, which is myself and the world. Tom Wolfe was trying to
> say everything, get everything, the world plus 'I' or filtered through
> 'I' or the effort of 'I' to embrace the world in which he was born and
> walked a little while and then lay down again, into one volume. I am
> trying to go a step further. This I think accounts for what people call
> the obscurity, the involved formless 'style,' endless sentences. I'm try-
> ing to say it all in one sentence, between one Cap and one period. I'm
> still trying, to put it all, if possible, on one pinhead. I don't know how
> to do it. All I know to do is to keep on trying in a new way. I'm inclined
> to think that my material, the South, is not very important to me. I
> just happen to know it, and don't have time in one life to learn another
> one and write at the same time. Though the one I know is probably as
> good as another, life is a phenomenon but not a novelty, the same fran-
> tic steeplechase toward nothing everywhere and man stinks the same
> stink no matter where in time.

In his statement to Cowley, Faulkner essentially says that cen-
tering his work in the Yoknapatawpha stories as a collectivity
amounts to a reduction of his own view of it as a series of discrete
endeavors to render the story of the self as literary artist attempting
to confront and to order a desacralized world, in which everything
and everybody—every aspect of nature and of human existence as
apprehended by the human consciousness—have become historical. The telling of this story demands an art more strenuous than
that which Thomas Wolfe brought to it, an art of the word that
may appear to be formless but that is designed to seize human ex-

istence in history in the tight and irrevocable grasp of one long sentence. Although Faulkner's remarks to Cowley may be partly a spoof, they give us a less distorted view of his purpose as a novelist than the view that conforms his intention to the standard of Balzacian diversity and monumentality. Taken symbolically, Faulkner's compulsion, as he says in the same letter to Cowley, "to put all mankind's history in one sentence" accords with James Joyce's motive in *Ulysses*—that is to say, through the strength of art to make a novel which is an intricate metaphorical perception of the differentiation of the historical self from a mythic-traditionalist community.

Seeking a way to dramatize and explore the relation of self, history, and art in a society divested of the sacramental, Faulkner wrote his first novels, *Soldiers' Pay* and *Mosquitoes*, not, as he sometimes said, for fun but as serious, meditated attempts to grasp his subject. In the first novel Faulkner daringly uses a fictitious town in Georgia called Charleston as a quasi-wasteland setting. Donald Mahon, a wounded and comatose First World War aviator-faun, and Januarius Jones, a plumpish satyr at loose in the twentieth century, are among the characters who appear on the scene as symbols of alienation. In the second novel the scene of the wasteland, more appropriate if less imaginatively daring, is New Orleans. An ambitious effort to encompass the whole subject of artist, critic, and patron under the modern condition, *Mosquitoes*, like *Soldiers' Pay*, does not develop the drama of differentiation beyond a superficial symbolic level. The self's experience of historical existence fails of embodiment in any character, though Faulkner makes a half-convincing try in the case of Gordon, the sculptor.

The imperative need of a maturing literary artist for a way to embody the experience of the modern self brought Faulkner to the matter belonging to the land of his nativity. In a memoir of Sherwood Anderson published in 1953, Faulkner acknowledges his motive in pursuing the South as his material; but he does so in a typically curious and indirect manner, attributing to Anderson's influence what he himself indubitably perceived.

I learned . . . from   [Anderson] . . . that, to be a writer, one has first
got to be what he is, what he was born; that to be an American and a
writer, one does not necessarily have to pay lip-service to any conventional American image. . . . You had only to remember what you were.
'You have to have somewhere to start from: then you begin to learn,'
he told me. 'It dont matter where it was, just so you remember it and
aint ashamed of it. Because one place to start from is just as important
as any other. You're a country boy; all you know is that little patch up
there in Mississippi where you started from. But that's all right too.
It's America too; pull it out, as little and unknown as it is, and the
whole thing will collapse, like when you prize a brick out of a wall.'
    'Not a cemented, plastered wall,' I said.
    'Yes, but America aint cemented and plastered yet. They're still
building it. That's why a man with ink in his veins not only still can
but sometimes has still got to keep on moving around in it, keeping
moving around and listening and looking and learning. That's why ignorant unschooled fellows like you and me not only have a chance to
write, they must write. All America asks is to look at it and listen to it
and understand it if you can. Only the understanding aint important
either: the important thing is to believe in it even if you dont understand it, and then try to tell it, put it down. It wont ever be quite right,
but there is always next time; there's always more ink and paper, and
something else to try to understand and tell. And that one probably
wont be exactly right either, but there is a next time to that one, too.
Because tomorrow America is going to be something different, something more and new to watch and listen to and try to understand; and,
even if you cant understand, believe.'

Whatever basis it may have in fact, Faulkner's account of Anderson's sage advice to him is another one of his fables about his career. An ignorant American country boy who wants to be a writer
learns from a successful writer, also of country origin, that the
way to be a genuine literary artist is to keep on being an ignorant
American country boy. Faulkner is talking about how a relatively
sophisticated, highly gifted, widely read young writer, from an
educated and locally prominent family resident in the southern
university community of Oxford, Mississippi, realized that what
he knew as actuality—the life in the community of his rearing,
the life of his own family, his own life—embodied the subject he
had been pursuing. His comprehension of this subject was not, as
he had assumed in his first writings, to be derived from literary

records. He had already comprehended it in his inner consciousness of himself and the world. He was inside the drama of differentiation, both as participant and observer. Like Anderson, and no doubt partly because of his association with the author of *Winesburg, Ohio*, Faulkner intuited in the American microcosm of the Western society of history and science a profound intimacy between self and history. Like no other American writers save Poe, Mark Twain, and Wolfe, he intuited that this intimacy assumed its typical form—an internalization of history in the self—with a singular intensity in the microcosm of American culture, the South.

Flags in the Dust, the first of the Yoknapatawpha novels (published in abridged form as *Sartoris* in 1929 and published in the original form in 1973) essays a full-scale version of the matter of north Mississippi as the embodiment of the drama of differentiation. This novel postulates a South that is not and never was the traditionalist society presented in the standard literary image of the South. The southern society represented in *Flags in the Dust*, specifically that of the years right after World War I, is continuous with the society transplanted a hundred years earlier under frontier conditions from an older South. It is a society which, like that of the older South, has harbored an illusion of itself as a perpetuation under New World conditions of European traditionalism. As the novel makes plain, modern history would not tolerate such an illusion; the Civil War killed the South, leaving it to live its death in history—an experience of which World War I is an integral part. In this society, in which the self is not only isolated in history but in which history is isolated in the self, the connections among individuals give the impression of being assumed and formalistic, of being unspoken save in the public voice of the orator and storyteller. But these connections are in truth deeply personal, for each person in Faulkner's southern society experiences his existence as a story that must be told.

This compulsion is not autobiographical, or at any rate, not confessional. It is a historical, or biographical, imperative. Faulkner once described its influence on the novelist—by clear implication on his own method as a novelist—as follows: "But then, every time any character gets into a book, no matter how minor, he's actually telling his own biography—that's all anyone ever does, he tells his own biography, talking about himself, in a thousand different terms, but himself." This comment was a reply to a question about Quentin Compson, but Quentin is no more than the richest distillation of Faulkner's method of novelistic development. He attempted this method in his first two novels; but he could not come into possession of it until he yielded his imagination to the image of self and history implicit in his north Mississippi homeland.

Flags in the Dust begins with a scene in which old man Falls, for the millionth time perhaps, is telling a story about Colonel John Sartoris and the Civil War to old Bayard Sartoris. As the novel progresses it becomes apparent that this kind of biographical garrulity is deceptive. The South revealed in the characters in *Flags in the Dust* is not an open but a deeply introverted culture. Hidden under a masking flow of words is a world enclosed in a long series of illusions about self and history that extend back into the illusions of the South's European forebears. Faulkner never more successfully emblematized what may be called the biographical mode of southern culture than in the scene in *Flags in the Dust* when old Bayard goes to the secluded upper room of the Sartoris home, opens the chest of family memorials, and contemplating the faded list of Sartoris names in the back of the brass-bound Bible thinks about the list as a gesture made in the name of destiny. He thinks, too, about the illusion of destiny and the ultimate illusion of the heaven that is claimed as part of man's destiny: "heaven, filled with every man's illusion of himself and with the conflicting illusions of him that parade through the minds of other illusions."

Feeling his way into the self-contained and reclusive world of the Sartorises—a world dominated by the past tense, by the fatality of *was*—Faulkner uncovered in the southern embodiment of modern history the same motive he had sought to explore in *Soldiers' Pay* and *Mosquitoes*, the deep narcissism of the modern self. Thus in *Flags in the Dust* he wrote a novel he valued not as the inauguration of a saga of the South but, in his judgment, as a more successful attainment of what he had tried to do in the earlier works. These were, he said strangely, the "foals" of *Flags in the Dust*. He had paradoxically created the immature offspring before he brought into visible existence the mare that had given them birth, a novel in which the characters are no longer symbols of history but its flesh and blood creatures, complex human beings who interiorize history in the passions of human nature. *Flags in the Dust*, Faulkner declared to his publisher Horace Liveright, "is the damndest best book you'll look at this year, and any other publisher." But the publisher did not think so. Failing to understand Faulkner's intention to create a drama based on the biographical structure of history, he turned the novel down with the suggestion that it was so lacking in plot and character development that it was unpublishable.

In spite of his disappointment in the rejection of *Flags in the Dust*, Faulkner plunged more deeply into the matter of the South. Having got hold of it, he had found, in a powerful and almost inextricable combination, not only a novelistic method but the experiential center of history in the modern literary consciousness: the one in the biographical mode of southern culture, the other in the internalization of history in the southern self. Now his struggle to encapsulate the self and the world (implicit in the self-consciousness of history he had been seeking to express since he conceived the poems in *The Marble Faun*) came into its most intense phase. Within a period of about seven years Faulkner wrote the five greatest Yoknapatawpha novels: *The Sound and the Fury, As I Lay Dying, Sanctuary, Light in August*, and *Absalom, Absalom!* Each of these works is distinctly marked by its character as an autonomous experiment in novelistic composition, yet each finds its focus and movement in characters who, directly or indirectly, tell their own biographies. In each novel, it is to be noted, there is one character who serves to some degree as a surrogate of the authorial figure: Quentin Compson in *The Sound and the Fury* and *Absalom, Absalom!*, Darl Bundren in *As I Lay Dying*, Horace Benbow in *Sanctuary*, and Gail Hightower in *Light in August*. Both as participant in and observer of the biographical movement of a given novel, the surrogate serves not so much as a voice of the author but as eyes through which he looks at the inside of his story. Then, too, he serves to suggest that there is an authorial self, a literary artist, a controlling authorial presence in the story. This presence may be as explicit as that of Quentin in *The Sound and the Fury* and *Absalom, Absalom!*; or it may be as tenuous as that of Darl in *As I Lay Dying*. Yet it is there, an assertion that a self-conscious, poetic, historical, perhaps prophetic imagination is intrinsically existent in Yoknapatawpha County.

Yoknapatawpha is no more an unself-conscious traditionalist culture than is the culture of the Old Testament. Pursuing meaning in human history through the biographical mode, Faulkner was, to be sure, adhering to a major source of the post-Civil War culture, the biblical sense of history, especially as this is expressed in what Erich Auerbach in *Mimesis* terms the "biographical element" of the Old Testament. Unlike the heroic or epical mode, Auerbach observes, the Old Testament charges the lives it records with "historical intensity." Even when a life is no more than a fragmentary legend, even when a life is plainly a composite of different legends, it becomes historically credible in the context of other biblical stories. As Auerbach says:

> The claim of the Old Testament stories to represent universal history, their insistent relation—a relation constantly redefined by conflicts—to a single and hidden God, who yet shows himself and who guides universal history by promise and exaction, gives these stories an entirely different perspective from any the Homeric poems can possess. As a composition, the Old Testament is incomparably less unified than the Homeric poems, it is more obviously pieced together —but the various components all belong to the one concept of universal history and its interpretation. . . . The greater the separateness and horizontal disconnection of the stories and groups of stories in relation to one another, compared with the *Iliad* and *Odyssey*, the stronger is their general vertical connection, which holds them all together and which is entirely lacking in Homer. Each of the great figures of the Old Testament, from Adam to the prophets, embodies a moment of this vertical connection.

In the composition of each of the five Yoknapatawpha novels after *Flags in the Dust*, Faulkner's commitment to an autonomous thematic and artistic endeavor was in a strong tension with the sense of a larger endeavor that was beginning to take on a compulsive aspect in his imagination—a many-dimensioned story about all kinds and conditions of Yoknapatawpha inhabitants, red, white, and black, through the several generations, from the time of the antebellum South's expansion into the north Mississippi wilderness to the present. Faulkner became quite aware of the deepening interrelation of the Yoknapatawpha novels; as early as 1933 he thought of making a Golden Book of Yoknapatawpha, in which he would record the genealogies of his characters. But he had no impulse during the period of their origination (which was also the period of Faulkner's triumph as a literary artist) to conform the Yoknapatawpha tales to a chronological scheme, not even to the simple narrative pattern of legend. Imprecisely yet assuredly Faulkner's historical sensibility imposed on the evolving Yoknapatawpha saga a structure resembling the vertical structure of the Old Testament. Just as the biblical characters respond to the will of the hidden God, the Yoknapatawpha people respond to the artist's will to make history yield its meaning in the intensity of their lives. In their inward images of themselves as historical beings, in the historical images other characters make of them, and those the author himself may make of them, they become representative moments in the vertical connection of the great Yoknapatawpha novels.

The climactic moment is embodied in the character of Quentin Compson in *Absalom, Absalom!*, where the biographical mode is brought into full play as Miss Rosa Coldfield, Mr. Compson, and Quentin tell the biography of Thomas Sutpen, and in the telling reveal their own biographies. As the talking proceeds, wandering around and around, it discloses with the force of fate the burden of Yoknapatawpha's history: the introverted illusion of itself as a representation of the old, familial, corporate, sacramental community. The truth that is Sutpen comes out: the origins of Yoknapatawpha (and of the South) lie in the ruthless drive of the modern historical ego, which, unleashed from all societal bonds, has founded a modern slave society in a wilderness; and yet in its isolation must seek to emulate not the substance but the appearance of the old community. Witnessing the incredible struggle of Quentin to assume the whole burden of the South's tangled psychic history, Shreve McCannon, the Canadian interrogator and commentator, exclaims, "The South . . . .Jesus. No wonder you folks all outlive yourselves by years and years and years." And Quentin says, "I am older at twenty than a lot of people who have died."

Although *Absalom, Absalom!* is the closest Faulkner would come to getting history, figuratively speaking, onto a pinhead, his will to comprehend its intricate complexities in the modern age dictated his motive and method in each Yoknapatawpha novel through *Go Down, Moses* (1942). But the historical emphasis is altered and diminished in the later Yoknapatawpha works. Auerbach, in connection with his remarks on the Old Testament structure quoted above, also observes that the Hebraic "classification and interpretation of human history is so passionately apprehended" that it "eventually shatters the framework of historical composition and completely overruns it with prophecy." An analogous phenomenon influenced the course of the Yoknapatawpha saga. Not long after *Go Down, Moses* appeared in the year in which America actively entered the Second World War, Faulkner became fascinated with a legend about the identity of the French Unknown Soldier of the First World War. His interest resulted in ten years of labor on *A Fable*, a work he often called his "big book." When he finished *A Fable* in 1954, Faulkner believed it to be the one work that unqualifiedly confirmed his genius. Although not many of his critics have supported the author's high opinion of it and have ranked it as inferior to most of the Yoknapatawpha novels, *A Fable* is the logical outgrowth of Faulkner's fervent examination of the drama of differentiation in the Yoknapatawpha stories. In its own way a study of history, a philosophy or humanistic theology of history, this singular book is primarily a work of prophecy. Its message is the triumph of mankind over the modern historical society—with its destructive divisions into self-interpreted nation-states—through the eventual acceptance, not of the Son of God, but of the Son of Man. *A Fable* proclaims the triumph over history of a humanistic myth of man. The hero of this myth transcends the consequence of the differentiation of the historical from the sacramental order, the closure of history in the narcissistic modern society, the kind of society so graphically represented in the Yoknapatawphan image of the South.

Yet withal, *A Fable* is a dark book. To redeem history from its descent into the self, Faulkner identifies the Unknown Soldier with a Christ who as the Son of Man is the son of Satan, the fallen angel, who in his passions is the symbol of man. Unable to control the endless ramifications of his portentous identification, Faulkner ends up with a passionate but unconvincing assertion of man's capacity to transcend his historical condition, and, by paradoxical implication, with a passionate and convincing assertion that he never will. The reason for this passionate irresolution in *A Fable* can hardly be stated simply, but in summation it amounts to the fact that the Old General (Satan) tells his biography with an eloquence and conviction that submerges the biography of his son, the Corporal (the Christ figure).

Faulkner's struggle to give desacralized history a transcendent spiritual quality in *A Fable* demarcates a line between the Yoknapatawpha novels through *Go Down, Moses* and the ones that follow. We may appropriately speak of a first and second cycle of Yoknapatawpha tales. The second begins in 1948 with the publication of *Intruder in the Dust* and includes *Requiem for a Nun, The Town, The Mansion* (the latter being the second and third volumes of the Snopes trilogy), and *The Reivers: A Reminiscence*.

This is by no means to suggest that the second cycle of Yoknapatawpha stories may be distinguished from the first by an inclination to prophetic frenzy in the second. Faulkner's large-scale and prolonged adventure in prophecy during the writing of *A Fable* did not overwhelm the Yoknapatawpha saga. It simply quietly shattered Faulkner's sense of its temporal structure. In the novels of the second cycle the assignment of the South to the condition of a world living its death in history—a world composed, as Charles Bon said, of those "doomed to live"—is significantly modified. There is an assimilation of *was* to *is*. When Chick Mallison in *Intruder in the Dust* thinks "yesterday today and tomorrow are Is: Indivisible" and recalls Gavin Stevens' celebration of the great existent moment in the mind of every fourteen-year-old southern boy—the living instant right before the Battle of Gettysburg began ("Its all *now* you see. Yesterday wont be over until tomorrow and tomorrow began ten thousand years ago")—he speaks for the Faulkner of the second cycle. This is the Faulkner who explained to the University of Virginia students in 1957 that he subscribed to the "mystical belief that there is no such thing as *was* . . . no such thing as *will be*. That time is not a fixed condition, time is in a way the sum of the combined intelligences of all men who breathe at the moment."

Faulkner talked too about the philosophy of his long sentences: "There is no such thing really as was because the past is. It is a part of every man, every woman, and every moment. . . . And so . . . a character in a story at any moment of action is not just himself as he is then, he is all that made him, and the long sentence is an attempt to get his past and possibly his future into the instant in which he does something." Regarded as the expression of a mutant moment in history conceived as *is*, the long sentence no longer bears the burden (as it did in the earlier Faulkner's imagination) of serving as an integral symbolic recapitulation of man's history conceived as a sundering of the tenses. Abolishing the fatality of *was*, Faulkner abolishes the differentiation of the historical self and the narcissism of history, thereby abolishing the grievous burden of the alienation of the self from the world, and so leaving his imagination free to conceive of Yoknapatawpha as the embodied design of *is*—as a microcosm of the universal, a fictional yet a timeless structure of reality created by the literary artist.

Several times the later Faulkner affirms the *is* with a sense of exaltation, nowhere more so than in the well-known interview with Jean Stein Vanden Heuvel in 1956:

> Beginning with *Sartoris* I discovered that my own little postage stamp of native soil was worth writing about and that I would never live long enough to exhaust it, and that by sublimating the actual into the apocryphal I would have complete liberty to use whatever talent I might have to its absolute top. It opened up a gold mine of other people, so I created a cosmos of my own. I can move these people around like God, not only in space but in time too. The fact that I have moved my characters around in time successfully, at least in my own estimation, proves to me my own theory that time is a fluid condition which has

no existence except in the momentary avatars of individual people. There is no such thing as *was*—only *is*. If *was* existed, there would be no grief or sorrow. I like to think of the world I created as being a kind of keystone in the universe; that, small as that keystone is, if it were ever taken away the universe itself would collapse. My last book will be the Doomsday Book, the Golden Book, of Yoknapatawpha County. Then I shall break the pencil and I'll have to stop.

Yet implied in Faulkner's serene, retrospective vision of Yoknapatawpha as a transcendent autonomy of the artist is all the pathos of the literary myth of modern history—of the drama of the artist and the historical differentiation of the self. The vision reveals what it denies: the unremitting tension between self and history. Yoknapatawpha is in truth no sublimation of the actual but the embodiment of the profoundest reality: the terrifying modern internalization of history—which in its ineffable and pervasive dominion comprises man and nature, God, world, and universe—in the self. Faulkner hid the truth of Yoknapatawpha from himself at times, particularly in his later career. But he acknowledged it all the same—in the term that he used to describe Yoknapatawpha: "my apocryphal county." Sometimes he called the Yoknapatawpha stories "my apocrypha." He meant more than "my fictions." He meant my stories in which there are "hidden things," and notable among the things he hid in the tales is the story of the artist and his struggle against modern history. In this struggle Faulkner followed the defiant Joycean dream of sacramentalizing the role of the artist by means of grace self-bestowed. But Faulkner knew, perhaps more surely than Joyce knew, that dreaming his biography was only a part of his being as a creature of history. He understood this irony as an American, and especially as a southerner. He grasped it so well that in his final novel, *The Reivers*, subtitled *A Reminiscence*, though trying not to do so, he virtually surrenders to the pathos of history: creating a Yoknapatawpha existing neither in the *was* of Quentin Compson nor in the *is* of Gavin Stevens but in a mingled *is-was* that, transcending all tense, is yet the truest tense for Americans, the tense of nostalgia—the tense Americans use when they speak of America as "home sweet home," the place beyond all grief and sorrow.

WALTER SULLIVAN

The Fading Memory
of the
Civil War

One thing is certain: the American Civil War did more than any other event to shape the consciousness of the South. To repeat what has already been said many times, the South that produced the southern literary renascence was a peculiar section of the United States that gloried in its own peculiarity and clung to its sectional identity. Southern society at the time of the renascence was homogeneous, agrarian, religious, and inclined to see life and history in terms of images rather than according to theory and abstraction. For those who had experienced it and for those who heard the stories firsthand from those who had lived through it, the Civil War was the most concrete of all images of what one meant when he claimed to be a southerner. For one thing, the war was a flat contradiction of the American mythology of continuing national success. The United States had won the conflict, but the South had lost; the United States had known prosperity, but the South had suffered economic oppression during and after the Reconstruction; the United States, except for rare instances, had read about the war in newspapers, but the South had been the battlefield and had endured the accompanying desolation. In short, the South had had the agony. But the South had gained a myth.

From a literary point of view, the myth in its first delineations was too simple. It was a myth of the past, and southern society at large supported itself through difficult times by cherishing the memory of southern heroism and Yankee injustice and the dream of what might have been if the South had prevailed. Southern intellectuals and artists were divided between those such as John Esten Cooke and Thomas Nelson Page who defended the Old South as the most perfect of all civilizations and those such as Henry Grady and Walter Hines Page who called for a new political and social structure built on values contrary to those that informed the commonly held southern legend of the past. Both points of view were simplistic, both denied the essential complexity of history and of the human condition. As a result, southern literature of the late nineteenth and early twentieth centuries was generally inferior to that of the renascence. After World War I, the two disparate strains of southern culture—on one hand, a legend of the past fraught with a sense of form and honor and courage; on the other, the harsh lot of the black man under slavery and subsequent discrimination—combined in the minds of southern artists to create the familiar, and to the writer indispensable, "argument with oneself."

Look, for example, at the work of William Faulkner. Although he wrote only one novel that is devoted entirely to the Civil War and its aftermath—*The Unvanquished*—the conflict, both immediate and remembered, is an essential part of the public and private dimensions of his fiction: it shapes the enveloping action; it lingers in the air that the characters breathe. The McCaslin twins, seen in *Go Down, Moses* and elsewhere in the Faulkner canon, are firm opponents of slavery; but though they are past sixty at the beginning of hostilities, they compete to determine which of them will be allowed to join the fight. Thomas Sutpen in *Absalom, Absalom!* sees his ambition thwarted and his life destroyed by the racial aspect of the typically southern dream he pursues. Even in his later works, when he was most deeply conscious of the moral discrepancies at the foundations of southern culture, Faulkner continued to struggle for a reconciliation of the flawed present with the idealized past. Chick Mallison in *Intruder in the Dust* remains deeply conscious of every southern boy's heritage—the right not only to remember the war, but to believe that somehow the past can be recaptured, that the fatal charge has not yet been made at Gettysburg, that the South can be saved. But even as the past encroaches on his consciousness, he works to preserve the life of an arrogant, but innocent, Negro man.

In his only novel and in one of his most famous poems, Allen Tate takes the Civil War for his theme. Both *The Fathers* and "Ode to the Confederate Dead" balance the purposelessness and absurdity of modern civilization against the ordered though tainted society of the antebellum South. George Posey of *The Fathers* is the incarnation of twentieth-century barbarism and efficiency against whom the forces of tradition, represented by Major Buchan, cannot stand. The tension developed by these opposing forces is joined in Lacy Buchan, who loves and admires both his father and Posey, his brother-in-law. At the end of the novel, with the guns of the Battle of First Manassas sounding in his ears, Lacy determines that he will follow Posey, but in actual fact the decision had been made for him—he has no choice. The burning of his ancestral home by a party of Union soldiers symbolizes the destruction of a South that cannot rise again. Lacy must move into the modern world, but a part of him will be forever looking backward.

So it is with the voice that speaks to us in "Ode to the Confederate Dead." The time of the poem is much later than that of the novel. The gravestones of the Confederate soldiers are chipped and weathered, and the modern man who stands in the cemetery pondering human mortality and his own spiritual ineffectualness knows the Old South and the courage of its soldiers only as a rumor, but a rumor that approaches the force of memory: he accepts the heroism of the Confederacy as an article of faith. But he knows too that his own sense of moral uncertainty results, in part at least, from the ambiguities of his past. Being, like Lacy Buchan, caught between the old and the new, he discerns that his despair is not only a gift of the modern world: it is a part of his birthright, a vestige of the past that he reveres.

One of the most interesting of all Civil War novels, and one that deserves a wider audience than it has yet gained, is Andrew Lytle's *The Long Night*. Nothing could be more typically southern than Lytle's basic theme of revenge. In Alabama, before the Civil War, Pleasant McIvor sets out to avenge his father's death at the hands of a criminal syndicate. He will kill everyone even remotely involved with his father's murder and in doing so, he will not only restore the family honor; he will rid the community of a band of criminals and therefore serve society as well. But when the war comes, public and private duty cease to coincide. By continuing to pursue his own personal vendetta, Pleasant transgresses his responsibilities as a soldier and brings about the death of innocent men. Thus the war, which is the beginning of a new social and political dispensation, renders inoperative the old system under which Pleasant formerly lived. Again, the tension between old and new meet in the main character of the novel.

Robert Penn Warren, Stark Young, Caroline Gordon, and Donald Davidson wrote works that are based directly on the war, all of which probe the conflict between past and present and the rich tensions that result when the old comes into conflict with the new. Even those writers who have not made much direct use of the war in their work—Thomas Wolfe and Katherine Anne Porter, for example—still retain a consciousness of southern uniqueness that came out of defeat and the knowledge that a new world with new values had been imposed upon the old. The war and its ramifications are a part of the background and ambience of their writing.

And of course, there is *Gone With the Wind*. Margaret Mitchell was not a finished novelist. The author of a single book, and it imperfectly written, she nonetheless made available to the world at large some of the themes that inhere in southern history. Regaled by her grandmother with stories of before and after, taken when she was young to visit impoverished old ladies who as girls had lived in indolent luxury, she saw with her own eyes what a division in southern life the war had wrought. So when she came to write her book, her material was at hand, and within the limits of her restricted abilities, she did her job well.

Her characters are stereotypes, but as such, they represent in a general way the people who composed southern society both before and after the war. There are landed aristocrats and poor whites, belles and beaux and dashing buccaneers, slaves faithful and otherwise, and after the war, carpetbaggers, opportunists, prostitutes. Miss Mitchell exaggerates and romanticizes the South in the same way—though much less skillfully—that Dickens exaggerates and romanticizes London. But such distortion is the nature of art. Most people, of whatever place or time, are drab figures who plod their ways through the workaday world. The good writer finds those who are most interesting and thrusts them forward to stand for the rest. Miss Mitchell's portrayal of the South is not inaccurate, and her sense of the social milieu both before and after the war is perceptive and complete. What her book lacks, other than a high degree of literary skill, is the modern sensibility—an apprehension on the part of author and characters of the significance of that moment in history when the Old and the New South stood poised side by side.

Lost causes lend themselves to romantic revision. Once they are rendered harmless by defeat, enemies are humanized in the eyes of the victors. We are more likely to remember that they fought well than that the interests for which they fought were opposed to ours. Those who lose, like the dead, are freed of all responsibility. The winners have the real world to deal with, which being the real world, filled with complicated problems, is likely to prove recalcitrant. The North won the Civil War; the Union was preserved; the Negro was granted *de jure* freedom. The victors, weary of the whole procedure, rested on their laurels for half a century while southerners, absolved by their defeat from having any influence over the course of politics and history, created a literary renascence that lasted at least until World War II. With that upheaval and the events that followed, the South was swept into the mainstream of history, and for southern writers, as well as for southerners in general, the memory of the Civil War began to fade.

First of all, the passage of time blurs the recollection. But there are at least two other reasons that the war began to diminish in importance for the southern mind. Among the developed populations of the West—and here the South found itself, like it or not —there was a decline in the spirit of nationalism. Patriotic fervor was distrusted, the ambitions of empire were repudiated, the loyalties, particularly those of intellectuals and artists, were claimed by ideologies, rather than by geography or memories of a heroic past. It was no longer every southern boy's heritage to be a part of the continuing attack up Cemetery Ridge. The events of the war, which would necessarily have been less clear in the thoughts of each passing generation, were hastened to rest by a new orientation that denigrated national causes. And the Civil War was a fight for southern independence, an effort to set up a separate Confederate state.

Of even more consequence was the struggle for racial justice in the South that began not long after the surrender of Japan in 1945. Bus boycotts, lunch counter sit-ins, marches, and demonstrations directed at every manifestation of racial discrimination were met in some quarters by an appeal to confederate tradition that many southerners—including a number who were not sympathetic to the aims of black people—could not abide. Yet, tawdry as they were in many instances, the appeals that intransigent whites made to the values of the Old South were essentially correct. Certainly, the Civil War was fought for a number of complex reasons, some of them social, some political, some economic. But at the heart of the disagreement between North and South was the question of slavery. It was not only the immediate cause of the war: it was the *sine qua non*. Consequently, seen in the context of the civil rights movement, the war took on meanings and delineations it had not theretofore assumed.

When Robert Penn Warren, whose early work had been in the traditional southern mold, came to deal directly with the Civil War in 1955, his cast of characters was vastly different from those of Tate or Lytle or Faulkner or Margaret Mitchell. His heroine is a girl of mixed blood, sold into slavery at the death of her father. Her first benefactor and later her lover is a retired slave trader, who comes to her bed during the successful Union attack on New Orleans. Other actors in Warren's narrative are a Yankee captain, abolitionist son of a northern industrialist, whom Amantha marries, and an escaped slave who has become an officer in the Union army. Warren's portrayal of the South in *Band of Angels* is hardly less romantic than those of John Esten Cooke and Walter Hines Page, who celebrated and glorified the Old South as the best of all possible cultures. The *donné* of Warren's novel is difficult to accept: that the girl should have been sold into slavery while her neighbors looked on strains our credulity. That having been sold, she could have remained unharmed until she found herself safely

in the custody of Hamish Bond seems even less likely. Scarlett
O'Hara and Rhett Butler, farfetched as they may seem to modern
readers, are more typical of the Old South than any of the people
that Warren shows us in *Band of Angels*.

Or take another example. William Styron's *The Confessions of
Nat Turner* is not strictly speaking a treatment of the Civil War,
but it deals directly with the antebellum South and with the question of slavery, which, as I have said, was both an underlying and
immediate cause of the war. The success of *Nat Turner* as a work
of art continues to be debated, but that need not concern us here.
What is important is that the hero and only really major character
in the novel is a black slave. This represents an enormous departure from the approach that was taken to the South and the war
by the writers of the 1930s. All art distorts, and no one can say
with finality which distortion leads us closest to the truth. But in
reading Styron's book, one misses the sense of a fully portrayed
culture. It is true that the slaves and later the free blacks are given
short shrift in many novels about the South. But at his best, Faulkner presents what appears to be a complete recapitulation of southern society—its strata, the relationships of the people, the perfidy
and strength, the meanness and generosity of those involved.

In Warren's novel, Amantha Starr, herself a victim of racial prejudice, follows and supports her husband in his struggle to gain
justice for the black man. Forced by her mixed blood to face the
question of her own identity, she cannot discover who she is until
she has fathomed the mystery of our common humanity, regardless of belief or background or color of skin. Styron's Nat Turner
embarks on his own quest for self when he inaugurates a slave revolt by killing the master who has treated him with relative kindness. I do not wish to denigrate these novels or to minimize the
importance of the themes they seek to explore. A writer of the
present age who chooses to eschew the existential agony or to
feign ignorance of the race question will separate himself from
the major impulses of his own time and risk thereby grave impov-
erishment of his art. But to impose these same concerns on the
customs and history of another era is to commit a dangerous sort
of anachronism. The resulting artistic and historical distortion

may not so much move us toward the truth as shield us from it.

In the 1920s and 1930s, the most productive years of the southern renascence, Faulkner and Tate and Lytle and Margaret Mitchell were obsessed by a culture whose fruits they had known. Conscious of the changes that passing time had effected, they looked backward to tell the truth, to describe with as much accuracy as possible a civilization they had observed. But it is important to remember that in America—and particularly in the South —even those who felt the encroachments of the modern period most keenly persisted in a kind of innocence of what modernism was composed of and what it would mean. The southern writers of the thirties felt the change viscerally, but the philosophy, the intellectual codification was yet to come. During this time, it is true, Tate, Warren, and others were writing essays; those by Tate were particularly prophetic; but no one could yet see the exact structure of the future. Concern, rather, was with protecting and analyzing what was considered good in the past.

To what extent, then, can southern writers of the present and the future make use of the Civil War? My own speculation is that though the war will continue to engage the attention of historians, both professional and amateur, it will be less and less frequently used as a subject for poetry and fiction. The rush of modern history takes the present-day author farther and farther away from the events of more than a hundred years ago. With each war, each government scandal, each social crisis, we are taken more fully into a modern orientation and the memory of the war recedes. Yet, the basic issues over which the Civil War was fought are with us still and the questions that the war raised remain unanswered.

Chief among those issues and questions is that of race relations and the struggle for racial justice that continues to this day and constitutes a not entirely bloodless second civil war. Contemporary southern writers realize this, and just as in the 1920s and 1930s every southern author dealt sooner or later with the struggle of the 1860s, now southern writers of every degree of competence seek their plots and themes in the continuing quest for total racial justice. As one would expect, novels based on the race question vary enormously in seriousness of intention and competence of execution. On one hand, there are such gifted artists as Carson McCullers, Shirley Ann Grau, Elizabeth Spencer, and, as I have mentioned, Styron and Warren; on the other, there are those such as Harper Lee, Jesse Hill Ford, and Lillian Smith whose shallow efforts appear for a time on best-seller lists and then sink into oblivion. But in almost every case, literature that is based on the contemporary struggle for racial justice is not as good as it should be.

The failure is not the fault of the material. It seems obvious to me that the stuff of many good novels and many fine poems abides in the social and political experience of the South during the past thirty years. This material has not yet been put to the proper use because southern novelists and poets remain too close to the historical events and too deeply committed to the cause of social progress. Which is to say, the novels and poems remain polemical: the argument with self has not begun. We know that the struggles of the 1850s and 1860s were fraught with drama and they were conducted by people of all sorts, the good and the bad, the honest and the dishonest on both sides. And though it will be considered heresy for me to say so, some element of fundamental right attended the efforts of all who were and are involved in the agonies that move us now toward social change. Until we reassert in our literature these truths that are inherent in the human condition, we will remain in the situation of those writers who immediately following the Civil War glorified the Old South as it had never been and as nothing ever could be. Time and experience cured their romanticism and perhaps it will cure ours. Our past experience gives us reason to hope.

C. HUGH HOLMAN

The Southern Provincial
in
Metropolis

One of the most common American experiences in the nineteenth and twentieth centuries has been the movement of young men of ambition and intelligence from the remote, simple, and unsophisticated places of their birth and childhood to great centers of culture, art, industry, and intellect. Such centers have been, as Theodore Dreiser once called Chicago, magnets attracting with almost irresistible force the young and ambitious who come within their orbit. New York, Boston, Philadelphia, Chicago, Los Angeles—these cities have been powerfully attractive for the eager and hopeful. Such a movement has naturally been the subject of fiction, particularly when it has an autobiographical element.

To describe this movement is to follow a tradition that has been strong in French, English, and American writing, and one that Lionel Trilling called the story of the Young Man from the Provinces. It is the story of Julien Sorel, which Stendhal tells in *The Red and the Black*. It is the story of Eugène Rastignac, which Balzac tells in *Père Goriot* and other of his novels in *La comédie humaine*, and the story of Lucien Chardon, which he tells in his trilogy *Lost Illusions*. It is the story of Pip, which Dickens tells in *Great Expectations*. It is the story that Gustave Flaubert tells in *Sentimental Education*. It is the story of Jay Gatsby, which Scott Fitzgerald tells in *The Great Gatsby*, and it is, with certain changes that Mr. Trilling notes, the story of Hyacinth Robinson, which Henry James tells in *The Princess Casamassima*.

This Young Man from the Provinces, born and raised in simple, often rural settings, is a person of intelligence, sensitivity, high

hopes, and strong ambition, but he lacks a knowledge of the ways
of the world. He approaches life with directness, simplicity, and
pride, and he makes great demands upon life. He is overwhelmed
with wonder at its greatness and its complexities, and he sets out
to seek his fortune by moving toward a metropolis. Once there he
usually moves from a very obscure and poverty-stricken position
to a position of some importance. In the city he is confronted with
situations that he does not understand but which seem to have
for him dark meanings. He wants to know how the world is run,
to understand the sources of its power, to comprehend the mecha-
nisms of its society, to be at home among its social rituals. Usually he meets a person or persons who have positions of power
in this society and who lift him out of his obscurity and set him
down in places of some importance. In the city he will realize his
fate, whether it be grim like that of Julien Sorel or Jay Gatsby, or
whether it be glorious like that of Pip. Such a form seems to be
naturally suited to the frequent American experience.

The southerner, whatever his other disjunctions with the national experience, has differed from the rest of the nation in feeling this necessary attraction only in intensity; yet he has been the
provincial approaching the large city in a special and different
way from the midwesterner or the up-state New Yorker. In a sense
New York, Boston, Chicago, San Francisco, and Los Angeles are
the cultural and spiritual capitals of the regions from which most
of the American provincials have come, but these cities have until very recently by no means been spiritual capitals for the southerner. The South has been until the last few decades primarily an
agricultural region of communities rather than of cities. Though
it has had small cities that were commercial, transportation, and
shipping centers—Richmond, Baltimore, Charleston, New Orleans, and Atlanta, where the railroads began to cross in the middle
of the nineteenth century—these centers have been, in a sense,
the doorways to an outer world. It can be said with a reasonable
degree of accuracy that the South had within its borders no cultural and intellectual capitals of the sort that London was for Englishmen, Paris for the French, Berlin for the Germans, or Boston
for the New Englanders. When the southerner has gone to the

metropolis, when he has felt the strong pull of the cultural and intellectual forces concentrated in a great city, it has been to what was in many respects to him a foreign land. This fact has had a very important effect upon southern writers.

William Gilmore Simms, the most prolific and most representative of antebellum southern men of letters, had to find in New York and Philadelphia the cultural home for his work, and the pattern of his life became established so that he spent the time from October to May at his plantation seventy miles inland from Charleston and then spent the summer months in New York making contracts for the publication of his work, reading proofs, seeing books through the press, attending concerts and plays, being for a while virtually a member of the Knickerbocker group of writers and storing up a special kind of stimulus to see him through the months when he went back home. Yet he remained quintessentially a southerner, and though the issue that sharpened the difference for him was slavery, he was always a sojourner in the city, never truly a resident. The city intensified rather than weakened his sense of what he was as a southerner and sharpened rather than diminished his awareness of his differences from his fellow Americans.

Allen Tate, in the 1920s, also went to New York City, and there he found a wider range of intellectual experiences than he had found before he left, although Nashville and Vanderbilt University were hardly rural environments. Yet his experiences with the intelligentsia of New York City, with its magazines and publications, served not to wean him away from the southernness he felt to be his most distinctive characteristic but rather to intensify it. Stark Young of Mississippi spent much of his mature life as a New York drama critic for the *New Republic*, but while he was seeing plays and criticizing them for a liberal and very urban weekly, he was also reconstructing the beautiful and ordered Old South of his imagination which is the subject of *So Red the Rose* and his other novels. Richard Wright, a black man from the Deep South, found himself in Chicago, then New York, and finally Paris. He never came back home again, but essentially it was the experience of being southern and black that proved to be one of the most effective subjects of his work. Hamilton Basso traveled from Louisiana to New York, from the New Orleans *Picayune* to the *New Yorker*, but at the end of his career he returned with a heightened sense of its meaning to the South of *The View from Pompey's Head* and *The Light Infantry Ball*. Such a list might be extended a great deal, but a sufficient number of writers have been named to indicate that the experience of the southern writer in going to the metropolis has a certain consistency.

It is not, therefore, surprising that Thomas Wolfe, one of the major southern writers, should have made the story of the Young Man from the Provinces in the great city one of the basic themes in his fiction. Indeed, after *Look Homeward, Angel*, which ends as Eugene Gant lifts his eyes upward and outward toward the North of which he has dreamed, Thomas Wolfe's work deals in large measure with the southerner in the city. First it is the city of Boston, then New York, then London, then Paris, and then Berlin, but always the intensely autobiographical record that Wolfe makes in his novels is a record of the outward movement of a southern boy from the mountains of North Carolina to the great cities of the world.

The story of this outward journey constitutes the greater portion of three massive novels that Thomas Wolfe produced after *Look Homeward, Angel*. In *Of Time and the River*, Eugene Gant leaves Altamont, travels to Boston, experiences "the coming on of the great earth, the new lands, the enchanted city, the approach, so smokey, blind and stifled, to the ancient web, the old grimed thrilling barricades of Boston . . . He saw the furious streets of life with their unending flood-tide of a million faces." In Boston, for the first time, he experienced the "fury" that the city created in him:

> And from that moment on blind fury seized him. . . . Of this fury, which was to lash and drive him on for fifteen years, the thousandth part could not be told. . . . He was driven by hunger so literal, cruel and physical that it wanted to devour the earth and all things and people in it, and when it failed in this attempt his spirit would drown in an ocean of horror and desolation, smothered below the overwhelming tides of

this great earth, sickened and made sterile, hopeless, dead with a stul-
tifying weight of men and objects of the world, the everlasting flock
and flood of the crowd.

Seldom has the intense involvement of a young provincial with a
city been described in more extravagantly rhetorical terms than
Wolfe uses here and throughout *Of Time and the River*.

In Boston Eugene Gant attends a great university, tries to understand the nature of life through watching his uncle Bascom
Pentland, returns home to Altamont in the southern mountains
on the occasion of the death of his father and finds his sense of
home sharpened and deepened by his experiences in the North.
After completing his graduate work, he goes to New York City,
teaches English in another university, and becomes acquainted
with that most representative child of the city, Abe Jones. He also
becomes acquainted with the rich and privileged people who live
in the great houses along the Hudson River. Thus Boston and New
York show him a rich culture and acquaint him with a great variety of urban people. In his friends Francis Starwick, in Boston and
later Paris, and Joel Pierce, in New York, he has guides who in-
struct him and open doors for him. Then he travels to Europe and
has to find himself once more, this time in another, a different
and, in many ways, richer culture than he had known before. First
in London, then in Paris, and at last in southern France, as he came
to know the land, the people, and their cultures, he also came to
turn increasingly in upon himself. As he expresses it, "At morning in a foreign land . . . he wakes and thinks of home . . . and the
wilderness, the things that are in his blood, his heart, his brain, in
every atom of his flesh and tissue, the things for which he draws
his breath in labor, the things that madden him with an intolerable and nameless pain." In later works the extravagance of such
rhetoric is to be reduced, but the essential situation there described
does not change. No Young Man from the Provinces—in Stendhal, in Balzac, in Dickens, in Flaubert—has had his experiences
of self-discovery and self-knowledge detailed more consistently,
more thoroughly, or more passionately than Eugene Gant's are in
Of Time and the River. The seeming lack of structure in the novel
has puzzled its critics, leading them to seek new terms to use in

characterizing it; Richard S. Kennedy, for example, has called it a *thesaurus* rather than a novel. However, when we look at the persistence in it of the theme of the Young Man from the Provinces, it becomes clearly a very loosely plotted example of that genre of fiction.

Wolfe was self-conscious about this pattern in his later fiction, as he was self-conscious about the Joycean pattern in *Look Homeward, Angel*. He says in *The Web and the Rock*,

> There is no truer legend in the world than the one about the country boy, the provincial innocent, in his first contact with the city. . . .It has found inspired and glorious tongues in Tolstoy and in Goethe, in Balzac and Dickens, in Fielding and Mark Twain. . . . And day after day the great cities of the world are being fed, enriched, and replenished ceaselessly with the life-blood of the nation, with all the passion, aspiration, eagerness, faith, and high imagining that youth can know or that the tenement of life can hold.

The further the Wolfe protagonists move into urban lives remote from the world of their childhood and youth, the more completely that world reasserts itself in memory in contrast to the city around them.

After *Of Time and the River* Wolfe abandoned Eugene Gant as his protagonist and substituted for him George Webber, who was the central figure in Wolfe's last two novels, *The Web and the Rock* and *You Can't Go Home Again*. *The Web and the Rock* in its early pages repeats in slightly modified form a brief record of the protagonist's childhood in what is now called Libya Hill, a mountain town in North Carolina, and his college experiences at Pulpit Hill. Then George Webber goes to New York City. Wolfe sees Webber's entry into New York in terms quite explicitly those of the story of the provincial in the city. He says, "for one like George Webber, born to the obscure village and brought up within the narrow geography of provincial ways, the city experience is such as no city man himself can ever know." And he adds,

> When such a man, therefore, comes first to the great city—but how can we speak of such a man coming first to the great city, when really the great city is within him, encysted in his heart, built up in all the flaming images of his brain: a symbol of his hope, the image of his high desire, the final crown, the citadel of all that he has ever dreamed of or

longed for or imagined that life could bring to him? For such a man as this, there really is no coming to the city. He brings the city with him everywhere he goes, and when that final moment comes when he at last breathes in the city's air, feels his foot upon the city street . . . looks around him at the city's pinnacles, pinches himself to make sure he is really there—for such a man as this, and for such a moment, it will always be a question . . . which city is the real one, which city he has found and seen, which city for this man is really there.

This statement, with its clear juxtaposition of two cities—one of dreams and hopes, the other of actuality—defines one of the major themes of *The Web and the Rock* and its sequel *You Can't Go Home Again*, for they are accounts of George Webber's gradual and painful discovery that the two are not the same and that the first, tested by the second, always proves false. This steady testing process—which had been present for Eugene Gant only to a limited degree, chiefly in his sense of the suffering of the poor—seems always to turn the thoughts of George Webber back to the simplicity, beauty, and calm of the provincial world of his childhood. This theme, bluntly announced as George enters New York, is a dominant and shaping motif for the remainder of *The Web and the Rock* and for *You Can't Go Home Again*, where it is explained in great detail. In the latter novel George returns to the South briefly on the occasion of the death of his aunt, but the greater portion of the book deals with his experiences among the great and near-great in New York City, as the result of the success of his first novel and his entry into the world of artists, writers, and the theater through the tutelage of his mistress Esther Jack. Then he travels to Europe and in London meets Lloyd McHarg, plainly a fictional portrait of Sinclair Lewis. He travels on to Germany and in Berlin is forced into an acknowledgment of the darkness and depravity that is, he now sees, a part of all human beings. Before the conclusion of this book he comes to recognize that the city is not the enchanted place that he had once dreamed it was and that he had celebrated with so much passion on first approaching it. He sums up what the life of the real city he now sees is through the representative figure of C. Green, who commits suicide by leaping twelve stories from a hotel to the street. He says of Green, "He was a dweller in mean streets, was Green, a man-mote in the jungle of the city, a resident of grimy steel and stone, a mole who burrowed in rusty brick, a stunned spectator of enormous salmon-colored towers, hued palely with the morning. He was a renter of shabby wooden houses. . . . He was a waker in bleak streets at morning." The world that C. Green commits suicide to escape is a far cry indeed from the enfabled rock that Eugene Gant approached at the beginning of *Of Time and the River*, but in discovering its nature, Wolfe's protagonists, and Wolfe himself, were carried back closer to the simpler world of the South.

Provincials from other parts of the nation can approach New York or Los Angeles much as provincials from Rouen approach Paris or natives of Lichfield approach London, as in a sense coming —"at last"—to their own capitals. Wolfe was intensely aware of how different it was with southerners. He described Webber's entry into the North, which for Wolfe was usually synonymous with northern cities: "always the feeling was the same—an exact, pointed, physical feeling marking the frontiers of his conscious-ness with a geographical precision. . . . It was a geographical divi-sion of the spirit that was sharply, physically exact, as if it had been severed by a sword. . . . He ducked his head a little as if he was passing through a web." The metaphor of the web, in *The Web and the Rock*, consistently refers to the South, as the meta-phor of the rock refers to a metropolis. The feeling Wolfe assigns his protagonist here is, he believes, in no sense unique to Webber: "Every young man from the South has felt this precise and formal geography of the spirit," he asserts, "but few city people are famil-iar with it." He speculates on why this feeling is always there: "they felt they were invading a foreign country. . . . they were steeling themselves for conflict. . . . they were looking forward with an almost desperate apprehension to their encounter with the city." And he asks, "How many people in the city realize how much the life of the great city meant to him . . . how, long ago in little towns down South . . . something was always burning in [his] heart at night—the image of the shining city." Thus the south-erner approaches the city as a foreign land and to some extent a hostile one. Perhaps because of the almost paranoid sense of being not merely provincial but an outsider, he remains, even over long periods of time, a sojourner.

Such a sojourner is different, and Wolfe explores the special characteristics that a southern provincial brings to this experience. George Webber decides that "there is no one on earth who is more patriotically devoted—verbally, at least—to the region from which he came than the American of the Southern portion of the United States. Once he leaves it to take up his living in other, less fair and fortunate, sections of the country, he is willing to fight for the honor of the Southland at the drop of a hat." He goes on to argue that a transplanted southerner is likely to be lonely in a great city and to look up others from his region and to "form a Community of the South which has no parallel in city life. . . . The most obvious reason for the existence of this Community is to be found in the deep-rooted and provincial insularity of Southern life." People from other regions are more readily and easily absorbed into the life of the city. The southerner, he says—and what southerner in a northern city has not experienced it?—remains a stranger to some degree and always a sojourner. If Wolfe's account is that of the Young Man from the Provinces moving out to the great city, it is also an account of a man whose sense of the health, beauty, and dignity of the provinces grows steadily, first in contrast to the complexity and glitter of the great cities, then as a consolation to one lonely in the city as only in the city one can be alone.

Upon his death, Wolfe left the first ten chapters of an incomplete novel entitled *The Hills Beyond*. The story returns to the mountains of western North Carolina and to the kinds of people who had been a major part of the background of *Look Homeward, Angel*. *The Hills Beyond* is a story that celebrates the simple people of the mountain region. Gone now is much of the condescension and dislike that Wolfe had heaped upon them in *Look Homeward, Angel* and in the early pages of *The Web and the Rock*. Now he celebrates them as large folk characters drawn bigger than life with great gusto, vitality, and health. The author of this fragment had demonstrated very clearly that the further he got away from home and the more completely he realized the impossibility of attempting to go home again, the more vividly home and the South and its special qualities and characteristics existed in his mind.

The more deeply Wolfe became immersed in the life of the busy

North, the more completely he became acquainted with and came
to understand the rich culture of Europe, the more totally he described the interior life of his provincial protagonist as he confronted the great cultural centers of the world, the more a self-
consciousness about his region grew in his own mind. Wolfe was
very much the traditional southerner outside the South, one who
is usually a recognizably uncomfortable creature whose southernness tends to become exaggerated. The comic figure of the "professional southerner" is a part of the response of this southern
provincial to a world that is truly not his own, and the metropolis
becomes for him a sounding board for realizing what his region
truly is. Thomas Wolfe was thus both the major writer who most
consistently used the frame of the southerner as provincial in the
metropolis to order his work and the sharpest definer of the differences between that southern provincial and other American provincials approaching the great cities of the world. As the portrayer
of that experience, he became the recorder of the common experience of many of his fellow southerners.

His career also became in one sense an adumbration of the future relation of his region to the larger nation. In the years since
World War II the South has increasingly moved out of its insularity toward being an integral part of the larger nation. It has played
a steadily growing role in national affairs at the same time that it
has retained most of its distinctively regional characteristics. Its
sense of difference has resulted in a consciousness of characteristics that a more homogeneous or less self-conscious people might
have ignored. Thus it has brought new perspectives and has served
from time to time as a conscience. These aspects of the South in
recent history Wolfe's career foreshadowed and his work defined
with startling clarity.

J. LEE GREENE

The Pain and the Beauty:
The South, the Black Writer,
and Conventions of
the Picaresque

Long before social, political, and economic changes in the 1960s and 1970s greatly altered the pattern of southern life and race relations, the South as depicted in literature by black writers of southern origin had both its negative and positive sides. Indeed, a positive image of the South in southern black literature has been pervasive throughout this century. This is not to say that southern black writers ever condoned the social, political, and economic restraints of living black in the South or ever as a group espoused the romantic, idealistic image of the South advanced by the white Plantation School writers who idealized antebellum society during the last quarter of the nineteenth century. Rather, southern black writers since the turn of the century consistently have written about a spiritual component of black life exclusively identified with a southern black experience. In doing so, these writers have made a clear distinction between the South as a region and its white population.

Southern black literature since the turn of the century has shown that the southern black character who lives close to his natural surroundings is nurtured and sustained by forces that minister to his spiritual being. His *soul* (a term with multiple meanings in black American culture) is shielded from the dehumanizing and spiritually deadening onslaught of a twentieth-century materialistic and technological culture—a culture that some might term the New South and others might view as a thinly veiled Old South. It is within the context of twentieth-century artistic expressions of primitivism or the nineteenth-century back-to-nature aspect of

romanticism that southern life as it affects blacks is treated positively in this literature. While his soul is nourished by his natural
environment, the body of the southern black character is victimized by "the Man," by the white South that tempts him with its
increasing materialistic assets. Tempted and then seduced by the
tantalizing rewards of the new society's materialism and technology, the black character is primed for the destruction of his body
and soul when he tries to gain access to the fruits of this society
through its social, political, and economic institutions. His nem-
esis is "the Man," those who control the societal institutions that
provide the only access to egalitarian participation in the prosperity of the New South. It is, therefore, from this context that the
negative side of southern life for blacks is presented in the literature.

There is a close affinity between the life and the literature of
southern blacks. Movements in southern black literature are not
as clear-cut as those in the literature of many other American
groups or regions, perhaps because, unlike that of the country
in general, the life of southern blacks did not experience drastic
change until the past fifteen years or so. Yet the publication of
certain works and the careers of certain authors do indicate peaks
in the concerns of, approaches to, and development of southern
black literature, particularly fiction. James Weldon Johnson's *The
Autobiography of an Ex-Coloured Man* in 1912, Jean Toomer's
Cane in 1923, Richard Wright's *Black Boy* in 1945, Ralph Ellison's *Invisible Man* in 1952, and Ernest Gaines's *The Autobiography of Miss Jane Pittman* in 1971 historically documented the
uniformity of and differences in southern black writers' treatment of the South. Of these five representative works *Black Boy*,
a product of the 1930s and 1940s Protest Era and of the chief southern black writer of the period, stands apart from the other four
works in that it deals almost exclusively with the negative side of
living black in the South, the side that perhaps has been overly
stressed in critical interpretations of southern black literature. It
is my intent here, therefore, to concentrate on the ways in which
"the South" is treated as a positive force by four representative
southern black writers.

Southern black fiction had its genesis in the prose narratives of the lives of blacks who had escaped a slave existence. The conventions of the slave narrative were central to the development of black American fiction (which for the most part is of and about the South) in the second half of the nineteenth century and the early decades of the twentieth century. The slave narrative was primarily an "autobiographical" account of a slave's life in the South, usually ghost-written by a white northerner. The form became so popular in the first half of the nineteenth century that it enjoyed relatively widespread use by white writers in the North, and its conventions continued to be adapted by white writers such as William Dean Howells (An Imperative Duty, 1892) and Mark Twain (The Tragedy of Pudd'nhead Wilson, 1894) well after chattel slavery had ended.

While the central function of the slave narrative was to expose the brutal existence of a typical slave's life, the narrative frequently effected this by focusing on the experiences of a person too white to be black and yet not white, ostensibly to excite the abolitionist sentiments of northern readers, a large number of whom were women. Given the moral code of the time, the northern female gentility could empathize (or at the least sympathize) with any woman, white or black, whose sexual honor was in constant threat of violation by men. Consequently, the dehumanizing effect of slavery presented through the perilous life of a young quadroon or octoroon became a stock device in the slave narrative, and was repeated in many fiction works by whites that were based either on slavery or on the slave narrative (Harriet Beecher Stowe's Uncle Tom's Cabin is the most prominent example). Black fiction writers in turn picked up the convention, which easily evolved into the "tragic mulatto" novels of the late nineteenth century and the "passing" novels of the early twentieth century.

William Wells Brown, born in Kentucky, was the first acknowledged black American and black southerner to publish a novel—Clotel; or the President's Daughter (1853). Clotel served in many ways as a prototype of the black American novel from Frances Ellen Watkins Harper's Iola Leroy; or Shadows Uplifted (1892) to Charles Waddell Chesnutt's The House Behind the Cedars (1900) and many later southern black novels. The thematic structure of the slave narrative included the escape of the protagonist from a brutal existence in the South to freedom in the Promised Land of the North. *Clotel* alters this linear pattern in that after escaping to freedom Clotel returns to the South to search for and be reunited with her children. This return motif continues through Chesnutt's *The House Behind the Cedars*, where it takes a twist that is thematically emphasized in Johnson's *Ex-Coloured Man* and reaches a zenith in Toomer's *Cane*: the protagonist learns that he has roots that sink deeply into the southern experience and reach all the way back to Africa. The result of his return South is that his soul is rejuvenated by a southern environment.

The autobiographical mode, the tragic mulatto strain, and the theme of passing merge in Johnson's classic (but underrated) short novel *The Autobiography of an Ex-Coloured Man*, first published anonymously in 1912. This seminal novel marks a definite beginning in the contrasting thematic treatment of the South by southern black fiction writers. By 1912 the Great Black Migration to the North was well under way. It began at the close of the Civil War and rapidly accelerated during Reconstruction and the rise of the repressive Jim Crow segregation laws. By the 1920s it reached a peak. Frightened, discouraged, and disillusioned by the repressive measures of the postbellum South and the enactment of Jim Crow laws, blacks steadily migrated from the South to the North. It took over a century for the pattern to be reversed, for only in the early 1970s did more blacks migrate South than North. The steady migration of blacks to the North—increasing and subsiding, depending on the conditions in the society—is a dominant feature of southern black literature. It is within the context of this migratory pattern that southern black writers contrast the South with the North and thus through the thematic structure of their works contrast the two contradictory yet complementary sides of living black in the South.

The fictional treatment of the southern black experience incorporates the conventions of picaresque literature, especially as these conventions were practiced by English novelists of the eighteenth century. This is not to say that southern black fiction writers consciously model their works after the English picaresque novel. Rather, the fidelity with which these writers describe southern black life closely resembles life in picaresque literature. Virtually all of the conventions of the genre can be used, then, to elucidate the concerns and achievements of southern black fiction writers. The four representative works included in this discussion—*Ex-Coloured Man, Cane, Invisible Man, Jane Pittman* —contain variations of the following picaresque conventions: the narrative is usually autobiographical; the hero is a foundling, a bastard, or an outcast; he undergoes a journey; on his journey he comes into contact with various levels of society and affords the author opportunity to comment (usually satirically) on them; on his own with no ancestral fortune to sustain him, the hero must survive by his wits; his odyssey provides for a loose, episodic structure in the narrative. These and other picaresque conventions help define the pattern of southern black life and fiction.

One characteristic of the picaresque novel is that it is usually written in the first person and as such is considered autobiographical. Though in its literal definition autobiography refers to the life of one person written by himself, the form as used in the slave narrative and as adapted by southern black fiction writers (who found it particularly suitable to their needs and intents) includes the life experiences of an individual but also incorporates incidents, characters, themes, and experiences that are applicable to the lives of a large group of individuals—often to the race itself—and emphasizes the uniformity of experiences shared by blacks in the South and in America in general.

Neither Johnson's nor Gaines's novel is an autobiography in any literal sense, but the inclusion of the term autobiography in the title of each is indicative of the inclusive approach each writer takes to the lives of blacks in American culture. To be sure, the incidents, themes, and concerns in both novels are true not just for the central character in each but for a large segment of the race. These simulated autobiographies, to different degrees and in different ways, are twentieth-century outgrowths of the antebellum slave narrative. The ex-coloured man's experiences apply not only to him but to a large group of blacks on the color line who are forced to cross because of racial and social repression. While the narrator objects to writers who precede his volume for exaggerating the vices and virtues of a black protagonist in order to prove a case about the race as a whole, he nevertheless quickly points out that his autobiography is "a composite and proportionate presentation of the entire race, embodying all its various groups and elements, showing their relations with each other and to whites." The editorial persona in the "Introduction" to *The Autobiography of Miss Jane Pittman* points out that "this is not only Miss Jane's autobiography," but that it is also an account of life experiences intimately shared by many other blacks.

Considering the extent to which each novel incorporates the life of its author, *The Autobiography of an Ex-Coloured Man* and *The Autobiography of Miss Jane Pittman* are less autobiographical than Jean Toomer's *Cane* or Ralph Ellison's *Invisible Man*. Not only do *Cane* and *Invisible Man* draw extensively from the respective author's personal experiences, but each novel thematically encompasses the experiences of a large portion of the race, if not of the entire race. In developing the theme of racial or ethnic identity, for instance, each novel becomes a biography of the race, and within this cultural context the autobiography of the author and his protagonist is a generic autobiography of the race. Echoing the poetry of Walt Whitman throughout, the narrator of *Invisible Man* sings of himself as well as of countless others, as the last line of the novel suggests: "Who knows but that, on the lower frequencies, I speak for you?" The sentence echoes the beginning of Whitman's "Song of Myself." Toomer's "Song of the Son," the poem in *Cane* that best capsulizes the major theme in this largely autobiographical book, celebrates the "song-lit race of slaves," black Americans in general; the poem embodies the thematic approach the author takes to his material in order to produce a work that in essence is a spiritual and historical biography of black Americans.

Perhaps one can argue convincingly that most American fiction, especially that of the first half of the twentieth century, is autobiographical. But the use of the elements of autobiography in black American fiction—in particular that fiction which emanates from a southern experience—differs from the autobiographical import of mainstream American fiction in that, to use Johnson's words, it is essentially "a composite and proportionate presentation of the entire race," not just the life of its author or central character. The use of autobiography varies in degree among black writers, as it does among nonblack writers, but for black writers the composite approach and representational intent in their use of the autobiographical form are clearly in focus.

The typical hero in picaresque literature is a foundling, an orphan, a bastard, or an outcast, and this characteristic is especially applicable to the protagonists in the four works considered here as well as to the group they represent. The conditions of slavery in the South created many orphans like Jane Pittman, a child whose father was from a plantation other than the one on which her mother lived, and whose mother was beaten to death by a cruel overseer. Left alone in the world to fend for herself with the limited assistance of the slave community, Jane Pittman is forced to survive by her wits, like the conventional picaro (or picaroon) and like countless blacks (orphans and otherwise) after slavery. Johnson's ex-coloured man, who also must make his way alone in the world, typifies the dilemma of a large group of blacks during and after slavery. The illegitimate son of a well-to-do southern gentleman and a woman whose black ancestry is barely visible, he is reared fatherless and becomes acutely aware of the bastardy of his birth, and thus of the reason for his and his mother's estrangement from both the black and white communities. He shares with Toomer's character Kabnis the heritage of the southern white aristocracy, and the two share with practically every other black American a miscegenated ancestry. In speaking of his lack of racial identity and the cause thereof, Kabnis speaks for all black Americans in that African-Americans as a group are historically the offspring of white American fathers and black African mothers, and, therefore, being neither completely white nor completely black, are indeed members of a "bastard race": "I'm th victim of their sin. I'm what sin is": "that bastard race thats roamin round th country." We are told less about the parentage of Ellison's invisible man than about the parentage of the other three protagonists. Having violated the code of living black in the South, Ellison's invisible man becomes an outcast and is forced to make his way in New York, where because he is black he remains outcast from mainstream society. He breaks all ties with his family once he leaves the South and in effect becomes an orphan in the city; even the semblance of a family that he finds with Mary Rambo is short-lived. Like the picaro, all four of these characters, then, are outcasts from the dominant culture, and in that are representative of the position of blacks in America.

Even as a young child Jane Pittman's independence separates her from the slave community, and it is only after she begins her senior years on the Samson plantation that we see her as an integral part of a social community. The ex-coloured man ever remains estranged from blacks due to the circumstances of his birth and of his childhood in Georgia and Connecticut. Even when on his own after his mother's death—a bastard who has now become in effect an orphan—he finds it virtually impossible—certainly not to his "taste"—to become an integral part of the black community. He gains the friendship and patronage of a white benefactor, yet he assumes the subservient role of a black valet. Though he marries a white and then passes for white himself with relative success, he still remains psychologically distant from whites and physically separated from blacks.

The ex-coloured man, Kabnis, and invisible man are all spiritual and cultural orphans in that they are cut off from their past and its traditions, cannot come to terms with their southern black heritage, and as blacks cannot become a part of the mainstream culture. Yet all three are drawn to the roots of their southern black heritage. Years after achieving his desire to alienate himself from blacks, the ex-coloured man finds himself somewhat psychologically uncomfortable in the white world; and the tenuousness of his psychological state as a white man causes him to write his narrative. While he is able to deny being black, to reject the pains and sorrows that emanate from southern black life, he cannot sever the ties that psychologically bind him to his racial or ethnic past and give him identity. Ironically, he cannot become an ex-coloured man. The yellowing manuscripts (symbolic of black spirituality) that have haunted him for years will not disappear from his psyche. It is that negative image of the South, the lynching scene, symbolic of southern violence and inhumanity, that makes him decide to deny his black heritage. But the ever-present manuscripts will not allow him to do this with spiritual impunity. Because Kabnis cannot come to terms with his southern and black heritage, because he cannot—as the character Lewis says—hold the pain and beauty of the South, he cannot reconcile the forces that give him identity. The conflict between the negative force of the South (his fear of being lynched) and the positive South (the spiritual power of the landscape) places him in a limbo: "If I could feel that I came to the South to face it. If I, the dream (not what is weak and afraid in me) could become the face of the South. How my lips would sing for it, my songs being the lips of its soul." But, like the ex-coloured man, he represses the spiritual force: "Oh, no, I wont let that emotion come up in me. Stay down. Stay down, I tell you." Invisible man, too, cannot reconcile the two forces. He cannot bear to be near the manifestations of his spiritual past (Susie Gresham, the girl singer, and Dvořák's *New World Symphony* in chapter five of the novel) and cannot rid himself of the symbols of the negative South that he collects in his briefcase (the cast-iron Negro bank and Tarp's leg iron). At the end of *Cane* and *Invisible Man* there is some indication that the protagonists will be able to accept their black heritage, will be able to reconcile the conflicting forces of their being, and will be able to achieve a positive identity. There is no such indication at the end of *Ex-Coloured Man*; he has "sold [his] birthright for a mess of pottage."

Seen in mythic terms as an outcast, as a wanderer and vagabond, the hero of these and many other black American fiction works is depicted as the biblical Cain. The pun in the title of Toomer's *Cane* points to this biblical analogy on which the book's thematic structure is based, an analogy that is strongly rooted in southern culture, if indeed it does not have its origin there. Kabnis, who sees God as exacting punishment on him because of his racial identity, internalizes the myth that mainstream American (specifically southern) society has used to justify his oppression. Unlike many of the protagonists in white American fiction, the black

American, uprooted from his native Africa, bastardized by miscegenation, is forced to flee from the South to northern cities to
seek release from racial oppression. The mainstream society sees
him as the embodiment of the curse and mark of Cain—much as
it sees its own fictional heroes as New World Adams. In Genesis,
God cursed Cain for killing his brother, Abel, by decreeing that
henceforth Cain should be a vagabond and a wanderer. But to protect Cain from those who would do him harm as a result of the
curse, God placed a mark on Cain so that all those who came into
contact with him should not slay him. Though the Bible does not
state exactly what the mark was or its color, those in America
who used the Bible to justify slavery identified it as a black mark
and consequently identified blacks as the descendants of Cain,
heirs to his supposed curse and mark. It is probably this perver-
sion of biblical lore that Father John speaks of when in *Cane* he
utters his haunting only sentence: "Th sin whats fixed . . . upon
th white folks—f tellin Jesus—lies. O th sin th white folks 'mitted
when they made the Bible lie."

The mainstream culture used basically three stories from Genesis to justify and explain the enslavement of black Africans. The
stories that generated racial myths based on arbitrary interpretations of biblical lore became so intrenched in antebellum religion
and culture that remnants of them still remain in popular thought.
The Cain-Abel story, the Abraham-Isaac-Ishmael story, and the
Noah-Ham-Canaan story were used, singularly and collectively,
to account for the color of blacks, their enslavement, and their
perennial outcast state. These same biblical stories (whose details
may vary according to different editions of the King James Bible)
are used with technical skill in the literature by and about southern blacks.

Southerners who were sympathetic to the slave system could
easily reconcile any conflict they might have between their attitudes toward blacks as people and their moral teachings by be-
lieving that the culture's attitudes toward and treatment of blacks
were sanctioned by the Bible. In fact, the supposed biblical sanc-
tion of slavery became so deeply rooted in the southern mind that
many people enthusiastically defended slavery by asserting with

confidence that God decreed blacks be slaves. No doubt a major reason for this belief was the interpretative confusion of the Cain-Abel and the Noah-Ham stories. For having looked upon his father's (Noah's) nakedness, Ham is cursed to have his sons become "servants of servants." The son of Ham on whom the curse is placed is Canaan, whose descendants separate from others of Noah's line. Combining the curse on Cain and that on Canaan and his descendants, perhaps confusing the names of Cain and Canaan, and interpreting "servants of servants" to mean "slave of slaves" (the terms are used in some editions of the Bible), it was a short step for the would-be Christian southerner to conclude that blacks were cursed by God to be slaves, notwithstanding other biblical passages to the contrary.

Details of the story of Abraham and his sons closely parallel southern society as it stems from a slave system. The Old Testament patriarch Abraham is one of God's chosen. He fathers two sons: the first-born, illegitimate Ishmael is born from his union with his wife Sarah's handmaiden, the Egyptian (African) slave Hagar; the second son, Isaac, is born to Sarah and, as the legitimate heir to the house of Abraham, is the one who will carry down through his seed the royal line of the chosen people. The implications and ramifications for the application of this story to black-white relations in the South are many. The elements of this story relevant for this discussion are briefly outlined: Abraham, Sarah, and Isaac are identified with southern whites, with the "chosen" race; Hagar and Ishmael are identified with southern blacks, with slaves, and thus with the outcast race. While the southern white man (Abraham) is the father of southern whites (Isaac) and of southern blacks (Ishmael), the heirs to his kingdom are whites only, while blacks, because they are "the son of the bondwoman," are rejected. The survival of Calvinism in the antebellum southern mind made it even easier for these three biblical stories to coalesce and produce the image of blacks as wanderers and vagabonds, eternally outcast because their inherited curse and mark of blackness separate them from God's chosen people—from the Elect. Metaphorically, this is the picaresque plight—Ishmaelism —of the representative protagonist in the southern black novel.

The ex-coloured man, the central intelligence in *Cane* (usually considered to be Kabnis), invisible man, and Jane Pittman each undergoes a physical journey that historically parallels (with slight thematic variations) the migration of blacks from the South in search of the Promised Land of the North, and in this sense each one's odyssey conforms to the journey motif in picaresque literature. In all four works the protagonist's physical journey evolves into a spiritual quest. The wanderings of Jane Pittman are closely connected with her quest for identity, her desire to shake off the shackles of her southern slave past, to rid herself of an identity imposed upon her, and to seek self-knowledge and identity in a land of freedom. Corporal Brown, who gives her the name Jane to substitute for her slave name Ticy, sets her off on a physical journey that soon becomes one with her spiritual quest. And her quest is inseparable from the symbolic North and the dehumanizing South. But like Mark Twain's Jim and Huck, Jane's and Ned's physical attempts to get North only entangle them more deeply in the South. And it is, consequently, in the South that both Jane and Ned eventually affirm their identity.

Jane Pittman's physical journey never takes her to the North, but the protagonists in *Ex-Coloured Man, Cane,* and *Invisible Man* do get there, only to discover that the relative physical freedom in the North is symbolic or superficial, that it negates too much of their affinity for things black and southern. Each then is drawn back to the spirituality of his black roots, back to the South. Folk art becomes in all three works indicative of the luring powers of southern black life, a life that may brutalize the body but one that nourishes the soul. Foremost among these arts is music, the black American affinity for song and rhythm (in both music and dance) that is a distinct aspect of the southern black experience. Toomer iterates the theme in *Cane* when in "Song of the Son" and elsewhere he praises the spiritual art of the slave songs (in the culture appropriately designated spirituals) created by "some genius of the South" who makes "folk-songs from soul sounds" ("Georgia Dusk"). These slave songs are at the heart of black American art forms. It is these same slave songs that draw the ex-coloured man to the South. But, like Kabnis, spiritually too weak to embrace what these "soul sounds" mean, to embrace the very thing that would spiritually rejuvenate him, he allows the manuscripts he has collected to fade and thus his soul festers; he is a character who easily could fit into *Cane*, one whose soul is dying for a lack of contact with his spiritual past. When the ex-coloured man is in Germany, he realizes that high art is embedded in these folk songs. His dilemma is the same as that of invisible man. Reference to Dvořák's *New World Symphony* (a classical adaptation of black American slave songs) in *Invisible Man* (and in other black American works) underscores this idea and indicates how difficult it is for those who estrange themselves from the southern black past to sever completely their psychological and spiritual ties.

In *Invisible Man*, Susie Gresham, that "relic of slavery," represents for the protagonist the "warm and vital and all-enduring" quality of the black soul, though at the time his desire to deny his past prevents him from embracing what she represents. And though he wishes to deny his spiritual past, he cannot do so. In the North he meets in Mary Rambo an extension of Susie Gresham, for in Mary he recognizes "a force, a stable, familiar force like something out of my past." It is in chapter five especially that the spiritual force of his ethnic past is manifested in music: in the "thin brown girl" who sings in the chapel and whose "voice seemed to become a disembodied force that sought to enter her, to violate her, shaking her, rocking rhythmically, as though it had become the source of her being, rather than the fluid web of her own creation"; or in the organist who, apparently playing "white" music, "twisted and turned on his bench, with his feet flying beneath him as though dancing to rhythms totally unrelated to the decorous thunder of his organ." Ellison's "brown girl" and organist have been forged by the same spiritual mold as that used for the characters in *Cane* whose spiritual essence is manifested in song, dance, and rhythm.

The journey-quest motif of the outcast protagonists is congruent with the picaresque convention of a loose, episodic structure, which is applicable to these works. Such an episodic structure brings the protagonists into contact with many people and environments and, as in the picaresque novel, allows the authors to comment on various levels of American society and thus emphasizes the social import of southern black fiction. (Unfortunately, it is probably the extensive social commentary in southern black fiction that has caused many of its literary aspects and achievements to receive less critical attention than they deserve.)

Among these four works the fullest delineation of this picaresque convention is in *The Autobiography of an Ex-Coloured Man*, a novel in which the protagonist comes into contact with and comments on practically all socioeconomic levels of black and white society. In the first half of the novel the ex-coloured man in a flashback surveys his experiences in the South and classifies southern black society into three primary groups, pointing out that his categorizations "apply generally to every Southern community." His first category is the "desperate class," those who "conform to the requirements of civilization much as a trained lion"; they "cherish a sullen hatred for all white men, and they value life as cheap." It is out of this same class that Richard Wright a quarter of a century later created Bigger Thomas from a composite of five southern black characters; indeed, conditions in the South had changed little in the interval between Johnson's novel in 1912 and Wright's *Native Son* in 1940. In his naturalistic approach to the life and death of Bigger Thomas, Wright concretizes Johnson's statement in *Ex-Coloured Man*: "these men are but the creatures of conditions, as much so as the slum and criminal elements of all the great cities of the world are creatures of conditions." Probably voicing the sentiments of the tiny, educated, and mobile minority of black people known as the Talented Tenth at the turn of the century, Johnson maintains that these members of the race "[represent] the black people of the South far below their normal physical and moral condition." Charles Waddell Chesnutt (another member of the Talented Tenth and the first major southern black fiction writer) through the character Josh Green in *The Marrow of Tradition* (1901) and Wright in *Native Son* and other of his works show that in the increase of this class, as Johnson states, "lies the possibility of grave dangers." "This class of blacks hate everything covered by a white skin, and in return they are loathed by the whites.

The whites regard them just about as a man would a vicious mule, a thing to be worked, driven, and beaten, and killed for kicking." Johnson's statement here points to the conditions that have produced many protagonists in southern black life and fiction. Yet it was not until after the late 1930s that major works in southern black fiction included a large number of protagonists from the "desperate class."

Johnson's "second class, as regards the relation between blacks and whites, comprises the servants, the washerwomen, the waiters, the cooks, the coachmen, and all who are connected with the whites by domestic service. . . . Between this class of blacks and whites there is little or no friction." This class is well represented in the fiction of southerners, especially that of white southerners. Faulkner's Dilsey (*The Sound and the Fury*) is a well-known example of a member of this class, to which belong secondary characters in Chesnutt's works, most of the characters who populate the first and third sections of *Cane*, and most of those in *Jane Pittman*. From Reconstruction to the mid-1960s a majority of southern blacks belonged to this class. After the Civil Rights Movement of the 1960s, the proportionate number of southern blacks belonging to this class sharply decreased. However, in southern black fiction prior to the 1930s, members of this class were not chosen as central characters as frequently as those from the third class Johnson cites.

Johnson's "third class is composed of the independent workmen and tradesmen, and of the well-to-do and educated coloured people," people "as far removed from the whites as the members of the first class." The lives of blacks in this class dominated southern black fiction before Richard Wright. Blacks on the color line (who usually were the protagonists in the fiction) most often belonged to this class, a class that produced Harper's Iola Leroy, Sutton Griggs's Bernard Belgrave and Belton Piedmond (a dark-skinned hero), Chesnutt's Rena Walden and Dr. William Miller, Johnson's ex-coloured man, and several of the characters in *Cane*. Though most members of this class are not in daily contact with the white community at large, in much of the fiction in which they are included the racial tension is effected as a result of their physical or psychological identification with whites. "These people," says Johnson, "live in a little world of their own," basically separated from the other classes of blacks as well as from whites. This is the class that formed the southern black bourgeoisie. Its members were able to avoid many of the burdens of living Jim Crow by forming among themselves a network of relations and associations that spread throughout the eastern half of the nation and remained intact until well into the 1960s, when improvements in human and civil rights brought a decrease in racial discrimination in the public sector and thus removed one of its primary functions. The practice of southern Jim Crow in particular and national Jim Crow in general was largely responsible for the genesis and continuation of this class, whose forebears often were the direct descendants of the slave masters or the white overseers. While the gaining of civil rights, access to better education, to employment, and to public facilities for blacks decreased the primary purposes of this class, these same improvements increased the number of its prospective members as more blacks acquired the requisite money, education, and culture for membership in this class.

From the late nineteenth century to the present, southern black novels have included characters from all three of these categories. After about 1940, though, the southern black writer seldom chose his protagonist from the third class described above, because the intent of most southern black fiction was to dramatize the oppressive plight of the masses rather than to show the problems of an elite, well-to-do class of blacks.

In addition to a survey of the different classes of blacks, practically all southern black novels comment on the various levels of white society, and though conditions in the South have changed markedly from the turn of this century until today, the literary representation of the classes of southern blacks and whites remains essentially the same. There is the southern poor white who, like Toomer's Becky or Gaines's Job, is sympathetic to the plight of blacks. Yet the degree of hostility that southern poor whites historically have held for blacks in the South is not proportionately represented in the fiction that includes this class. Though perhaps more brutally racist than the other classes of southern whites, poor whites apparently had little power to improve the quality of life for blacks. And given the sociopolitical intent of much of the fiction, members of this class were ostensibly not as important to the southern black writer as were those whites who could effect political and civil changes in the society.

There is the middle-class southern white, most often depicted as a bigot or a paternalistic figure, who is amiable to blacks only as long as blacks know and keep their assigned places. The black writer gives significant attention to this class when he sees its members as having the power to effect social and political changes. Then there is the aristocratic white southerner, one who most often is a bigot and who exploits the labor of the southern black. He holds deep-seated prejudices, often displays overt hostilities, and firmly believes in the innate depravity of blacks. Gaines's Colonel Dye, Toomer's Bob Stone, and Ellison's city fathers in the battle royal episode are among the varied representatives of this class. At times, though, we see the aristocratic white southerner rising above prejudices and bigotry (as do whites in the other classes) and going against popular opinion in his community. Many times his position in the society allows him control over other whites, and often he is chastised by the writer for not using his power to better the lives of blacks.

Since in most southern black novels the protagonist journeys to the North in search of a better life, the author is allowed the opportunity to comment on northern whites, who almost always belong to the middle or upper class. Treatment of these northern characters is usually sympathetic as far as their relations with blacks are concerned, perhaps in order to emphasize by contrast the racism rampant in the South. Corporal Brown from *Jane Pittman* represents the attitudes of many members of this class (though there is no indication of his socioeconomic class). Quite often, however, southern black writers emphasize the shortcomings of the wealthy white northerners. The widow and the benefactor in *Ex-Coloured Man* are representatives of aristocratic northern whites who on the surface are depicted relatively favorably in their relations with blacks but who are drawn to blacks primarily because they suffer from a lack of fulfillment in their own lives,

whites who often prey on the vitality of black life as it is lived by
the southern black migrant in the urban North. The liberality of
members of this class is often a threat to those blacks whom they
supposedly befriend; Sybil's attitude toward invisible man and
Mary Dalton's treatment of Bigger Thomas, which leads to both
their deaths, are examples. The hypocrisy, depravity, and bigotry
of the northern white aristocrat many times are scorned. Wright's
Mr. Dalton and Ellison's Mr. Norton, Brother Jack and other members of the Brotherhood belong to this class of northern whites
whose lives and life styles are ridiculed in southern black novels.
These are characters taken from life, people whose dubious altru-
ism and philanthropy do more to aggrandize themselves or to pla-
cate the white South than to move the southern black masses
into the American mainstream. Indeed, as a work of art that derives much of its technical artistry directly from the culture in
general, it seems a natural consequence that the southern black
novel would be inclusive in its survey of different levels of social
classes, black and white, South and North. The survival of the
southern black character has depended to a large extent on his
acute knowledge of racial attitudes associated with socioeconomic
classes, classes of both blacks and whites.

The picaro's ability (and necessity) to survive by his wits is one
of his most distinguishing characteristics, one that is shared by
southern black characters in life and in literature. The black American has endured the brutalities of a slave existence, the oppressive practices of Jim Crow, the lynching mania that spread over
the South from the end of the Civil War until the end of the third
decade of this century, and other threats to his survival. The New
World African learned to adapt to his New World conditions,
taught his descendants how to survive under these conditions,
and never accepted these conditions as definitive of his proper
station in American life. Out of the folk culture come tales of this
adaptation, tales used to literary advantage by both black and white
writers of the nineteenth and twentieth centuries, writers from
the South and from the North. From these tales in the oral culture
and the written literature based on them comes what I term the
mask device. The device is apparent in several accounts of slave

life and slave escapes. To be sure, the various disguises slaves used to deceive their masters and whites in general are indicative of the strategy blacks have used for centuries to survive in America.

One of the most skillful adaptations of the mask device is in Chesnutt's *The Conjure Woman* (1899) in which an old ex-slave, Uncle Julius, effects his own security by outwitting his employer, John, an Ohioan who has migrated South. Working primarily through John's wife, Annie, Uncle Julius quickly recognizes the psychology of his white employers and gradually gains control over them (and thus over his own life) by catering to Annie's romantic mind and to John's stereotypes of blacks. In his ability to survive by his wits, Uncle Julius is much like Br'er Rabbit of the black American folk tales, tales popularized by Joel Chandler Harris and others in the nineteenth century which have antecedents in black African cultures.

Of the four works treated in this discussion, Ellison's *Invisible Man* is the one that uses most fully in the technique of the novel the mask device as it has evolved from black American folk culture in the South. Central to the novel's thematic structure is the statement the protagonist finds in his briefcase at the end of chapter one: "Keep This Nigger-Boy Running." The statement alludes to Br'er Rabbit, that black American folk picaroon who constantly had to flee or outwit his more physically powerful opponents, and who often was the persona through which the slave commented on his own predicament in his struggles to survive in the South. The line thematically suggests through the dream motif the nightmare quality of invisible man's attempts to be included in the Great American Dream.

Each of the novel's episodes is a thematic variation on this statement, for in each invisible man, alternately Jack-the-Rabbit and Jack-the-Bear, is kept running until he learns, or thinks he learns, exactly how to cope with and survive in the system of whiteness. The method for coping and surviving is given in his grandfather's death-bed "curse," which comes at the beginning of chapter one and combines with the statement at the end of the chapter to emphasize further the Br'er Rabbit analogy: as a black, invisible man must learn to play the games of his opponents but must never believe in those games, as a veteran at the Golden Day puts it. Invisible man's declaration in chapter 24 of his intention to undermine the Brotherhood by grinning and yessing them to death and destruction emanates from his grandfather's curse, a device that was originated in the South as an effective means for blacks to survive in a system controlled by whites.

What invisible man learns by the end of the novel in his movement from innocence to experience is, appropriately, what his grandfather, Bledsoe, the veteran, and others have told him, and what every black born into and reared by the southern system must learn if he is to have any control over his life: he must survive by his wits. The three-fold Br'er Rabbit metaphor shows that the dilemma of Br'er Rabbit is the dilemma of invisible man, and his dilemma is that of black Americans in general, as the novel's last line suggests.

One of the most interesting thematic uses of the mask device in the novel is in the factory hospital episode where the white doctors consider a prefrontal lobotomy to curb the potentially violent nature of the protagonist, whose sense of self (though subdued) is a threat to the survival of this system of white supremacy. The protagonist's identity stems from his knowledge of his ethnic past, a past which in turn is presented through memories of Mother, that universal, sacred, and unifying force among blacks, and of Br'er Rabbit, the trickster device that allows black identity to survive in a hostile world. "When I discover who I am, I'll be free," says invisible man, underscoring the theme of identity so prominent in black American literature and emphasizing the idea that black survival depends on keeping intact the symbols and meanings of the black ethnic past, a past that when lost would cause the black American to be absorbed into or in other ways be destroyed by whiteness.

In exploring various thematic implications of this device, Ellison focuses on the danger of allowing the mask to become self-destructive. Bledsoe has used the mask device to such an extent that he is indistinguishable from his masks. He is one who has deferred to whites for so long that his deference has become an instinctive part of his psyche. The ambivalence inherent in blacks' use of the mask is presented in Ellison's allusions to Booker T. Washington, particularly in his barely veiled reference to the statue of Washington at Tuskegee Institute. In the novel the statue of the college Founder is described as holding a veil over a kneeling slave. One cannot tell if the Founder is lifting the veil or lowering it more firmly in place. The symbolic statue suggests the time-lessness or fixity of this condition in black-white relations, and that this has been the problem of many so-called black leaders in the South whose compromises with the white power structure have no doubt been detrimental to the black community.

The mask device as it stems from the Br'er Rabbit metaphor permeates the novel and can be seen in various symbols, motifs, situations, and characters. In the character Rinehart, the thematic and technical ramifications of this device culminate. Rinehart is a man who wears so many masks in his attempts to outwit and survive in a white world that, ironically, he destroys the very thing that would insure his survival—his blackness. He allows his outer self—the rind—to obliterate his inner self—the heart; he takes the act of survival to the point of self-destruction. The various uses of the mask device in the craft of *Invisible Man* are so intricate that the technique can appropriately be termed Rinehartism.

The Autobiography of an Ex-Coloured Man, Cane, and *The Autobiography of Miss Jane Pittman* do not make nearly as much thematic and technical use of the mask device as does *Invisible Man* or other works by black southerners. Yet Johnson, Toomer, and Gaines use variations of this device to relate the strategies blacks have used to secure a position in a hostile white-dominated society. In the first paragraph of *Ex-Coloured Man* the protagonist iterates the theme of the mask device: "I feel the thrill which accompanies that most fascinating pastime; and, back of it all, I think I find a sort of savage and diabolical desire to gather up all the little tragedies of my life, and turn them into a practical joke on society." It is of white society that he speaks here; and in so doing his statement recalls the "diabolical desire" of Br'er Rabbit, that master trickster, to let his opponents know they have been foiled, the same impulse invisible man has in the hospital episode, in his encounter with Sybil, and elsewhere in the novel, or the "joke" he is playing on the Monopolated Light and Power Company. In *Cane* the device can be seen in the character Layman, who knows more than any black man should know about whites, but who is able to possess this knowledge with impunity. It is also used in the character of Professor Hanby, whose mask, like that of Bledsoe, threatens to become the person.

The ability and necessity of the black character to use his wits to survive is thematically prominent in numerous works by other southern black writers. The second half of Wright's *Black Boy* brings the device into focus, and Book Two of *Native Son* is constructed on the device, for it is Bigger's instinctive knowledge of white psychology that allows him to outwit his pursuers and thus postpone his capture and death. Though the mask device is deeply rooted in southern black folk culture, its literary use has not been confined to writers in and of the South. Born to a couple in Chicago who had migrated from the Deep South, Sam Greenlee knew well the mask device as practiced in the South and used it with thematic skill as the basis of his novel *The Spook Who Sat By the Door* (1969). In Melville's Babo from "Benito Cereno" (1856), in Faulkner's Deacon from *The Sound and the Fury* (1929); in Sutton Griggs's *Imperium in Imperio* (1889), in William Melvin Kelley's *dem* (1967), in Reed's *Flight to Canada* (1976), and in several works by southerners and nonsoutherners, by blacks and nonblacks, the mask device, which parallels the picaresque convention of the hero's ability to survive by his wits, has been widely used and often is at the core of works that deal with black Americans' need and will to survive. The device is pervasive in the life and the literature of southern blacks.

That the protagonist is cut off from the past and from tradition is a picaresque convention that can be readily applied to the ex-coloured man, to Kabnis, to invisible man, and to many other protagonists in southern black fiction. The past and its traditions for these protagonists and their counterparts is a southern black past and a tradition that includes the survival of Africanisms in southern black culture. The typical situation in many southern black novels is that the protagonist has accepted the mainstream culture's denigration of a valuable black past, but while on his journey-quest he rediscovers and affirms the glory and sustaining powers of his ethnic past and its tradition.

The picaresque conventions discussed above are not the only ones applicable to southern black life and its fictional representation. But although a superimposed formula based on European literary traditions can be used to help elucidate approaches to southern black fiction, no such formulaic critical approach in itself is sufficient to explain generically the concerns of and technical achievements in southern black fiction, especially since that fiction derives directly from a southern culture which itself has undergone various changes in this century.

Southern black literature in general has tended to follow closely the social, political, and economic trends in the society that have affected the lives of blacks, and in doing so the literature, while it does not adhere to clear-cut movements, certainly conforms to historical cycles in southern black life. Southern black literature in the first two decades of this century in its often apologetic or propagandistic approach reflected not only the country's attitudes toward the treatment of the somewhat privileged 10 percent and the definitely deprived 90 percent of the black population, but also the attitudes the black populace had toward itself. With the Harlem Renaissance came the second cycle in southern black literature. Although the literary component of this renaissance is identified with Harlem, its literature cannot be separated from the black South. Many of the Harlem Renaissance writers were southern migrants, and many of the works of southern and non-southern blacks of the period were specifically about the South or about the continuity and survival of Africanisms in southern black culture. (The southern black writer living outside the South but writing about it has been the typical situation since World War II.) Toomer's *Cane*, often considered the harbinger of the Harlem Renaissance, remains foremost among book-length works that concentrate on the beauty of living black in the South. In the poetry of the period (a period dominated by poetry), Langston Hughes and James Weldon Johnson are paramount among several poets for whom the positive forces of the black South are central to their art. The trend continued with post-Harlem Renaissance writers such as Zora Neale Hurston, Arna Bontemps, and William Attaway, and with black writers of the 1950s, 1960s, and 1970s who were of southern origin and who, like their protagonists and personae, looked to the black South for spiritual and artistic inspiration.

By the late 1930s southern black literature entered a third cycle in which the pains of living in a racist society are a dominant theme in the literature. Richard Wright and the school of writers identified with him reflect the intensified racism that afflicted the lives of blacks during the economic depression and its aftermath. With the publication of *Invisible Man* in 1952, Ralph Ellison broke with this trend, and the positive quality of southern black life came again to the fore in major works by southern blacks. Within a decade after the publication of Ellison's novel, however, black American literature in general began to focus on the urban North with the advent of such talented writers as James Baldwin and LeRoi Jones (Amiri Baraka). But even in the works of Baldwin, a nonsoutherner and the most prominent black American writer of the 1960s, the South remained in focus and actually dominates *Go Tell It on the Mountain*, a novel about the coming of age of a young urban black whose identity is inseparable from that of his southern migrant family. In many of the works between the mid-1950s and the late 1960s, the South is used as a symbol of the racism that afflicts black life in this country.

Southern black literature entered its present and fourth cycle in the late 1960s and early 1970s, when writers of southern origin were among the leading black American writers. The most dramatic results of the Civil Rights Movement of the 1950s and 1960s were in the South. When by 1970 civil and human rights had become more a fact than a distant hope for black Americans, the effect on black American literature was that the young, urban, black male persona of the 1950s and 1960s who articulated the pains of living in a racist America gave way to a more concentrated focus on the beauty of living black. Southern themes, settings, characters, and authors again came to the fore: Rufus Scott gave way to Jane Pittman; James Baldwin gave way to Ernest Gaines. It is significant that with the emergence of this cycle the works of earlier writers who concentrated on the beauty of southern black life—Jean Toomer's *Cane* and Zora Neale Hurston's *Their Eyes Were Watching God* (1937), for example—were "rediscovered" and stood unabashedly with the best of Richard Wright and of James Baldwin.

Within the cycles of southern black literature that positive force of the South that is ever present in black life has never been totally absent. Even during the protest periods of the 1940s and the 1960s, southern black writers deprecated southern white racism but at the same time affirmed the spiritual essence that sprang from southern black life. And except for these two periods, the South, whether positive or negative, has been foremost in the fiction of black Americans. It began formally with William Wells Brown and has maintained a thematic continuity ever since. From Brown's *Clotel* to Gaines's *Jane Pittman*, from Brown's *The Escape; or a Leap for Freedom* to Reed's *Flight to Canada*, the southern black writer has held his place in American literature, and the contrasting yet complementary images of the South, its pain and its beauty, have remained the subject of and inspiration for the literary arts of black Americans.

There are those who will argue with validity that southern whites have not changed. Yet none can contend justifiably that overt racism in America has not been noticeably curtailed within the last decade. And as an index to black life, southern black fiction has basically paralleled the increasing and diminishing intensity with which racism has oppressed the lives of black Americans. It seems, then, a natural consequence that among the foremost black American fiction writers of the present period are writers of southern origin such as Ernest Gaines and Ishmael Reed, writers who look to the beauty of the black South for inspiration and aesthetic direction.

GEORGE CORE

The Dominion of
the Fugitives
and Agrarians

The incidence of genius is mysterious and inexplicable, but the occurrence of an extraordinary range of talent in groups as diverse and numerous as the Nashville Fugitives and Agrarians of the 1920s and thereafter is rarer and more unaccountable. As Donald Davidson pointed out in his argument with the sociologist Howard W. Odum, no social scientist can explain the presence of a writer so great as William Faulkner in a state so poor and benighted as Mississippi. Davidson could have said the same thing about Eudora Welty; and, to a lesser extent, his argument would have held true for many other twentieth-century southern writers in and out of Mississippi, himself included. Faulkner is the greatest southern writer—and also the greatest American writer—of his time; but the upper South—Kentucky and Tennessee—produced during the same period at least four writers who were more intelligent in a literary sense and who were far better educated: Davidson, John Crowe Ransom, Allen Tate, and Robert Penn Warren, the leading members of both the Fugitives and the Agrarians and the only ones who were members of both groups. Among the other members of the Nashville Fugitives were a psychiatrist (Merrill Moore), a Harvard political scientist (William Yandell Elliott), several prominent businessmen (Ridley Wills, Jesse Wills, and Alfred Starr), and a medieval and renaissance scholar (Walter Clyde Curry). All of these men achieved success well beyond the average for their professions, and the same is true of many of the Agrarians who were not poets and men of letters. Lyle Lanier is a distinguished psychologist; Frank L. Owsley was a leading American historian; and John Donald Wade was a fine biographer and critic.

The focus of the Fugitives was poetry, with a secondary emphasis on criticism; in contrast the Agrarians, who in 1930 published the symposium *I'll Take My Stand*, were interested chiefly in the political impact of social and economic ideas, of their proposals for an ideal society. The most profound effect that Agrarianism had was in the realm of ideas—not in the realm of action. The contributions of both groups were literary and philosophical, not political, economic, sociological; their continuing significance rests on a plane that is of a literary and theoretical order, not a practical one, with the exception of the influence that the New Criticism has made in the classroom—but I am getting ahead of the story.

The Fugitives were chiefly students and teachers at Vanderbilt University, which in their day in the 1910s and 1920s was endowed with an extraordinarily gifted faculty that performed brilliantly despite an obtuse and autocratic administration. The younger faculty included recent graduates of Vanderbilt—first Ransom and then Davidson and (briefly) Warren—and for that time (or for any time since) a remarkable camaraderie and equality obtained among the members, who ranged from a Nashville merchant (James Frank) and his brother-in-law, a mystic and world traveler (Sidney Hirsch), to members of the English department (Ransom, Curry, Davidson), to young students (first Tate, then Moore, and finally Warren). The usual barriers—between town and gown, between students and faculty—were put aside in the interest of ideas and then, increasingly, of poetry.

In general the Fugitives and Agrarians came from Tennessee and Kentucky, from the bluegrass region in central Kentucky to middle Tennessee, with many of the members having grown up along the border between the two states. None of them came from a wealthy family, but Tate and Andrew Lytle both had some pretensions to having derived from planter or aristocratic stock. What Ransom said of Cleanth Brooks, a Vanderbilt alumnus and literary critic (who contributed to the second Agrarian symposium), and himself—"Brooks and I were about as like as two peas from the same pod in respect to our native region, our stock (we were sons of ministers of the same faith, and equally had theology in our blood), the kind of homes we lived in, the kind of small towns; and perhaps we were most like in the unusual parallel of our formal educations"—could be applied, *mutatis mutandis*, to nearly all the members of the Nashville groups. They were from a cultural backwater that had fortuitously and suddenly found itself with a respectable (but by no means first-rate) university, and they were drawn to it because it represented the best education that most of them could afford. (Both Ransom and Davidson temporarily were forced to discontinue their undergraduate education in order to work and make money for tuition at Vanderbilt. Both taught in the kind of preparatory schools that many of the Fugitives and Agrarians attended, schools modeled on Sawney Webb's academy at Bell Buckle, Tennessee.)

Virtually all the Fugitives and many of the Agrarians had classical educations, with a deep knowledge of Greek and Latin, languages that they continued to read all their lives. Ransom, Davidson, Tate, Warren, and Brooks—any or all of them might have taught classics with great distinction. (As a Rhodes scholar at Oxford Ransom won honors in the Greats course, but he never matriculated in a single course in English literature at either Vanderbilt or Oxford.) And their general knowledge of languages meant that they were all comparativists to a considerable extent, although they seldom wrote on classical or modern European authors. All were widely read in the humanities, especially philosophy (Ransom's principal interest after poetry and the ground of his and Tate's criticism) and history (which attracted Davidson and Warren). All learned writing as a discipline not through "creative" writing courses (Tate, in fact, was one of the first writers-in-residence in the country when he joined the faculty at Princeton University in 1939) but by independent application that profited from the criticism of others. The kind of education that Vanderbilt afforded in the first two or three decades of this century was perfect for their interests and their purposes—despite the provinciality of both Nashville and its leading university.

The commitment to literature was instinctive but by no means undisciplined. It led naturally to the principal Fugitives' and Agrarians' becoming men of letters—not mere academic specialists on the one hand or writers whose ability was confined to a single mode on the other—neither professors writing historical scholarship nor amateur poets. "The man of letters pursues literature as a vocation—seeing no difference between his vocation and his avocation," Tate has observed. ("Journalism is a career; literature is, or ought to be, a vocation," John Gross has argued in *The Rise and Fall of the Man of Letters*.) He is no more confined to writing in a single form than he is limited to the classroom if he happens also to be a professor. For him the community of letters is more important than the academic world; his true commitment is to the life of the mind. "The true province of the man of letters is," as Tate has said, "nothing less (as it is nothing more) than culture itself." The man of letters both creates literature and interprets it in the context of culture so that he is devoted to the vitality not only of art but of language and civilization.

Allen Tate personifies this commitment to art and to the realm of letters: he has probably done more than any American of his time to elevate, enhance, and secure the profession of letters; and his influence on other writers—such as Robert Lowell, Peter Taylor, and Howard Nemerov—has been almost incalculable. Tate has been so devoted to the literary world as to be oblivious a good part of his life to the mundane considerations of everyday living. Davidson's commitment to letters was far more remote in terms of the human dimension (he was very nearly antisocial) but no less profound. In the lives of Ransom and Warren one sees a healthier attitude toward writing and publishing, but the engagement is no less deep, lasting, and unequivocal. I do not wish to become enmeshed in biography, but I will say that Ransom, a cheerful naturalist and Aristotelian, achieved distinction as poet, critic, and editor; that Davidson, a dour Puritan, was a good poet, essayist, and historian; that Tate, a bizarre combination of Catholic religionist and sophisticated sensualist, is a superb critic, poet, and editor who wrote a fine novel; and that Warren, the most talented and worldly of the Nashville group, has performed brilliantly as poet, novelist, critic, and editor and has written good work in history, children's literature, biography, and journalism. I describe these men in religious terms because their quest for a literary community and their involvement in the realm of letters has had a definite spiritual dimension. As Lewis P. Simpson has argued, they founded a southern clerisy (similar to the New England clerisy of Ralph Waldo Emerson's day), and their quest for a literary order in the South is religious as well as intellectual in nature.

Such, then, is the general complexion of the Fugitives and Agrarians. I should add a further point—that all of them were fiercely independent and powerful personalities, and that even though some of them yearned for a community of shared belief (especially Davidson), none of the principal members was ever threatened by a loss of identity or by having his identity becoming subservient upon the mind and will of another person. Ransom was the acknowledged leader of the group, the man to whom the others looked; but no one of them modeled himself upon Ransom or parroted his ideas. The groups were significant collective and personal experiences precisely to the extent that the members honestly gave and took criticism and exchanged information and ideas. The meetings of the groups and the correspondence among the members show an astonishing frankness as well as a shared sense of vocation.

In the first number of the magazine they published from 1922 through 1925, *The Fugitive,* the founders announced (in a statement that has since been quoted endlessly) that they fled "from nothing faster than the high-caste Brahmins of the Old South." Today that statement appears to be a little misleading. In any case, if the Fugitives fled from the aristocrats and bogus aristocrats of the Old South (whose creed in some respects might best be represented in the moonlight-and-magnolia South of Thomas Nelson Page), they engaged the advocates of an industrialized New South at every opportunity after 1929; and throughout their careers they conducted a running battle with Edwin Mims, chairman of the Vanderbilt English department and spokesman for the New South. Mims was a natural enemy since he represented the New South philosophy and a New South administration at Vanderbilt. The Fugitives realized quickly that there is a basic difference, even an antagonism, between the complexion of the literary community and the nature of a university. They were all men of letters first and academicians second.

The Fugitives and Agrarians also reacted powerfully against other groups and other ideas: the New Humanists (especially Irving Babbitt and Paul Elmer More), H. L. Mencken and his followers, who to some extent included the Chapel Hill regionalists (Howard W. Odum, Rupert Vance, and others of like spirit, especially W. J. Cash), positivists and positivism, science and technology (including industrialism), and neo-Aristotelian criticism. Time diminishes certain deep and apparently irreconcilable differences, and today one can see plainly that the Nashville group had a good deal more in common with the New Humanists and the Chapel Hill regionalists than any of them realized in the 1920s and 1930s. The same is true of the common ground with the *Scrutiny* group in England, although there has been little or no intercourse between the New Critics and Leavis and his followers. The Fugitives and Agrarians have remained consistently opposed to big business or industrial capitalism; to science and technology; to totalitarian government, whether of the left or the right (including fascism); and to views of the South differing from their own, including the Piedmont perspectives of Thomas Wolfe, Erskine Caldwell, and James Agee, and the New South creeds of various editors and apologists beginning with Henry W. Grady and Walter Hines Page. This is to state the force of their ideas and values in a negative way—to say what they were against rather than what they believed in.

Before turning to the positive side of the ledger, I want to glance at some of the important historical events that strongly affected the Nashville writers. In the first place there was the world war of 1914–1918. Ransom and Davison were directly involved in it as officers serving in Pershing's expeditionary force (Ransom managed all the same to have his first book published—*Poems about God*—in 1919). Tate was a boy when the war began, but it made a strong impact on his life (and that of Warren) all the same; he wrote at the end of World War II: "With the war of 1914–1918, the South reentered the world—but gave a backward glance as it stepped over the border: that backward glance gave us the Southern renascence, a literature conscious of the past in the present." That event enabled the Fugitives and Agrarians to understand the Civil War in an immediate sense.

The other two historical events that made an enormous impact on some of the Fugitives and Agrarians were the Scopes trial at Dayton, Tennessee, in 1925 (which involved the teaching of Darwin's theory of evolution and its collision with Old Testament doctrine) and the Great Depression of the 1930s, which proved their prophesies to be true and which led in part to the second agrarian symposium, *Who Owns America?* (1936).

The literary events of greatest importance were the publication of H. L. Mencken's broadside "The Sahara of the Bozart" in 1920 (and his related attacks on the South) and the publication of major literary works of modernism, especially *The Waste Land, Ulysses,* and many of Yeats's most important poems. These appeared in the early 1920s, during the years that R. P. Blackmur called *anni mirabiles*. Much of the Fugitives' poetry and criticism was forged in large part by their reaction—largely negative—to modernism. Against this general background one can see the catalysts that precipitated the thought and the writing of the Nashville group.

Before turning to the ideas as such, I want to mention the vehicles of those ideas. First came *The Fugitive* magazine, which was published from 1922 through 1925 and was suspended because the Fugitives were too busy by 1925 with their own work to have time for a magazine. The principal vehicles for the Agrarians were the symposia *I'll Take My Stand* and *Who Owns America?* and a magazine edited by Seward Collins, the *American Review*. By 1937 Agrarianism as a formal movement had ended, and Ransom, Tate, Warren, and Cleanth Brooks turned their energy to criticism. Ransom founded the *Kenyon Review* in 1940 and edited it for the next quarter century; by 1940 the *Southern Review* under Brooks and Warren had already been published for five years, and in 1942 it was suspended. In 1944 Tate redefined the *Sewanee Review* along the lines of the *Kenyon Review* and the *Southern Review*, as a quarterly that was primarily literary and critical. Through the agency of these magazines and by means of the criticism of Ransom, Tate, Warren, Brooks, and other critics of similar persuasion such as Blackmur, Francis Fergusson, and Yvor Winters, the hegemony of the New Criticism was established by the mid–1940s. The Nashville group, by now largely dispersed in the Midwest and the East, had moved from social criticism (Agrarianism) to the study of literature (the New Criticism). Poetry remained important but for the moment was secondary. The Fugitive-Agrarians had by the late 1930s and early 1940s not only created publishing outlets for themselves through founding and editing magazines, but they had also published their work with the leading southern publisher, the University of North Carolina Press, and with the leading trade houses in the East, especially Harper, Houghton, Mifflin, and Scribners. Few other literary groups have understood so well the importance of the literary marketplace.

What of the ideas that were disseminated in wide commonality through that marketplace? In a letter written to Davidson in August, 1922, Tate said that he believed that no "man can write without a theory of some kind, and a metaphysical theory at that!" This proved true for the Fugitives and Agrarians. Tate himself has defined their common pursuits better than anyone else. "There was a sort of unity of feeling, of which we were not then very much aware," he has written, "which came out of—to give it a big name —a common historical myth." Elsewhere he has defined it as the Greco-Trojan myth—"Northerners as the upstart Greeks, Southerners as the older, more civilized Trojans"—saying of myth in general that it is "a dramatic projection of heroic action, or of the tragic failure of heroic action, upon the reality of the common life of a society, so that the myth *is* reality." Tate goes on to say that he sees the southern myth along these lines:

> The South, afflicted with the curse of slavery—a curse, like that of Original Sin, for which no single person is responsible—has to be destroyed, the good along with the evil. The old order had a great deal of good, one of the "goods" being a result of the evil; for slavery itself entailed a certain moral responsibility. . . . This old order, in which the good could not be salvaged from the bad, was replaced by a new order which was in many ways worse than the old. The Negro, legally free,

was not prepared for freedom. . . . The carpetbaggers, "foreign" exploiters, and their collaborators, the native rascals called "scalawags," gave the Old South its final agonies. The cynical materialism of the new order brought the South the American standard of living, but it also brought about a society similar to that which Matthew Arnold saw in the North in the eighties and called vigorous and uninteresting.

Tate quite properly sees William Faulkner, of all modern southern writers, as bringing the greatest pressure to bear on this myth and at the same time exploring it the most successfully within the limits of literary form. He believes that what sets Faulkner apart from Warren, Lytle, Stark Young (also a contributor to *I'll Take My Stand*), Caroline Gordon, Katherine Anne Porter, and Eudora Welty is Faulkner's brilliant and characteristic theme of man's obsessive exploitation of nature. That theme in Tate's judgment "adds a philosophical, even a mystical, dimension to the conventional Southern myth. *For most of us the myth is merely historical and secular*" (italics mine). The Fugitives and Agrarians did not incorporate the theme of nature's exploitation into their literary works, as Faulkner did; they could only inveigh against the rape of the land in their Agrarian tracts. But I do not wish to obscure the larger point—that Faulkner, the Fugitives, and other important southern writers of the same time had not only a common theme but a shared mythology to draw upon. In Faulkner's greatest fiction the mythology has a genuinely religious dimension: it is instinctive and original; but the same myth in the fiction and poetry of Ransom, Davidson, Tate, Lytle, and Warren is the product of the historical imagination rather than the religious imagination: it is willed, conscious, and derivative. One would expect this, for the Fugitives and Agrarians were enormously conscious and sophisticated in their writing. This is nowhere more evident than in their views toward the South. Once they became men of letters, they willed themselves into the southern community: they were in it but never again quite of it. In this respect they lost their innocence much more quickly than Faulkner, but Faulkner felt the same deprivation and pretended most of his mature life that he was a farmer rather than a writer.

The myth of the South as Tate describes it constitutes the substantive foundation for the fiction and poetry of the Fugitives and Agrarians: for Ransom's "Antique Harvesters," for Tate's *The Fathers* and "Ode to the Confederate Dead," for Warren's *Brother to Dragons* and *Band of Angels*, for Davidson's "Lee in the Mountains," for Lytle's *The Velvet Horn*. The Nashville writers did not invent the myth: they seized upon its availability and its vitality. The myth was a common property that could be inherited by their generation of southerners, but we should remember, as Lewis P. Simpson has observed, that no literary group has ever worked quite so hard at inheriting its inheritance as did the Fugitives and Agrarians.

The use of the Greco-Trojan legend as Tate describes it provides a concrete example of what he meant in writing to Davidson in May, 1926: "There is one fundamental law of poetry, and it is negative: you can't *create* a theme. Themes are or are not available." The situation for the literary or social critic is different from that of the poet, however; and the Nashville writers created social and critical themes in Agrarianism and in the New Criticism.

In its simplest sense Agrarianism was an effort to project the possibilities of a life in the South based on the family and the land. The Agrarians were among the first literate and vocal ecologists in the United States, for they recognized that industrialism is founded on what Ransom called "a principle of boundless aggression against nature." One of the pillars of Agrarianism, as Frank Owsley termed it, was to conserve land for future generations. But the Agrarians were unable to work out a complete social program or to answer the crucial question of how the land could be bought from holding companies and banks and then distributed to small farmers. The movement succeeded brilliantly on the plane of ideas, but failed dismally on the plane of action. As they looked back on the experience in 1952 in a symposium published in *Shenandoah*, Ransom, Davidson, Tate, Lytle, and others agreed that the emphasis in the movement should have been placed more firmly on religion. They were not concerned about the failure of the practical aspect of the enterprise, and they thought, quite properly, that Agrarianism in the 1950s had a greater intellectual following than in the 1930s. It has a still greater influence today.

More and more people are embracing the idea that science, technology, and industry are the gods of a capitalist state, and they deplore the worship of materialistic progress.

The Agrarians gradually turned away from social reform back to literature, and in the course of doing so they almost accidentally and unconsciously, as it were, founded the New Criticism, which has had a revolutionary and epoch-making effect on the teaching of English literature and the interpretation of that literature. At the heart of its philosophical complexion lies the simple but firm belief in the autonomy of the literary work. The insistence on that autonomy probably springs in part from the Fugitives' and Agrarians' belief in the inviolability of the literary community and their commitment to the literary vocation. The stress on the integrity and independence of the literary work does not mean, as Walter Ong has argued in *Interfaces of the Word* (to name one of many critics of like mind), that the New Critics argue that the poem is a closed field. There is stress on structure, to be sure; but as Brooks has recently said, "Nobody in his right mind, of course, is really interested in empty formality. . . . The 'arrangement of words' about which I am talking is a kind of special reflection of manifold humanity itself." In order to consider manifold humanity the critic must bring his knowledge of history, of biography, and so forth to bear on the given poem or fiction. Brooks and Warren therefore agree that "all the information we can get . . . is valuable, provided that we do not make it reductive." Anyone who has read the criticism of Ransom, Tate, Warren, and Brooks with any degree of care knows that the criticism is not antihistorical or antibiographical, as has often been charged. What Tate has said of the criticism of William Empson and of Cleanth Brooks—in neither "is history left out; it ceases to appear methodologically; it no longer devours the literary text; it survives as contributory knowledge"—is true of the New Critics as a whole.

This brings us naturally to what is the central informing idea in the criticism of the Fugitives and Agrarians: the concept that literature is a unique form of knowledge. Ransom said it best in *The World's Body*: Poetry "only wants to realize the world, to see it better. Poetry is the kind of knowledge by which we must know

... that we shall not know otherwise. . . . There is no reason why it should not offer an absolute knowledge of this object, so far as the adjective is ever applicable to a human knowledge, including a scientific knowledge." Brooks and Warren have recently agreed that literature is "immediate knowledge by imaginative enactment." Tate concludes his essay on the subject, "Literature as Knowledge," by quoting I. A. Richards—"Poetry is the completest form of utterance"—and extrapolating from that text. Tate argues that the value of poetry is cognitive: it offers knowledge by bringing order to our experience through the limits of form. This experienced order in its highest realm is mythic—which returns us to Tate's judgment that the Fugitives were "an intensive and historical group as opposed to the eclectic and cosmopolitan groups that flourished in the East. There was a sort of unity of feeling . . . which came out of . . . a common historical myth." That myth we have already considered: it concerns, as Tate said of Davidson's poetry, the "opposition of an heroic myth to the secularization of man in our age." It is, therefore, like Agrarianism, a powerful response to the cross-currents of modernism. (The New Criticism was created in part as a means of coping with a strange new literature—modernism.) The myth is ultimately the subject not only of the fiction and poetry but of the Agrarian essays, of the Confederate biographies of Stonewall Jackson and Jefferson Davis by Tate, the biography of John Brown by Warren and his *The Legacy of the Civil War*, *Bedford Forrest and His Critter Company* by Lytle, and various other books such as the fiction of Stark Young and Caroline Gordon and the biography of the antebellum humorist A. B. Longstreet by John Donald Wade.

That myth, founded on memory and history as Lewis Simpson has shrewdly observed, has now been replaced by a new and opposing view of man in the South, which, as Mr. Simpson has also remarked, rests on the tension between a gnostic society and the existential self. The myth has for the time at least passed into literary and cultural history like the myths and civilizations upon which it and the South were modeled: Troy, Sparta, Republican Rome, and medieval Europe.

What of the balance sheet? The influence of the Fugitives and Agrarians has reached far beyond the borders of the southern United States. Through their writing, their editing (which includes not only four important quarterlies but many fine textbooks, particularly Brooks and Warren's *Understanding Poetry*), and their teaching, especially at Vanderbilt, Louisiana State University, Kenyon, the University of Minnesota, Bread Loaf, and Yale, the Fugitives and Agrarians have reached a wide audience not only in the United States but in Europe and the British Isles. Indeed their importance was recognized outside Vanderbilt, Nashville, and the South well before it was within southern borders. The intellectual center that they provided for their time and the succeeding generations (the peak of their influence occurred in the late 1940s and the 1950s) was by no means limited to the South (the geographical center moved from Nashville to Baton Rouge, Louisiana, to Gambier, Ohio, and New Haven, Connecticut).

The Nashville writers have made a deep impress on the community of letters. The universality of their impact paradoxically may have seemed to dilute the local and regional origins of the literature and the men who made it. Such an argument might be advanced by the critic who strongly emphasizes the departure of most of the Fugitives and Agrarians from the South. That critic might say that the South for these men—Ransom, Tate, Warren, and Brooks especially—had been repudiated actually or symbolically, and that they wrote about a South that became increasingly remote and foreign to them. This is to distort the fact that the South has always remained the spiritual homeland of the Fugitives and the Agrarians, and that by leaving the South the Fugitives and Agrarians were able in many senses not only to see it more clearly but to use their positions in the Midwest and Northeast as vantage points from which to advance the acceptance of their work and of the South in general. The highwater mark of international recognition for their success may have come in the historic issue of the London *Times Literary Supplement* devoted to contemporary American writing (September 17, 1954), an issue dominated by consideration of southern writers.

The collective contributions of the Fugitives and Agrarians are far easier to detail than their individual works: *The Fugitive*, the two Agrarian symposia, the old *Southern Review* (1935–1942), the *Kenyon Review* (1940–1969), the *Sewanee Review* since 1944, the School of English at Kenyon College (later the School of Letters at Indiana University) where a generation of students learned criticism, and the New Criticism as a whole (which was much more the result of a collective but largely unorganized effort than any of the fiction or poetry). The greatest impact that the Nashville writers made collectively is the effect of the New Criticism, which even today in its beleaguered, misunderstood, and maligned state continues to exercise a far-reaching influence and to be the most important criticism of this century.

The most important contributions of the leading Fugitives and Agrarians can be briefly described. Ransom, as his student and colleague Randall Jarrell once pointed out, wrote a handful of almost perfect poems that will be read as long as poetry in English is valued; he is the most important southern writer of this century after Faulkner in consequence of his writing (including the literary criticism) and his editing. Tate has had an almost equally great authority and influence through his writing and by means of his relations in the literary world. He is not so good a poet as Ransom but is a slightly more astute critic, and his editing has been almost as far-reaching in its impact as Ransom's. Warren is a novelist of considerable power and a poet who (unlike Ransom and Tate, each of whom wrote too little poetry to be considered more than minor poets) has some claim to being major. At this moment he is probably the greatest living American poet. With his friend Brooks he has revolutionized the teaching of college English. Brooks is a brilliant practical critic, probably the best in the world; he does not have the philosophical grasp of Ransom and Tate. Davidson did not achieve major stature in any given field except as a teacher. In a group of people known for brilliance in college teaching, he was the best. (He also wrote the finest expository prose of any of his colleagues.) Of the remaining Fugitives and Agrarians who wrote as a career, Lytle is the most important, but he has never written a novel of the first order, and his literary criticism is slighter than that of the others, excepting Davidson's. The best of this distinguished body of work is quite likely to endure: Ransom's *Selected Poems* (1945) and some of his essays (especially those in *The World's Body*); Tate's *The Fathers* (perhaps), some of his poems (especially "Ode to the Confederate Dead," "The Swimmers," and "Seasons of the Soul"), and a half dozen of his essays; Warren's *All the King's Men, Brother to Dragons,* and *Selected Poems 1923–1975;* possibly Davidson's *Attack on Leviathan* and a few of his poems; and Brooks's best criticism (chiefly essays in *Modern Poetry and the Tradition* and *The Well Wrought Urn*). With the exception of Ransom's best poems, *I'll Take My Stand* will probably last as long any of these works. It would be easy to overestimate the writers and their work in this context. None of them is major in the sense of a Hawthorne, Melville, Whitman, or James; and only Warren could be considered a major writer by any reasonable and convincing standard.

The most significant contribution of the Fugitives and Agrarians may have been to show the South the possibilities of the southern experience for a vital southern art. As John Peale Bishop observed, until 1920 the South's arts were limited to manners and cooking —a judgment that oddly complements Mencken's famous attacks. The Nashville group not only made it possible for the southern writer in succeeding generations to stay home and pursue his profession, but created a literary marketplace in the South. In this and other ways the Fugitives and Agrarians and the other leading southern writers of their generation—especially Faulkner—gave the South back to the South and made it at the same time the most important country of the American imagination in the twentieth century.

The South: Distance and Change.
A Conversation with
Robert Penn Warren, William Styron, and Louis D. Rubin, Jr.

RUBIN: The two southern authors who are with me here to talk about the South might be said to be of different literary generations. Robert Penn Warren was born in 1905. As a youthful member of the Nashville Fugitive poets he was publishing verse in 1924, a year before William Styron was born. Red Warren's first novel, *Night Rider*, came out before the Second World War, in 1939. Bill Styron published *Lie Down in Darkness*, his first novel, in 1951. Yet in addition to a close personal friendship, they share many things together, among them a fascination with southern history. What is interesting to me here is that neither of them has lived in the southern states for a number of years. Bill, you left Newport News, Virginia, well before your first novel came out, didn't you?

STYRON: Well, I'll put it this way: there's a split. I spent my childhood, boyhood, youth, and education entirely in the South, and in my early twenties I left. I've visited a lot, but I've never really been back.

RUBIN: And, Red Warren, you grew up in Guthrie, Kentucky, and then you went to Vanderbilt University in Nashville, Tennessee . . .

WARREN: Fifty miles away. It was in the same part of the world.

RUBIN: But then when you graduated from Vanderbilt you went to California, and Yale, and then Oxford, and then you came back to the South to teach.

WARREN: In 1930. And I lived in the South until 1942, with some trips abroad and other trips around the country—a lot of trips to the Far West during that period, and abroad a couple of times.

RUBIN: You left Louisiana State University, where you and Cleanth Brooks edited the *Southern Review*, in 1942, and you went to Minnesota. So you've been away from the South for over thirty years.

WARREN: Yes, I left Minnesota for Yale, and I've lived in New England now for twenty-five years, for twenty-seven years.

RUBIN: And, Bill, you've been away almost that long yourself.

STYRON: Yes.

RUBIN: Yet what strikes me now is this: Red, you recently published a new novel, *A Place to Come To*. And, Bill, I've seen excerpts from the novel that you've been working on. Red's novel involves a southerner who's been away from the South for a long time, going back and leaving. And while Bill's novel takes place in New York and Europe and involves a concentration camp experience of the Second World War, nevertheless the meaning of the experience is "happening," insofar as the narrator is involved, to a southerner from Virginia. So obviously the experience outside of the South still seems to mean a great deal to both of you in terms of what it signifies to you *as* southerners. Your imagination seems to be still very thoroughly grounded in an identity that geographically at least you abandoned a long time ago. Could you say that, as a fiction writer, Red, this is still the experience that is most real to you?

WARREN: Well, "reality," I guess, is one word to describe it. Actually, it seems to me that though your basic images and attitudes may change in many ways, they are always fundamentally conditioned by what you knew in small and large ways very early in life. This remains important, at least to me. Now take a small, trivial thing. If I were writing a story about a Connecticut farmer, I wouldn't know where to begin. But writing a story about such a family, rich or poor, grand or miserable, in the South, I wouldn't have any hesitation. It would be as natural as breathing to me. I'd know what they did, I'd know what they ate, I'd know what they'd say. And also the matter of landscape is extremely important. I suppose I'm bringing in something now that may be irrelevant, but the nature of the land itself, in relation to the landscape of other parts of the world, other places, is very important to me, particularly in poems.

RUBIN: Bill, most of your fiction has not taken place *in* the South, but has involved southerners away from the South, or else, in the case of *The Confessions of Nat Turner*, it takes place in the South but you elected to take a completely different social view of the thing, looking at it from the standpoint of a black slave, rather than that of a white man in your own time. So in a sense, your fiction seems to involve either a way of looking at the South from outside, or a southerner away from the South trying to get his bearings. If you identify it in a moment of history, it would be the confrontation of the provincial southern experience of the past with the wide world outside. That seems to be your subject.

STYRON: I think a lot of it has to do with the change which has taken place in America and the kind of homogeneity of the regions—the idea that the South is no longer the South that it once was. Maybe I arrived on the historical scene at a crucial juncture, at least for myself. When I got out of college and World War II was over, I decided I was not going to live in the South, because my pull was elsewhere. The magnet was northward. So I moved North, and as a result—I don't mean to say it's been a conflict— I've always had a fluid feeling about the South merging with the North, and the North with the South, and so on. I've had to acknowledge my own southern roots throughout, and I've never lost sight of them. I know deep down that I'm very much the writer I am because of my origins, which were southern. But I've had to reassess my experience as I've gone along, to be quite honest, because I have not lived in the South.

RUBIN: It seems to me that there is a historical significance involved. One of the most moving scenes in any of your novels is that scene early in *Set This House on Fire* when you have your narrator go to a place where he had once been crabbing in a skiff in the tidal marshes around Newport News and Hampton, and he finds that on the very spot where he had once almost drowned, there is now a filling station, an Esso station, and a shopping center. The tremendous fact of that change seems to demand a kind of redefinition. Red Warren, I notice that several of your recent novels have involved a man going back a long time later to the place where he grew up and noticing the difference, having had the experience of being out in the world. In one instance the old place has been covered by flood waters. In your most recent novel he comes back at the very end to the town he had been fleeing from all his life, where his mother had lived.

WARREN: She had driven him out, because she hated where she was.

RUBIN: In one of your poems there is an image that I find very striking—it has come to my mind again and again. It is the image of the man who has returned home and walks out by the railroad tracks at night and watches the Pullman cars on the train go by— that memory. In both cases it seems to me that so much of your experience of the South, and Bill Styron's experience of the South, involves this sense of "who am I?" in terms of "how far have I gone from the South and where did I start from and how did I come back?"

WARREN: There's one difference between us; I don't know how important it is. I wanted to live in the South, you see; I'm a refugee from the South, driven out, as it were. The place I wanted to live, the place I thought was heaven to me, after my years of wandering, was Middle Tennessee, which is a beautiful country, or *was* a beautiful country—it's rapidly being ruined. But I couldn't make it work. When I went back to teach for three years there, I enjoyed living in the country, and driving in to do my teaching, and this was fine. But I was let out of Vanderbilt University, and had to go elsewhere for a job. I went to Louisiana State University, which was quite fortunately a very exciting place. And I left Louisiana only because I felt I wasn't wanted. I felt pressure to leave. It wasn't a choice. I had settled myself down and bought a house in the country—settled down for life, I assumed. I left, shall we say, under pressure of some kind or another. I wasn't fired. I left out of pride. I went to Minnesota, which I enjoyed.

I've quit teaching several times—"never again." But I fell in love with teaching along the way, so I always drifted back in again. I was out as long as six years one time, two years another time, and again a year or so at a time. But that's not the point. The point is that I, unlike Bill, didn't make a choice of living outside the South. I always felt myself somehow squeezed out of the South, which is a very different thing from Bill's conscious choice. That is a generational matter, perhaps; I don't know.

RUBIN: But I wonder whether Bill's choice was entirely a free one? In other words, didn't the choice really mean: "can I be myself and do what I want to do while living here?" And the answer was no.

STYRON: I think that was my decision. The decision I made had nothing to do with any antipathy toward the South; quite the contrary. It so happened that I didn't have many friends left in the South. I had very few connections in the South that I felt deeply. I was not in teaching. After I left Duke University I hung around Durham for a while and enjoyed it, oddly enough, because it's not the most attractive of southern cities. But I left simply because most of the profounder contacts I had made with other human beings were in the North, and that was my decision. I hope we will discuss later the experience of the southerner up North, and the southerner as an intermediary for his fellow southerners, and so on. That's a different kettle of fish. But I felt—it may be a generational matter—I left on my own volition, just for the reason I mentioned.

RUBIN: I wouldn't say it's simply a generational matter. Certainly there are writers of Red's generation, and older than Red, who did the same thing you did, while there are writers of your own generation, Walker Percy, for example, who have stayed and lived in the South—though significantly, not in the place where he grew up. Walker lives right outside of New Orleans, but he didn't grow up there, he grew up in the Mississippi Delta. But you and Red Warren both left something which was called "the South," and now when you go back you don't go to something called "the South," you go back to something which is now called "the Sun Belt."

WARREN: Just recently.

RUBIN: Now it's "the Sun Belt." Something profound has supposedly happened to make "the South" into "the Sun Belt," and it seems to have something to do with the cultivation of peanuts, as far as I can tell, and sunburn. But now, all of a sudden, the South is the Sun Belt.

STYRON: That's a jazzy modern expression, and I think it has something to do with what you mentioned just now. Also, it has to do with the disappearance of the Pullman train and the arrival of Eastern Airlines. I think things like that make all the difference. You can readily utter a very jazzy phrase like "the Sun Belt" if you're travelling by Whisperjet to Atlanta—it seems to be appropriate—but you couldn't in the old days, which we still remember, of the Pullman trains and that lonesome whistle that Thomas Wolfe was always describing.

RUBIN: The significance of the change of the name, it seems to me, is that now, for the first time since the days of Thomas Jefferson, you no longer quite find yourself in the position of having to do what I notice Bill Styron has one of the characters in his new novel do, in the excerpt I read the other day: *apologize* to his northern contemporary for coming from that barbarous place down there. That's no longer quite necessary, is it? You're from the South, but they don't look to see whether you're carrying your slave whip any more. You're in a different situation. Now you come from Where The Action Is.

WARREN: By the way, this term "Sun Belt" is a realtor's term, and that captures the whole story.

RUBIN: It is true still, though, that "red-necks" came from the Sun Belt, didn't they? That's how their necks got red.

STYRON: There is a huge emotional and historical chasm between 1947, let us say, when I first arrived as a very young man in New York, and the attitude toward the South at that point, and the attitude that prevails now. I think it's a very interesting contrast. At least my own experience tells me that there used to be a very distinct tangible hostility in certain areas of New York life toward people who came from the South. It's in my experience.

WARREN: It's in *my* experience, too.

STYRON: And I think Louis is right, that it no longer applies, at least certainly not with the intensity that it once did. In fact, it may have almost disappeared altogether.

WARREN: Too bad!

STYRON: Too bad. Well, at least it takes some of the abrasiveness out of life.

RUBIN: It takes some of that experience of identity. After all, part of your identity can be shaped by a sense of what you're not, as well as what you are. And I think many people became aware of the fact that they were southerners when they got out of the South, and found that many things they assumed were not ordinarily assumed by a lot of other people.

WARREN: The South never crossed my mind except as an imaginative construct before I left it. I was raised on the battles and leaders of the Civil War by a grandfather veteran who had a very active part in the Civil War, but he was also mad for Napoleon's campaigns, so I got a great dose of Napoleon's campaigns and General Forrest's operations all mixed up together. I could draw the battlefields of Austerlitz or of Fort Donelson, or the attack on this, or the other. I had it all tangled up together in my earliest years.

RUBIN: That is also what the Confederates themselves did, you know. They thought of their Civil War experience, when they wrote about it, in Napoleonic terms. You know that story about the Battle of Shiloh, the surprise march, when the sun's coming up and the officers are saying "This is the sun of Austerlitz," and the soldiers didn't know what they were talking about—they thought they were saying "the Son of Oyster Itch."

WARREN: This leads to another question. The South has one peculiarity: it was a nation once, and that makes a vast difference, though it can be forgotten that it makes a difference. Another thing that's forgotten that makes a difference is that southerners felt that they had created the Union—Washington and Jefferson had created the Union—and the North was going to take it away from them. There were many Unionists in the Civil War who were still fighting in the Confederate army because they were fighting for their country, which was the United States of America.

STYRON: Wasn't Robert E. Lee's conflict in 1861 based on that?

WARREN: I guess it was based on that; many were. It was a double nationality that was involved there, and there's a vast complication—I don't pretend to settle it now—an emotional tangle in the role of the South in fighting the United States, and the role of the South as an independent nation. This is a complicated issue, and it has strong emotional ramifications, even for ignorant people.

STYRON: The very idea that such an intense nationalism existed almost defines the individuality that the South still thinks itself to have, whether rightly or wrongly.

RUBIN: I think it's still very much there. I don't think it's eroding. The fact that the South is becoming urbanized and industrialized, so that, let's say, the suburbs of Atlanta seem to resemble the suburbs of Detroit, or something like that—I don't think that they *are* the suburbs of Detroit. I don't think the South is losing its identity at all.

STYRON: I don't think it's losing its identity, but I think it tends to be less well defined in certain areas. I've spent recently a lot of time in North Carolina, and I notice that in the larger urban areas, there is a blur. I mean, except for the accents, and so on, you find a kind of northern overlay. On the other hand, the small towns, where I've also been, in eastern North Carolina, are maybe even more southern than I once remembered, for some reason. A little town like Goldsboro, where I've spent a lot of time, which is in the heart of the Tobacco Belt, has barely changed an iota since the time I remember it as a little boy in the 1930s. So I think it's a matter of where you are in the South.

WARREN: That may be true. I think there are vast changes in the parts of the South I knew best—Middle Tennessee and the Cumberland River Valley—vast changes and changes of attitude. Now some are for the good, and I would be the first to grant that. I faced the question, actually, when I started to buy a farm in Tennessee, where I would spend half the year. I felt I'd be isolated. A lot of friends are dead and gone. But I also felt a real change in the whole nature of the world. And I felt it would be an idle dream for me to go back there. It would be ridiculous.

STYRON: I feel the same way.

WARREN: The one friend I know who did so shot himself.

STYRON: *That*'s the end of a dream.

RUBIN: Aren't you really talking about the nature of time, though? I mean, about your experience of your childhood and the people you knew when you grew up as a child. If you had stayed there, they wouldn't have continued the same way, either. When you go back to Guthrie, Red, or you go back to Newport News, Bill, in a sense you are going back to your memories of a time. There are a number of physical objects around that can trigger those memories, but you're really going back to a time even more than to a place. You say that everything has changed. What you're saying is that so many years have elapsed, aren't you? As for the people who have been there all along and who haven't left, they've changed too. They're not the same. You're now fifty-one, I believe. Let's say you had been fifty-one in the year 1935 instead of 1977. Don't you think that if you had come back to Newport News in 1935 at the age of fifty-one, you might also have said, "This has all changed. It's all gone. It's not like what it was"? In other words, isn't part of what we're dealing with here the nature of time, and when you look back it always seems that everything has changed?

WARREN: Part of it is. That's partly true. But there are also other elements involved in it. One element for me was that I had no attachments to a town. My attachment was always to the country, and that made a difference. I was attached to the countryside, to rural life, not town life. I couldn't abide small town life from the start. I was always against it.

RUBIN: In some ways it seems to me that a good deal of the strength of twentieth-century southern writing in general, and your own work in particular, may lie in the fact that the literature itself has had to, and still has to, confront the tremendous phenomenon of change in time. It becomes almost an exemplar of the American experience as a whole. The change has been so swift, so bewildering, and in so short a period of time—in your own lifetimes—that a good deal of the strength of southern literature comes out of the intensity and the power of that change.

STYRON: I think you must include in that the quite obvious and single most significant social change in the South, which we haven't touched on yet—the rapidity with which the whole racial dilemma has been turned around, within the lifetimes of most all of us. Certainly that has been one of the most bewildering and, I might add, amazing and benignly revolutionary things that I think have ever happened in a civilized country.

WARREN: And now Jimmy Carter can be elected president by black support, as he was.

STYRON: Yes, of course.

RUBIN: It seems to me that actually the South—and I don't just mean the urban South, I mean the *rural* South, in many ways more so the rural South and the small town South—is more integrated now than almost any place else in the country. I mean *integrated*. I see this all the time. It may be true that I live in an academic community myself, but one of my interests is youth baseball. I have been running a four-county baseball league, and we go around the several counties and play various teams. Those teams we play are interracial teams, and it never occurs to anybody when they're

selecting a baseball player that that's a black boy or a white boy.
It's a matter of how fast he can run and how well he can hit. You
know, that's rather amazing. I don't mean to say that our racial
problems are solved, or anything like that. I don't know that they
ever will be solved—if they are, it will be the only important moral
problem in the world that ever was solved. But it seems to me
that the South has become a more genuinely integrated society
than anywhere else in the world.

WARREN: Back in the 1960s I was traveling a great deal in the South,
more than in the North for a while, interviewing Negroes for a
book I was writing—all kinds of Negroes. More than once I heard
Negroes say, "There's a personal relationship here, bad or good,
which gives reality and holds some hope for the future. If a sheriff
shoots you in Alabama, he probably knows your name. If a cop
brains you in Detroit, he doesn't know your name. That makes a
big difference." This was actually said to me by an Alabama black.
"I see some hope in that," he said. "He knows what he's doing;
he's stuck with it."

STYRON: He might be a black sheriff now.

WARREN: Yes, now he might be a sheriff himself.

STYRON: Well, I notice this, again very intensely, in Goldsboro,
North Carolina, to be specific. If you wanted to have a movie version of a typical small coastal southern town, Goldsboro would be
it. I'm thinking of the Down Towner Motel there—you know,
they have them all over. Well, it was hard for me to adjust at first,
coming from the totally white precincts of Litchfield County,
Connecticut, to the Down Towner's dining room, which is so
completely integrated that no one even gives it any thought; most
of the diners—I'd say 60 percent because of the heavily black population down there—are black. And it's as casual as you can imagine. There is no thought, no concern, no friction, there's no nothing. And when any of us compares that to the environment we
were accustomed to in the segregated South, the one that I remember and that I'm sure all of us remember, it's just astonishing. If you had told me, as a growing boy during the depression

years in Virginia, that that could happen, I would have called you a nut, crazy.

WARREN: Don't forget that segregation was a very late development in America, and it was not true of the Old South. There was slavery, but not segregation. Segregation did not come in until quite late. In the 1880s and 1890s, according to Vann Woodward's book *The Strange Career of Jim Crow*, the Charleston, South Carolina, papers, for example, were against segregation. They said, "After you segregate the trains, the next thing is there will be two Bibles to kiss in court." And it happened.

RUBIN: That's true. On the other hand, I think that can be interpreted a little differently. Isn't it true that laws demanding segregation, and all these little artifacts—the front and the back of the streetcar—came about because with the end of slavery there was no longer any enormous institutionalized social fact which would create the distance, maintain the barrier, and therefore the white South felt it had to enact these things into little laws, and things like that? It wasn't even questioned, before, so that there wasn't any need for it in that sense.

WARREN: Well, there was no need up north, because there was enforced segregation already.

STYRON: But there was also the fact of Reconstruction, which was a trauma in many ways to the South, with on the surface often a very shocking insult to white southern sensibilities. The idea of black men being in power, and being artificially put in power, was a traumatic experience after the hegemony of the whites. Certainly one of the reasons for Jim Crow, at least one of the elements in Jim Crow, was a redressing of that grievance.

WARREN: It was also a change in the class system in the South, part of it.

RUBIN: Very much so.

STYRON: But all this aside, the fact still remains that for many of us, if we could have lived to be two hundred years old today, we would have known a phase in our lives when strict segregation would have been an unheard-of strangeness because in antebellum times it would have made no sense, emotionally or otherwise. But for those of us who are caught up in history, the experience of being brought up in the South, born and raised any time from 1900 right on through to World War II, was the equivalent—I don't think it's stretching it too far to say—of living in South Africa, certainly in the Black Belt part of the South where I was brought up. You had a total *apartheid*, and it had a severe, lacerating, and wounding effect on both races, black and white.

WARREN: I agree with you about that.

STYRON: And it wasn't our fault. I'm not trying to get off the hook. I'm simply saying that history treated a whole generation of us—maybe two generations—to this.

WARREN: One other very important element in it, too, is the flinch from black flesh, dark flesh. Now the flinch was not part of slavery. The flinch from black flesh was very strong in the North. The word "miscegenation," for example, was a word cooked up by Copperheads and New York journalists, according to the *Journal of Negro History*, which is my only authority for this. They tried to get Lincoln and various other people to sign a document saying it would be nice to have miscegenation. They couldn't get a signer.

RUBIN: What you're saying is that nineteenth-century America, North and South, was racist.

WARREN: What I'm saying is that in the South there was little flinch from black flesh compared to that in the North, where there was a great flinch from black flesh, and concubinage occurred quite frequently.

STYRON: Aren't you saying also that this repulsion did not exist much in antebellum times, but did exist afterwards, even in the South?

WARREN: That's exactly what I'm saying. It grew up afterwards in the South.

STYRON: I remember noting this to my own surprise once, when I wrote an essay on this for *Harper's* a long time ago. When I reflected on my boyhood in a southern town, not a southern rural environment, in retrospect I was astounded by my total unfamiliarity with black flesh. I mean, even as a presence, even as a part of the ambiance of my life. It was nonexistent, except for the ones who worked in the kitchen. After the day was done they evaporated, they went somewhere else. The myth was quite the opposite. This miscegenation myth you're talking about *was* a myth, because after the modern South began and after Jim Crow began, everything legislated against any contact.

WARREN: In the earlier agricultural South, a lot of children played together. They had their black nurse. This was very common, in many segments of society.

RUBIN: It seems to me that in your imaginative writings and in your journalism, too, both of you have chronicled this change. I don't say that you sat down consciously with the intention of doing so, but this is what your work shows. In Bill Styron's case, his first novel involves someone growing up in the South and leaving the South. His next novel involves someone who again grew up in the South but is a long way away from it and is trying to learn how to go back, but not really back to the same place—how to find a place, or a place to come to, to use the title of Red Warren's latest book. And in your next novel, Bill, you took a black man, a slave; here is the southern racial experience, but looked at from a completely different point of view. In the novel you're working on now there is a man brought up with southern sensibilities, coming to grips with a different kind of horror, a completely different kind of horrible situation—the concentration camps of the Second World War. And he says, "the particular kind of injustices which I'm indignant about may not be nearly so important as what race hatred can do to people like this." That's the insight to be drawn out of that experience of separation. And, Red, it seems to me in your instance, there are few if any other authors who have written as much as you have, consciously, about the problems of the South and the southerner, the southerner going away and returning, the southerner living in the change from the Old South to the New South, and the various problems this involves. If I were a social historian, let's say fifty years from now, and I wanted to chronicle how all this happened, in both instances your works would be one of the best places to look, even though I would doubt very much that either one of you, especially when you are writing fiction or poetry, ever sat down with that conscious intention in mind.

WARREN: Certainly it never crosses my mind. It's the story that counts. If it has a story it has a cocklebur in it, that you can't understand, and that you want to understand. It has a nag in it; that becomes the reason you write it, the nag in it.

RUBIN: You wrote your first fiction about the South when you were in England, didn't you?

WARREN: I did, and I did it because I was asked to write it. The farther I got away from the South, the more I thought about it. I never read any southern history until I was well away from the South.

RUBIN: And you, Bill, wrote your first fiction at Duke, in Durham, though that was apprentice fiction.

STYRON: Yes, very much so.

RUBIN: And you wrote most of *Lie Down in Darkness* living in New York, didn't you?

STYRON: I wrote practically all of it somewhere in New York.

RUBIN: So in both cases it's been the fact that you were away from the scene that triggered the reexamination, and then you have kept reexamining it, and it's provided a sort of nourishment, an index of reality if you want to call it that, all the way. You can measure "who am I?" in terms of the kind of ambiance that you grow up in. What I'm getting at is this: the fact that neither you, Red, nor you, Bill, has been living in the geographical South for a number of years, may make you into a different kind of southern writer, but nevertheless that very experience itself is a part of the southern experience—the moving out from and looking back at the past.

WARREN: I don't want to talk about myself too much, but something you've said triggers this thought. For ten years I couldn't finish a poem, even a short poem—I have stacks of them unfinished, four lines or six lines or eight lines, and then they go off in a folder somewhere. Now I began writing poems again in Italy, at a ruined castle over the sea, when I remarried, and the poems began when I had a child there. That year I wrote *Promises* and two sonnets, and spent the winter revising them. That book is half Kentucky-Tennessee, and half Italy. There's medieval Italy and boyhood—they make a book. Do you see what I'm getting at? It's the long withdrawal from South Kentucky. But the book is really on that theme as much as any other theme, the other being father-child, father-daughter, father-son, as infants.

RUBIN: Don't you think the same thing is true of your most recent novel?

WARREN: It's quite deliberately true of it, though it's autobiographical only in the deep way that all books are autobiographical. I want to come back to one other thing. You said a southerner asks "who am I?" but "who am I?" strikes me as ultimately the question all writers are asking. In the southern case it's only an especially acute one; it's pointed up more sharply. But "who am I?" is a basic human question. I just add that as a footnote to what you said.

RUBIN: That's quite true. But the extent to which it is a problem is what's involved, and it seems to me that when you look at the great body of nineteenth-century southern literature, that question could be answered very easily, they thought, and the fact that it was answered so very easily accounts for the fact that the literature has so little tension in it, because the answer is rhetorical. In your generation and Bill's generation this is not a rhetorical question; the indices are all moved around and changed around and mixed up, and therefore you're wrestling with it all the time. You don't wrestle with it literally, in terms of the question "Who am I, Robert Penn Warren?" or "Who am I, William Styron?" but "Who is this person or that person in this dramatic situation?" It comes to the same thing, though.

WARREN: Yes, you transfer it.

STYRON: You're quite accurate when you point out the huge chasm between nineteenth-century southern sensibility and twentieth century. I'm speaking in general. Apart from Edgar Allan Poe and one or two others, don't we tend to localize nineteenth-century southern writing in sensibilities like Thomas Nelson Page, who were delightfully satisfied with the status quo? And possibly for good reason—the status quo often looked pretty good to them.

WARREN: Or their dream of it.

RUBIN: That's really more like it. Thomas Nelson Page was writing about the beauties of life on the old plantation, and his best stories are told by the faithful black retainer. Here is a man who is married to the sister of Marshall Field, lives in Washington, D.C., travels abroad all the time, goes up to New England in the summers, serves as the ambassador to Italy during the First World War—a thoroughgoing cosmopolite, and yet when he sits down with a pen and writes there is the dream of the old thing—he's not looking at his own experience.

WARREN: It's a pastoral.

STYRON: He's not looking, because even at that time the horrors were commencing. To localize history in one single type of event, lynchings were very rare things in the first half of the nineteenth century. It was a post-Civil War phenomenon; it came with Jim Crow. Page was writing during the heyday of lynching. We in the twentieth century, let's face it, have had strange and unearthly experiences that were not dreamed of by and large by our nineteenth-century forebears. The Civil War is an exception to that, but I'm talking about the experience between black and white, the tension—the power and the glory and the horrors and all that reached their crescendo in the twentieth century.

WARREN: It's not black or white in the twentieth century, it's everybody.

STYRON: It's anybody. You're talking about the whole world.

WARREN: About the Dresden fire raid, and a lot of other such things.

STYRON: And to me that's another thing that my own imagination has been captured by—a thing that's totally extraneous to my experience, namely, what happened in the Nazi concentration camps, which seems to epitomize humanity at its nadir in all of its history. And I have been able I think to come at it through whatever sensibility I created in myself as a southerner.

WARREN: This is an important point, Bill. It seems to me that the whole problem of modernity, of all modernity, is that of how can the person hang on to the fact that he's a person, and not become simply a thing being shoved here and shoved there, caught in a vast, complicated machine, and depersonalized in the process. The very strong personal sense in the South that makes tales worth telling—sitting around and talking about some*body*, Mr. Smith versus Mr. Jones, or why did this man do this crazy thing, because he's that kind of a person—is involved somehow in the question of how personality is preserved in the face of the more and more mechanized, computerized world of technology.

RUBIN: In other words, a gas oven is so much more efficient than a lash, isn't it?

STYRON: It's another thing that's just being apprehended, really. It's fascinating to me that a place like Auschwitz is in a curious way an extension of Western chattel slavery. It was of course a place for extermination, but it was equally a place in which slavery was practiced, of a monstrous sort, which was a logical extension of the *relatively* benign slavery practiced in the South—I say "relatively" because slavery in the South was not, inhuman as it was, practiced as a method to extract everything that one could out of a body and then let it perish, whereas Auschwitz was a place in which slavery was practiced with the idea in mind that people were disposable and that after you got the work out of them they died. I don't think it's possible to make any direct comparisons between southern slavery and Nazi slavery, but the two are somehow linked in what you, Red, were describing as a kind of evolutionary dehumanizing process which is all around us.

WARREN: Yes, that's what I'm getting at.

RUBIN: The struggle to preserve one's humanity, one's identity, within this—a constant struggle which goes on all the time—in a sense constitutes the burden of a great deal of twentieth-century southern literature.

WARREN: It becomes acute there because the mark of individuality was strong and old-fashioned.

RUBIN: It seems to me that your work, and the work of your generation of southern writers, is a place to look to see this process going on, and continuing, and being imaginatively explored. At least, I know that's where I look.

NANCY M. TISCHLER

The South Stage Center: Hellman and Williams

Popular cinematic and dramatic productions in the early decades of the twentieth century had portrayed the American South as the brooding and romantic home of heroic aristocrats, witless black men, and silly white women. From *Birth of a Nation* to *Gone with the Wind*, the films had developed the image of the magnolia South defeated in war and outraged in Reconstruction. By the 1930s, Broadway had enlarged its southern imagery with *Abraham's Bosom* and *Green Pastures*, sympathetic and moving, though condescending, portrayals of tragic mulattoes, simple peasants, and depraved whites. *Tobacco Road*, also set in the South and written by a southerner, provided amusement for the sophisticated at the expense of lecherous, foulmouthed poor whites. These plays and films, along with their inevitable sequels, provided a set of stereotyped characters and situations within which more sophisticated authors could develop, contradict, or combine elements for an audience already hungry for the exotic, bawdy, violent stories of this alien land. The poets and novelists had already demonstrated with subtlety and virtuosity that great wealth lay in southern lore. The more public form of the drama, requiring an urban audience, was slower to adopt the southern accent and matter. It awaited the moment that combined audience, opportunity, and artist.

Lillian Hellman had already worked for years on films and plays before she turned to the subject of her native South. To her as to her audience, this land of Spanish moss and elephant ear leaves seemed alien in climate, mood, and psychology. Though her mother was from a landed Alabama family, her father was a German Jew—and it was with his people that the playwright identified. Spending half her early years in New Orleans and half in New York made her feel an outsider in her native South. She was therefore the natural interpreter for the New York audience —comfortable in the urban northern culture where the plays were produced and criticized, and steeped in the southern culture that provided a rich lode of dramatic materials.

From her memories of her mother's family and her impressions of Alabama, she planned a trilogy, which she wrote only partially and in curious order (second and then first). The first of Hellman's plays about the South, *The Little Foxes*, produced in 1939, was a great success, a triumph of idea and craftsmanship. Using the fourth-wall realism of nineteenth-century Europe, she developed a well-made play in the manner of Ibsen's *Hedda Gabler*. The central character is a turn-of-the-century Medusa with a southern accent, Regina Hubbard Giddens, a woman capable of enslaving her community, robbing her brothers, and killing her husband for money. Her cruel and materialistic brothers help explain her own more subtle form of evil. The three Hubbards, Regina, Ben, and Oscar, in cooperation with a northern industrialist, plan to bring the cotton gin to the cotton. The story, set in 1900, is a miniature of the New South's problems. Though prosperity should benefit the whole depressed community, these "little foxes" will gobble up all the profits, cheating poor blacks and poor whites without discrimination. Other characters provide further insights into southern history and economy: Birdie, Regina's sister-in-law, is a gentle, weak, ineffectual relic of the old plantation South. Still in love with a culture long since dead, and unable to battle the mercantile evils of the New South, Birdie retreats into a cloud of liquor and music. Addie, the black housekeeper, is a choric figure common to southern literature, who serves as spokesman for the exploited groups. And Alexandra, Regina's daughter, provides an unlikely but comfortingly sentimental hope that the younger generation may in time blend the best features of the Hubbard and the Giddens families—the realistic toughness of the one and the romantic idealism of the other.

The play is a melodrama, hanging on a trick, a death, and a double game of blackmail. After watching the shrewd manipulations of the Hubbard clan, we discover some unexpected toughness in the decent people, which predictably cannot effectually counter the devices of their unscrupulous adversaries. It is therefore unlikely that such a story would in fact end (as this one does) with the sinister forces temporarily halted and the decent folks— at least those who survive—in a position of power. The ending, however, reinforces the thematic core of the play, summed up in Addie's judgment on the Old South and the New: "Well, there are people who eat the earth and eat all the people on it like in the Bible with the locusts. Then there are people who stand around and watch them eat it. Sometimes I think it ain't right to stand and watch them do it." The speech, while universalizing the exploiting urge of the Hubbards (who remind us of Faulkner's Snopeses), also judges the old aristocrats. If there are obligations in nobility (albeit "nobility" only two generations deep), then these decent people have no right to retreat into gentility and alcohol when action is needed. Given this moral position, Hellman must provide a situation in which action is possible and a character capable of acting decisively and responsibly. Alexandra is her only hope; she must free herself from her mother and the threat of marriage. Sensitivity is not enough to an author who believes that morality must result in action.

The sinister portrait of the shrewd, cold, manipulating Regina was to lead Miss Hellman into her second (and, in fact, last) play of the proposed trilogy eight years later. *Another Part of the Forest* traces the early womanhood of Regina, portrays her dominating father, her guilt-ridden, slightly demented mother (who is rather like Birdie in the other play), her aristocratic, war-ravaged lover, and her already conniving, vicious brothers. At twenty Regina is a more pathetic figure that at forty—more vulnerable, blind to the incestuous feelings of her father and their peril for her life, still open to love and sexual joy, still full of illusions about life. She is already a manipulator, an actress, a materialist, but she is not so hard.

Apart from Regina, the other dominating character studies in

the play are Marcus, her father, and John, her lover—two images
of southern manhood. John Bagtry, Birdie's brother, is a Confederate veteran and victim, less heroic than in war mythology, more
like the shell-shock victims of twentieth-century wars. His experience of death and defeat has left him with tunnel vision, concerned with nothing but the dream of heroic action. Rather than
helping his women to rebuild their plantation or accepting the
passionate proposal of Regina, he elects to seek new wars in Bra-
zil, where he can again don the uniform and fight for slavery. Old
Marcus caustically suggests that he choose the other side this
time—"Every man needs to win once in his life."

If John is symbolic of the southern psychology of defeat without discovery, Marcus is symbolic of survival without honor. For
Marcus is a survivor: he used the Civil War to build his own fortune, to feed his appetite for power and elegance and beauty. We
see in the old man an ironic parody of Jefferson's "natural aristocracy." As one of his sons notes in *The Little Foxes*, the Hubbards
are not aristocrats in the southern sense. They came too late, grew
rich off trade, and built their mansion before they won acceptance.
But the plays reveal their deficiencies in other ways: they lack the
love of the land, the sense of noblesse oblige, the dignity and consideration and culture that go with the term *aristocrat*. As Ben
explains, though the distinction between a Hubbard and a Bagtry
may seem a fine one to an outsider, it is a real one to a southerner
—and one that has been made for the Hubbards. They, in turn,
sneer at the southern aristocrat's inability to adjust to the new
world and their own triumph:

> When the war comes these fine gentlemen ride off and leave the cot-
> ton, *and* the women, to rot. . . .
>
> Well, sir, the war ends. Lionnet is almost ruined, and the sons finish
> ruining it. And there were thousands like them. Why? Because the
> Southern aristocrat can adapt himself to nothing. Too high-tone to
> try. . . .
>
> It is difficult to learn new ways. But maybe that's why it's so profit-
> able. *Our* grandfather and *our* father learned the new ways and learned
> how to make them pay. They work. *They* are in trade. Hubbard Sons,
> Merchandise. Others, Birdie's family, for example, look down on them.

To make a long story short, Lionnet now belongs to *us*. Twenty years ago we took over their land, their cotton, and their daughter. . . .

The Hubbards grow more debased with each generation: their frontier vigor turns to mercantile craftiness and finally degenerates into nastiness and sadism. (In some ways, they remind us of the Sutpen "dynasty" in *Absalom, Absalom!*). They tend to be frigid or perverse sexually, cruel to animals, blacks, and helpless whites, and without aesthetic taste. Old Marcus loves music, but his sons and grandson are deaf to its pleasures. Their cynicism and unmitigated evil is as unreal as John's empty and simpleminded lust for heroism, but Miss Hellman prefers balanced contrasts of clearly defined symbols to the messiness of human experience. Complex individuals do appear in her work, but she more characteristically sees people as types, defined socially and historically and economically, judged by clear moral standards.

Tennessee Williams, on the other hand, who began his halting theatrical career shortly after the success of *The Little Foxes*, can seldom judge clearly or define exactly. His first play of significance, *Battle of Angels*, was to fail primarily for his inability to define and to simplify. It is a clutter of southern characters and themes set in a small southern town, a messy, melodramatic, poetic portrayal of occidental and oriental mythology, Freudian psychology, and Bohemian protest. Williams insists that the play failed because it mixed sex and religion, but that is far too simple an explanation. He has revised the play as *Orpheus Descending* and *Something Wild in the Country*, but it is clearly not destined for successful production.

His next play, *The Glass Menagerie* (1945), exposes Williams' full dramatic strengths. This gentle vignette of a southern family living in exile is individualized, compassionate, and real. Though set in the depression at the time of the Spanish Civil War, the play itself is a timeless expression of the individual confrontation with despair—not a regional or economic or political or historic commentary. The city of St. Louis is used as a painful symbol of their exile: from the Deep South and its values, from the landscape and the flowers, from the past, from meaningful work, from position in family and community, from security and beauty and romance.

Amanda, the mother, draws on an idealized past for her aristocratic values; and like Hellman's Birdie, she is blind to the exploitation of blacks. Both casually assume a class structure in which
white ladies lead idle, genteel lives. But this is by no means the
most important quality about Amanda, who does in fact do the
housework and seek to earn a living. She is an anachronism who
has the tenacity to survive in the new world and is groping for the
means. She tries to protect her gentle daughter Laura from her
own fate by providing her with a career and self-sufficiency. She is
enough of a realist to recognize (though not usually to admit) that
Laura will probably not marry, and that the modern world has no
role for dependent old maids. She realizes that her son is unhappy
in his work and will in time "fall in love with long distance" as
did his runaway father. In the meantime, she relies on his income,
nags him to adjust to the modern, mechanical world (which is foreign to the whole Wingfield family), and prods him to help her
marry off Laura. In this loving and cruel struggle for survival, the
mother expects ultimate defeat, but her defiance in the face of impossible odds makes her stature all the more heroic. At the end,
when the son has gone even deeper into exile, becoming even more
rootless, he looks back at her and acknowledges her beauty and
her stature. Without insisting on a plantation background or talking of slaves, Amanda demonstrates an aristocracy of spirit. And
without mention of the Civil War, she portrays a spiritual beauty
that can come out of defeat. Williams, developing the themes of
the South in the complex and subtle mode of Chekhov, in this
play captures the network of often unexpressed ideas and attitudes that enmesh a family and a culture.

His compassion and sensitivity take on a more intense color
with *A Streetcar Named Desire*. In this far more brutal play, using
techniques of "epic" theatre, Williams repeats his portrait of the
antiquated belle, but isolates her from family and places her near
the completion of her fall. Instead of the memory of a romantic
courtship, a briefly happy marriage, and two children to comfort
her, Blanche has only the memory of one day of love, culminating
in the discovery that her husband is a homosexual, ending in her
outraged accusation and his suicide. Without support of family or

hope of romance, she moves deeper into alcoholism, nymphomania, and fantasy. Within the play, she grasps for one last man she might marry, one last family member who might love her, one last ideal of beauty and dignity and hope for mankind before she is demolished by rape and sinks into madness.

Although the play deals with extremes, it is not a clear battle of good and evil. Our affection and compassion necessarily go to the moth-figure Blanche, whose heroic defense of old values has a quixotic beauty. But her pretentiousness, her duplicity, her cruelty, her venality, her selfishness, and her occasional bawdiness keep her from being a romantic heroine in the clutches of an ogre. Stanley Kowalski is by no means as gentle and pleasant as Laura's Gentleman Caller, but he is not the anthropological study that Blanche insists. Until we come to see him, as does Stella, from Blanche's point of view, he appears a healthy, loving, sexual, intelligent man. His exchanges with Blanche offer comic counterpoint in the manner of Tom's with Amanda. He is shrewd enough to see that Stella can be influenced by her sister, that Blanche is a liar, that he must fight for the survival of his home and family. His brutal rape of Blanche is the climax of her prim flirtation with him, the semiserious game of the perennial belle; she seeks her own destruction through sexuality. Thus, Stella appears justified at the end in rejecting Blanche's sterile romanticism for Stanley's crude realism. Stella has deliberately refused to acknowledge the ravaging of the old southern culture by the virile new forces. Outsiders in Williams, as in Hellman, have less beauty than the anachronistic aristocrats, but more vitality. Williams' sympathy always goes to the fragile victims of the world, leading him to a rejection of Stanley or Big Daddy, but not always to a moral judgment.

While Hellman does not cotton to defeat, Williams dotes on the defeated, helpless, disinherited refugees of the world, his precious people. His heroes and heroines often retreat from the modern world, finding in it or within themselves no means to alter human history. In his explanation of the alternate (and more sombre) ending for *Cat on a Hot Tin Roof*, Williams explains that he does not believe people change radically. The numerous variations on his particular southern mythology reveal his faith in discovery, but not in clear, rational, moral decision followed by decisive action. Occasionally his heroes break out of the "solitary confinement within their own skins" and communicate briefly with one another. He asks no more than this, that we try to understand ourselves and feel compassion for one another. Social and political evils are of almost no importance in Williams' plays: Big Daddy's wealth means nothing to Brick, his understanding and love mean everything. Williams' characters seldom seek or expect any future beyond the next sunset; they are people of the past who tolerate the present with reluctance. No Alexandra Giddens points to a new day a-coming in Williams. His Alexandra del Largo searches passionately for a means of reliving a victorious past and delaying a horrifying future.

The later Williams plays, like the later Hellman plays, become more interesting, personal, and autobiographical—though not so artistic. Both *Toys in the Attic* and *Autumn Garden* are more individualized and experimental technically than Hellman's earlier plays. The Chekhovian *Autumn Garden* uses the Gulf Coast, but with none of the atmosphere Williams had captured in *Summer and Smoke. Toys in the Attic* (based on childhood memories chronicled in her autobiographical essays) uses her native New Orleans, but again little sense of place permeates the play. Except for the stereotypical red-neck violence and the eating of local fish dishes, the characters might have been anywhere in the South. Williams invariably uses the southern setting with more immediacy, specificity, and power than does Hellman, an assertion that can be substantiated by exploring their contrasting use of New Orleans.

Whereas Hellman spent half of her formative years in New Orleans, Williams discovered it only after college, when he established his spiritual kinship with its artistic community. In his flight from shoe factories and progress, he discovered a home among the artists and eccentrics who shared his own anarchy of spirit. In the Vieux Carré, he found musicians, prostitutes, drug addicts, homosexuals, poets, and dreamers who had withdrawn from or been cast out of the conservative culture of the South. The physical presence of the city, with its historic French elegance, its decaying splendor, its walled wealth, and its crowded filth provides symbolic equivalents to the life of its people. It is the perfect place for Blanche du Bois to end her tragic journey through history: from the plantation called Belle Rêve, taking the streetcar named Desire, transferring at the cemetery, getting off at the Elysian Fields, where her once-aristocratic sister shares a rundown apartment with a first-generation Polish immigrant. Outside their flat, we hear the trains and the Spanish flower vendor in this hodgepodge of modernity and antiquity. Whether in Garden District or Vieux Carré, among the rich or the poor, Williams sees the city as a mine of materials for the artist. Although Hellman describes New Orleans with some vividness in *Pentimento*, she views it simply as the setting for her childhood, bearing none of the riches exploited by the more symbolic imagination of Williams. Human action and consciousness take precedence over habitat for Hellman except when she thinks of her lost farm which she shared with her lost lover. Other places have little significance to her—an indication that she does not share the traditional southern trait of a strong sense of place.

Two playwrights using the same geographical region and the same era in human history, writing their plays seriatim, must be expected to overlap. Their domineering paterfamilias, and their languishing belles echo both social history and personal experience. Both authors describe homosexual sons tied to possessive mothers, both use grotesque old maids and religious fanatics. Neither makes much use of black characters, hill or rural folk. For both, a shadowy plantation South explains present discontent. Change is inevitable, and the southerner, like most people, finds the change painful. For both authors, the sense of lost values and the need to create new ones provide the unstable mental climate for their human drama.

Both believe that strength of will and independence of spirit can triumph to some degree, and both admire those who (like the Princess in *Sweet Bird of Youth* or Maggie in *Cat on a Hot Tin Roof*) have the courage to battle against impossible odds. Williams sees the enemy as time or fate, while Hellman is more inclined to see it as human malevolence. Therefore Hellman's victories are more possible and her plays more hopeful; Williams' victories are rare moments of relief before tragic conclusions. Thus, Williams has turned the South's "burden" of history into a metaphysic. The entire universe lumbers toward the destruction of fragile beauty. The lost antebellum world becomes a symbol of the loss of all beauty, youth, and romance. The region becomes a microcosm of human destiny, and the artist turns his compassionate gaze on all those who face the end with courage, dignity, and grace.

Williams enjoys the speech of the South more than Hellman, loving the vivid imagery, the expansive rhetoric, the poetic rhythms. She is more economical verbally than he, using the southern speech with precision, but blurring it quickly into general American dialect. He uses the southern dialects in a manner parallel to Synge's use of Irish and Lorca's of Spanish, as a fount of beauty and natural symbolism. This "collaboration" between the artist and the folk of his region has been the source of enormous artistic power in an age increasingly uniform and drab. Williams cherishes this individuality in imagery, cadence, word choice, and pronunciation. Like the neo-Confederates who resist the uniformity implied in union, Williams sympathizes with the sturdy independence of spirit mirrored in the "eccentricities of a nightingale." In his weaker moments, he is inclined to overindulge his lyricism, neglecting his drama for his poetry. But even here, his vice is indigenous to his region: his abundant verbiage and cluttered plots mirror the vegetation of his native Mississippi.

Lillian Hellman's range of interests has been wider than Williams'. She has written of economics and politics and history. She has been a supporter of the Spanish Civil War, an interpreter for Russia during World War II, a strong spokesman against fascism, and a vocal antagonist to investigating committees. Her career and her plays, which appear to be approaching their end as she meanders through old memories and rekindles old angers, have demonstrated a toughness of mind and a courage that another age would have applauded as "masculine."

Williams's interests have been narrower, more personal and obsessive. He continues to develop the same themes and characters, adding an occasional relative or friend—his grandfather or his favorite actress. He laces his tragedy with comedy and experiments with absurdity. His sexual saviors become Freudian Christ figures, his eccentric prostitutes are portrayed as madonnas. His interests invariably contradict the sweep of history. When the Spanish Civil War absorbed Hellman, Williams worried about a glass menagerie. His compassionate, whimsical, perverse, poetic vision is one that a less enlightened people would have labeled "feminine." His subjectivity, emotionalism, and idolatry of the past mark him as southern.

Together, Hellman and Williams demonstrate that the artist develops as he/she must, not as man or woman, but as humans confronting levels of personal and social experience, responding to those elements that thrill them. The artist most often finds himself, as have these two, an alien in his homeland; for separation is one of the marks of the creative act. Immersion is another: for Williams, especially, the southern homeland is more than a place, it is an experience of the heart.

No one can deny the importance of either of these giants of the modern theatre, as interpreters of the South or as American artists. Lillian Hellman is the only woman playwright of prominence in modern America—or in theatre history. Her portrayals of her native South are effective vignettes of "home and frightening land." But "Tennessee Williams' voice," as Walter Kerr noted recently, "is the most distinctively poetic, the most idiosyncratically moving, and at the same time the most firmly dramatic to have come the American theatre's way—ever. No point in calling the man our best living playwright. He is our best playwright, and let qualifications go hang."

WILLIAM HARMON

Southern Poetry in the Last Quarter of the Twentieth Century

Twentieth-century poetry in English falls pretty neatly into quarter-century periods. The Golden Age of 1900–1925 saw the appearance or flourishing of a number of first-rate poets, none born later than 1890, whose work during these years is generally considered their best—whether it was their last phase (as it was for Thomas Hardy) or their first (as for T. S. Eliot, Ezra Pound, William Carlos Williams, Wallace Stevens, Robert Frost, Conrad Aiken, John Crowe Ransom, Hilda Doolittle, and a few others). The Silver Age between 1925 and 1950 witnessed two main classes of poetry: valedictory syntheses by the established masters (*Four Quartets*, *The Pisan Cantos*, *Paterson*, and so forth) along with the emergence and perfection of the next generation, those poets about twenty years younger than the giants of the Golden Age; W. H. Auden and Theodore Roethke now look like *the* typical poets of this period. The next age, 1950–1975—Bronze enough for a rough-and-ready sketch—witnessed diverse phenomena, most influentially the old age and death of almost all of the giants, some of whom (Williams, Stevens, and Pound, for example) continued to produce distinguished work right up to the end. The Silver Age poets and their epigones (such as Randall Jarrell, Karl Shapiro, William Stafford, and John Berryman) entered their later years, and quite a few of them died. Around 1950 younger poets began to appear more or less on the model of Robert Lowell, and a case of historical reversal took place: the dominant, fashionable poetry written by people born after 1920 ignored the technical and thematic pioneering carried out so courageously and brilliantly by Eliot, Pound, Williams, Stevens, and other giants. For several years after World War II, praise, prizes, jobs, and attention went to such Landoresque poets as Richard Wilbur, who specialized in conservatively husbanded emotions expressed—expertly but maybe a bit too slickly —in canonical verse forms that permitted a virtuoso display of wit, irony, and stoical understatement. A majority of American poets born in the 1920s began their careers as crafters of this symmetrical poesy (for example, Louis Simpson, James Wright, John Hollander, Donald Hall, W. S. Merwin, Robert Bly, Anthony Hecht, Galway Kinnell, Howard Nemerov, X. J. Kennedy, and Carolyn Kizer); but around 1960 most of them followed Lowell away from elegantly grieving symmetry into inelegantly grieving surrealist asymmetry, when the public world of poetry felt the onslaught from the anarchist Beatniks, Black Mountain innovators, and a handful of talented (if anomalous) old-line imagists like Alan Dugan and Denise Levertov. During most of the 1960s, after the settling of the dust from the lurid Beatnik crusade, the typical magazine poem (whether in the *New Yorker* or a thousand little journals) was a clearly derivative, nicely mannered imitation of W. S. Merwin's spacious, honest-sounding quietist idiom of neo-surrealist recombinations of such romantic sentiments as love, lonesomeness, and pacifism.

Through all of those seventy-five years of poetic development and devolution, the place of the American South remained peripheral. None of the real giants was particularly southern, and by the time Ransom, Jarrell, Allen Tate, and Robert Penn Warren achieved any reputation at all it was for the most part as *national* figures who spent a good deal of time away from the South and worked in areas away from poetry. In the South, scholarship and criticism were somewhat stronger than poetry, and it was in their native South, for example, that two of the finest students of Eliot's work—Professors Grover Smith and Marion Montgomery—did the work on their first-rate commentaries. But the most interesting poets were not southerners at any time during these three Ages until the very end of the third Age—that is, around 1970, by which time it was obvious that three American poets of major importance were southerners and also distinctively southern in much of their writing—I mean Jonathan Williams (b. 1929), James

Dickey (b. 1923), and A. R. Ammons (b. 1926)—and at the same time a large number of younger American poets were southerners: Robert Morgan, Charles Wright, Ellen Bryant Voigt, Henry Taylor, Coleman Barks, A. B. Spellman, James Seay, Fred Chappell, James Applewhite, Van K. Brock, Charleen Whisnant, and John Ower come readily to mind. It is too early to decide anything definitive about such younger poets, but I can enter here my own testimony that many of them impress me as consistently interesting and exciting. The state of poetry seems healthy. I believe that the spell between 1975 and 2000 can see a new flowering of poetry in the South.

But the future is a bucket of air. Let me concentrate on the three senior poets I have mentioned already; their achievement is a matter of record, not speculation.

Jonathan Williams excels in two kinds of verse: expert little satirical pieces that float like a butterfly and sting like a scorpion with perfect pitch, and oddly formed aesthetic exercises that record the eerily focused impression of some special instant. In hundreds of poems published in dozens of beautifully produced books and broadsides, Williams is elegant, alert, sensitive, coarse, playful, varied, and cultivated. Buckminster Fuller, the avant-garde engineer-artist, has compared Williams to Johnny Appleseed, and the comparison is just. Williams has labored for thirty years, with only meager support from individuals and institutions, in the service of art, especially poetry but also printing, painting, photography, jazz, instrumental "serious" music, and art education. His Jargon Press has published nearly a hundred items since 1950, including important early works by well-known figures like Charles Olson, Robert Creeley, and Denise Levertov. At the same time, Williams has criss-crossed America and Europe by car and even on foot, giving lectures, showing slides, and reading poetry in a tireless effort to keep the arts of civilization alive.

Coming from Highlands, North Carolina, Williams preserves a good many of the mountaineer's habits and virtues: he is aloof, versatile, ornery, independent, stubborn, footloose, open-handed, forthcoming, and—like many cultured southerners—countrified in a complex way that tells you little about how much of his behavior is genuine and how much is put on for the sake of amusement or defense. A protean artist in many media, he combines the urbane tradition of self-conscious craftsmanship promoted by Poe and William Morris and the rustic tradition of profound self-reliance still found among isolated people in rural North Carolina. Williams is the only poet I know of who is really capable of *thoroughly* realizing a poetic work from scratch. With only a minimum of artificial resources, Williams can compose a poem, make his own ink and paper, do his own printing and binding, add his own graphic work, manage the production, distribution, advertising, and marketing, and deliver a creditable reading to any sort of audience at the drop of a hat; he could even add some learned annotations, if such things were called for. Purist and loner, he respects the integrity and dignity inherent in the creatures of the wilderness, but he feels free to appropriate and arrogate whatever he pleases from the language in whatever way he pleases—puns, rebuses, anagrams, transliterations, pig Latin—all in the same pioneering spirit that found a creek christened "Purgatoire" by some fanciful Frenchman and changed it to "Picketwire," which makes somewhat more sense. Elegantly, Williams fools around with language and type, sometimes rather idly but sometimes, in his best poems, in ways that maintain the authenticity of his native Appalachian landscape and the style with which his neighbors use words. He has recorded the "Most Astonishing Sign in Recent American Letters":

O'NAN'S
AUTO
SERVICE

—and the idiosyncrasies of the journalistic manner of the "Pigeon Roost News":

that snake were such
peculiar looking
to me I'm afraid I
couldn't give it justice
trying to describing it but it
didn't act mean like
it tryed to be
pretty like
it did

—as well as the spontaneous "sayings" of people as they philoso-
phize:

> but pretty though as
> roses is
> you can put up with
> the thorns
> —*Doris Talley, Housewife & Gardener*

In a poem called "Uncle Iv Surveys His Domain from His Rocker
of a Sunday Afternoon as Aunt Dory Starts to Chop Kindling,"
there is a full disclosure of many southern mountain qualities, including hospitality, courtesy, acute observation, economy of eloquence, and a touch of old-fashioned discrimination now stigma-
tized as sexism:

> Mister Williams
> lets youn me move
> tother side the house
>
> the woman
> choppin woods
> mite nigh the awkerdist thing
> I seen.

Williams, Dickey, and Ammons all missed or bypassed the fashion of rhymed verse that dominated American poetry for a while
just after World War II; on infrequent occasions, all three can turn
out a regular rhyme, but their ordinary mode is one or another
kind of free verse, and all have explored various tracts of the territory of the experimental (including, in Williams' case, the fad
of "Concrete" poetry that came—and, I think, went—a few seasons ago). Dickey spent the 1960s experimenting with a strange
mode of verse—highly charged, emotional, personal, sentimental, primitive or pseudoprimitive, a poetry that devotedly looked
inward and saw in oneself a gloriously animated beastly creature
motivated by lusts, fears, hatreds, and habits of killing so thoroughly ingrained that they rose to the status of totemic ritual.
Dickey's central theme was the prestige of death in any form—
accident, disease, hunting, fishing, homicide, suicide, combat—
realized in a rather awestruck idiom that committed sacramen-

tal mayhem on language and the "line" of poetry, which, under Dickey's *Field-and-Stream* musculature and dexterity, tended to come unglued. With such a limited (but potent) theme and style, it may have been predictable that Dickey would suffer the fate that he did: he used up the virtues and values of his best poetry and had then to turn to other, lesser, closer, safer investments: perfunctory poems (especially the unofficial laureate's piece he turned out for the inauguration of his fellow Georgian, Jimmy Carter), coffee-table picture books, popular fiction, screenplays, and the wasteful business of being a celebrity. But none of this decay of intensity has to breed a corresponding decay of respect, because a fair number of Dickey's poems, particularly those in *Buckdancer's Choice*, remain very fine indeed, and his contribution to one area of criticism ought to remain notable, too. I mean the immediate review of the single volume by a living poet, often a young one. Everybody tends to ignore this kind of reviewing, because in ninety-nine cases out of a hundred it is merely a grubbily vestigial branch of journalism, and probably the most ephemeral and most partisan branch, at that. The fact is that most volumes of poetry are not (within a year of publication) reviewed in, of, for, and by themselves. Many are not reviewed at all. Many receive one otiose notice by a crony, former teacher, or former student of the author. Many are placed in a corral with as many as fifty other volumes and given the "omnibus" treatment. But now and then, here and there, magazines run a review of some new volume of poetry, and for about ten years—say, 1955 to 1965—James Dickey was the best practitioner of this specialty: the most articulate and the most sensitive. By and by he stopped doing it. There's no money or anything else in it, unless you count certain species of chauvinistic or spiteful experience. But Dickey did it, and he did it very faithfully. He also, rather like Williams in his Johnny Appleseed role, "barnstormed" for poetry at scores of colleges where the audiences and accommodations were, in more than one sense, limited. But Dickey did it, and he did it with style and power.

Dickey was an aviator during World War II and the Korean War, and it seems now that his strongest poetry, that of his mature years during the 1960s, developed step-by-step as this country's Mercury, Gemini, and Apollo enterprises went forward, climaxing in the lunar landing in the summer of 1969. To use an old figure, one could call Dickey "air-minded": the imagination strongly at work in his finest poems seems to be a miniaturized version of some aeronautical and space administration, habitually viewing people, cities, and the earth itself from an altitude so great that personality and civilization are stripped away. In "Fire-Bombing" (the theme and setting of which invite comparison with Vonnegut's *Slaughterhouse-Five*), a veteran, now comfortably dwelling in the suburbs, recalls the mixture of distressing terror and satisfying power that filled him when he was on a night-bombing flight over Japan twenty years earlier. "Falling" is the fanciful account of an airline stewardess who has by accident fallen from a plane in flight. As she falls, she goes through a ritualized experience of undressing and returning herself to a primal condition of animal innocence as her uniform and undergarments fall dreamily to the same mid-American Kansas countryside that forms the actual setting of *The Wizard of Oz*; this nameless woman is the dead dark side of the myth of Dorothy. Falling and dying are the worst things, but, by a zanily imagined otherworldly presence of mind, the woman does not panic; instead, she reverses the Fall of Man by ridding herself of the artificiality of culture. It was acute of Dickey to perceive in the airline stewardess the unique perfection of mechanical culture—an ideal doll as lovely and efficient as a robot (Teflon, say, with a sparkling drop of Retsyn) programmed to combine the functions of mother, nurse, wife, teacher, waitress, mistress, goddess, and blanket five or six tipsy miles above the workaday world. But her fall is an iconic mistake strengthened by a sheer act of the animal will and turned into a rising into innocence and—by a pretty corny piece of irony that approaches the Aviational Sublime—a virtually orgasmic rebirth.

In any event, aircraft, the dream-toys and terrible swift swords of the twentieth century, furnish Dickey with his most workable settings and themes, and "Firebombing" and "Falling" are both (literally) *terrific* poems. For such displays, Dickey hammered out an extravagant manner that derives at least in part from southern rhetorical traditions, such as the (literally) tall tale, the urban belief tale, the Pentecostally stem-winding revival sermon, and the self-loathing, self-vaunting confessional that involves elementary encounters with animals, wild people, and nature. Applied to subjects other than hyperbolic visions of the world from some lofty gadget or grotesque mishap, Dickey's idiom seems painfully overblown, as when he tries to write about such mundane matters as sunburn, adultery, or kudzu. In his latest works—a long fat poem called *Zodiac* and the Jimmy Carter Ad—Dickey is repeating gestures memorized in his air-minded successes, but, without a fully answerable subject or occasion, the style is just noisy.

"Air-mindedness" may be what prompted Dickey to write quite a few of his poems in long lines with occasional four-em spaces at melodramatically arranged intervals, a device that somehow cuts the line loose from its normal earthly gravity of conventional punctuation so that the words seem to float and drift. For example, here is Dickey's poor stewardess after she has hit the ground:

                    but she is lying like a sunbather at the last
Of moonlight   half-buried in her impact on the earth   not far
From a railroad trestle   a water tank   she could see if she could
Raise her head from her modest hole   with her clothes beginning
To come down all over Kansas   into bushes   on the dewy sixth green
Of a golf course   one shoe   her girdle coming down fantastically
On a clothesline, where it belongs   her blouse on a lightning rod. . . .

The gaps generate a "sprung" line that gives the effect of discontinuity, of aesthetic space shimmeringly occupied or airily left unoccupied. This effect seems more or less the opposite of Ammons' favorite quotation mark, the colon; nevertheless, both Dickey's space administration and Ammons' colons can overdo their appointed effect if they are used too gimmickily.

As far as I know, personal contacts among Williams, Dickey, and Ammons have been sparse. They have probably met one another; most American poets meet, sooner or later. Williams, who seems to have corresponded with just about everybody, has corresponded with both Dickey and Ammons. Lately, though, he has taken to referring to Sheriff Dim Jickey and to writing poems in answer to Ammons' rare public announcements (or misquoted responses in telephone interviews). Dickey and Ammons seem not

to know each other or each other's work very well. The three are
southern poets of a single generation, but they do not constitute
any sort of school or movement. Each tends towards uniqueness
and its accompanying isolation, which seems to be the prevailing
mode of American poets nowadays.

Ammons impresses me as the best American poet now writing.
He is the most versatile, his range is greatest, his excellence in
the subsidiary arts included in poetry is the most distinguished,
he is funny, and he has been wonderfully abundant. His published
work now runs to almost a thousand pages, and he is nowhere
near retirement. As of this writing—August 1977—his big *Collected Poems, 1951–1971* and four other volumes are available,
and he is said to have three other volumes ready for publication.

In his best poems, Ammons chips away at the oldest obstacle
confronting American writers: the thing itself. Remotely in Eliot
and Pound, indirectly in Stevens and Frost, and directly in William Carlos Williams, American-born writers have sought, sometimes with a desperation approaching hysteria, to escape the fictions of language and art so as to come as close as possible to the
actual physical concrete things of the earth. This profound sentiment unites Dickey's fallen stewardess—finally, in her estatic return to earth, glad to shuck her confining, degrading uniform and
foundation garments—with Thoreau, so starved for Reality that
he told a few little white lies to assist him in his flight from the
Unreal. (If he had really meant what he said—"Simplify, simplify"
—he would simply have said "Simplify" and been done with it;
the rest—"to live deliberately, to front only the essential facts of
life," to "stand right fronting face to face to a fact"—is political
rhetoric for a splinter party, not untainted by the silliness of Sierra
Club chic and back-to-nature by means of a mobile home.) As
purely as can be, Ammons belongs to the American tradition of
using language and culture to reach ends that language and culture do not seem designed to reach. "Be it life or death, we crave
only reality," Thoreau morbidly wrote in a message now grimly
glossed by most of Ammons' poems (as by most of Whitman's,
Stevens', and Eliot's). Consider, for example, this cheerfully fatal-
istic lyric called "Utensil" that opens up what Ammons has called
the "freedom of each event to occur as itself":

How does the pot pray:
wash me, so I gleam?

prays, crack my enamel:
let the rust in.

The poems in Ammons' first volume, *Ommateum* (1955), are assigned to a specific persona, "Ezra," who moves through history with an ideal, mythic freedom from temporal, spatial, and linguistic boundaries. The poems are mature and on the whole well realized, but the volume represents a false start in the entire Ammons canon. After *Ommateum*, the poet turned exclusively to the voice that was to endure and become peculiarly his own: a modern man, now and then called "Archie," who devotes virtually all of his poetry to one goal, the accurate registration of truth. It sounds simple and American, so much so that the unvarying and unyielding pursuit of it may seem foolish (and "fool" is an important noun in Ammons' vocabulary). To tell the truth: that was the distinguishing virtue of Washington and Lincoln. It is the burden of the motto of Ammons' home state, North Carolina: ESSE QUAM VIDERI, "To Be Rather Than To Seem." And it is easy enough to make immediate contact with the facts of your daily life—an enterprise that we normally picture as knocking on a solid wooden table or picking up a rock or piece of earth in the bare hands. But, with us Americans and our secondhand language still miscalled "English" and our polymorphous culture, the removal from the real world that language creates is even greater than usual. We may be accused of resembling that endless succession of Scottish philosophers who keep worrying about whether or not the real Real is really real. Thanks to certain literary conventions, poetry has a couple of real physical dimensions: what you hear in the air and what you see on the page, but neither the graphic nor the acoustic dimension bears any radical, necessary relation to what the language semantically *means*. If we can say that a football player is "very physical," we should be allowed to observe that a poet is "very verbal"; American poetry, famished for unsuperstitious realities, tends to emphasize both the physical sound of the verse, rooted in real speech, and the physical appearance of writing on a page. With these two fantastically developed physical dimensions, our poetry again and again drills through its self-created and self-constituting experience, looking for the actual. Ours is a bizarre literature.

The impulse toward the physical sides of poetry can be seen at work in both Longfellow and Whitman, closing the immensely overpaid accounts between us and an ostensibly obsolete system of myths and rhythms, opening fresh credit accounts with a muse installed amid the smithies and kitchenware (like Ammons' "Utensil"); it is easy to see the impulse at work in Frost and Williams, in Sandburg and Marianne Moore, even though those poets are quite different in many ways. Pound, for all his divagations and eccentricities, set the bit of his rock-drill to the task of chipping away old rhetoric and nonsense to find the bedrock of actuality. Eliot may seem out of place in a discussion of the impulse to physical actuality, but behind all of his writing we can see the old American preoccupation with the philosophy of experience and knowledge; after all, the most important things in the world for Eliot were physical: the Objective Correlative and the Incarnation, which may turn out to be two versions of one single thing. And Stevens, for all his hoobla-hoo about the Imagination and the world-not-world, did say a nicely Republican maxim: "The greatest poverty is not to live / In a physical world."

It is probably a good thing that Ammons was born in the South, for several elements of that particular background seem to have outfitted him ideally for his distinguished participation in the general American debate about the physical world. Ammons can recall a landscape and a language of a bleakness and splendor hard to match anywhere else in the country. His home county (Columbus) has always been poor. Many of his autobiographical poems suggest pitiful depths of poverty on a southern farm during the depression, a time so miserable that a young boy had to do hard jobs with practically no recreations. A sow, a mule, and an injured wild songbird were his pets. Living utterly in a physical world given spiky contours by hunger, cold, illness, and misfortune, the poet grew into a chastened vocabulary that is now about 90 percent horse sense and 10 percent rustic clowning around. Both the dead-level speech and the ornate goofing off are qualities of southern speech, and both gloss the actual world in its weirdnesses as well as in its routines.

Now in his fifties and wearing the honor of the Goldwin Smith Professorship of Poetry at Cornell University, Ammons has emerged as the ideal heir to the strongest fortune of American poetry, and his work synthesizes the best experiments of all of his precursors, especially the ones who stayed at home—Whitman, Sandburg, Williams, Jeffers, Stevens, and Frost. With a southerner's innate skepticism and peculiarly efficient sense of irony, Ammons is at once the flattest of writers and the fanciest. Southerners, black and white, rich and poor, have all suffered too damned many indignities, humiliations, setbacks, and defeats to speak directly, except when you are least expecting directness. Idle conversation in the South—not to mention stories, jokes, graffiti, songs, nicknames, and official artworks—depends on a maniacal degree of indirectness. Equipped with the tools of indirection and irony, Ammons has been beautifully enlarging the scope of old-time naturalism and realism, so that now his work has come to resemble the serial experiments of Claude Monet and other relativist-impressionist painters, luminists who used primary colors to render the effects of changing light in simple scenes. Ammons' latest book, *The Snow Poems*, is a long work in 120 parts mostly devoted to rendering a single elm tree through changing lights and circumstances from autumn through winter to spring. The concentration, intensity, and scope—and even some of the humor and doodling—all resemble the surfaces of Monet's series of paintings of poplars, haystacks, and (preeminently) water lilies. Like the greatest painters, Ammons even includes large tracts of idleness and emptiness, and the effect for me is one of uncanny veracity and charm. For a while now, the greatest living American poet will be a benevolent southern genius.

LOUIS D. RUBIN, JR.

The Boll Weevil, the Iron Horse, and the End of the Line: Thoughts on the South

1. *The Boll Weevil*

On hot afternoons in the summertime—this was in the middle-to-late 1930s—I sat in the bleachers at College Park in Charleston and when the baseball game was not too interesting I watched for the Boll Weevil at the Seaboard Air Line railway station. It was called the Boll Weevil because when the little gas-electric locomotive-coach was placed in service in the early 1920s the black folk of the South Carolina sea-islands through which the little train passed fancied its resemblance to the bug that had moved northward and then eastward from Mexico to devastate the cotton crops.

The little Seaboard gas-electric coach, of course, devastated no cotton crops. As a railroad train the Boll Weevil wasn't much. There were two of them in actuality, a northbound and a southbound train, operating each day between Savannah, Georgia, and Hamlet, North Carolina, the latter being a railroad junction point a few miles beyond the border between the two Carolinas. The trackage they traversed was not the Seaboard's main line, which was the New York-Florida route that crossed through South Carolina well to the interior. Rather, the railroad's low country branch constituted a large bow in the line, a two-hundred-mile-long loop that dropped southward from the main line junction at Hamlet down toward the seacoast, then southwestward to Charleston and to Savannah not quite a hundred miles farther, where it rejoined the main line. It served the truck-farming and—until the coming of the little black bug—the cotton industry along the coast,

346

and transported passengers, mostly black, who wished to travel between the little way stations, towns, and flag-stops and Charleston or Savannah, the only two communities of any size along the route.

The northbound Boll Weevil came through Charleston from Savannah shortly before midday. Its southbound counterpart from Hamlet customarily arrived about three o'clock in the afternoon. It was the latter that I watched for. At some point during the weekend double-header Municipal League baseball games it would make its appearance, clattering across Rutledge Avenue and rolling to a halt at the little stucco railroad station at Grove Street just beyond the left-field limits. No ceremony attended its advent. Perhaps there would be a taxicab or two, but usually only a railroad baggageman and a handful of outward-bound passengers were there to greet it.

The Boll Weevil's route lay closer to the coast than the Coast Line's. Until the 1900s the only way to travel between Charleston and the numerous coastal islands had been by slow boat: shallow-draft launches with steam and later make-and-break gasoline engines had traversed the creeks, estuaries, bays, and rivers with passengers and cargoes from the islands, made their way to the city, and tied up at Adger's Wharf. But now most of the sea-islands were linked to the mainland by bridges, and the remoteness of the low country, which had lasted from colonial times, was coming to an end.

The Boll Weevil, however unprepossessing in appearance, thus represented a phase in the process whereby the several centuries of comparative isolation that had characterized the life of the Carolina seacoast were giving way to the mobility of modern industrial America. No longer were goods dependent upon water transport, or upon horse and mule drayage along rutted, sandy roads, to get into the hinterlands. And if there was no job for a black farm-hand in the low country—no need, for example, to pick cotton any more, thanks to the little black bug from Mexico—the train was there to take him to the city.

So the sleepy little Boll Weevil gas-electric train that waited around for such an interminably long time at the stucco station up at College Park, just beyond left field, and which I would watch on summer afternoons during the 1930s, was in its own way emblematic of something perhaps every bit as disruptive, as devastating, as the insect that had moved up from Mexico in the 1910s to eradicate the cotton crop. What it represented and embodied was *change*.

Throughout the South there were many trains like the little Boll Weevil. In Eudora Welty's beautiful novel *Delta Wedding*, a little train named the Yellow Dog—in actuality the Yazoo and Delta—brings cousin Laura McRaven from the city of Jackson to the cottonlands of the Mississippi Delta—a mixed train, "four cars, freight, white, colored, and caboose, its smoke like a poodle tail curled overhead." Into the flat plantation country of the Delta it transported travelers from Jackson and from the world beyond, and though it seemed so diminutive and harmless, with its friendly engineer Mr. Dolittle who occasionally halted the train en route so that the conductor could gather goldenrod, it was not harmless but instead powerful and inexorable, as Miss Welty suggested, and what it brought and signified was ultimately irresistible: time and change, the world outside the confines of the plantation.

Nowadays there is no more Yellow Dog, and no more Boll Weevil. Even when I sat in the bleachers at the baseball games in the 1930s and watched the little train arrive at the Seaboard station, it was already outmoded, for the trains had been an earlier phase of the change. By the 1930s automobiles, buses, and trucks were the principal means of conveyance between the city and the islands. The dirt roads were being widened and paved. There were highway bridges connecting most of the sea-islands with the mainland. Few places in the low country were really remote any more. All over the South this was taking place—had, indeed, already taken place by the middle 1930s.

The old isolation was ended, and the towns and cities were expanding into the open countryside. When I had first begun attending the games at College Park I had walked home through fields, leaving the built-up area along Grove Street to cut through a mile of open land, crossed a marsh creek over a little wooden bridge, then walked through a grove of trees to our house on a bluff overlooking the Ashley River. But by the late 1930s the entire area was rapidly being built up, and where for two hundred years there had been planted fields and marshland there were now frame houses and multiple-occupancy dwellings. For there was a growing need for new housing in Charleston, occasioned by the influx of new people into the city to work at the Navy Yard, the steel mill, and other industrial installations to the north of the city limits. True, those city limits were still where they had been located at the time of the Civil War, along Mount Pleasant Street, a block north of our house. But now there was a sprawling and largely unlovely industrial community stretching out for ten miles and more to the northward.

One day I was waiting for a bus—the trolley cars were gone by then—at the corner of King and Wentworth Streets downtown. When it pulled up to the curb there were already so many riders aboard that there was no room for anyone else. It was the going-home hour and another bus would be along shortly, I knew, so I prepared to wait. A woman who was standing near me was not willing to wait, however. She went up to the closed doors of the bus and began rapping on the glass panels in a vain attempt to gain admittance. "I want in!" she called. "I want in!"

She could not be a native Charlestonian, I knew, because she would never have said it that way if she were. She would have called, "I want to come in!" or "I want to get in!" No doubt she and her family had come from Ohio or somewhere else in the Midwest to work at the Navy Yard. Many people were moving to Charleston, from the Upstate, the other southern states, and the Midwest and North as well, for there were imminent signs of another war, and a tremendous defense industry was getting into high gear. There were many more buses in service, but also more waiting, because the area north of the city was becoming so thickly populated that the South Carolina Power Company simply could not purchase new buses rapidly enough to accommodate the demand.

Meanwhile the Boll Weevil kept to its rounds. I would catch sight of it from time to time while riding downtown or coming home on the bus. Sometimes I wished I might go for a trip aboard the little train. I wanted to board it at the station on Grove Street and make the journey with it up the coast and then inland, all the way to its northern terminus at Hamlet, North Carolina. I could then transfer to a mainline Seaboard train such as the streamliner, the Silver Meteor, and continue on to Richmond, where my aunts, uncles, and cousins lived. But of course that was not the way to travel from Charleston to Richmond. To go there one drove up to North Charleston and boarded one of the Atlantic Coast Line trains.

By then the Second World War had come. My family moved from Charleston to Richmond, where my mother had come from, and soon after that I was in the Army. I was stationed first in Alabama and then in Connecticut, and most of my fellow soldiers were from the North and Midwest. Some were quick to point out to me, when I attempted to describe what I so liked about life back home, that many of the more pleasant qualities of that life were possible because of the availability of a disadvantaged labor force to do the unpleasant work and thus permit the famous 'Gracious Living' enjoyed by the white folks. But if that were true—and I began to see that in certain crucial respects it was all too true—I could not feel that it was a sufficient explanation for what I felt about life in my part of the country.

Later I was sent to Fort Benning, and for almost two years I lived near the city of Columbus, Georgia. Here was a community of less than 50,000 which almost overnight was the civilian adjunct of an army camp of 120,000 troops! Housing, transportation, business, entertainment, recreation facilities were inconceivably overcrowded and inadequate. From my occasional visits to Columbus I could understand why it was that when sometimes I encountered a fellow soldier who had been stationed at or near Charleston, his attitude toward my own home city as a place to visit was usually so very hostile. Of course the city he had found so unpleasant and inhospitable was not the real Charleston, as I always hastened to explain, but a place that within a matter of several years had suddenly been forced to accommodate itself to the presence of three times its own population, ringed as it was with military installations. The chances were that on his visits to the city he had encountered very few actual Charlestonians; most of those store-keepers, taxi drivers, USO workers, shop girls and other civilians he had met were recent arrivals.

I doubt that the question ever occurred to me whether, when the war was done, my native city could or would go back to being what it had been just a few years ago. Yet had it not been changing even when I was living there? "I want in!" the woman at the bus stop had declared in her midwestern accent and idiom. Was the city I remembered, with the fishing boats and the White Stack tugboats tied up at Adger's Wharf, the little train waiting at the station just past the ball park, the barber shop which like my father I always patronized (with its familiar clientele and its barbers who conducted themselves so professionally and yet so accommodatingly), Broad Street with its lawyers, bankers, realtors, insurance men, the local "establishment" as it were, where my aunt was a secretary and where there were so many persons I knew and who knew me and my family—was this place, which I knew so well and liked so much, both for its virtues and its vices (and both were numerous), not the real, unchanging Charleston? And after the war was won would I not go back there to live, as I was sure I wanted to do?

Several times when I visited my relatives in Charleston during the war while on leave from Fort Benning, I had seen the little Boll Weevil in its familiar setting up by the station at College Park. But there was one occasion when I caught sight of the little train in a very different context. It was when I was on furlough to Richmond, where my parents were living. The train to Richmond, which I boarded at Atlanta, stopped at Hamlet, North Carolina, sometime after midnight to change crews and engines, and I made my way out of the crowded coach, which was filled with sleeping travelers, and stepped down onto the platform to look around. It was cold. The station was a large, old-fashioned wooden affair, with tracks on both sides. I walked back along the platform, past the station and toward the rear of the train, and gazed out into the winter night at the town's main thoroughfare. Except for the lights in the lobby of a railroad hotel, all was dark. After a minute I strolled back toward the station, and on the way I happened to glance down a section of track along a side street that crossed the main line, whereupon I spied a familiar silhouette. It was the Boll Weevil, waiting overnight for the next day's run down to Charleston and through the low country to Savannah.

Unlit and unnoticed, on a siding, not far from a station which even though the hour was well past midnight was crowded with servicemen, civilians, railroad crewmen, porters, passengers on the main line passenger train from Atlanta paused there en route northward, the little Boll Weevil seemed out of place, far from its proper element. To come upon it here, waiting mutely and, as it seemed, forlornly on a side track, was a shock. It belonged to sunny afternoons and the stucco station at College Park.

I went back to my coach, made my way to my seat, and waited for my journey to resume.

When the war was done and the troops came home, the South did not go back to being what it had been. Cities such as Charleston did not shrink back to prewar size; with only minor interruptions they proceeded to develop peacetime industries and enterprises to replace the war installations, and not only retained their prosperity and population but kept right on expanding in size and importance. The small cities of the South became large cities, the towns became smaller cities, the countryside, joined to the cities by networks of highways, lost what still remained of its remoteness and isolation. The traditional patterns of southern agriculture were being diversified. Cotton was king no more. Sharecropping and tenant farming no longer characterized much of the land-use arrangements. The rural population, in particular the blacks, moved to the cities as never before, and there was also a steady outmigration of blacks and whites to the big industrial cities of the North. The tractor, the mechanical cotton picker, the mechanized tobacco harvester displaced the mule and the field hand. There was money available in the South now. The postwar boom was on, but on a much more solid foundation than in the years just after the First World War.

As for myself, I did not go back to Charleston to live after all. There was no job for me there, for I was now a newspaperman and the Charleston newspapers had no place for me, nor, after I had left journalism for graduate study and teaching, was there a teaching position at home until long after I was at the stage in the profession that would make it impossible for me to go back. I realized a little later that even if I had been able to return home to live, the chances are that I should not have remained there for long. Charleston had changed in many ways, and my loyalty and attachment were really not so much to a place as to a time—to the years when I had been a child and an adolescent growing up in a small southern city. And Charleston was not that any more: this was borne in on me whenever I went back to visit. The familiar, medium-sized southern community that I had known was now only the center of a vast, sprawling metropolitan area of suburbs, subdivisions, manufacturing plants, shopping centers. Once I went outside the downtown area I hardly knew my way around. What had been fields, woods, marshland, open country now were urban areas. Many of the people I knew best, in particular most of those with whom I had attended high school and college and in whose company I had passed most of my time, were gone; like myself they had not come back home after the war.

As for the little Boll Weevil train, it had long since gone. I found this out rather vividly in the early 1950s. Returning to Charleston for a visit I decided that just for the fun of it I would not ride the Coast Line train but instead take the Seaboard down to Hamlet, spend the night in the railroad hotel near the station, and the next day get on board the Boll Weevil and ride down through the low country to Charleston. I checked the timetables; the little train was still listed as operating. So I rode down to Hamlet, stopped overnight in the railroad hotel, and the next morning went over to the passenger station to purchase my ticket. Instead of the familiar little gas-electric combine, I found a train made up of a diesel locomotive, a baggage car, and several air-conditioned coaches.

As the train rolled along down the single track line into South Carolina the conductor told me that the Boll Weevils had been removed from service several months ago. Nor was he regretful of their passing; the gas-electric combination coaches had always given much trouble, he said, and were constantly breaking down and falling behind schedule, so that he and his fellow trainmen had been happy to see them go. So I rode from Hamlet to Charleston in an air-conditioned coach. When the train arrived at the stucco station at College Park I got off and walked over to Rutledge Avenue to take the bus downtown. I thought to myself that even if the Boll Weevil was gone, at least I had finally made the trip.

It was none too soon, for within a few years all passenger service on the Hamlet-Charleston-Savannah branch was discontinued. And in the 1960s when the Seaboard and Atlantic Coast Line railroads were merged, even freight traffic along the tracks that led by the ball park and over the trestle at the foot of Grove Street was ended. The old wooden bridge across the Ashley River was torn down. No longer would young Charlestonians lie in bed at night as I had once done and hear the night freight train from the south whistling far off in the darkness, and then gradually draw near the bridge, until as the wheels rolled onto the timbered structure the iron flanges set up a deep, singing reverberation on the rails, which grew hoarser as the train crossed over the river and entered the city.

No, the train was gone for good, as indeed were steam locomotives, the Boll Weevil, Adger's Wharf down on the waterfront with the shrimp boats and tugboats and little cargo launches with their make-and-break engines, and many another artifact of youth and young manhood. And each separate visit, over the years, seemed to broaden the loss. The barber shop down on King Street, where once there had been eight barbers, all of whom I knew by name and who knew me, was now down to one elderly man, tending shop by himself. The comfortable old Fort Sumter Hotel on the Battery was converted into condominium apartments. The hulk of the ferryboat *Sappho*, moored throughout my youth in the tidal flats just beyond Gadsden Street, had long since disappeared under a landfill. The old Southern Railway roundhouse on Columbus Street, where on Sunday mornings my father used to take us to see the trains, was gone, and a supermarket occupied its former place. East Bay Street, where the wholesale houses had been located in antebellum buildings, had lost its hegemony to more accessible places in the built-up northern area; there was little but empty store fronts and a few conversions into apartments. Missing in particular was a red wagon wheel which had always hung suspended from a bracket above the entrance to one hardware dealer. My father had installed it in 1913, when he had been a youth working there.

Gone, too, along with the places and the emblems were those Charlestonians of my father's generation who had once lived among these things and made them substantial and significant. For almost all of those men and women, my elders, the adult citizens of the city when I was a child, and whose lives and positions and concerns and opinions had seemed so important and so formidable, were dead now, while the few who still survived and whom I sometimes encountered here and there were frail and old, human relics as it seemed, more like tourists such as myself than inhabitants, now that their onetime peers and companions, the social context in which they had fitted, were gone. They appeared oddly diminished and shrunken in stature, caricatures of their former selves. So that on each successive visit to what had once been my home, I found that what had constituted its substance and accidence both had dwindled. To the extent that the places, objects, people, and associations of my childhood—a southern childhood, in and of a southern city—had constituted whatever there was of reality and permanence to my younger experience, then that reality was becoming more and more a matter of absence, loss, and alienation. I was, that is, steadily being dispossessed.

2. Bill Barrett's Iron Horse

The experience recounted thus far, however intensely felt by myself, is in no sense unique. It differs from similar experience for others only in the particular details in which it has been presented. Insofar as it is appropriate to most persons who, like myself, have grown away from a community that has been very much caught up in social transition and widespread change, it is valid for numerous modern southerners. Moreover, though its meaning lies, I think, at the center of the southern literary experience of our time, in the form that I have reported it so far it is inert, useless: merely a species of nostalgia. As presented, it presupposes a kind of absolute cultural, social, and historical order, designed and believed to exist permanently, and then interprets all subsequent changes within that order, all alteration in the complex substance of its embodiment, as a diminution of reality, an erosion of what should by rights have been immutable: in short, as disorder, loss, chaos.

But while such a way of viewing one's experience is perhaps unavoidable as a starting point, it is also partial, superficial, and really a distortion of reality rather than an evocation of it. And if that were all there was to the southern literary imagination as it views the past, there would be little point in paying much heed to it. For the truth is that, as I have suggested earlier on, just as there was at no time an absolute, unchanging, permanent form to the life of the Carolina low country, but instead at all times change and alteration, so my own memories of places, people, institutions, and artifacts of my own childhood and young manhood are composed not of fixity and diuturnity but of elements that were very much caught up in change, however they may have once seemed immutable to me.

I had thought of the little Boll Weevil train as fixed and determined in its arrivals and departures at the Seaboard station. But the railroad crew that operated it reported that it had constantly broken down and been behind schedule, and what it meant for the agricultural life of the low country had been mobility, change, the coming of the city to the sea-islands and the movement of the black folk to the city. When during the war I had caught sight of the Boll Weevil late one winter night in North Carolina, and had felt so powerfully that it belonged not there on the unfamiliar siding but to summer afternoons at the stucco station in Charleston, I had been facile. It was not the little train, but myself, who was in what seemed to be the wrong place and wrong season. And what made the present time and place seem unsatisfactory was that I was attributing a greater emotional importance, a more self-sufficient identity and a freedom from contingency, to the earlier experience. Whereas the truth was that only *because* of the later experience—because I *saw* the little train in Hamlet that night—

was the earlier experience made to seem so important, so intense, to seem, in short, so very *real*. In actuality the authenticity of the experience, and its importance for me, lay neither in the isolated memory of the little train at College Park as such, which was an act of mere nostalgia, nor in my reencounter with the train at Hamlet, which because of its seeming inappropriateness was so pathetic. Rather, the authenticity and importance resided in the relation of the one to the other—in the profound vividness of the experience of time and change, a vividness that I myself, through my participation, was able to bring to it. And it has been just such vividness, but magnified and enriched many times through artistic genius, that has constituted the achievement of the best of the modern southern writers.

There comes immediately to mind a scene from a brilliant novel by Walker Percy, *The Last Gentleman*, in which precisely this kind of perception is delineated, and which I now propose to discuss at some length. The novel, which like much of Percy's fiction contains strong autobiographical elements, involves the hegira of one Williston Bibb Barrett from Mississippi to New York City and then back southward and later westward in search of a way to unite action and conviction, and much of the motivation for Barrett's journey is ascribable to the collapse and futility, as he sees it, of the old southern stoic attitude of aristocratic fortitude he had been taught to believe in, a collapse exemplified by his own father's suicide.

Like more than one young man in southern literature, Bill Barrett has the expectation of a proper and assured role for himself, but cannot identify the possibility of any such role existing in his own changed circumstance, even while he remains unwilling and unable to accept the kind of moral and social wasteland in which no such assurance is available. Like the speaker in Allen Tate's beautiful "Ode to the Confederate Dead," he stands at the cemetery gate, as it were, grieves at the inescapability of the fact that he cannot believe in the validity of the communal pieties, yet also cannot settle for an existence in which no such pieties are possible. "What shall we say who have knowledge / Carried to the heart?" Tate's protagonist asks. "Shall we take the act / To the grave?" In Bill Barrett's instance he manages to stop, en route west-ward, outside his old home in Mississippi one night and look on from the darkness of the oak trees while his aunts sit out on the porch in traditional southern style—watching a give-away quiz show on television!

He remembers the night when his father, a lawyer (and much resembling Percy's uncle, William Alexander Percy), had walked up and down the street beneath the oak trees as usual, awaiting the outcome of a public battle he has led against a lower-class fac-tion that seems to resemble the Ku Klux Klan of the 1920s. His son sat on the steps, tending the old-fashioned 78-rpm drop-record phonograph, on which a Brahms symphony was being played in the darkness. By and by the police come to tell the father that his fight has been won, the riffraff have broken up their meeting and left town. Instead of rejoicing in his victory, however, the father tells his son that its price has been the destruction of any pretense to superior moral and ethical standards on the part of his own class of onetime ladies and gentlemen. The illusion of aristocratic virtue and rectitude having been shattered, the father has only his private isolated sensibility to fall back upon. "In the last analy-sis, you are alone," he tells his son, and walks off again. "*Don't leave,*" his son begs. But the father goes into the house, climbs the stairs up to the attic, places the muzzle end of a shotgun against his breast, and pulls the trigger.

Now an older Bill Barrett stands among the oaks remembering the sound of the shot, and meanwhile hearing the television com-mercial that his aunts are watching. He reaches out in the dark-ness and his hand encounters an iron hitching post, moulded in the form of a horse's head, about the base of which an oak tree has grown until now it entirely surrounds it. He touches the tree bark:

> *Wait.* While his fingers explored the juncture of iron and bark, his eyes narrowed as if he caught a glimmer of light on the cold iron skull. *Wait.* I think he was wrong and that he was looking in the wrong place. No, not he but the times. The times were wrong and one looked in the wrong place. It wasn't even his fault because that was the way he was and the way the times were, and there was no other place a man could look. It was the worst of times, a time of fake beauty and fake victory. *Wait.* He had missed it! It was not in the Brahms that one looked and not in solitariness and not in the old sad poetry but—he wrung out his

ear—but here, under your nose, here in the very curiousness and drollness and extraness of the iron and the bark that—he shook his head—
that— (Signet Book ed., p. 260)

This is a marvelous passage. What Bill Barrett wishes he could
tell his dead father is that those public values and truths upon
which his life and conduct had been predicated, and which had finally seemed to have so eroded that he had killed himself, were
false, or at best only partial and ancillary. *Wait*, he keeps telling
his father in his imaginary expostulation, in repetition of that
traumatic moment in the past when he had vainly begged his father not to leave. The triumph over the riffraff, the great horn
theme of Brahms, he insists, were false victory and false loveli-
ness because the ideals they were being made to embody were il-
lusory, a species of ideality removed from the world, as it were.
His father had felt that his struggle with the red-necks (corresponding, one should note, to Walker Percy's grandfather's victory over the Klan in the 1920s, as described by Will Percy in *Lanterns On the Levee*) was the assertion of absolute integrity in a
graceless modern world. In being achieved it had revealed to his
father his own isolation, since it had forced him to see that those
who were on his side in the dispute, and who supposedly represented the lofty morality that he believed in, were in no way absolutely superior in ethics and morality to those they had defeated.
He tells his son that the lower orders had once been "the fornica-
tors and the bribers and the takers of bribes and we were not and
that was why they hated us. Now we are like them" (p. 258).

But what Bill Barrett knows, out of his own subsequent experience and observation, is that there never was any such generation
of earlier heroes who were exempt from human stain and contingency, so that his father's ideal of aristocratic virtue, however
nobly motivated, was actually a romantic escape from the com-
promised actuality of human life in time. Such a view necessarily
presupposed a former time in which men were better and wiser,
more disinterested and virtuous than humans could ever be, as
well as a society that had been more nearly free from all temptations to covetousness, avarice, lust, and cruelty than had ever existed on earth.

Thus any change in circumstances and conduct would have to

constitute a falling away from perfection, and to the extent that the change continued in time, the arrival of crass days, a moral and social wasteland, the death of the gods. So his father's belief that a mere political victory would reaffirm the antique virtues and insure their permanence was doomed to disappointment once his father realized that the golden age had not thereby been recreated. What his father had done was to attempt to insulate himself from time, change, and mortality by retreating into a private code of aristocratic virtue and honor, truth and beauty that gave him the illusion of human perfectibility, and when this was shattered by being tested in the actual world, there seemed nothing left for him but to be destroyed with it.

In the same way, the notion that the great horn theme of Brahms, to which the father had been listening on the night of his suicide, enunciated an ideal of absolute and timeless beauty was also ultimately self-contradictory. For as Bill Barrett sensed, "the mellowness of Brahms had gone overripe, the victorious serenity of the Great Horn Theme was false, oh fake fake" (p. 259). Percy is alluding, I think, to a characteristic of Brahms' symphonic music that I have also noticed. Brahms builds up to huge, slow-moving thematic statements that seen to assert a kind of hard-won triumph of spirit, and which in their massive harmonics pronounce an ultimate resolution superior to merely human difficulties and leaving no further occasion for striving or disruption. Thus when the last notes of the symphony die out, one has a sense not of triumph but of sadness, for since so supernal a resolution cannot be continued indefinitely but must come to an end, one feels, as it were, alone and abandoned in a jaded world. The quality that Bill Barrett identifies and deplores in Brahms seems to be a sort of victorious exhaustion, an elimination of all further possibility of growth or extension, that corresponds mightily to the *fin de siècle* romanticism of Swinburne, Dowson, the *Rubaiyat*, "The City of Dreadful Night," and, be it noted, of the poetry of William Alexander Percy himself. Thus, in having Bill Barrett declare that his father had looked for beauty in the wrong place, what Walker Percy means, I think, is that music that asserts as an ideal a quality of perfection that seems to rule out all further human involvement can only become hollow and intolerable.

The place to look for beauty and for truth, rather, is "here, right under your nose, here in the very curiousness and drollness and extraness of the iron and the bark . . ." For the iron horse's head of the hitching post, though ornamental, was cast for use by men, while the oak that has grown around it has drawn it into time and change rather than abstracted it from all future contingency, and in the union of the two is the miracle of growth and fusion, producing a quality of excess and uniqueness that goes beyond the merely usable or fortuitously natural, even while deriving its strength and beauty from time and change.

Such an achievement cannot ever involve a static perfection. The iron hitching post was given its form by men, to serve a purpose and yet to be ornamental as well, and though that purpose is outmoded, the very element that has outmoded it—change—has given it its marvelous new possibility: of being as one with the oak tree.

All this, it seems to me, is implicit in that remarkable passage from *The Last Gentleman. Wait!* Bill Barrett begs his father. *Don't leave!* For the boy needed his father, but the father's way of seeing himself and his duty did not, finally, encompass any obligation to or need for a future so fallen from perfection as to seem meaningless. The father could not see that the presence of the boy there with him in the dark, tending the phonograph as he walked back and forth beneath the trees, was itself a refutation of his premise that *"in the last analysis,* you are alone" (italics mine)—for human virtue and meaning were not to be found solely within oneself, as measured against an autonomous, static ideal of timeless perfection, but instead were human qualities growing out of continuing existence in time, never perfect, never complete and self-sufficient in themselves, but always in vital relationship with ongoing experience.

The great horn theme seemed to separate itself from all regeneration, assert an ideal of pure, abstract beauty that mocked mere human striving. Similarly, the worship of the past as an age of superhuman heroes made the present into a time of certain decline and fall, and the future into something meaningless. Instead of the past being allowed to illuminate and strengthen the authenticity of the present, it is made to destroy it. For the presence of the boy there on the steps, overseeing the drop-record phonograph

and watching his father, is what the past has created; and the boy's
need of his father—*don't leave!*—validates the genuineness of
the past, because it provides a means for the best qualities of that
past to continue to have meaning in time. And it is *that* kind of
continuity, and not the blind preservation of what had once been
human existence in time as static, changeless icon, untouched by
the hurly-burly of continued experience, that keeps the past meaningful and makes its exemplars truly heroic. Otherwise that past,
which Bill Barrett's father saw as the sole repository of virtue, is
rendered empty and abstract—as futile as the world-weary, life-
denying "victory" of the great horn theme, a beauty so removed
and isolated from human need and desire as to produce emptiness
and despair.

Looking out from under the shadow of the oaks, Bill Barrett
does not blame his father for having left him. On the contrary, he
is filled with love and pity for his father, for he knows that his father, like himself, was caught in a situation not of his own making, and was unable to extricate himself from it. Indeed, it might
even be said that it was *because* his father had taken his life, in
despair over what he considered the impossibility of being able to
stay with him, that he was now able to recognize the murderous
falseness and inadequacy of the ideal of the solitary man. The
sound of that shotgun blast in the night, the hopelessness that had
caused his father to pull the triggers of the twelve-gauge Greener,
was what had sent him on his own search, which however prolonged and agonizing represented the only way that he might ever
learn to break through the walls of solitude that might otherwise
have imprisoned him as well.

What he learns, finally, is that solitary integrity is not enough
for a man, that one cannot live merely in private measurement
against a personal ideal. There can be no *I* without a *Thou*. The
plea, "Wait. Don't leave!" is the recognition of human need, and
the heeding of the plea is the acknowledgment not only that one
is needed by another, but that acceptance of another's need is *in
itself an assertion of need*. It is there, in ongoing involvement with
what is outside of one's own otherwise solitary self, that one's identity in time can be affirmed: not through a strong-willed transcend-

ing of life but *in* and *through* life, immanently: the iron horse encircled by the living cortex of the great oak, the two elements become extraordinary in their marvelous need-in-separateness: unique and mysterious in their configuration—the handiwork of God.

The difference, as I see it, between my experience with the Boll Weevil and that given by Walker Percy to Williston Bibb Barrett in *The Last Gentleman* is that in effect the novel commences where I was willing to leave off. What I had done was to see the past—the little Seaboard gas-electric coach in its place at the station in Charleston—as something absolute and completely self-contained, in and of itself. And God said, Let there be Light, one might say; and He created the Boll Weevil. Because the train was there for me to see, it became part of my experience, and it belonged there at the ball park. But since, being human, I existed in time, I grew away from the experience it symbolized, and because its vivid, emblematic quality was important to me, I could only interpret any change in my relationship to it, any distancing of its image in time, as a falling away from perfection. Each subsequent stage in my relationship to it—seeing it at night on the siding, far from its familiar context; finding the diesel locomotive in its place when I went to board it at Hamlet; and finally, seeing the tracks along which it ran and the trestle over which it crossed the river torn up and removed—constituted a diminution of its reality to me. For I had associated the little train, to repeat, with a time and place that had seemed very real and permanent to me. The memory of the train was nostalgic, in that it revived the memory of the time and place, as a kind of golden age before the Fall; but since it was no more than that, I had to confront the fact that it was gone forever, with nothing in my present experience seemingly able to replace it in its vividness and solidity.

In the same way, Bill Barrett's father in *The Last Gentleman*, confronting the fact that the old times, the old standards of aristocratic probity, were gone, and not even the temporary victory over the rabble can restore them, saw no further hope, no standard of moral conduct that could adequately replace what had been lost.

But not so his son, who out of his grief and loss at his father's death is made to see the limitations of such a way of viewing one-self and one's place in time in the inevitable hopelessness of his father's plight. Through an act of the resolute will his father had managed for a period of time to convince himself that the old times were not gone; but the evidence of his eyes and senses finally shattered the illusion. Bill Barrett will make no such attempt, because he cannot; his father's suicide made it impossible for him to be satisfied with any repetition of his father's way. What he comes to see, therefore, after a long and painful search, is that no man may impose his heart's-desire view of reality upon the world without isolating himself from that world. Human reality in time, and his relationship to it, must be found in one's continuing engagement with the world, an engagement that because it takes place in human time must accept and incorporate change as well as continuity. Acceptance of that relationship involves an acceptance of one's need for what is outside oneself, and the obligation to seek to be oneself *in* that exterior world. A difficult task, truly, requiring as it does neither abject surrender nor prideful disdain, but ongoing engagement.

3. *End of the Line*

And what has that to do with the present and future South, whether Walker Percy's or mine or anyone else's? Simply (yet with what complication!) that we live in a region upon which history has enforced so pervasive a heritage of order and form and community, so powerful a set of loyalties and expectations, that we cannot sidestep the extraordinary strength of our identification with it. So decisive is that sense of identification, even today, that to an important degree it determines our personality. When I say, "I am a southerner," or "I am from Charleston," I am, no matter how I may disguise it, uttering an expression of pride in identity. It matters not that Walker Percy's experience of the South and his role within it may be in certain respects very different from mine or someone else's (his grandfather owned plantations in the Delta and served in the Senate of the United States, while mine owned a little grocery store down by the railroad tracks in Florence, South Carolina, and spoke in a German Jewish accent); the similarities are far more important than the differences, and that fact of itself might help to explain *why* the region could and still can exert so strong an influence upon its inhabitants and command so much of their loyalties. For genuine human communities, as contrasted with mere economic and social combinations, are hard to come by in this world, and that is what the South has been.

But the temptations and dangers involved in such an identification are perilous, too. It is too easy, and too tempting, to surrender one's own individual personality to it, to construct an absolute moral and ethical entity out of a relationship which, because it is human and in time, cannot ever afford absolute certainty to one. That way lies idolatry. This is what Allen Tate meant when he wrote to his friend Donald Davidson in 1942 that "you have always seemed to me to hold to a kind of mystical secularism, which has made you impatient and angry at the lack of results. We live in a bad age in which we cannot give our best; but no age is good." Donald Davidson, like Bill Barrett's father, sought valiantly to fuse his own identity with the community he loved in its time and place, and when, as was inevitable, that community, being made up of humans, changed, he saw the change as a fall from perfection, and thus as a betrayal, and he spent his energies in a vain attempt to arrest the change and deny its manifestations. Increasingly the South that he loved became a heart's-desire land which bore less and less relationship to the actual Tennessee community he lived in, until his life became almost totally a rear guard action against any accommodation with change, and in which each engagement was fought as if it were Armageddon, or perhaps Gettysburg. Entered into with the noblest of motives, waged with unremitting courage and high personal honor, Donald Davidson's battle ultimately deprived him of all contact with the real world that poetry must inhabit if it is to take its images and meanings from life.

It is temptingly easy to forget what Stark Young warned his fellow Nashville Agrarians about when he declared in his contribution to the Agrarian symposium *I'll Take My Stand* that "we must remember that we are concerned first with a quality itself, not as our own but as found anywhere; and that we defend certain qualities not because they belong to the South, but because the South belongs to them." But it is also rather too easy to pursue the opposite course: to give in utterly and uncritically to change, to attempt to abdicate any responsibility for determining one's own moral and ethical relationship to it. For one's identity lies not in the change as such, but in what is undergoing change, and though we cannot arrest change, neither can we yield ourselves over to it entirely and still hope to retain any worthwhile integrity or identity in time. We are, in human terms at least, the product of our past, and our task is always therefore to adapt what we are to the inevitability of change, so as to secure and strengthen what we are and can be: to seek to control and shape change so as to help it become part of *us*. In that transaction lies human identity in time, and it would be foolish indeed for us not to attempt to preserve such hard-won virtues and accomplishments as we possess. For we have no way of knowing that adequate and acceptable replacements will be available if we give them up uncritically in exchange for the unknown.

The South has been with us for some time now, and there seems to be little reason not to assume that it will continue to be the South for many years to come. It has changed a great deal—it is always changing, and in recent decades the change has been especially dramatic. But there is little conclusive evidence that it is changing into something that is less markedly southern than in the past. After all, why should it? Does anyone, for example, seriously believe that the liberation of an entire segment of its population, its black folk, into full participation in the region's political and economic life will make the region *less* distinctively southern in its ways? Is not the reverse more likely? Does it seem plausible that, merely because they now live and work in towns and cities rather than in rural areas, the bulk of the southern population both white and black will abruptly cease to hold and to share most of the values, attitudes, concerns, and opinions that have hitherto characterized their lives?

Is the South becoming the "no-South"? Does the southern community cease to exist once it becomes urban and industrial? Not if we are to place any stock in what the sociological and political indices report, or what Walker Percy and other novelists and poets tell us. To think of change simply as destruction of the South's distinctiveness is misleading. Instead of concentrating our attention solely upon what industrialization, urbanization, racial integration, and so forth are going to do to the South, we might consider what so powerful and complex a community as our South is going to do to and with them. For the South has long had a habit of incorporating seemingly disruptive change within itself, and continuing to be the South. The historian George Tindall wryly records the long chronology of supposed demises of the "Old South." Each juncture in the region's history—the Civil War, the end of slavery, Reconstruction, the New South movement of the 1880s and 1890s, the Populist revolt, the impact of the First World War, the boosterism and business expansion of the 1920s, the Great Depression, the New Deal, the downfall of King Cotton and the rise of a more diversified agriculture, the break-up of the one-party system and the Solid South, *Brown* v. *Board of Education* and the end of legal segregation, the sweeping industrialization and urbanization of the 1960s and 1970s, the newfound prosperity of the so-called "Sun Belt," the election of Jimmy Carter as president with strong backing from black southerners—has been proclaimed as signalizing the end of the line, so far as the preservation of regional identity and distinctiveness are concerned. Yet an identifiable and visible South remains, and its inhabitants continue to face the same underlying human problems as before, however much the particular issues may change.

At the conclusion of *The Last Gentleman*, Bill Barrett, having lived in New York and journeyed to Sante Fe, will presumably go back to Birmingham, Alabama. He will not return to Things As They Were; but then, things are never as they once were. Those who proclaim Walker Percy's fiction as existential, thereby symbolizing the passing of the South and the conclusion of the twentieth-century southern literary mode as such, miss the point, it seems to me. The details of the southern heritage are deeply embodied in Percy's imagination, and in taking on the continuing human problems of self-definition, belief, good and evil, man's place in society from the perspective of a changed set of social and historical circumstances, Percy is doing what every major southern author before him has done. For at no time was there ever a static, changeless society known as the South, inhabited by fully-realized, timeless human exemplars known as southerners, for whom there was no problem of self-definition in changing times. The evidence of southern literature, it seems to me—of which Percy is the latest practitioner—is that in every time and place men have faced the task of reconciling individual and private virtue with an inescapable need for fulfillment within a community of men and women, and there is always the requirement to redefine the ethical and moral assumptions of one's rearing and one's present social circumstance amid change. In *The Last Gentleman* Bill Barrett has no doubt, really, that he wants to live a "normal" life; his consuming problem is the discovery of a way whereby he can believe in the virtue and value of such a life, rather than merely viewing his role in it as a kind of game plan, a calculated, abstract exercise of the will in which he imposes a private meaning upon what is outside and around him entirely in terms of its usefulness for himself. What he realizes, finally, is his absolute need for what goes on and is involved in that life—for what is ultimately outside of and unknown to him. Only with this acknowledgment of absolute dependence can he go back to his girl and his job and his life in Birmingham.

Now it seems to me that far from representing an end to the so-called "traditional" southern literary mode, *The Last Gentleman* is a redefinition of it, one that is necessary if it is to continue to have any significance. It represents, on its author's part, a reassessment of certain fundamental human truths, involving community, order, mutability and belief, in a changed social circumstance. Without such a reassessment, whereby ethical and moral assumptions are translated into a usable idiom, the assumptions would soon become empty and meaningless. And as Bill Barrett well reccognizes, any such redefinition can be only partial and inexact, for the human beings who hold to the assumptions and seek to act upon them are finite men and women.

Once more, and for the last time, the Boll Weevil: for its demise, the merger of the Seaboard and Coast Line Railroads, the discontinuance of all railroading along the trackage that led by the baseball field in Charleston, the removal of the old wooden trestle across the Ashley River, were not after all the end of my imaginative involvement with the little gas-electric coach that plays so inordinately emblematic a role in my memory of the past. There was a summer day, only several years ago, when I was driving from Charleston back to my home in North Carolina. The route led through the town of Hamlet, and since it was getting on toward midday when I neared there, I decided that I would leave the marked route, drive over to where the railway passenger station had been located, have a look around, and then find a place to eat lunch.

It had been twenty-five years since the day I had ridden down from Richmond, spent the night at the railroad hotel, and then gone to board the Boll Weevil, only to find it replaced by a diesel locomotive and air-conditioned coaches. Now I found the station itself, looking much as it had in the past, except that save for one small area reserved for Amtrak passengers, it was all boarded up. I went over to look at the train announcement board. There were only two passenger trains a day each way listed upon it. Not only had the branch line service to Charleston been long since discontinued, along with other such branches, but with the takeover of all passenger service by Amtrak, the onetime Seaboard service to Atlanta and Birmingham had been eliminated. Now the only passenger trains were New York-to-Florida runs.

The station platform was empty. I remembered it as it had been during the war, when the station had been filled with travelers, the lunch room crowded, porters busy with baggage carts along the ramps, railroad workers checking the condition of the wheels and braking equipment on the strings of coaches, switch engines shunting coaches, pullmans, baggage and mail cars back and forth to make up consists for the northbound, southbound, westbound, and eastbound runs. The life of the town of Hamlet, I thought, had once centered upon the activities at this station. Now it was deserted, boarded up.

I found the place where one night during the war I had spied the little Boll Weevil waiting alone in the darkness, far away from where in my mind's eye I felt it ought to be. Now there was only an empty stretch of siding next to an old brick warehouse, with the weeds grown high about the crossties and the rails rusty from long disuse.

I wondered whether the old wooden railroad hotel was still functioning. I walked a block southward. It was still there and, surprisingly, still doing business. No doubt its clientele of trainmen still found it useful for overnight stays between freight runs.

The restaurant was open, so I went in and sat down at a booth to order lunch. The room was crowded, and as I waited for my meal to be served, I looked around at my fellow customers. To judge from their age and appearance, most were not railroad workers but employees in the stores and offices along the main street nearby. What caught my eye, however, were four young women installed in a booth diagonally across from where I sat, eating lunch together while several youths stood nearby bantering with them. Three of the girls were white. One was black.

Twenty-five years ago, if I had been here at lunchtime, such a sight would have been inconceivable. As they talked away, eating, chattering, making jokes, laughing, giggling, I thought of how much political rhetoric, how much scheming and planning and denouncing and defying and editorializing and drawing up of legal briefs and passing laws and the like had been expended in my part of the country in the vain effort to prevent those four girls from eating lunch together in that restaurant. How many dire predictions of social catastrophe, how many lamentations over the imminent destruction of the Southern Way of Life, the violation of all that was sacred and noble, had come thundering forth on all sides!

Yet here they were now, eating lunch together, and here was this restaurant in a southeastern North Carolina town on a summer day, with the clientele laughing and talking and eating, and the waitresses serving up the hamburgers and salads and cokes and coffee and iced tea and pie, and the floor fans droning away, and except for the presence of the black girl there and several other black customers at other tables, whom I now saw, nothing seemed importantly different from what I might have seen there had I stopped in for lunch on that day when I rode the successor to the

Boll Weevil down to Charleston, or for that matter, from what I would have seen if a decade before that I had been able to board the train at the station near the ball park as I had dreamed of doing, and made the trip all the way up to Hamlet.

How remarkable it was, to have been part of all that had happened since then! For indeed I had been part of it; nor was it yet concluded. Here was I, at the place where a third of a century earlier I had known that the train was bound for, and had wanted to go there with it. Only now there was no more train. Those same years that had contained the stress and struggle and strife which had ultimately made it possible for those four girls, three white and one black, to go out for lunch together after three centuries of law and tradition to the contrary, had also witnessed the decline and the demise of the little passenger train that I had once so admired and loved. Yet could I honestly say, if in effect the end of a place for the Boll Weevil in the scheme of things had been, symbolically, the price that had to be paid in order for me to see those four girls eating lunch together in this restaurant, that the cost had been too high?

So that I could not and must not think of the memory of the little train as something unique and unqualified, frozen in time and inviolate, and of which all subsequent encounters and experiences were a species of decline and fall. For both I and the train had been part of a complex fabric of social experience, having moral and ethical validity, whose form had been the shape of time. It had been *real*, it had *existed*, and for me the little train was process: identity *in* time, not outside it. Its diminution did not represent merely loss, but change, of which I was a part, and which, because it had happened to me in my time, was mine to cherish. And it was not ghostly and subjective, with no further existence except as I could remember it, but substantial and in the world, authentic *because* it was part of time and change, emblematic of my own involvement in that world, and proof that I had been and still was alive. It was *in* time that it was able to be what it was for me, *in* its contingency: droll in its extraordinary extraness—the oak tree growing around the iron horse's head. And if I wanted to understand who I was, what my country was and why, it was there that I must learn to look.

Notes on Contributors

Cleanth Brooks was born in Kentucky in 1906 and studied at Vanderbilt University and Tulane University and as a Rhodes Scholar at Oxford University. Now professor emeritus at Yale University, he has also taught at Louisiana State University, the University of Texas, and the University of Southern California. He was one of the founders of the *Southern Review* and is author of several distinguished works of literary criticism, including *The Well Wrought Urn; A Shaping Joy: Studies in the Writer's Craft; Understanding Poetry* (with Robert Penn Warren); *William Faulkner: The Yoknapatawpha Country;* and *William Faulkner: Toward Yoknapatawpha and Beyond.*

George Core, editor of the *Sewanee Review*, was born in 1939 and grew up in Lexington, Kentucky. He was educated at Vanderbilt University (B.A., M.A.) and the University of North Carolina (Ph.D.). He has written extensively, chiefly on modern American literature, for the *Virginia Quarterly*, the *Southern Review*, and other quarterlies, and is the editor of two books on southern literature.

Shelby Foote is a native of Greenville, Mississippi, where he was born in 1916, and attended the University of North Carolina. A novelist, historian, and playwright, he is the author of a three-volume historical narrative, *The Civil War*, and several novels, including *Follow Me Down, Love in a Dry Season, Jordan Country*, and *September, September*. The recipient of several Guggenheim fellowships and a Ford Foundation grant, he lives in Memphis, Tennessee.

J. Lee Greene, associate professor of English at the University of North Carolina at Chapel Hill, was born in Forest City, North Carolina, in 1944. He received his M.A. and Ph.D. from UNC and has also taught at the University of Michigan. A specialist in black American literature, he is the author of several scholarly articles and of *Time's Unfading Garden: Anne Spencer's Life and Poetry*, and is also managing editor of the *Southern Literary Journal*.

William Harmon, born in North Carolina in 1938, received M.A. degrees from the University of Chicago and the University of North Carolina and a Ph.D. from the University of Cincinnati. He is professor of English at the University of North Carolina at Chapel Hill, where he was chairman of the Department of English between 1972 and 1977. An award-winning poet, he has also published essays, reviews, and articles in several journals, including *PMLA* and *The American Anthropologist*. His books include three volumes of poems and a critical study of Ezra Pound's work; and he is the editor of the forthcoming *Oxford Book of American Light Verse*.

William C. Havard, Jr., born in 1923, is professor of political science and chairman of the Political Science Department at Vanderbilt University. His M.A. is from Louisiana State University and his Ph.D. from the London School of Economics. A specialist in political theory and American politics, he has taught at LSU, the University of Florida, the University of Massachusetts, Virginia Polytechnic Institute and State University, and as a Fulbright lecturer at the University of Munich. His publications include books, articles, and scholarly reviews, many of them on aspects of southern politics. His most recent book is *The Changing Politics of the South*.

C. Hugh Holman was born in Cross Anchor, South Carolina, in 1914, and received his Ph.D. from the University of North Carolina. He has served on the faculty and administration of UNC at Chapel Hill since 1946 and is presently Kenan Professor of English. His numerous publications include *The Roots of Southern Writing; Three Modes of Modern Southern Fiction; The Loneli-*

ness at the Core: Studies in Thomas Wolfe; The Immoderate Past: The Southern Writer and History; editions of Thomas Wolfe's correspondence and works; and a play, *37 Octobers*, based on Wolfe's life.

Blyden Jackson, professor of English at the University of North Carolina, was born in Paducah, Kentucky, in 1910 and grew up in Louisville. He received his M.A. and Ph.D. degrees from the University of Michigan and has also taught at Fisk University and at Southern University, where he was dean of the Graduate School, before moving to UNC in 1969. A specialist in black American literature, his publications include *Totem* and *The Waiting Years: Essays on American Negro Literature.*

Robert D. Jacobs was born in Vicksburg, Mississippi, in 1918 and has an M.A. from the University of Mississippi and a Ph.D. from Johns Hopkins University. Currently Callaway Professor of Language and Literature at Georgia State University, he has also taught at Johns Hopkins and at the University of Kentucky. He is author of *Poe: Journalist and Critic* and coeditor (with Louis D. Rubin, Jr.) of *Southern Renascence: The Literature of the Modern South* and *South: Modern Southern Literature.*

Katie Letcher Lyle was born in China in 1938, grew up in Virginia, and graduated from Hollins College and Johns Hopkins University. She teaches English and is chairman of the Liberal Arts Division at Southern Seminary Junior College in Buena Vista, Virginia. A poet, newspaper columnist, and professional folksinger, she has written several articles on country music, novels for teenagers, and *The Golden Stones of Heaven*, a novel about the country music industry in Nashville.

Mary E. Mebane, born in Durham, North Carolina, received both her M.A. and her Ph.D. from the University of North Carolina. She has taught in several public school systems in North Carolina, at North Carolina College at Durham, at South Carolina State College in Orangeburg, and at the University of South Carolina in Columbia. She has contributed to several anthologies: *A Galaxy of Black Writing, The Eloquence of Protest: Voices of the*

70's, and *Southern Writers: A Biographical Guide*. She is presently under contract to Viking Penguin, Inc., for a book tentatively titled *Mary*.

John Shelton Reed was born in 1942, grew up in Kingsport, Tennessee, and received his Ph.D. from Columbia University. He is associate professor of sociology at the University of North Carolina at Chapel Hill, a research associate of the Institute for Research in Social Science, and book review editor of *Social Forces*. He has held visiting positions at the Hebrew University of Jerusalem and at St. Antony's College, Oxford. A specialist in the sociology of the South, he is author of numerous scholarly articles and books, including *The Enduring South: Subcultural Persistence in Mass Society*.

Louis D. Rubin, Jr., University Distinguished Professor of English at the University of North Carolina, was born in Charleston, South Carolina, in 1923. He received his M.A. and Ph.D. degrees from Johns Hopkins University and has taught at Johns Hopkins, the University of Pennsylvania, Louisiana State University, and Hollins College. An editor, literary critic, and novelist, he is author of a number of studies of southern literature, including *The Writer in the South*, *The Wary Fugitives: Four Poets and the South*, and *William Elliott Shoots a Bear: Essays on the Southern Literary Imagination*.

James Seay was born in 1939 in Panola County, Mississippi. An award-winning poet, he earned an M.A. at the University of Virginia and has taught at Vanderbilt University, the University of Alabama, Virginia Military Institute, and the University of Virginia School of General Studies. He is at present lecturer in English at the University of North Carolina. He has published poems and articles in several literary reviews, as well as two books of poetry, *Let Not Your Hart* and *Water Tables*.

Lewis P. Simpson, born in Jacksboro, Texas, in 1916, is William A. Read Professor of English Literature at Louisiana State University and coeditor of the *Southern Review*. He received his M.A. and Ph.D. degrees from the University of Texas and has taught at LSU since 1948. Author of *The Dispossessed Garden: Pastoral and History in Southern Literature* and of *The Man of Letters in New England and The South: Essays on the Literary Vocation in America*, as well as numerous articles and reviews, he has also edited several collections of essays of literary criticism and is the series editor of the LSU Press Library of Southern Civilization.

William Styron, author of the 1968 Pulitzer Prize-winning novel, *The Confessions of Nat Turner*, was born in Newport News, Virginia, in 1925. He has an A.B. from Duke University and was a fellow of the American Academy in Rome. He has been a fellow at Yale University since 1964 and is also a literary critic, dramatist, and editor. His other novels include *Lie Down in Darkness*, *The Long March*, *Set This House on Fire*, and *In the Clap Shack*, and, most recently, *Sophie's Choice*.

Walter Sullivan was born in Nashville, Tennessee, in 1924. He received his M.F.A. from the University of Iowa and has taught at Vanderbilt University since 1949, where he is now professor of English. Author of two novels and several short stories, he has also published numerous articles and several books about southern literature, including *Death By Melancholy: Essays on Modern Southern Fiction* and *A Requiem for the Renascence: The State of Fiction in the Modern South*.

George B. Tindall, Kenan Professor of History at the University of North Carolina, is a native of Greenville, South Carolina, where he was born in 1921. He earned his M.A. and Ph.D. degrees at UNC and has also taught at Eastern Kentucky State College, the University of Mississippi, Louisiana State University, and the University of Vienna. A specialist in the history of the South since 1865, his numerous publications include *The Emergence of the New South*, *The Disruption of the Solid South*, and *The Ethnic Southerners*.

Nancy M. Tischler, born in Arkansas in 1931, received her M.A. and Ph.D. degrees from the University of Arkansas. She has taught at George Washington University and Susquehanna University, and is presently professor of English and Humanities and former chairman of the humanities program at Pennsylvania State University—Capitol Campus. Her publications include *Tennessee Williams: Rebellious Puritan*, *Black Masks: Negro Characters in Modern Southern Fiction*, and *The Legacy of Eve*.

Robert Penn Warren was born in Guthrie, Kentucky, in 1905. He studied at Vanderbilt University, where he was a member of the Fugitive group of poets; at the University of California, where he earned a M.A.; and as a Rhodes Scholar at Oxford University. He has taught at Vanderbilt, Louisiana State University (where he was a founder of the *Southern Review*), the University of Minnesota, and at Yale University. The only writer to win Pulitzer Prizes for both poetry (*Promises: Poems 1954–56* in 1958 and *Now and Then: Poems, 1976–1978* in 1979) and fiction (*All The King's Men* in 1947), he has also held the Library of Congress chair for poetry and has won a number of other literary prizes. His publications include literary criticism, biography, political and social commentary, short stories, plays, and most recently a novel, *A Place to Come To*.

Eudora Welty, a native and resident of Jackson, Mississippi, won a Pulitzer Prize in 1973 for her novel, *The Optimist's Daughter*. She studied at the Mississippi State College for Women and received a B.A. from the University of Wisconsin. Her short stories and novels, which have won her a preeminent position in American literature, include *The Golden Apples*, *Losing Battles*, *Delta Wedding*, and *The Ponder Heart*. Her most recent book is a collection of essays on fiction, *The Eye of the Story*.

Sylvia Wilkinson was born in Durham, North Carolina, in 1940. She studied under Randall Jarrell at the University of North Carolina at Greensboro, received her M.A. from Hollins College, and attended Stanford University under a Wallace Stegner Creative Writing Fellowship. She has taught at the Asheville and Chapel Hill campuses of the University of North Carolina and at the College of William and Mary, and has been writer-in-residence at Hollins College and Sweet Briar College. A member of the Sports Car Club of America, she has published a number of articles about auto racing, as well as a book, *The Stainless Steel Carrot*, about her experiences traveling with a sports car racing team. Her novels are *Moss on the North Side*, *A Killing Frost*, *Cale*, and *Shadow of the Mountain*. She is presently working on a fifth novel under a Guggenheim fellowship.

Thomas Daniel Young is the Gertrude Conaway Vanderbilt Professor of English at Vanderbilt University. He was born in Louisville, Mississippi, in 1919 and earned his M.A. at the University of Mississippi and his Ph.D. at Vanderbilt. He has also taught at the University of Mississippi, the University of Southern Mississippi, and Delta State College. A specialist in southern literature, he has written numerous essays and books, including his most recent, *Gentleman in a Dustcoat: A Biography of John Crowe Ransom*, and has edited many others, including *The New Criticism and After*.